Economics
for CSEC® Examinations

Robert Greenwood

Terry Cook

Dave Ramsingh
Naparima College, Trinidad

Karen Radcliffe
Glenmuir High School, Jamaica

Yvonne Harvey
Glenmuir High School, Jamaica

CSEC® is a registered trade mark of the Caribbean Examinations Council (CXC).

Cambridge Economics for CSEC® Examinations is an independent publication and has not been authorised, sponsored, or otherwise approved by CXC.

CAMBRIDGE UNIVERSITY PRESS

CAMBRIDGE UNIVERSITY PRESS
Cambridge, New York, Melbourne, Madrid, Cape Town,
Singapore, São Paulo, Delhi, Mexico City

Cambridge University Press
The Edinburgh Building, Cambridge CB2 8RU, UK

www.cambridge.org
Information on this title: www.cambridge.org/9780521701174

© Cambridge University Press 2007

This publication is in copyright. Subject to statutory exception
and to the provisions of relevant collective licensing agreements,
no reproduction of any part may take place without the written
permission of Cambridge University Press.

First published 2007
4th printing 2012

Printed in the United Kingdom at the University Press, Cambridge

ISBN 978-0-521-70117-4 Paperback

Designer:
Cover designer: Richard Jervis Design
Typesetter and Illustrators: Oxford Designers & Illustrators

Cambridge University Press has no responsibility for the persistence or
accuracy of URLs for external or third-party internet websites referred to in
this publication, and does not guarantee that any content on such websites is,
or will remain, accurate or appropriate. Information regarding prices, travel
timetables and other factual information given in this work is correct at
the time of first printing but Cambridge University Press does not guarantee
the accuracy of such information thereafter.

Every effort has been made to trace copyright holders. Should any
infringements have occurred, please inform the publishers who will correct
these in the event of a reprint.

Contents

Preface v
Acknowledgements vi

Part one: The nature of Economics — 1

  1 The nature of Economics 3
  2 Production possibility 15
  3 Influences on economic decisions 24

Part two: Products, economic resources and resource allocation — 37

  4 The factors of production 39
  5 The costs of production 57
  6 Goods and services 67

Part three: Markets and prices — 77

  7 Economic systems 79
  8 The price mechanism 96
  9 Elasticity 116
  10 Market structures 132
  11 Market failure 146

Part four: The financial sector — 165

  12 Money 167
  13 The financial sector 177

Part five: Economic management: policies and goals — 193

  14 Public finance: national income 195
  15 Public finance: the national budget 208
  16 Inflation and causes and consequences of inflation 220
  17 Policies to deal with inflation 230
  18 Unemployment: the role of trade unions 241

Part six: International trade — 251

  19 International trade 253
  20 Terms of trade, exchange rates and the balance of payments 271

Part seven: Caribbean economies in a global environment — 286

  21 Caribbean economies at present 289
  22 Trade liberalisation, globalisation and their effects on Caribbean economies – E-commerce 309

Answers to exercises and examination questions — 333

Index 365

I wish to thank my wife Margaret for her support and encouragement in writing this book, and my son Edward and daughter Emily for helping me at the end of a 'phone with my problems in handling computer technology.

Preface

This book has been written to meet the requirements of the CSEC (Caribbean Secondary Education Certificate) in Economics.

The author is an experienced Economics teacher and was an international examiner for many years. He also taught in the Social Studies Department, Cayman Islands High School. He is well aware that Economics can be a mysterious subject for secondary school students so he devotes much space at the start of the book to explaining the nature of Economics. He also realises the difficulties students new to the subject encounter, both with the subject matter and the methodology, and that it can take some students a whole year before they feel at ease with the subject. However, once the student has a grasp of Economics, he or she will have no regrets in opting for the subject and will benefit from a greater understanding of the world around him or her.

The changing nature of economic realities in the Caribbean is a theme throughout the book but before they can be discussed, the student must have a sound knowledge of the principles of Economics. In the early part of the course, there must be patience while the principles are learnt: the theory must be grasped before it can be applied. In the second year, the student should begin to discuss economic issues informatively and be moving towards what will be required for the higher examination grades. However, there is often more than one side to any problem, and Economics does not always provide one definitive answer. For example, within the Caribbean, there are two completely contrasting economies: Cayman is a good example of a free market

Free Market and Command Economies are Caribbean neighbours

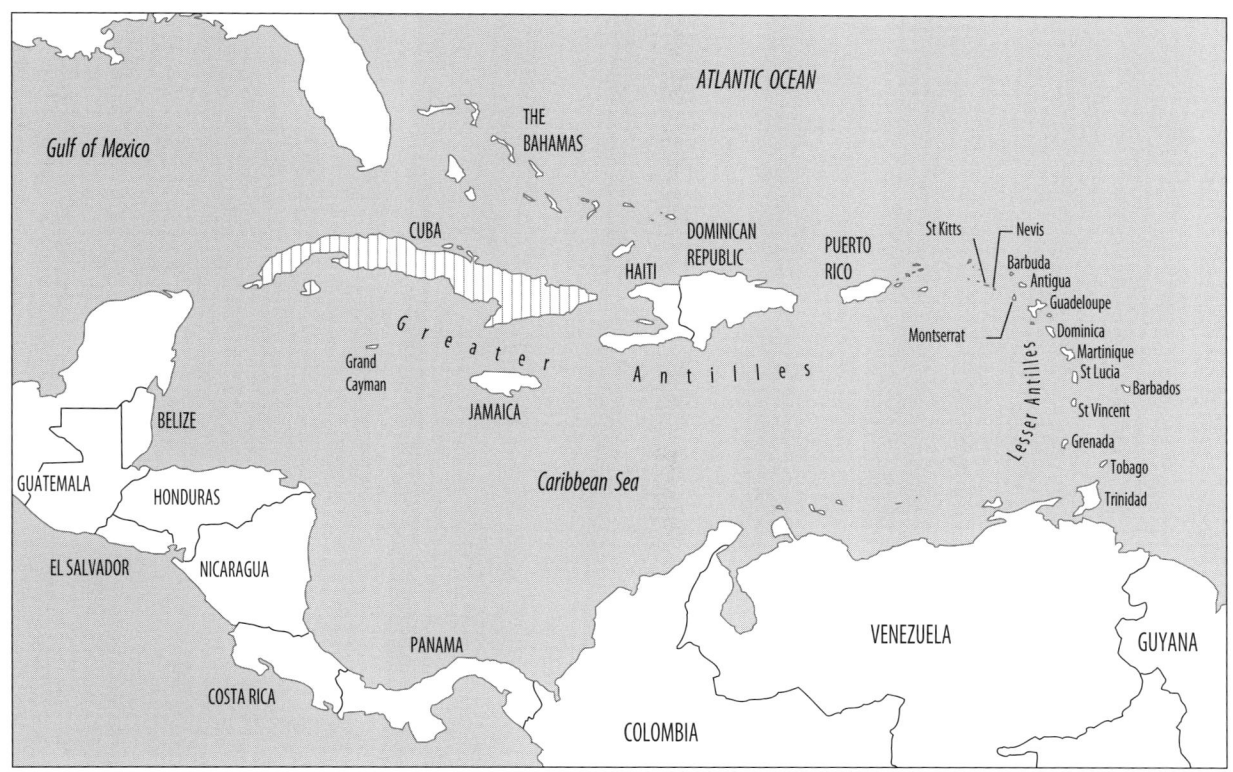

economy and Cuba of a command economy (you will find out what these two expressions mean in the first chapter). Which country has it right? Economists and students will disagree on this and many other issues and it is hoped that by the end of the two year course students will be able to support their arguments with a good knowledge and understanding of the subject.

The author has followed closely the order of sections and topics in the CSEC Economics Syllabus and their subdivisions. He has provided an introduction to each chapter, included many definitions, examination tips and exercises and provided some examples of examination type questions at the end of each chapter.

Finally, it is hoped that this book will stimulate the study of Economics and help to make students appreciate the rewards of studying it.

Acknowledgements

We would like to thank the foll,owing for permission to reproduce photographs: Alamy, BP, Empics, PA Photos, SA Photos, and Stillpictures.

Part one

The nature of Economics

CHAPTER 1

The nature of Economics

In this chapter, you will be learning:
- What Economics is about
- Choice and opportunity cost
- What is meant by an 'economy'
- Positive and normative statements
- Classification of economies in terms of free market, command or mixed
- Micro- and macro-economics

What Economics is about

Definition of the Economic problem
Man has infinite or unlimited wants but finite or limited resources.

Definition of Economics
Economics is the study of scarcity and choice.

The key issue in Economics is how to allocate those resources in the best possible way. Even Bill Gates, the founder of Microsoft and one of the richest men in the world, has limited resources, although he would be thought by most people to be wanting for nothing.

Even Bill Gates has an economic problem.

There would be no Economics without scarcity. In other words, if everyone had all they could possibly want, there would be no Economics. As with individuals, so with countries. Governments have to allocate their limited resources in what they see as the best way. The United States, with its abundant resources, still has an 'economic problem'. Burkina Faso, a very poor country in West Africa, has very limited resources and a much more obvious 'economic problem'.

If we consider the two Caribbean countries the Cayman Islands and Cuba, we will see that these two countries deal with their 'economic problem' in very different ways. It may be simply put at this stage that Cayman allows the free market mechanism to determine the allocation of its resources, i.e. goods and services to go to who can

Burkino Faso has a huge economic problem.

Source: Stillpictures.

or will pay for them, thereby letting there be 'haves' and 'have-nots' in its society. On the other hand, the Cuban government directs where the resources go, aiming for a more equal distribution of resources, a socialist solution. Cuba is known as a command economy because the government issues directives for the distribution of resources and overrides the free market mechanism, which it would consider allocates resources 'unfairly'. We shall look at this more closely later in the chapter when considering what an economy is.

EXERCISE Consider why you, Bill Gates, the USA, Burkino Faso, Cuba and the Cayman Islands all face an economic problem.

Choice

Let us go back to the definition: 'Economics is the study of scarcity and choice'. It is because there is scarcity that there must be choice. Choice is an economic problem because of limited resources. We must be clear at this stage that resources are not just monetary resources. Time is a scarce resource. We cannot do two things at once. We have to choose between a movie and a disco for the evening's entertainment. We cannot go to both because they occur at the same time. We have to make an 'economic decision' but it does not involve money in that money is not the scarce resource – time is.

Energy is also a scarce resource. In the school sports day, the 800 metres and the 1500 metres are not run at the same time but we do not have the energy to run in both. We have to make a choice between one race or the other. When we make our CSEC decisions, we have to make a choice. If we choose Economics, we cannot choose Biology; this is because the two subjects are placed against each other in option columns whereby only one subject can be chosen in a column. Finally, of course, money is commonly the scarce resource. We have JM$50 as our resource and our wants are a can of Coca Cola and a meat patty, but our money will not stretch to both. We have to choose either the Coke or the patty. We make economic decisions like this every day.

Choice and opportunity cost.

Opportunity cost

In the above examples, if we choose a movie we have to forgo the disco; if we choose the 800 metres we have to forgo the 1500; if we choose Economics we have to forgo Biology; and, finally, if we choose the can of Coke we have to forgo the meat patty. Our scarce resources, time, energy and money have forced us into making a choice. The alternative choice forgone is known in Economics as the **opportunity cost**.

Opportunity cost is a very important concept in Economics. When you start thinking in terms of opportunity cost, you are beginning to think like an economist. Here is a test to see whether you are thinking like an economist: What is the opportunity cost of living in your own house? (It is the cost of the rent you are forgoing by not letting it out to a tenant. In monetary terms it could be JM$10,000 if that would be the rent you could command, but remember that opportunity cost does not have to be in monetary terms. Think like an economist!)

Definition of opportunity cost
Opportunity cost is the cost of the next best alternative forgone.

'Next best' is very important because there are often two or more alternatives and the opportunity cost is never the worst alternative forgone. Suppose a qualified woman could be a nurse, a personal assistant or a primary school teacher. First let us assume that there are no monetary considerations. She chooses to be a primary school teacher. She has forgone being a nurse or a personal assistant. She cannot face up to suffering therefore being a nurse is not an option, and the personal assistant is the opportunity cost of choosing to be a primary school teacher because it is the '*next best* alternative forgone'.

Examination Tip

Some students explain the concept of opportunity cost generally in terms of alternatives foregone. You need to be more precise and state clearly that it is the cost of the **next best** alternative forgone.

We can use the same example and bring in monetary considerations as the basis of her choice. The rates of pay are as follows:

Nurse: JM$500,000 per annum
Primary teacher: JM$600,000 per annum
Personal assistant: JM$800,000 per annum

On purely monetary considerations she would choose to be a personal assistant. The opportunity cost of being a personal assistant would be not being a primary teacher because $600,000 is the next best rate of pay. However, if we say that she is very attracted to the prospect of long school holidays … and if we say that she has a very strong humanitarian instinct …, then the opportunity cost question would have to weigh up all the considerations: money, free time, dedication to health care; and it would be very difficult. She could choose to be a nurse even though the rate of pay is lowest.

We shall come back to opportunity cost again and again in the syllabus. It is important to grasp opportunity cost as a pure concept now in dealing with scarcity and choice before we apply it to other parts of Economics.

EXERCISE Write down as many examples as you can of opportunity cost decisions you have taken in the last week or month, stating both what you chose and what you didn't choose.

Economics and money

Before studying Economics, students commonly associate it with money and think that the only resource the subject deals with is money. This would be a typical clue for 'Economics' in a crossword puzzle: 'Money management (9)'. The non-Economist will give the right answer in the crossword because he or she associates 'Money' with 'Economics'.

There is a branch of Economics known as 'Monetary Economics' which deals with the functions and characteristics of money, banking and monetary policy (money supply and interest rates), currencies and exchange rates and so on, but it is just a branch of Economics and not the whole study.

Hong Kong. The world's most free market economy?

An economy

An economy refers to the way the economic resources of a country are managed, e.g. the economy of Cuba is the way Cuba manages its resources. On a smaller scale, a community also has an economy, e.g. the economy of Kingston, Jamaica.

There are three broad categories of economy:

1. A free market economy; also known as a capitalist or a laissez-faire economy.

2. A command economy; also known as a planned or a communist economy.

3. A mixed economy; such an economy combines features of a free market economy and a command economy. Most economies in the world fall into this category. It is virtually impossible to be exclusively a free market economy or a command economy. Hong Kong is usually taken as a good example of a free market economy, but it has some features of state control, e.g. the provision of education. On the other hand, Cuba is often taken as a good example of a command economy, yet it has some free market features, e.g. the operation of private, small-scale restaurants.

EXERCISE Consider the likely advantages and disadvantages of private and state provision of education in society.

Positive and normative statements

Discussion of the different types of economy provides a good opportunity to inform the student more about the nature of Economics. Economists like to deal with positive statements. A positive statement is verifiable. It can be tested and proved to be correct, e.g. 'at a lower price, more will be sold than at a higher price, other things being equal.' (Economists always consider people to be rational; it would not be rational to buy more when the price rises.) The statement can be tested by going to a market and seeing the effects of lowering or raising prices on the amount of goods sold.

> **Definition of a positive statement**
> A positive statement is one which is beyond the possibility of doubt.

A normative statement is one which expresses an opinion. Economists do make normative statements because they are often called on for advice, e.g. by a government on whether to raise or lower interest rates. However, economists can disagree with each other over a normative statement. In our current study of types of economy, one economist may give the opinion that the nationalisation of the tobacco industry in Cuba after 1959 was the right course of action for the good of the country. Another economist might completely disagree. The former made a normative statement; he was expressing his opinion. In connection with the Cuban tobacco industry, a positive statement could be that after nationalisation tobacco provided 75% of Cuba's export earnings. This statement can be verified by figures.

> **Definition of a normative statement**
> A normative statement is one which involves an opinion or value judgement.

When Economics deals with positive statements it is a science, as when the boiling point of water is said to be 100° Celsius. However, Economics also deals with decisions made by human beings; normative statements make Economics a social science.

EXERCISE Look at the following five statements. For each one, say whether you think it is an example of a positive or a normative statement.

1. The rate of interest today is 4.75%.
2. The government should lower the rate of interest.
3. The system of public transport on the island should be much better.
4. Partnerships are examples of firms in the private sector.
5. The West Indies cricket team should win the next World Cup.

> **Examination Tip**
>
> Normative statements can often be recognised by the use of the word 'should' or 'ought'. Positive statements can often be recognised by the use of the word 'is'.

We must now return to the different types of economy.

The classification of economies

The free market economy

The American economist, Paul Samuelson, referred to the money in our pockets as our 'dollar vote'. When we pull a dollar from our pocket, we are voting for the product we spend it on. Perhaps we decide to spend the dollars on eggs. We take the eggs off the shelf in the shop. The shop has to replace them so the buyer signals to the egg supplier that more eggs are wanted. The farmer wants to supply more eggs so he needs more chickens. The farmer's resources are put into egg production (land, feed, labour etc.). Therefore, by our spending of the dollars, we have played a part in deciding how resources will be allocated in the economy. No government directive has told the farmer to put resources into egg production. The market has told him.

> **Definition of a free market economy**
> An economy where resources are allocated through the price mechanism.

In 1776, Adam Smith, a Scottish philosopher who is often referred to as the first economist, published *An Inquiry into the Nature and Causes of the Wealth of Nations* (usually known as just *The Wealth of Nations*). He explained how the market works by saying that there was an **invisible hand** which directed the allocation of resources much as was described in the preceding paragraph. He argued strongly that there should be no interference in the working of the market. Adam Smith felt that the invisible hand should be allowed to work in all markets, even the international market. He therefore advocated free trade.

The price mechanism

At this stage the **price mechanism** must be mentioned although it will be dealt with at much greater length in a later chapter. To go back to our previous example with the buying of eggs. When we buy eggs we are expressing a vote for them. However, our vote is one of many and when many people buy eggs, the price of eggs will rise as people have 'bid up' the price of eggs. The higher price will attract suppliers so more eggs will be supplied and hence there will be more demand for the resources which go into egg production. In a free market, price is the signal for what shall be produced.

> **Definition of the price mechanism**
>
> Price changes, caused by changes in demand or supply or both, send out a signal which affects the allocation of resources in a market. These signals are what are known as the invisible hand.

However, some goods will not be demanded and therefore resources will not be put into these goods through the invisible hand (the price mechanism). Resources will be idle and there will be unemployment in that sector of the economy. It is the prospect of unemployment which the free market creates that has led other economists to insist that there must be government direction over the economy.

The free market economy allows for the creation of monopolies ('monopoly' strictly is where there is only one seller or supplier). This is considered undesirable. In Cayman, in the 1970s, there was a monopoly over the supply of gas. Monopoly is not necessarily a bad thing for an economy but it holds the potential for restricting supply, raising prices and giving poor service.

> **Definition of monopoly**
>
> A monopoly is a market in which there is only one seller or supplier.

A free market economy at the national level does not exist in the world today. There is a role for government to play. The free market would not supply defence, universal education, universal health care and law and order, to name just four sectors. Governments intervene in the economy of every country so all economies are, to some extent, mixed. For example, Jamaica has a mixed economy. Before 1992, the government played a large role in the economy, even controlling prices and having direct control over many enterprises. Since then, Prime Minister Patterson has made Jamaica much more of a free market economy.

Prime Minister Patterson introduced free market reforms in Jamaica.

Source: AP/EMPICS.

An approximate percentage split will give an indication of how to label an economy. A combination of 70% private sector and 30% public sector would definitely be classified a free market economy. Hong Kong would be in this position. Reverse the percentages and the economy would be classified a command economy. However, the percentages tell us that both economies are, to differing degrees, mixed.

EXERCISE Try and find out the private and public sector percentages in your country. The following internet sites should be helpful:

www.cia.gov
www.imf.org
www.un.org
www.worldbank.org
www.wto.org

The command economy

In a command economy, there is a central planning authority which issues directives for what is currently to be produced and what will be held back for investment in the future. A successful business will sacrifice current production for investment in future production, but in a command economy the central planning authority dictates this for the whole economy.

> **Definition of a command economy**
>
> An economy where resources are allocated by the state or government through a system of planning.

One economist, Karl Marx, believed it was vital that there was a large element of government direction over the economy.

The state decides what people need. If the state decides that people need tractors, tractors are produced. The people may want jeans, but jeans are not produced. Tractors can be over-produced and jeans under-produced. There can thus be wastage in a command economy.

Fidel Castro made Cuba a command economy in 1959.
Source: AP/EMPICS.

The state, through the central planning authority, may control prices. It may decide that the prices of essential foods are to be kept low, e.g. bread, corn and potato prices, and that the prices of domestic electrical goods be kept high. Low prices encourage consumption and hence there are long queues outside bread shops in communist countries. High prices discourage consumption and hence there is smuggling and black-marketeering.

The state provides services like education and health. Cuba is famous for its very high standards in education and health. In the Cuban revolution of 1959, the new government decided that it would turn its back on the 'haves' and 'have-nots' of the previous regime and bring about a greater equality of incomes and opportunities. It is not exactly true that a surgeon and a waitress earn equal incomes but the difference is relatively small. Perhaps a surgeon is rewarded with better quality of state housing (all housing is provided by the state). We are tempted to question why a person should spend years and years qualifying as a surgeon when he or she will not be rewarded financially, but a communist regime works on the Marxist principle of: 'From each according to his ability, to each according to his needs'.

In a large and complex command economy, like the former Soviet Union, which collapsed in 1991, the central planning authority has to be so large that there is excessive bureaucracy and 'red tape'. Decisions are slow and the costs of running such authorities are very high. In a perfectly free market economy, there would be no such bureaucracy.

EXERCISE Try and find out some information about the Cuban revolution of 1959. From what you have discovered, do you think that the revolution has been successful in achieving what it set out to do?

The mixed economy

All economies are, to some extent, mixed economies. Free market economies have features of command economies and command economies have features of free market economies. Most economies accept that access to education and health should not be based on the ability to pay. Therefore, the state provides education and health services free, or at very little cost, to all. The extent of this varies according to the resources that the state has available; for example, universal primary education is the target for even the poorest sub-Saharan African countries with their very limited resources, but secondary education is far from universal, usually reaching under 10% of the population. Caribbean countries consider education a priority and provide for universal education up to secondary level.

EXERCISE What do you think are the advantages of universal secondary education for both the individual and the economy?

Let us consider roads. All countries recognise that transport infrastructure is essential for the economy to prosper so the state provides roads. There are examples of roads being provided by the private sector, as with the turnpikes in the United States, but along with turnpikes are the state highways. In some free market economies, the trend is moving towards more private roads.

However, there are some parts of the economy which the state considers too vital for its safety and the well-being of the community to be left to the free market, such as the provision of defence and law and order (these are known as 'public goods' and we will discuss them in a later chapter). A free market firm would not provide defence because it would be unwilling to invest in an enterprise which would bring no return to itself. However, the state sees that defence is essential for the well-being of its citizens.

In mixed economies, there is private ownership of resources alongside public ownership. Let us take two examples from Jamaica.

1. The Jamaica Railway Corporation, a state company, owns 56% of the track, and the remaining 44% belongs to the private sector, chiefly the bauxite companies. (There are plans for privatisation but under these plans, the state will still hold 40% of the joint venture with 60% held by private companies.)

Definition of nationalisation
Nationalisation is the taking into state ownership of private sector firms.

Definition of privatisation
Privatisation is the sale of government-owned firms to the private sector.

2. The Ministry of Education administers the public schools, pre-primary through to high schools, but there are also 232 privately run schools in Jamaica that educate 7% of the school age population.

Finally, two further examples.

1. The Cayman Islands has no direct taxation, i.e. there is no income tax. The government is therefore without a government's usual source of revenue. Revenue comes from import duties, bank licences and indirect revenues from tourists. It is a mixed economy strongly leaning to the free market. The government provides state education through to secondary level and the Cayman Community College at post-secondary, but there are also private schools in the country. Electricity is provided by the Caribbean Utilities Company, a joint stock company. The tourist industry (before Hurricane Ivan) accounted for 70% of the Gross Domestic Product and is entirely in the private sector.

2. Cuba is a mixed economy leaning very strongly towards a command economy. In 1959, almost 100% of Cuba's land was brought under state control and farming became a nationalised industry. The state controlled almost all other parts of the economy. However, as we have seen, without profit and income incentives, workers tend to under-produce and there were food shortages in the 1990s. In October, 1994, the state liberalised agricultural markets and allowed private farmers who had reached their quotas to sell the excess at unrestricted prices (free market prices). This reduced the black markets which had appeared in agricultural products.

Definition of liberalisation
Liberalisation is the freeing up of previously state-controlled markets to allow the private sector to enter.

Micro- and macroeconomics

When the University of Cambridge first began examining in Economics in the 1960s, the syllabus and the examination papers were divided into microeconomics and macroeconomics, and students were familiar with these divisions. Nowadays these divisions are kept, but not as strictly.

Microeconomics is the study of individual markets and embraces key theories of Economics, like the price mechanism, e.g. the price of rooms in tourist hotels in Barbados is determined by demand and supply.

Macroeconomics is the study of the economy as a whole, e.g. discussion of the Gross Domestic Product of Cuba.

Most textbooks start with microeconomic topics and move on to macroeconomic topics as the understanding of macroeconomics usually requires the understanding of microeconomics. However, the topic we are moving to in the next chapter is a microeconomic topic in that it is part of economic theory, but macroeconomic in that it discusses the whole economy! It is called 'production possibility'.

Examination Tip

> Economics can be divided into micro and macro elements but it may be useful in certain examination questions to show the examiner that you are aware of the links between them, as well as the distinctions.

Examination questions

1 a Explain what is meant by a free market system. *(5 marks)*
   b Give three examples of opportunity cost in an economy. *(5 marks)*

2 Protestors sometimes oppose the building of new motorways or airport runways.
   Explain how the concept of opportunity cost could be applied to such situations. *(10 marks)*

3 Discuss the advantages and disadvantages of **(a)** a free market and **(b)** a planned economy *(10 marks)*

4 Explain, with the aid of examples, the distinction between normative and positive statements. *(5 marks)*

Production possibility

In this chapter, you will become used to working with graphs, an important part of the methodology of Economics:

- You will relate production possibility to the economic problem
- You will be introduced to what is meant by 'resources' in Economics
- As the chapter progresses, you should become accustomed to working with graphs
- The concept of 'trade off' will be explained
- You will learn about some aspects of 'efficiency' in Economics

Production possibility and the economic problem

The economic problem states that man has infinite wants but that an economy has finite resources. It would like to give its citizens all the goods and services they could possibly want but it does not have the resources to do so. Production possibility deals in theory with what an economy can produce with its limited resources. We must speak of the 'given' resources because, if we change the resources, we change the production possibilities.

Economic resources

Richard Branson, entrepreneur, celebratres inaugural Virgin flight to Caribbean.

Source: EMPICS.

A country has four types of resources, known as the factors of production. These are land, labour, capital and enterprise. They are categories because, for example, land includes the earth, the forests, the oceans and all therein. Labour includes the physical as well as the mental labour. Capital, in this sense, includes the factories and machinery. Finally, enterprise refers to the role of the entrepreneur in combining the other resources into production to make a profit. (More will be said about resources in the next chapter.)

> **Definition of the factors of production**
>
> These are the resources of land, labour, capital and enterprise which are combined together to produce goods and services.
>
> **Land** refers to the natural resources available for production.
>
> **Labour** refers to the human effort available for production.
>
> **Capital** refers to the man-made physical goods used to produce other goods and services.
>
> **Enterprise** refers to a worker who organises the factors of production and takes a risk in doing so.

The production possibility curve

> **Definition of the production possibility curve**
>
> This is a set of combinations of products which can be produced within an economy if all of its resources are being fully used. It is usually shown in the form of a curve, showing the possible combinations of two goods.

Production possibility can be shown in a diagram. On the axes, two goods are shown, consumer goods on the vertical axis and capital goods on the horizontal axis. A curve is drawn between the two axes which shows the production possibility combinations of the goods on the axes.

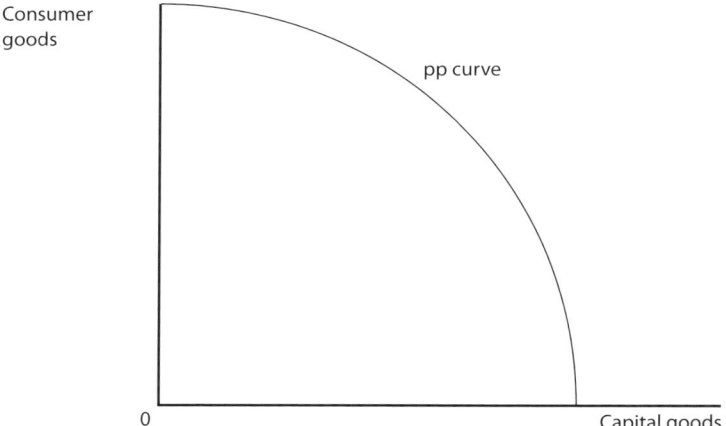

Fig. 2.1
The basic production possibility curve

> **Definition of a consumer good**
>
> A consumer good is one which satisfies a person's immediate needs.

> **Definition of a capital good**
>
> A capital good is one which goes into the production of other goods.

The production possibility curve can also be called a 'boundary' or a 'frontier'. 'Frontier' emphasises the fact that it is a frontier beyond which the economy cannot go because it does not have enough resources.

In the production possibility curve diagram below, we shall discuss certain combinations shown by the lettered points.

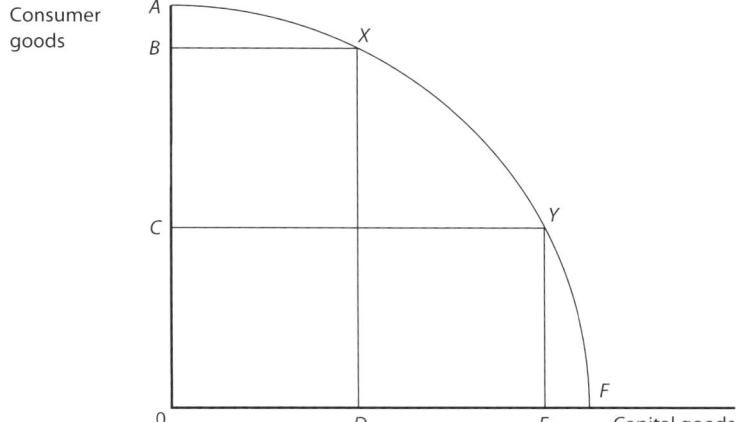

Fig. 2.2
Combinations of goods attainable with given resources

At point X, the economy, with its given resources, can produce the combination of 0B consumer goods and 0D capital goods. At point Y, it can produce the combination of 0C consumer goods and 0E capital goods. (Note that these are positive statements. We are not saying one combination is preferable to the other. If we said that X gives more consumer goods than Y and is therefore a better combination, that would be a normative statement.)

The economy can choose to produce at any point on its production possibility curve. There are many combinations possible on that curve. If it was at point A, it would produce only consumer goods and no capital goods.

The production possibility curve and opportunity cost

Opportunity cost is the cost of the next best alternative forgone. If the economy wants more consumer goods, it must forgo some capital goods. If it wants more capital goods, it must forgo some consumer goods. Consider these options:

1 The opportunity cost of 0A consumer goods is zero capital goods.

2 The opportunity cost of 0F capital goods is zero consumer goods.

3 (More difficult!) The opportunity cost of 0B consumer goods is DF capital goods. The economy can have the combination of 0B consumer goods and 0D capital goods, but it cannot have 0B consumer goods and 0F capital goods. If it wants 0B it must forgo DF.

4 The opportunity cost of 0D capital goods is AB consumer goods because you can have 0D capital goods and 0B consumer goods, but you have to forgo AB consumer goods.

5 The opportunity cost of CB consumer goods is DE capital goods. If it wants to increase consumer goods by CB it must forgo DE of capital goods ... and so on!

EXERCISE You have a certain amount of money to spend and this could be spent on a CD, a cinema ticket, a DVD or the entrance to a disco. Which would you choose? Consider the opportunity cost of your decision.

Trade off

Economists talk of a 'trade off'. There is a trade off between consumer goods and capital goods: the more consumer goods, the less capital goods. Consumer goods are traded off against capital goods and capital goods are traded off against consumer goods. The production possibility curve makes the idea of trade off very clear. You cannot have more of one without less of the other. More consumer goods means less capital goods and more capital goods means less consumer goods. (The rate of the trade off, i.e. how many consumer goods for a given quantity of capital goods, will be dealt with later.)

In the above diagram *BC* consumer goods are traded off against *DE* capital goods.

Economic efficiency

The production possibility curve diagram can also be used to show efficiency and waste.

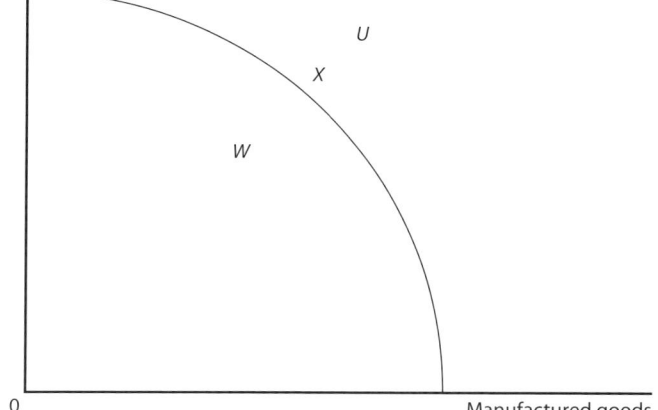

Fig. 2.3
Attainable and unattainable outputs

Note that the axes have been labelled differently!

Point *X* shows efficiency.* All the available resources are being used and the economy is achieving its maximum production at this point. No resources are being wasted.

---

* Efficiency at point *X* is also known as Pareto efficiency from the Italian economist Vilfredo Pareto. At point *X*, nobody can be better off without someone else being worse off. This is known as Pareto efficiency. If we moved up the production possibility curve, consumers would be better off at the moment, but future consumers would be worse off because there would be less capital goods, goods which would make other goods in the future.

> **Definition of economic efficiency**
>
> Efficiency generally means using resources in the most economical way possible.
>
> **Technical efficiency** is where the output from a given quantity of resources will be maximized.
>
> **Allocative efficiency** is the extent to which the allocation of resources coincides with the preferences of consumers.
>
> **Pareto efficiency** is where no one can be made better off without someone else being made worse off.

Point *W* shows a situation where resources are being left idle. It could signify unemployed labour, for example. The economy could produce more if the idle resources were employed.

Point *U* is unattainable. It is outside the production possibility curve. The economy has insufficient resources to reach this point. It is beyond the frontier. The economy would like to produce at that point but it does not have enough resources.

Examination Tip

> The examiner may ask you which point, *W*, *X* or *U*, is 'preferable'. The answer is *U* – it is preferable but unattainable. The economy would prefer to produce at point *U* but it cannot with its present resources.

More about point *W*

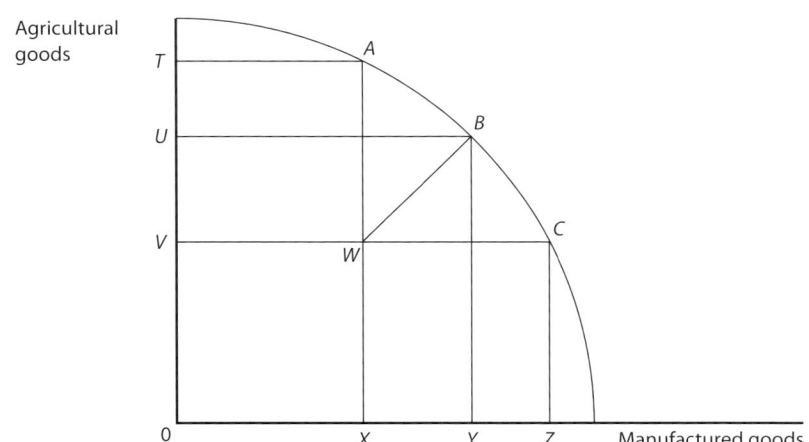

Fig. 2.4
Moving to points on the curve from a point inside the curve

At point *W*, resources are underemployed and the economy can move to the production possibility curve if it can bring these resources into production. There are three points on the curve which can be attained:

1. At point *A*, the economy could produce 0*T* agricultural goods and 0*X* manufactured goods. This is an increase of *TV* agricultural goods.

2. At point *C*, the economy could produce 0*V* agricultural goods and 0*Z* manufactured goods. This is an increase of *XZ* manufactured goods.

3. At point *B*, the economy can have more of both goods, an increase of *UV* agricultural goods and *XY* manufactured goods.

All these points are possible. Once again positive economic statements have been made in 1, 2 and 3. We are not saying what the economy should do, or what is the best point to move to. If we said that *B* was the better point because it gave more of both goods, we would be making a value judgement, a normative statement.

Shifting the production possibility curve

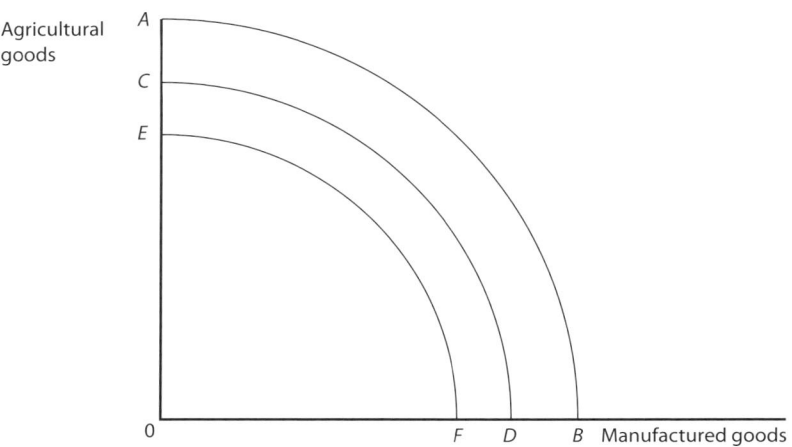

Fig. 2.5

Parallel shift outwards from the origin

The economy was originally on the production possibility curve *CD*. What could shift it to *AB*? The first answer is *improved technology*; for example, computerisation has shifted the production possibility curves of most countries outwards, improving the potential to produce more of both agricultural and manufactured goods.

Swivelling shift outwards from the origin

Land has been made to yield more with better fertilizer, more irrigation etc. This has happened in India and other developing countries with the 'green revolution', e.g. two crops of rice in one year instead of just one. However, on our graph this would shift the production possibility curve upwards from *C* to *A* on the agricultural goods axis, pivoting through point *B* and not giving a parallel of the curve. On the other hand, an improvement in manufacturing technology would shift the production possibility curve outwards from a point nearer the origin to *B* on the manufactured goods axis, pivoting from *A* on the Y-axis.

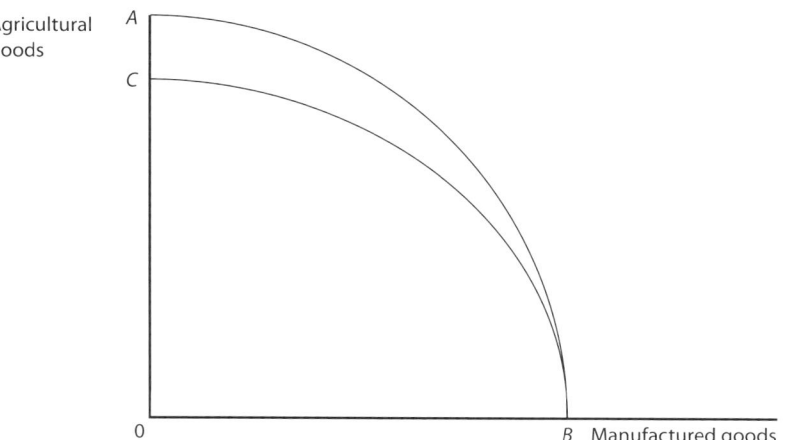

Fig. 2.6
Swivelling shift; out on one axis but not on the other axis

Parallel shift inwards to the origin

The production possibility curve shifts inwards to the origin parallel with itself, i.e. from *CD* to *EF* when there is a war or a natural disaster. On 7 September, 2004, Hurricane Ivan devastated Grenada and on 11 September, it devastated Grand Cayman. In the case of small islands, such a disaster would shift the production possibility curve of the whole economy massively inwards to the origin. Cayman's economy is heavily dependent on tourism and it is easy to illustrate on a diagram the inward shift of Cayman's production possibility curve.

Loss of resources due to natural disaster.

Source: AP/EMPICS.

Swivelling shifts inwards to the origin

On the agricultural goods axis, a plague of locusts would shift the production possibility curve downwards from A to C, pivoting through D because the manufacturing sector would not be affected. On the other hand, a permanent closure of factories would swivel the production possibility curve inwards on the manufactured goods axis from B to a point on the X-axis nearer the origin, pivoting through A on the Y-axis.

Conclusion

The production possibility curves of most countries are shifting outwards year by year because of technological progress. It certainly makes the news when an economy experiences a disaster which can shift the production possibility curve inwards.

The shape of the production possibility curve

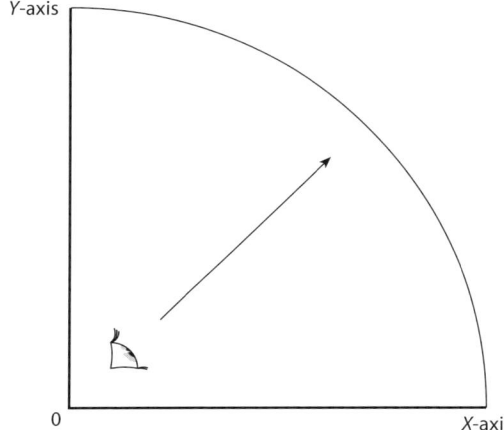

Fig. 2.7 *The concave shape of a production possibility curve*

The production possibility curve is *concave when viewed from the origin*.

Explanation of the shape

Economists are very interested in the concept of the **margin**. The marginal unit is the additional unit, the extra unit or the next unit. When an additional unit of resources is transferred from the Y-axis to the X-axis, it yields more of the product on the X-axis.

However, more and more units have to be transferred from the Y-axis to yield an additional unit of the X-axis as we descend the curve. *There is an increasing opportunity cost of producing another unit on the X-axis.* That is why the production possibility curve is concave when viewed from the origin.

> **Definition of the margin**
> The marginal unit is the additional or extra or next unit.

Examination questions

1. Explain, with the use of examples, what is meant by factors of production. *(5 marks)*

2. Distinguish, with the use of examples, between consumer and capital goods. *(5 marks)*

3. a Draw a production possibility curve. *(4 marks)*
   b Explain how it can be used to show the idea of a 'trade off'. *(6 marks)*

4. Explain what is meant by economic efficiency. *(5 marks)*

5. Explain the difference between a movement along a production possibility curve and a shift of the curve. *(10 marks)*

CHAPTER 3

Influences on economic decisions

In this chapter, you will study the economic influences on decision-making:

- You will understand the different influences on individuals and firms
- You will see the important influence that the government has in the economy
- You will then go into more detail about the role a government can play in the different areas of micro- and macroeconomics

Some of the topics will be dealt with at greater length later in the book.

Influences on individuals, firms and governments

In Chapter 1, when introduced to the concept of opportunity cost, you learnt that economic decisions are not always based on money, e.g. time is an important factor influencing economic decisions. In the first part of the previous chapter, you learnt how important the availability of resources are in production possibility decisions. Now we shall examine the important influences on economic decisions for individuals, firms and governments.

Influences on individuals

Economists assume that individuals are rational, i.e. they use their reason. For example, a person in St Kitts would not buy a CD for EC$ 40 in one shop if he or she could buy it elsewhere for EC$ 30. Economists therefore assume that individuals make decisions in their best interest. For example, the decision whether to smoke or not. To the medical profession, smoking is not rational but to the individual smoker, it may be a rational decision based on enjoyment, taking away stress or the idea of a cool image. An individual will weigh up all the benefits and costs before taking a decision. He or she is being rational.

Personal choice

Personal choice is an influence. Freedom of choice is an important principle. What we do in our leisure time is a personal choice. One person may like listening to music, another reading and another watching television. Is this an absolutely free choice? No, there are other constraints, e.g. you may like watching television but you may not have a television. Economists would say that a certain individual chooses to watch television in his or her leisure time, 'other things being equal'. This is called the **'ceteris paribus'** condition from the Latin words which mean 'other things being equal'.

> **Definition of ceteris paribus**
> The ceteris paribus condition means 'other things being equal'.

It is important to add this to many statements that are made in Economics because there are so many variables that could play a part, like the television being broken in our previous example.

There can be constraints on personal choice. An individual may be a nudist and want to walk around naked in public, but usually the government bans nudity in public places.

Income

This is a monetary influence on choice. A person with a larger income has more 'spending power' than a poor person and one aspect of this spending power is a wider choice of goods and services. So the higher the income, the more goods and services that can be chosen. On the other hand, if we equate quality with price, the higher income allows the choice of better quality goods. With 'normal' goods more are bought as income rises, e.g. CDs. The person on a low income is restricted in what he or she can buy and the income may be so low that they have to buy inferior goods, e.g. plastic shoes instead of leather shoes.

> **Definition of a normal good**
> A normal good is one more of which is bought as income rises.

> **Definition of an inferior good**
> An inferior good is one less of which is bought as income rises.

However, a very poor person has to spend all his or her income to survive. Some even have to beg, borrow or steal. The income is so low that there is no choice but to subsist or die. A higher income allows the choice between consumption spending and saving. Saving is what you do after consumption.

> **Definition of saving**
> Saving is where you refrain from consumption.

A high income gives this basic choice: to consume or to save, and a low income gives no choice in this matter.

Social pressures

Man is a social animal. Being a member of society brings peer pressure which influences choice in behaviour, taste and spending. Peer pressure leads to copying one's fellows in beliefs, fashion, lifestyle and spending. It can be very powerful, especially among the young. It takes a strong will 'to buck the trend', 'to stand out from the crowd' and thus choice is restricted. Peer pressure is very strong in schools, even in the choice of subjects at CSEC. Many 'go with the crowd' and opt for a subject that their friends have chosen. Teenagers sometimes hate to stand out. Therefore they are constrained in their choice by peer pressure.

Port-au-Prince. Supermarket for rich shoppers. The influence of income.

Source: Stillpictures.

Shanty town, Port-au-Prince.

Source: Stillpictures.

EXERCISE Can you think of any examples where you have been influenced by peer pressure?

Occupation

Occupation can be a strong influence on choice. Most people work for someone else, e.g. they are employed by a firm. Some people are self-employed, i.e. they work for themselves. This distinction will have a strong influence on choice. For example, a firm usually decides the hours of work whereas self-employed people can often decide their own hours, *other things being equal,* e.g. if you are running your own restaurant, you have to be open at lunch time.

Your occupation can take you away from home for long periods, such as service in the merchant navy. On board ship, choice is very restricted as regards leisure activities, spending (which may be limited to refreshments) and social contacts.

Some occupations dictate your dress. A banker usually has to wear a tie, even a suit, whereas a manual labourer may have his clothes provided and has no choice in style, colour etc.

Your occupation may be very stressful and so your choice of leisure activity will probably be one which provides the most relaxation. Merchant bankers under pressure in making financial decisions will seek to 'chill out' at the earliest opportunity.

Level of education

The level of educational achievement in the Caribbean ranges from illiterate to university graduate. In Jamaica, 85% of the population of 15 years and above have attended school so 15% have either not attended school or been so irregular in attendance that they do not qualify. However, it is dangerous to assume that the 15% non-attenders are illiterate. There are adult literacy programmes in Jamaica. The illiterate people have very different choices than the university graduates. Obviously the illiterate people will not read in their leisure time, nor will they buy books or newspapers.

The level of education certainly has much to do with earning power. It may not be the only objective of education but most people approach education with a view to increasing their earning power. Therefore, the university graduate has a wider choice of goods and services by the very fact that he or she has a higher income. In this respect, it is difficult to separate income, occupation and level of education. Certainly a lack of education or a low level of education does limit choice in lifestyle, leisure and spending. Conversely a high level of education does broaden choice in these matters.

EXERCISE Consider whether your education is just 'a means to an end' or whether it has a value of its own. Which subjects do you think might be more useful in terms of the eventual earning power of individuals?

EXERCISE Can you think of any other factors that could influence your decision to spend?

Influences on firms

The profit motive

The profit motive drives the majority of firms (some have environmental concerns but that will be dealt with in a later chapter when social benefits and costs are considered). Profit is the difference between revenue and costs.

> **Definition of profit**
> Profit is the difference between the revenue received and the cost involved in producing something.

Examination Tip

> You need to make it very clear that profit is not the same as revenue. Revenue is sales income. There will, however, be costs involved in production and these will need to be deducted from the revenue to establish the profit.

It is not enough for a firm to make profit. A rational firm maximises profit, i.e. it makes as much profit as possible. *Profit maximisation* is the goal of a firm. This is the chief influence on a firm. To do this, a firm must maximise revenue and minimise costs. Therefore, we can say that *revenue maximisation* is an influence on a firm's economic decisions as is *cost minimisation*.

> **Definition of profit maximisation**
> Profit maximisation means producing an output at the point where marginal cost is equal to marginal revenue.

Revenue maximisation

The firm aims to sell as much as it can at the highest possible price to maximise revenue (in this section we can make such a statement but we will need to qualify it when we have studied price theory).

Investment

Revenue maximisation could be 'jam today and no jam tomorrow' and so the position of the firm in the future is another influence over its behaviour. It could sell all the goods it has and leave nothing for the future. Holding back on present sales for future sales is another form of investment. Therefore *investment* is another influence on the firm's behaviour.

> **Definition of investment**
> Investment means spending now on something that can be expected to generate an income in the future, i.e. it is the spending of a firm not for present consumption.

Cost minimisation

Costs are a very important topic in Economics. Suffice it to say here that we are dealing with variable costs, i.e. the costs that are associated with the production of a product, such as the costs of raw materials and labour.

> **Definition of variable costs**
> A variable cost is one which varies directly with output.

The costs of raw materials are variable costs (as are labour). The firm seeks to keep these costs as low as possible (cost minimisation) in order to profit-maximise. Obviously a firm can use inferior materials at lower cost, but that is a short run influence because sales will soon fall when consumers reject the products.

Resources

Resources are the factors of production: land, labour, capital and enterprise. The resources available to a firm are a great influence on a firm's decisions. 'Land' includes the minerals therein. Let us concentrate on bauxite in Jamaica. Jamaica is rich in bauxite and is the third largest producer of bauxite in the world. At current production, its reserves will last another 100 years. Kaiser Aluminium, an American owned firm, handles much of Jamaica's bauxite. Clearly this firm will be little influenced at the present about its resource base in raw materials. It will be more influenced by its capital base, e.g. its refineries and its railways for transporting the bauxite.

Labour is another resource. The Jamaican bauxite industry employs thousands (the actual number goes up and down according to the world demand for aluminium) and the firms are major employers of labour. There is a ready supply of labour in the country.

Alpart Mines, Jamaica. Bauxite is an example of a resource.

Source: Stillpictures.

Environmental concerns are important. Industrial production is sometimes harmful to the environment. Again, the example of bauxite in Jamaica is relevant. The readily extractable bauxite is found on arable land so there is the conflict between farming and extraction. The disposal of waste material is also a big environmental issue. Jamaica is an island with a limited land mass. It cannot accommodate high volumes of waste material. Bauxite firms are profit maximisers and, in spite of the employment of environmental experts, there is still a conflict between profit maximisation and social cost minimisation.

EXERCISE What is the opportunity cost of extracting bauxite from the land in Jamaica?

EXERCISE Research your own country and see if you can find any examples of environmental degradation and pollution.

The Caribbean has some of the world's best resources for tourism and practically every area engages in tourism as a major industry. Cayman and Cuba both rely heavily on tourism for revenue. In Cuba, the tourist industry is state-owned. In Cayman, it is in private hands, often foreign hands. The resource base for tourism is land (including the sea!) and the climate. More hotels mean more revenue up to a point. More hotels, however, can spoil the resources and lead to less revenue.

EXERCISE What is the opportunity cost for a Caribbean island of developing its tourist facilities?

Capital, as mentioned in the previous chapter, includes factories and machinery. In a command economy, like Cuba, the state provides the capital but it is nevertheless an influence on economic decisions. In a free market economy, like the Cayman Islands, firms find their own capital investment and its availability is a big factor in decision making.

Land and capital are both relatively scarce resources in the Caribbean and therefore have strong influences on the economic decisions of firms in the region.

Labour is the human resource. It provides the skilled and unskilled labour force required in production. Labour is not generally considered to be a problem in decision making by most firms in the Caribbean. Unskilled labour is readily available and due to strong investment in secondary and further education, skilled labour is also available. However, the 'brain drain' is a problem in a country like Jamaica (and elsewhere in the Caribbean) as skilled labour is attracted abroad by higher wages.

> **Definition of a brain drain**
> The movement of well-educated and skilled people out of a country.

Industrial relations

Industrial relations can refer to either the relations between employers and workers nationwide or the relations between management and workers in a particular firm.

Industrial relations at the national level

Nationwide industrial relations are very much influenced by the government, even in a free market economy. There are three parties involved in industrial relations nationwide: the government, the employers and the workers, often represented by trade unions.

In the Caribbean there is a broad range of industrial relations from Cuba to Cayman. In Cuba, the government is the employer as all industries and services are state-owned. The government sets the hours of work, the holidays, the rates of pay, the housing, the education of workers' children, the health services for workers and so

Industrial area, Cuba

Source: Stillpictures.

on. The theory is that as the state knows what is best for the workers, the workers will receive the best possible conditions at work and at home.

On the other hand, there are no trade unions in Cayman. The government is thinking about introducing an Employment Bill to take effect in 2009, but there is strong opposition from the very powerful employers who up to now have had almost a free hand in industrial relations, hiring and firing as they please and exploiting foreign labour with low wages.

In the other parts of the Caribbean, there are trade unions of varying strength to represent the workers' rights and conditions. In Trinidad and Tobago, there is a long established trade union (founded in 1937), the Oilfields Workers' Trade Union (OWTU), which represents not only the oil workers but also gas, chemical, electricity, manufacturing and agriculture and forestry sector workers. It was born out of a general strike (all workers refusing to work) and was part of an anti-colonial revolt in Trinidad.

In relation to wages, if employers want to cost-minimise and workers want to wage-maximise, there is likely to be a conflict of aims. This can be settled amicably across the table and there can be said to be good industrial relations. The same good relations can be achieved over other employment issues, such as hours of work, holidays, pensions etc. There needs to be goodwill on both sides of the table.

If good industrial relations break down, the government may be called in to settle the dispute. Poor industrial relations, especially when strikes occur, are harmful to the economy and it is in the government's interest to keep industrial peace.

Industrial relations within the firm
This is the microeconomic view of industrial relations. In the absence of trade unions, employment is between the firm and the individual worker. Take wages for example. The profit-maximising firm offers a wage as low as possible. If the worker is not attracted by that wage, he or she will withhold the labour and the firm will have to offer more until the wage is sufficiently high to attract the labour that the firm requires. This is the market mechanism at work. Similarly with other conditions of employment. If the hours of work are unattractive or the holidays are insufficient or there is no pension on offer, the worker may withhold his or her labour and the firm will have to offer more attractive conditions.

If workers are organised into trade unions they have the strength of *collective bargaining* behind them. Then the firm (through the management) must meet the workers representatives around a bargaining table. The trade union gives the workers greater strength and higher wage rates and better conditions should result.

Definition of a trade union
A trade union is a group of workers who combine together to protect their interests.

Definition of collective bargaining
This is a situation where the representatives of the workers negotiate with the representatives of the employers.

If the collective bargaining is conducted with give and take on both sides, industrial relations will be good, but if there cannot be a resolution of the conflict, industrial relations will be less satisfactory. This is where either party to the dispute may be able to call in the government to arbitrate, i.e. judge, on the matter in dispute.

In a recent case in Cayman in 2004, the Ritz Carlton dispute over construction, the workers were on the losing side and many were dismissed. The workers had no trade union, no one to explain the situation and industrial relations reached 'rock bottom' between a firm and its workers.

EXERCISE — Consider the potential advantages and disadvantages of trade unions. When you go out to work, do you think you would be keen to join one, assuming that there was a trade union in existence for you to join?

The influence of government

The extent of the government's influence in the economy depends on what type of economy it is. In a command economy, the government influences many aspects of the economy. In a free market economy, the government allows the market to work and only plays a part in the macroeconomy. Of course, in a mixed economy, the government has a limited role in microeconomics.

Market failure

In a free market economy, the government only intervenes when things go wrong in the markets, i.e. when there is *market failure* (market failure is a subject in itself and we shall deal with it at length in a later chapter). The market fails to provide *public goods* such as street lighting, lighthouses, public parks, defence, and law and order. The government therefore provides them.

> **Definition of a public good**
>
> A public good is one the consumption of which by an individual does not reduce its supply to others.

When we walk down a pavement at night lit by street lighting, we are not depriving other pedestrians of that light.

Examination Tip: There is not always total agreement about what is and what isn't a public good. You could suggest this to the examiner. For example, is a pavement a public good because there might be limited space on a pavement? A road is not because a car takes up road space.

EXERCISE — Discuss whether a police force or a fire service should be run by the state or by private firms.

The market provides some goods insufficiently, e.g. education and health. These goods are called *merit goods*. The government steps in and provides merit goods to put the market failure right.

Definition of a merit good

A merit good is one which has both private and social benefit and which would be under-consumed if left to free market forces.

Private benefit is enjoyed by the person consuming the good and social benefit is that which the whole of society enjoys. Education increases a person's earning power, but also makes him or her more productive and so the economy as a whole benefits. The government does not think that education should depend on a person's ability to pay. Similarly, health should not depend on a person's ability to pay, but in a number of countries the individual must pay for health services.

EXERCISE Consider the advantages and disadvantages of the state provision of education.

EXERCISE Compare and contrast the private and social benefits of a meningitis inoculation.

The market over-supplies some goods like cigarettes. These are called *demerit goods*.

Definition of a demerit good

A demerit good is one which has a private benefit but a social cost and which would be over-consumed if left to free market forces.

Obviously the smoker must think there is a benefit in smoking, e.g. calming stress, but there is a cost to society from the pollution of the atmosphere, the costs to the health service of lung cancer, the loss of production resulting from sickness, and so on.

The government intervenes in the market by taxing demerit goods to reduce their consumption and to make the polluter pay for his or her pollution.

EXERCISE The price of a cigarette is often about 80% tax. Do you think it is right that governments tax such products so heavily?

Price floors and price ceilings

Government intervention in the market in the form of price floors and ceilings is controversial, but some so-called free market economies do have such intervention.

Definitions of price floors and ceilings

A price floor is a price below which the market cannot go.
A price ceiling is a price above which the market cannot go.

Minimum wage legislation is making a law to set a wage below which an employer cannot pay a worker. The justification for this interference is that wages must keep the worker out of poverty. The pressure on the government has come from organised labour, i.e. the trade unions. It involves interference in the labour market and its opponents consider it does more harm than good in the domestic and global economy.

Minimum wage legislation is common throughout the Caribbean. In September, 2003, the minimum wage in Jamaica was increased to JM$2,000 per week and this is still barely enough to keep a worker above the poverty line. In Trinidad and Tobago, there is a comprehensive list of minimum wages for nearly every category of employment; this is largely because the country has such strong labour unions.

EXERCISE Do you think wages should be entirely determined by the free market forces of demand and supply without any government intervention?

Maximum rents are an example of price ceilings. When accommodation is scarce and demand is high, the market price can be too high for some people and the government feels that it must set a maximum price. Again, such intervention is controversial and the free market economist would say that the market would solve the problem itself, if left alone. If the price of rented accommodation was high, more rented accommodation would be supplied and the price would fall, thus requiring no need for government intervention.

Taxes and subsidies

The government must have revenue to carry out its work, such as defence, roads, the health service and schools. Its revenue comes from taxes. There are two sorts of taxes, *direct and indirect*.

> **Definitions of taxes**
>
> A direct tax is one on the income of an individual or organisation.
> An indirect tax is one on the expenditure on a good or service.

One way of contrasting these taxes is that a direct tax is a tax on persons or organisations, an indirect tax is a tax on things.

In most countries there is a progressive income tax system which means that the higher the income, the higher the tax rate. The government considers that progressive tax is equitable (fair) according to the *sacrifice principle*, i.e. everyone should make equal sacrifice and therefore the rich should pay more than the poor.

Indirect taxes are levied on goods, e.g. a Value Added Tax (VAT) of 20% on all goods, except food, was proposed in Grenada in 1987 in order to change the tax structure completely. Direct tax (income tax) was to be ended and government revenue was to come largely from VAT. In Cayman, there are no direct taxes and all government revenue comes from indirect taxes like import duties. As very few goods are produced domestically, import duties raise considerable revenue.

Subsidies are monies paid by governments to suppliers to encourage them to supply more. In St Vincent and the Grenadines, bananas are subsidised in excess of EC$ 1.75 million. This subsidy was increased to help the industry recover after Hurricane Ivan, i.e. to keep the price of bananas low in the export market.

The government of St Vincent subsidises the banana crop.

Definition of a subsidy
An amount of money paid by a government to a producer so that the price to the customer is lower than it would otherwise have been.

The government in the macroeconomy

In all types of economies, the government has a major role to play in the economy as a whole, the macroeconomy.

Monetary policy

Apart from taxation, which we have already looked at, the government must provide a strong and stable currency in order to give confidence to individuals, firms and trading partners. The fall in the value of the Jamaican dollar has led to workers seeing their pay packets become less and less in terms of what they can buy. It has led to the prices of imported goods rising higher and higher in terms of the local currency and, in general, it has brought a lack of confidence in individuals and firms. The government must take steps through monetary policy to stabilise the value of the currency in domestic and foreign markets. Monetary policy involves the control of the money supply and interest rates.

Central Bank

The government must support a central bank at the head of the banking system. A central bank is responsible for the issuing of notes and coins, acting as banker to the commercial banks, supporting the currency through monetary policy (as discussed above), acting as banker to the government, i.e. to keep the government's bank accounts, and keeping the foreign currency reserves.

In the East Caribbean, there are eight political units (six are independent states and two are British Overseas Territories). In the Eastern Caribbean there is the Eastern

Caribbean Central Bank, based in St Kitts and Nevis. The Bank issues and supports the East Caribbean dollar. It determines the denominations of notes and coins in circulation and fixes the exchange rate between the EC$ and other foreign currencies such as the US$. This latter rate was fixed at EC$ 2.7 : US$ 1. The EC Central Bank must support this rate in order to create confidence in the currency.

Other government departments

There need to be a number of government departments, or 'ministries', such as Defence, Foreign Affairs, Education, Health, and so on. Some of these departments give assistance to business directly and others indirectly. There can be a Department of Trade which obviously assists business. However, the Education Department indirectly assists business by helping to improve the skills of the labour force.

Note
Many of the topics in this section have just been introduced briefly. They will be treated at greater length in later chapters. For example, the types of economy are considered again in the next chapter (they were introduced in Chapter 1), price floors and ceilings cannot be properly understood until the market system has been studied and macroeconomic topics like money and banking and international trade will be dealt with more fully in later chapters.

Examination questions

1 a Distinguish between the private and public sector of an economy. *(3 marks)*
   b Discuss the advantages and disadvantages of allocating resources through the public sector. *(7 marks)*

2 Distinguish, with the aid of examples, between direct and indirect taxes. *(10 marks)*

3 a Define a trade union. *(4 marks)*
   b Explain how membership of a trade union may be beneficial to a worker. *(6 marks)*

4 Distinguish clearly, with the aid of examples, between public goods, merit goods and demerit goods. *(10 marks)*

5 Compare and contrast the different influences on individuals in their spending decisions. *(10 marks)*

6 Compare and contrast the different influences on the behaviour of firms. *(10 marks)*

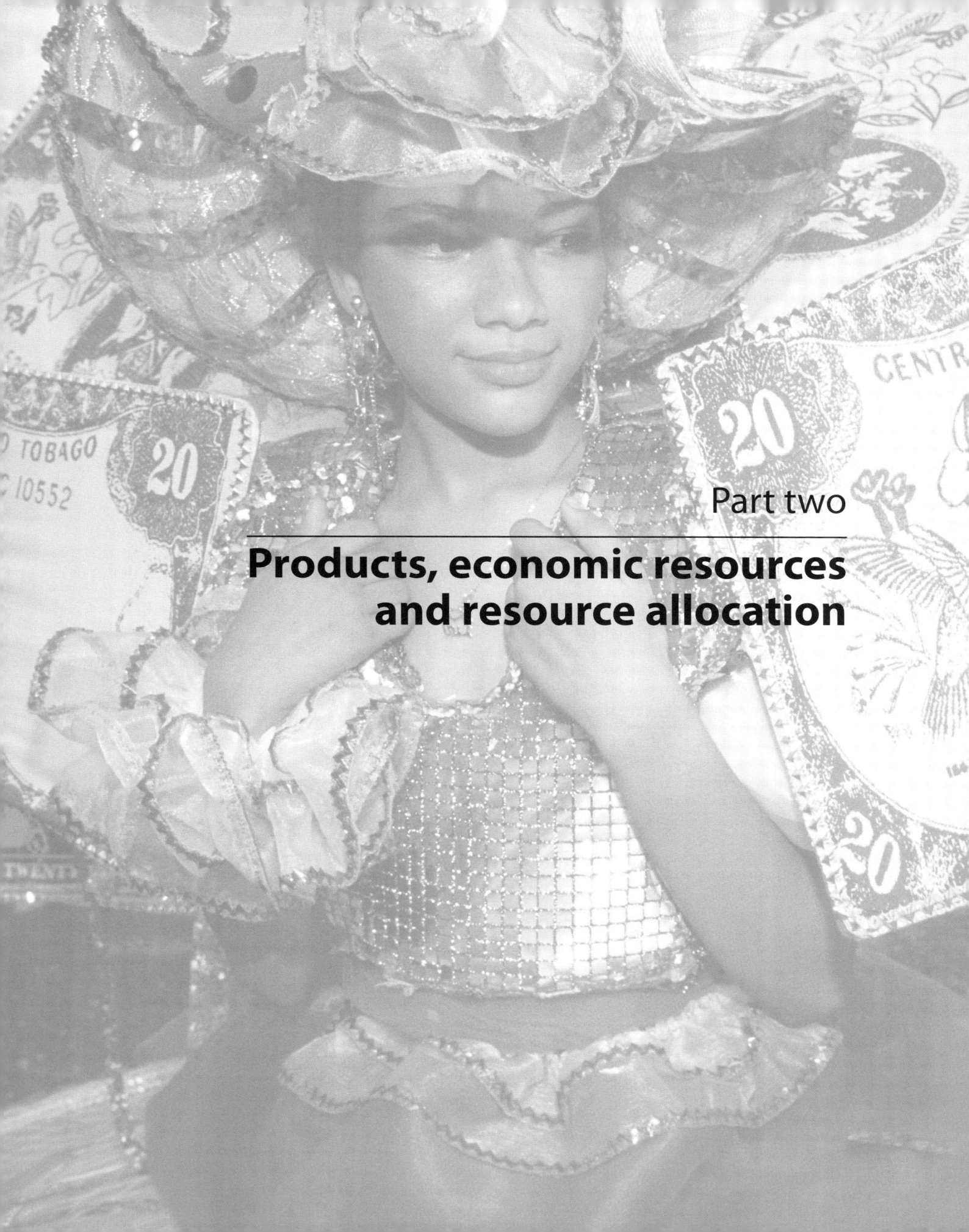

Part two

Products, economic resources and resource allocation

The factors of production

In this chapter, you will learn about land, labour, capital and enterprise, together known as the 'factors of production':

- You will learn what economists mean by 'land' and discover that it embraces more than just the land surface of the globe
- Labour is then examined from the Economist's point of view
- If you are a Business Studies student, you will have to revise your ideas on 'capital'
- Enterprise is the factor that brings all the others together in the best combinations
- Then you will learn about the returns, or rewards, to each of these factors: **rent** to land, **wages** to labour, **interest** to capital and **profit** to enterprise

Production

> **Definition of production**
> Production is the transformation of land, labour, capital and enterprise into goods and services.

Production is usually undertaken by firms, but it can be undertaken by the state or by individuals. When undertaken by individuals or firms, there is usually a **profit motive**.

It is rational behaviour by a producer to try to make as much profit as possible (**profit maximisation**), i.e. to be bringing in as much revenue from sales as possible while at the same time cutting costs as much as possible.

Production involves **adding value**. When a miller takes the corn and grinds it into flour, he or she is adding value to the corn. When the baker takes the flour and turns it into bread, he or she is also adding value. Production of a loaf of bread involves a series of adding values. Each part of the value added is the profit that goes to the producer for his or her enterprise.

> **Definition of productivity**
> Productivity is the rate or efficiency of work measured through output per worker.

The formula for productivity $= \dfrac{\text{Output}}{\text{Inputs}}$

If we take labour as the input, we often speak about the 'productivity of labour', i.e. how much each unit of labour can produce. For example:

$$\frac{1{,}000 \text{ loaves of bread}}{5 \text{ bakers}}$$

The productivity is 200 loaves per baker.

EXERCISE Consider the difference between 'production' and 'productivity'.

Inputs and outputs

There can be no output without input. In other words, to produce anything, you must put in some resources. Even the picking of wild fruit or nuts, e.g. coconuts, requires two inputs: land and labour. In fact, land is a necessary input for all output. Your Economics lesson requires land: the classroom.

The Jamaican novelist, Anthony C. Winkler, in his book, *The Lunatic* (1987), wrote about a village madman, Aloysius, who lived in the woods and fields and lived off wild fruits, berries and animals. He still needed land and labour.

Of course, some production needs all types of inputs. Producing a car needs land (the factory space) and the minerals like steel which comes from the iron ore out of the land. It needs capital (the machinery). It needs labour to work the machinery and perhaps apply the finishing touches. Even if the car is built by robots, labour is required to switch the machine on and off. Finally, there is enterprise, the managerial ability, to get the car plant up and running.

The inputs in production are called **the factors of production**. The output is what is produced.

Definition of factors of production
The factors of production are the inputs or resources used in the output of goods and services. They are land, labour, capital and enterprise.

Land

Definition of land
Land refers to the natural resources available for production.

Land refers to the land area of the earth which is in its natural state, i.e. unimproved by fertiliser. If it was fertilised, it would have had capital applied to it. It is limited in area. There is a finite amount of land. Land can be increased in size by reclamation from the sea, as has happened in the Netherlands, but this is not 'natural' because it has had capital (dredging machinery) applied to it.

Fertile land. Intercropping vegetables, cabbages and bananas in Cuba

Source: Stillpictures..

Land also includes the seas and lakes because the economist is really thinking of the whole of the globe's surface.

Land and sea are therefore both part of the factor, land. However, as a factor of production, land includes 'all that is therein'. It includes the minerals in the ground and in the sea and on the sea bed. It includes oil, as in Trinidad in both the land and offshore, and bauxite, as in Jamaica. It includes the virgin forests, but not the man-made forests. It includes the fish in the seas, lakes and rivers, but not those that have been stocked or the fish farms which have been made by the application of capital.

Therefore the factor land embraces all that is provided by nature on the earth. Let us repeat that there can be no production without land.

Land as a factor can be exhausted. Think of the minerals. The oil deposits are finite. Unless new reserves are discovered, Trinidad's oil reserves will be exhausted in ten years' time. (That is alarmist because the pattern has been for new reserves to be discovered offshore.) We have seen that at the current rate of extraction, bauxite deposits will last only 100 years in Jamaica.

The seas are being 'fished out'. These resources are finite. However, there can be **sustainable** use of land without the application of capital. If farmers do not overgraze the fields with their cattle and if fishermen conserve fish stocks by not overfishing, the resource, land, will not be exhausted and no capital has been applied.

The productivity of land

> **Definition of the productivity of land**
> The productivity of land is the ouput per acre or hectare.

The formula for the productivity of land is $= \dfrac{\text{Output}}{\text{Acres}}$

There is a difference in the productivity of types of land for farming purposes. (Remember that we are considering land that is provided by nature and not land that is improved by labour and capital.) Fertile land has the highest productivity per acre. Desert has the least productivity per acre.

One of Jamaica's problems is that the land rich in bauxite is also fertile arable land. However, we can still apply the formula of output per acre or hectare. If the dollar value of the output per acre from bauxite is higher than the dollar value of the output per acre from arable farming, then its productivity is higher from bauxite.

However, the productivity of land can be improved by the application of labour or capital or both labour and capital. Land can be made more productive by labour when it is cleared, levelled and drained. It can be made more productive by capital when it is fertilised and pesticides are applied. New crop varieties increase the productivity of land. This is well illustrated by the **'Green Revolution'** of the last forty years. In food production the world's productivity for land has increased by 1,000% or more. This can be shown in the graph below.

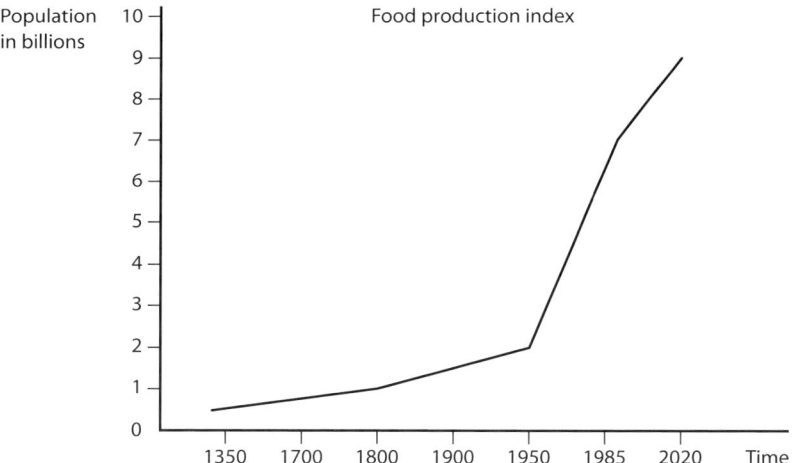

Fig. 4.1
The Green Revolution (not accurate)

From AD 0 until 1950, the world's food production barely kept pace with population growth. There were periods of famine and mass starvation. However, in the last forty years, agricultural scientists have introduced new crop varieties, fertilisers and pesticides that have greatly increased the productivity of land and kept world food production ahead of population growth. Of course, there have been areas of the world, Sub-Saharan Africa for example, which have experienced starvation during this time, but over the whole world food production has outstripped population growth.

This has been the so-called 'Green Revolution'. Its greatest impact has been on Asia where a large proportion of the world's population live and where the staple food is rice. Under the Green Revolution, scientists have enabled two crops of rice to be produced in one year on the same land.

EXERCISE Consider the extent to which the Green Revolution has affected your country.

Land is not just for agriculture. Land is also used for industry. Land near the centres of population is more productive for industry than land in the backwoods.

Labour

Definition of labour
Labour is the input from human beings, i.e. the human effort available for production.

The input can be physical, as in mining, or mental, as in the creative arts, or it can be a combination of the two, as in running a farm.

The labour force is limited in number. In most countries it is made up of the adult population, i.e. from 16 to 65 years. This is strictly the 'potential' labour force (those that can work in this age range) but many do not work for some reason or other. The most productive years are less in range, probably 25 to 35 or 40 years, but of course that depends on the nature of the labour.

Labour is classified in many ways: 'skilled', 'semi-skilled' and 'unskilled'; 'professional'; 'clerical' and 'manual'; 'white collar' and 'blue collar'. They are all parts of the labour force.

EXERCISE Place the following in the above categories of labour: surgeon, typist, builder, cane cutter, school teacher, architect, farmer and mechanic.

The labour force can be increased by the natural increase in population through the birth rate exceeding the death rate or by net immigration. For example, in Trinidad and Tobago, the population growth rate is negative by – 0.7%, i.e. the population is falling and thus labour as a factor of production is declining in numbers.

The size of the labour force is very important. The productive part of the population produces the goods and services for the whole population. What is more, it pays most of the taxes from which government revenue comes. This is called **the economically active part of the population**.

> **Definition of the economically active**
>
> The economically active part of the population is that part which produces the goods and services in the economy as a whole.

Education is very important for the productivity of the labour force. Labour is limited in skills. However, the skills base can be increased through education (or decreased by lack of education). Literacy and numeracy increase the output of labour. Universal primary education will increase the output of the labour force. Universal secondary education will make labour even more productive. University education will go a long way to providing all the skills in the labour force that the economy needs (this, of course, will to some extent depend on the particular subjects studied at university).

Therefore, the brain drain is a very big cause for concern. When Jamaica loses nurses to Canada, the United States and the United Kingdom, it is reducing its human resources. This is not just a problem for Jamaica but for all Caribbean countries. There are push and pull factors at work. The push factors are that there are not local jobs available to meet the demand, especially for highly qualified workers, and they have to seek work abroad. High levels of unemployment locally also drive even less-well qualified workers abroad. The pull factors are the higher wages abroad, sometimes better working conditions and the opportunity to advance skills in larger, more specialised job markets.

EXERCISE To what extent do you think the brain drain has affected your country?

Division of labour and specialisation

> **Definition of the division of labour and specialisation**
>
> The division of labour and specialisation involve the breaking down of production into simpler tasks, allowing workers to gain greater efficiency.

Most production can be divided into different tasks so that one worker performs the same task. He or she becomes 'specialised' in that task and performs it faster and with more skill. Also, the worker applies his or her mind to the task and thinks of ways in which the task could be performed better. Sooner or later the worker will have the idea for a tool or machine to aid him or her in the task. Technology is being introduced and production is improved still further.

Not only is output increased by the division of labour and specialisation but costs are reduced. If output is increased, yet the number of workers remains the same, unit costs go down assuming that wages remain the same:

$$\frac{\text{Labour costs (wages)}}{\text{Output}} = \text{Unit costs (average costs)}$$

For example:

(a) $\dfrac{\$500}{1{,}000 \text{ loaves}} = 50$ cents/loaf (b) $\dfrac{\$500}{10{,}000 \text{ loaves}} = 5$ cents/loaf

Therefore the division of labour and specialisation has four benefits:

1 Increased production (output).
2 Increased productivity (output per worker).
3 Lower costs of production.
4 Introduction of technology (new tools/machines).

Example A: Adam Smith and the pin factory

The increase in productivity that comes from the division of labour and specialisation was first recorded by Adam Smith in 1776 in his book *An Inquiry into the Nature and Causes of the Wealth of Nations*. He visited a pin factory in Britain. He called it a 'trifling manufacture' but it was a good example of the benefits of division of labour and specialisation.

Adam Smith doubted that a worker could make one pin a day and certainly not twenty pins if he was performing all the tasks required for making a pin. Therefore, the work was divided into a number of branches which were specialised tasks (Adam Smith called them 'trades'):

1 Drawing out the wire.
2 Straightening the wire.
3 Cutting it into the right lengths.
4 Putting a point on one end.
5 Grinding the other end for receiving the head.

The business of making a pin was thus divided into about ten operations, all performed by different individuals.

Output rose to 48,000 pins in a day, or 4,800 pins per worker. He therefore noted that with the division of labour and specialisation, productivity would increase at least 240 times!

By specialisation, each worker would invent a tool or machine to help in the task, e.g. a simple machine of cutting pins into the right length. Adam Smith attributed the invention of machinery to the division of labour.

Example B: Henry Ford and the Ford Model T

In the twentieth century, there was no better illustration of the benefits of the division of labour and specialisation than Henry Ford and the Model T. Henry Ford said, 'I will build a car for the great multitude.' This meant that he had to build a car at a low price that people could afford.

Model T Ford. Product of the assembly line

Source: EMPICS.

Between 1908 and 1927, Ford built 15,000,000 Model Ts. He introduced the assembly line where workers specialised in one task and passed on their finished article to the next worker in the line. Between 1909 and 1913 the speed of the assembly of the chassis had improved from 12 hours 8 minutes to 1 hour 33 minutes. In a single year, in 1914, 308,162 cars were produced. **By 1927, the Ford Motor Company was producing one Model T every 24 seconds!**

In 1909, a Model T was priced at $825. By 1927, the price had fallen to $290! Henry Ford had succeeded in what he set out to do. There is another lesson in Economics here apart from the benefits of division of labour and specialisation; lowering costs and cutting profit margins to increase demand made Henry Ford one of the richest men in the United States.

The supply of labour

It is necessary to make a distinction between the **market** supply of labour and the **individual** supply of labour.

The market supply of labour is the total supply of labour in a market for a particular job. This shows a normal supply curve rising from left to right because, in the market as a whole, the lower the wage the less supply and the higher the wage the more the supply. (Remember it is what workers would like to supply at given wage levels.)

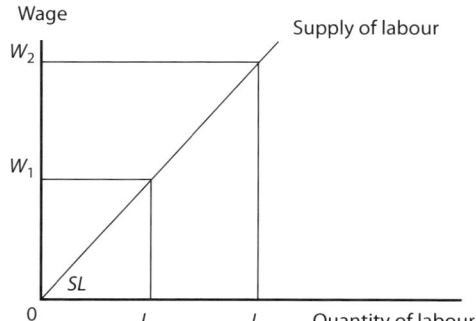

Fig. 4.2
The market supply curve of labour

When wages are low, at W_1, only L_1 quantity of labour is supplied. When wages are high, at W_2, L_2 of labour is supplied. The supply curve is showing the expected response – the higher the price, the more will be supplied, other things being equal.

However, the individual supply curve of labour is an entirely different matter. You must remember **'labour is human'**. When the returns are low a machine will not run for long, say 4 hours, but when the returns are high the machine will run for 24 hours a day, 7 days a week. Obviously a human being cannot work for 24 hours a day, 7 days a week. He or she needs sleep. Even a 'workaholic' has to sleep.

However, there is another consideration apart from sleep. A human being considers his or her quality of life and usually it is the leisure hours that contribute most to the quality of life. The game of cricket, the fishing, the reading and the partying enhance the quality of life. Therefore a human being has to weigh up wages against leisure. When he or she thinks that there is the right balance between money earnings and leisure, that will be the amount of labour supplied by an individual. This gives the phenomenon of the **'backward-sloping supply curve of labour'**. (Remember that this is the individual supply curve for labour.)

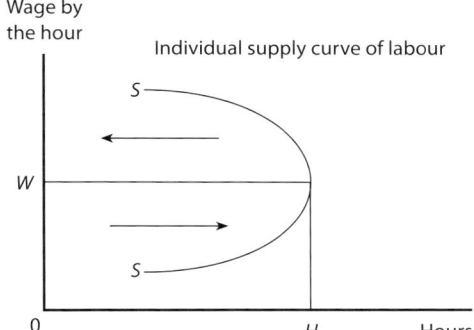

Fig. 4.3
The backward-sloping supply curve of labour

An individual will respond normally to higher wages between 0 and W, i.e. he or she will supply more hours of labour to obtain higher wages. However, there comes a point when he or she has enough wages and does not wish to offer more hours of work when wages rise beyond W. He or she wants leisure and will not work beyond H. In fact, if wages rise above W, the individual will say that he or she will take more and more leisure – a very happy state of affairs!

The supply of labour to a firm

If a construction company wishes to employ another builder, it will have to pay the **'going rate'** and will be able to go on hiring labour at this rate. This is because there is an infinite number of builders available in the labour market. This is one assumption of **perfect competition** (see Chapter 8: The price mechanism).

However, if there is not perfect competition, the construction company will have to pay higher and higher wages to attract more and more builders. The construction company will not only have to pay the higher wage to the additional worker, it will have to pay all its workers the higher wage (see Figure 4.4).

Figure 4.4(a) shows the situation in perfect competition when the firm is facing an horizontal supply curve. At wage W, it can recruit an infinite number of workers. It does not have to increase the wage to recruit another worker. However, below W it would not be able to recruit any workers. Figure 4.4(b) shows the situation in imperfect competition when the firm has to increase the wage to recruit another worker. The firm has to bid up wages to recruit an additional worker.

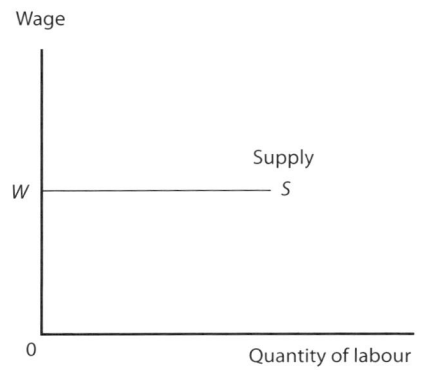

Fig. 4.4
The supply of labour to a firm in perfect and imperfect competition

(a) Perfect competition   (b) Imperfect competition

Capital

Capital is the man-made factor of production. Capital is the input that has itself been made. Capital consists of tools, machines and factories. In its simplest form, a machete is capital. In its most complex form, a computer is capital. In its largest form an oil refinery is capital. (Business Studies students accustomed to thinking of capital as money must revise their understanding of 'capital'.)

Examination Tip

Make sure that in an Economics examination, you give the economist's definition of capital and not any other.

Definition of capital

Capital refers to man-made physical goods which are used to produce other goods and services.

Primitive societies had land, labour but little capital (and enterprise). They did have primitive tools so there was not entirely an absence of capital. (They did have some enterprise, e.g. in the organisation of a hunting expedition.)

Capital is a limited resource in that an economy has a certain stock of capital, e.g. a certain number of factories. However, what is happening in the world today in capital is far more significant in productivity than what is happening in land or labour.

A container is being transferred from a ship to a truck. Transport is capital.

Source: Stillpictures.

Technology is making capital more and more productive. (You may argue that this is because capital is man-made and labour is becoming ever more skilled!) Loss of technology seldom ever happens. Once a process is discovered, it becomes recorded and cannot be lost. We can all understand how much computerisation has increased productivity.

Transport – road, rail, sea, air and pipeline – is capital. Transport has improved and increased productivity. The donkey-cart was capital, but jet freight is modern capital in transport.

Finally, stock is capital also. The stock of goods that are produced by a factory and waiting to be sold is a capital resource. When they are sold they will be turned into money, but until they are sold they are part of capital. Capital is a man-made resource.

Enterprise

Enterprise was identified as a factor of production by economists later than the other three. They recognised that there was a factor which added something to the other three to make them more productive in combination – the ability or skill of an 'entrepreneur'. Therefore, the factor was called 'entrepreneurship' or 'entrepreneurial ability' or, more simply, enterprise.

> **Definition of enterprise**
>
> Enterprise is the organisation of the factors of production by an entrepreneur who takes a risk in the expectation of making a profit.

Bill Gates is a good example of an entrepreneur. He introduced new products, new techniques and new software. He organised his land, labour and capital into the Microsoft empire and, in doing so, he took risks. In the Caribbean, Ernst & Young, an international accountancy firm, introduced a 'Caribbean Entrepreneur of the Year' (EOY) programme. Then a 'Master Entrepreneur of the Year' (MEY) was introduced. Some of the outstanding winners have been:

1999   Gordon 'Butch' Stewart of Jamaica, Chairman of Sandals Beach Resorts.
2000   Geoffrey Cave of Barbados, Chairman of Cave Shepherd & Company Limited.
2001   Arthur Lok Jack of Trinidad and Tobago, Chairman of Associated Brands Investments Ltd.

EXERCISE See if you can find some other examples of entrepreneurs. Explain what impact they have had in their particular industry.

Enterprise increases productivity. Without doubt this factor of production has become very important. Take two businesses producing the same good, e.g. cars. One is more productive than the other when other things are equal because of enterprise. The entrepreneur introduces new models, adopts new production techniques, organises labour, adopts new sales tactics, and so on, all the time taking risks, and he will increase productivity.

The returns to the factors of production

Land

The return to land is **rent**. The owner of land receives rent as his reward. The amount of rent received is determined by demand and supply.

> **Definition of rent**
>
> Rent is the income received for the use of land.

In England, at the beginning of the nineteenth century, the price of corn was a big issue and landowners were complaining about low prices. They did not understand Economics. They said that the price of corn was low because the price of land was low. An economist, David Ricardo, explained that the price of land was low because the price of corn was low. The price of land was derived from the price of corn. This introduced the idea of **derived demand**.

> **Definition of derived demand**
>
> Derived demand is when the demand for a factor production depends on the demand for the good it produces. For example, the demand for bauxite miners is derived from the demand for bauxite.

Rent is determined by demand and supply. The supply of land is fixed as the land area is fixed. This is easy to see in the islands of the Caribbean; for example, Jamaica has a fixed land area bounded by sea. (We are not considering reclamation. Remember we said earlier that we are talking about natural land unimproved by capital.) This means that the supply curve for land is a vertical straight line. Therefore, the price of land (the rent) will be determined solely by the demand for it.

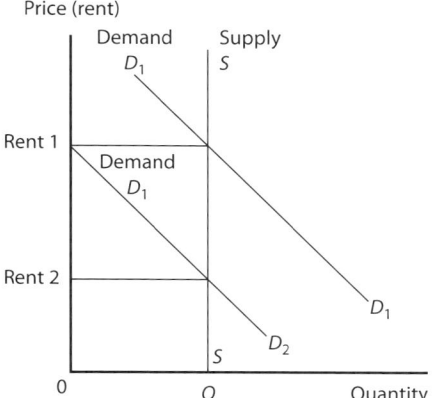

Fig. 4.5
The fixed supply of land

In the above diagram, *SS* is the supply curve for land. It is a vertical straight line because the supply of land is fixed. DD_1 illustrates the demand for land being high. This yields a high rent for the land, Rent 1. DD_2 illustrates a low demand for land and the rent is low at DD_2. This is the graphical representation for Ricardo's explanation.

When we say that the supply of land is fixed we are saying that land has no **supply price**, i.e. the amount of land on the market does not respond to price. This is not exactly true. Land can be reclaimed from the sea. It can be drained, fertilised, cleared and levelled to bring it into use. However, this is land with capital being applied.

Labour

Labour is the human resource and it is hired for wages. Economists use **'wage'** for the return to labour, whatever the nature of the labour.

Definition of wage
Wage is the income received for the use of labour.

The wage paid depends on the demand and supply in a market economy. If there is a very short supply of motor mechanics, the wage will be relatively high. If there is an abundant supply of farm labourers, the wage will be relatively low.

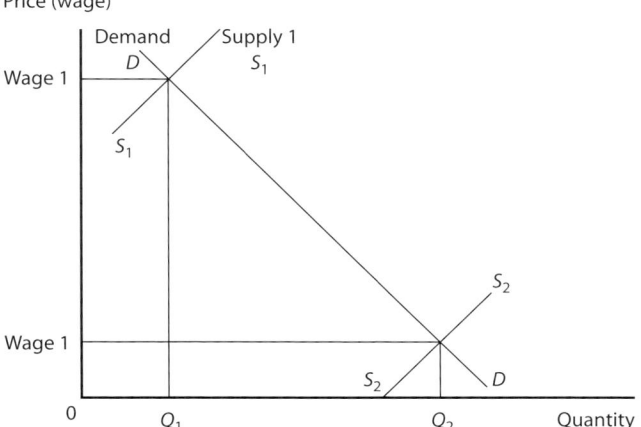

Fig. 4.6
Short v abundant supply of labour

The supply of labour, S_1S_1, is scarce so the wage, W_1, is high, e.g. rocket scientists. The supply of labour, S_2S_2, is abundant so the wage, W_2, is low (farm labourers).

You can use this diagram to explain the difference in wages between skilled and unskilled workers, assuming that skilled workers are in short supply and unskilled workers abundant. If the medical schools were turning out thousands of doctors, their wages would be relatively low!

Trade unions bargain for higher wages for their workers. They understand Economics. They know that if they can restrict the supply of labour, market forces will make wages go up. Therefore, they campaign for qualifications for each job, or for so many years of apprenticeship before a person can perform a certain job. Either approach restricts the supply of labour. Trade unions are in a very weak position when there are thousands of unemployed workers looking for work.

Farm workers preparing the ground for planting in Haiti. Labour is abundant.

Source: Stillpictures.

EXERCISE Choose three or four different occupations. Find out what the average wages are in those occupations and draw a demand and supply curve to explain them.

Capital

The return to capital is **interest**. Like rent and wage, interest is also a price.

> **Definition of interest**
> Interest is the price which has to be paid for the services of capital.

If a firm wants to buy a machine (capital), it can borrow the money. It will have to pay interest on the capital sum borrowed. If a firm uses its own funds to buy the machine, there is the **opportunity cost** of forgoing the interest that those funds could have earned in another investment. Therefore, either way, interest is the price of the machine.

The return to capital (the interest) must cover three things:

1 The opportunity cost of the next best alternative use for the money.

2 The risk involved. There is always a risk in a business venture and the calculation of the risk in money terms is called the 'risk premium'.

3 The cost of inflation. Money falls in value if there is inflation and the rate of interest must cover this. For example, if the **nominal** rate of interest is 5% and the rate of inflation is 8%, the **real** rate of interest is negative at −3%.

> **Definitions of nominal and real rates of interest**
> The nominal rate is the rate of interest in current terms.
> The real rate is the rate of interest corrected for inflation.

The determination of the rate of interest

There are two theories of the determination of the rate of interest: the loanable funds theory, which is a demand and supply explanation, and the liquidity preference theory.

The loanable funds theory

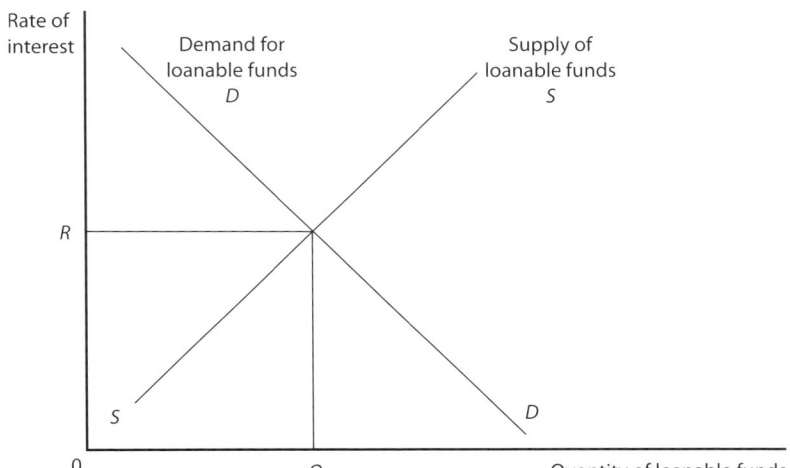

Fig. 4.7
Rate of interest determined by the demand and supply of loanable funds

The demand for loanable funds comes from firms wanting to borrow money for investment in capital goods from which they expect to gain profit. (There are other sectors who may demand loanable funds, e.g. households and governments, but let's assume it is just firms.)

The supply of loanable funds comes from individuals, firms and governments who wish to save. People will only save if the opportunity cost of not spending their funds is covered by the interest rate.

The liquidity preference theory

> **Definition of liquidity**
> Liquidity is the ability to turn an asset into cash.

Cash is the most liquid of all assets. A savings certificate is liquid in that it can be turned into cash within 24 hours. A stamp collection is not very liquid as a buyer has to be found and a price agreed on which may take months.

Therefore, the liquidity preference theory deals with people's desire to hold their wealth in the form of money. This very much depends on the rate of interest.

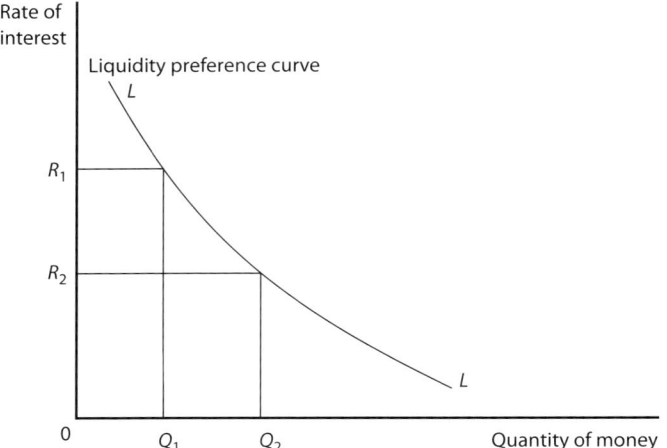

Fig. 4.8
The liquidity preference curve

At R_1, investors want to hold only Q_1 of money. When the rate of interest is high, investors will invest in capital goods because of the high rate of return and they will not want to hold money. The **opportunity cost** of holding money (the rate of interest forgone) is too high. Businesses will put up new factories or buy new machinery because the return on capital is high.

At R_2, investors will want to hold Q_2 of money. The rate of interest has fallen and money has become more attractive because the opportunity cost of holding money is low. Businessmen will hold off from building new factories and buying new machinery until the rate of return on capital is higher.

Definition of liquidity preference
The liquidity preference curve is the demand curve for money.

Enterprise

The return to the factor enterprise is profit. An entrepreneur takes risks and profit is the reward for risk-taking. In business ventures, there are risks and a businessman would not take these risks without the prospect of reward. The higher the risk, the greater the profit that would be needed to attract the entrepreneur.

Definition of profit
Profit is the reward to entrepreneurs for taking a risk in organising production.

Another way of looking at profit is that it is an incentive to go into business in the first place. Once in business, it is an incentive to expand, to increase the size of the business or to branch out into other goods and services or into new methods of production.

Some risks can be insured against but the probability of making a profit is uninsurable. If it was insurable, there would be no risk in business and no entrepreneurship.

Pure profit

Economists disagree with businessmen on what can be considered 'profit' so they come up with something that they can all agree on – the concept of pure profit. A business person thinks of profit as what is left to himself or herself after all the costs and expenses have been deducted. Economists call this **'accountants' profit'**.

An economist is more precise. If the money to be invested was put in a risk-free investment, let's say a post office savings account or a deposit account in a bank, it would earn interest, but the economist would call this the opportunity cost of capital and it would be deducted from profit. There is no risk in a bank or post office account and profit is a reward for risk. The economist would say that there is a normal profit which is the profit which keeps a business going without taking risks. Pure profit is the profit over and above these other two. It is the pure return on risk taking. It can be set out like this:

Pure profit = residual profit – the return of capital in a risk-free investment (usually referred to as interest) – normal profit.

Therefore, profit is the return for taking a risk above that taken by other entrepreneurs in an industry.

Finally, consider that there must be a risk of a loss, a negative profit. There is no risk if a positive profit is certain.

Examination questions

1. Explain what is meant by the four factors of production. *(10 marks)*

2. Describe the role of an entrepreneur. *(5 marks)*

3. Explain, with the use of examples, what is meant by a natural resource of a country. *(5 marks)*

4. Discuss why a company might change its combination of factors of production. *(10 marks)*

5. Why do you think a worker might be prepared to work for a relatively low wage? *(5 marks)*

6. Discuss why some occupations are paid more than others. *(10 marks)*

7 Distinguish between labour intensive and capital intensive production. *(5 marks)*

8 Explain the rewards that are paid to the different factors of production. *(10 marks)*

9 a What is meant by the specialisation of labour? *(4 marks)*
   b Explain how specialisation of labour can lead to greater productivity. *(6 marks)*

Chapter 5

The costs of production

The theory of the costs of production is covered comprehensively in this chapter and you will have more practice in reading graphs:

- You will first link Chapter 5 with Chapter 4 in that there can be no output without costs
- You will learn to distinguish between fixed costs and variable costs
- You will learn to distinguish between total costs, variable costs and marginal costs
- You will learn the relationship between the average and the margin
- Finally, you will see graphically what is meant by 'the economies of scale'

The link between output and inputs

There can be no output without input and inputs have costs. Therefore, there can be no output without costs. To a firm, the cost of its site is the rent it pays*, the cost of its labour is the wages paid, the cost of its capital is the interest and the cost of its entrepreneurship is its profit. Therefore, the costs of production are the rent, wages, interest and profit that a firm pays.

> **Definition of imputed rent**
>
> Imputed rent is the benefit that the owner-occupiers enjoy from living in their own property. It is the opportunity cost of not receiving rent from a tenant or it is the rent that would have to be paid for an equivalent property.

Fixed costs and variable costs

Fixed costs

Some costs have to be paid whether there is production or not and they stay the same whatever the level of production. These are called fixed costs, e.g. rent is a fixed cost because the landlord will demand rent whether anything is being produced.

> **Definition of fixed costs**
>
> Fixed costs are the costs of production that do not vary with output.

---

*Even if a firm owns the land it operates on, it must allow for rent. This is called **'imputed rent'**. (Remember **opportunity cost** and the problem of the opportunity cost of living in your own house.)

Fig. 5.1
Fixed costs

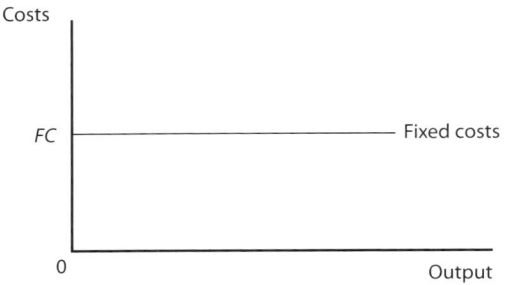

Fixed costs are shown on a graph as a horizontal straight line. They stay the same whatever the output. Fixed costs are also known as 'indirect costs' or 'overheads' but 'overheads' are loosely applied to electricity and other utilities (see later note about gas, water, electricity). Examples of fixed costs are:

Rent
Rates
Some forms of tax
Insurance
Interest on loans
Depreciation

Let us single one out for illustration. The bank will want its interest on a loan. It is not interested in whether the firm is producing or not. The firm borrowed the money and must repay the loan regularly.

All capital assets, such as buildings, machinery, furniture etc., decline in value and this must be seen as a cost to a firm. A firm should set aside money to cover this depreciation. One way of measuring depreciation is the cost of replacement.

Definition of depreciation
Depreciation is the fall in value of the existing stock of capital through wear and tear.

EXERCISE

Look in a newspaper and try and find examples of how the price of a particular model of a car changes over a number of years.

Variable costs

Variable costs vary with output. They increase with output, i.e. the greater the output, the higher the variable costs. They are also called 'direct costs' or 'prime costs'. When there is no output, there are no variable costs.

Definition of variable costs
These are the costs of production which vary directly with output.

Examples of variable costs include:

Raw materials (component costs)
Wages
Fuel and power*

Examination Tip: It would be good to get across to the examiner the idea that some costs combine a fixed and a variable element.

EXERCISE Consider why some costs, such as electricity or telephone, have both fixed and variable elements.

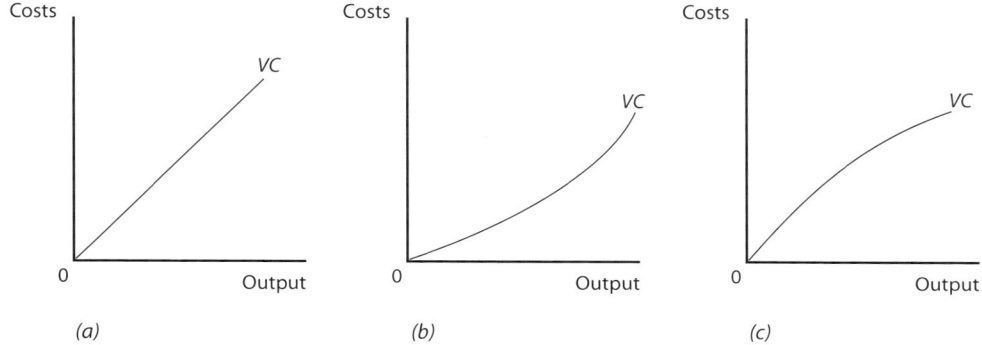

Fig. 5.2 Variable costs

(a)   (b)   (c)

In Figure 5.2(a), variable costs rise constantly with output.
In Figure 5.2(b), variable costs rise with output but they rise at a faster rate than output.
In Figure 5.2(c), variable costs rise with output but they rise at a slower rate than output.

Total costs

Definition of total costs

Total cost is the cost of producing a given amount of output. It is equal to total fixed costs plus total variable costs.

Total costs = fixed costs + variable costs. ($TC = FC + VC$). Total costs rise with output. This can be seen in the following graph.

---

* Electricity, gas and water have some elements of both fixed and variable cost. The fixed cost element is the charge for being connected to the supplier and the variable cost is the unit charge. For example, in the case of the telephone, the line rental is the fixed cost and the unit cost is the charge per call. Therefore, economists are wary about calling gas, water and electricity 'overheads' as if they are fixed costs. They are 'semi-fixed costs' (or 'semi-variable costs'!).

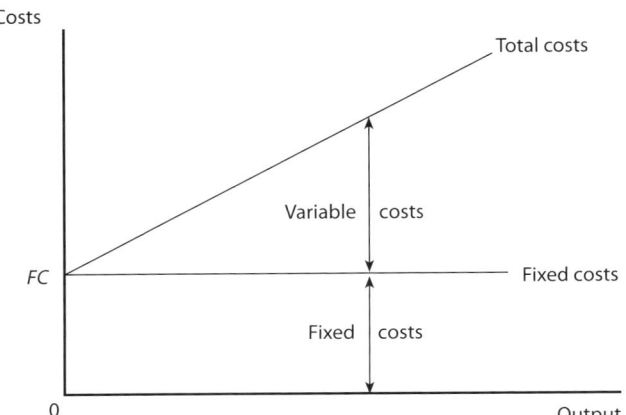

Fig. 5.3
Total costs

When output is zero there are fixed costs, 0 – FC. Variable costs can be measured by the distance between fixed costs and total costs at any level of output.

Total costs and average costs

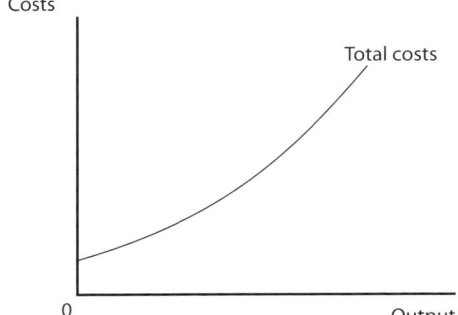

Fig. 5.4
Total costs rising at a slower rate then faster rate than output

The total cost curve above is more realistic than a straight line. When output is at zero, total costs = fixed costs. When output starts rising, variable costs rise.

$$\text{Average costs} = \frac{\text{total costs}}{\text{output}} \qquad AC = \frac{TC}{Q}$$

Definition of average costs

Average cost is the cost per unit of output. It is equal to total cost divided by total output.

When costs are rising at a slower rate than output, **average costs must be falling**. When they are rising at a faster rate than output, **average costs must be rising**. Therefore, the average cost curve is **U-shaped**, i.e. it goes down and then up. This is very important in Economics. As output increases, average costs will fall up to the point Q, but beyond this point, average costs begin to rise. This is shown in the graph below.

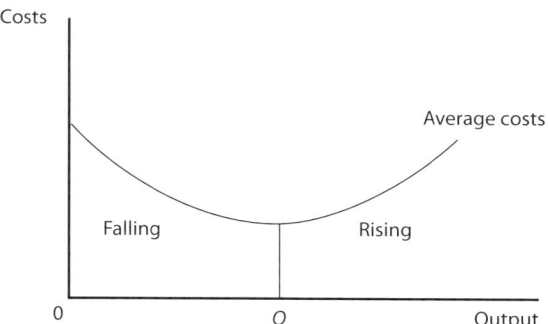

Fig. 5.5
U-shaped average cost curve

Marginal costs

> **Definition of marginal costs**
>
> Marginal cost is the cost of producing an additional unit of output.

Passat production in China.

Source: Stillpictures.

For example, if one more car is produced, there will be an addition to the raw materials and labour used by the firm, both of which will add to costs.

Marginal costs are very important to a firm. The manager may say: 'If I produce one more unit, how much will it add to my costs?' Of course, if that last unit adds more to costs than to revenue, the manager should not produce that unit.

The marginal cost curve is also 'U-shaped' but again it is only called 'U-shaped' because it falls and then rises. When output starts, an additional unit adds less to costs than the unit that went before and marginal costs are falling up to a point, Q. After that point, Q, an additional unit adds more to costs than the unit that went before and marginal costs are rising. This can be seen in the graph below.

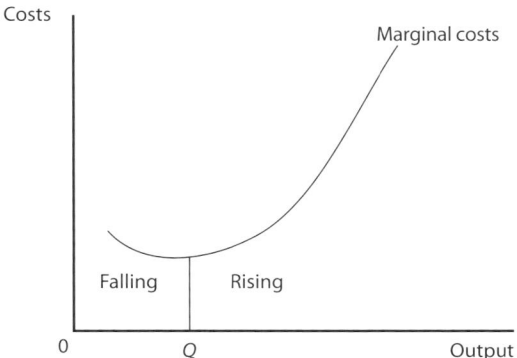

Fig. 5.6
U-shaped marginal cost curve

Average cost and marginal costs

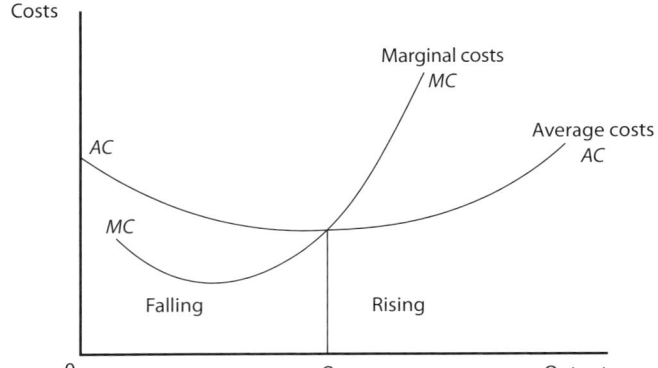

Fig. 5.7
Relationship between average costs, AC, and marginal costs, MC

When marginal costs are below average costs, average costs are falling. When marginal costs are above average costs, average costs are rising. **Therefore, the marginal cost curve cuts the average cost curve from below at the lowest point of the average cost curve.** When marginal cost is below average cost, it is pulling average cost downwards. When marginal cost is above average cost, it is pulling average cost upwards.

Examination Tip

> Examiners will want you to include diagrams to help support your explanations but make sure that they are drawn and labelled correctly.

This can be explained by taking an example from cricket. If a batsman scores 25 in the first match and 35 in the second match, the average score is 30 per match, and the marginal score is 35. In the third match the batsman scores 60. The average score is 40 and the marginal score is 60. The marginal score has pulled the average up. However, if in the fourth match the batsman makes 20, the average score is 35 (140/4) and the marginal score is 20. The marginal score is below the average score and has pulled the average down.

EXERCISE

Try and think of some other examples which show the relationship between the average and the margin, such as the number of goals scored by a particular footballer.

The short run and the long run

The terms 'short run' and 'long run' are very important in the theory of the costs of production.

Definitions of the short run and the long run

The short run is the period of time during which at least one factor of production is fixed.

The long run is the period of time during which all factors of production can be varied.

For example, in the short run, a firm may be able to vary the input of labour but the machinery cannot be varied – it is fixed. Perhaps more labour can be applied at short notice but the firm cannot buy and install another machine for a long time.

In the long run, a firm has enough time to juggle with labour, machinery and land as its inputs until it can achieve the least cost method of production.

The actual time period for short and long runs varies with the industry. The short run in a shop may be only a day or two. The short run in a car plant may be six months.

The long-run average total cost curve

This curve is very important to a firm. It shows the level of output at which the costs are lowest. A firm should aim to achieve this level of output, not less and not more, other things being equal.

In Economics, the lowest point on a firm's long-run average total cost curve is called **'capacity'**.

> **Definition of capacity**
>
> Capacity is the level of output at the lowest point on a firm's long-run average total cost curve.

At every level of output there is a short-run average total cost curve (at least one factor is fixed). These are shown as SRATCs 1–8 on the graph. The long-run average total cost curve, LRATC, is drawn **tangential to all the SRATCs**. It is therefore called an envelope or an umbrella curve. At each level of output, there is a short-run average total cost curve.

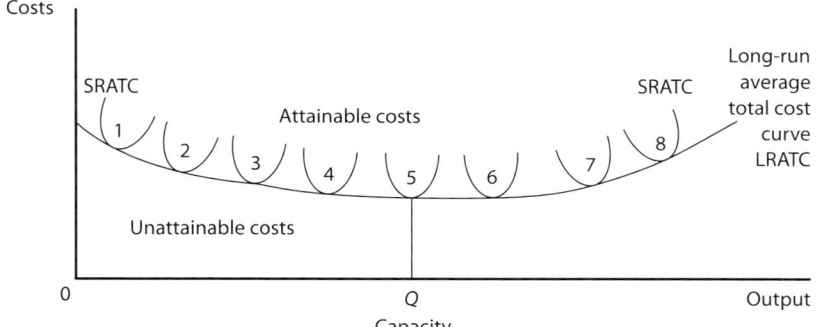

Fig. 5.8
The 'umbrella' of cost curves

Below the LRATC, costs are unattainable; above the LRATC, costs are attainable but the firm could achieve lower costs by reaching the curve. A firm can lower its LRATC by improving technology. In this way, it could enter the 'unattainable costs' area.

Economies of scale

A rational firm would like to achieve its lowest-cost output, but it may not be able to become big enough because of the restriction of the market. If the market is big enough, or if a firm can expand its market, e.g. by exporting, it may be able to achieve economies of scale.

> **Definition of economies of scale**
> Economies of scale refer to the reductions in long-run average costs as the scale of production and output of the firm increases.

A firm can increase output and enjoy falling costs up to a point. Up to this point, it is enjoying 'economies of scale'. It will achieve its maximum economies of scale at capacity. If the firm increases output beyond this point, it will experience diseconomies of scale, i.e. rising costs. The economies of scale in Economics is another way of saying 'big is best'!

There are a number of examples of economies of scale.

Technical or plant economies

1. The division of labour and specialisation. The larger the firm, the more opportunity there is for division of labour and specialisation.

2. Technical economies. Certain machines only become economical to use when the output is large. On a very large scale, we can think of the introduction of robots in a car plant. Another technical economy involves containers. The larger the container, the bigger the volume relative to surface area. Therefore, this economy of scale can only be achieved when large volumes have to be dealt with.

3. Large machines are more efficient. Only one worker has to switch the machine on and off whatever its size. Therefore, the lower the wage costs relative to output as the size of the machine increases.

4. Spin-offs. When output is sufficiently large, there may be spin-offs in the form of by-products, e.g. the by-products of the US Space Programme.

Spreading the overheads.

Spreading the overheads

The fixed costs have to be paid whether the firm is producing or not. The larger the output, the lower the fixed costs per unit. For example, a gas (petrol) station has fixed costs in the form of rent, electricity and depreciation. The more cars it serves, and the larger the number of gallons, the more the overheads are spread.

Financial economies

1. Large firms are able to buy in bulk. The bigger the bulk, the lower the price usually charged.

2. Large firms may be able to borrow money at lower rates of interest because they are considered more secure by the financial institutions.

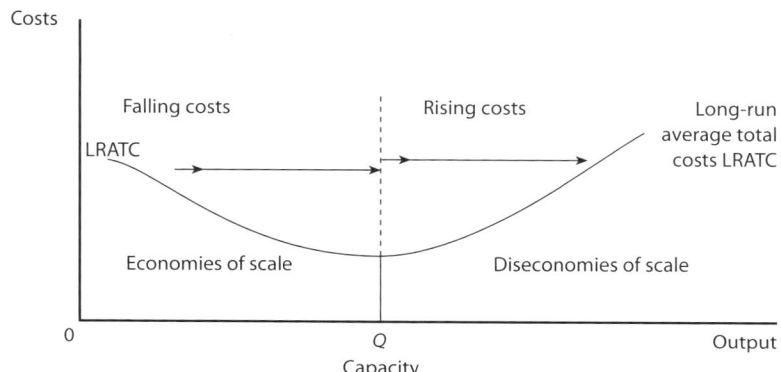

Fig. 5.9
The economies of scale

Diseconomies of scale

Definition of diseconomies of scale

This refers to the increases in long-run average costs as the scale of production and output of the firm increases.

The causes of diseconomies of scale include the following:

1. Simply, the business becomes unwieldy and there is poor communication. In a very large car plant, there can be difficulties in moving from one part of the plant to another.

2. Management problems. Management loses touch with the operations of the firm.

3. Workers lose their motivation because their roles appear insignificant in a large firm.

4. In mass production, especially in the assembly lines, a hold up in one section can lead to an expensive breakdown in production.

5. Very large trade union membership may lead to industrial action and stoppages.

EXERCISE Discuss whether the advantages of a large factory outweigh the disadvantages.

Examination questions

1 What are the advantages of a firm becoming large? *(10 marks)*

2 Distinguish, with the aid of examples, between fixed costs and variable costs. *(6 marks)*

3 Distinguish clearly between economies and diseconomies of scale. *(10 marks)*

4 Distinguish between average and marginal costs of production. *(6 marks)*

5 Explain why the distinction between the short run and the long run is so important. *(6 marks)*

Goods and services

In this chapter, the different types of goods that economists speak of will be explained as well as the services produced in an economy:

- Firstly the distinction between goods and services is explained
  Then the goods have been put in pairs to help you distinguish them
- Free goods and economic goods
- Consumer goods and capital goods
- Normal goods and inferior goods
- Giffen goods and Veblen goods
- Private goods and public goods
- Merit goods and demerit goods
- Finally you will learn about the different types of services in the economy

The distinction between goods and services

A good is a tangible thing, i.e. it can be touched, whereas a service is intangible. Two straightforward examples will make this distinction clear. This book is a good. Education is a service.

Other distinctions between goods and services are more confusing. A tangible good such as a television is not immediately consumed but provides a flow of services over time and for future consumption. In a health service, you may be given a tablet to swallow which, of course, is tangible.

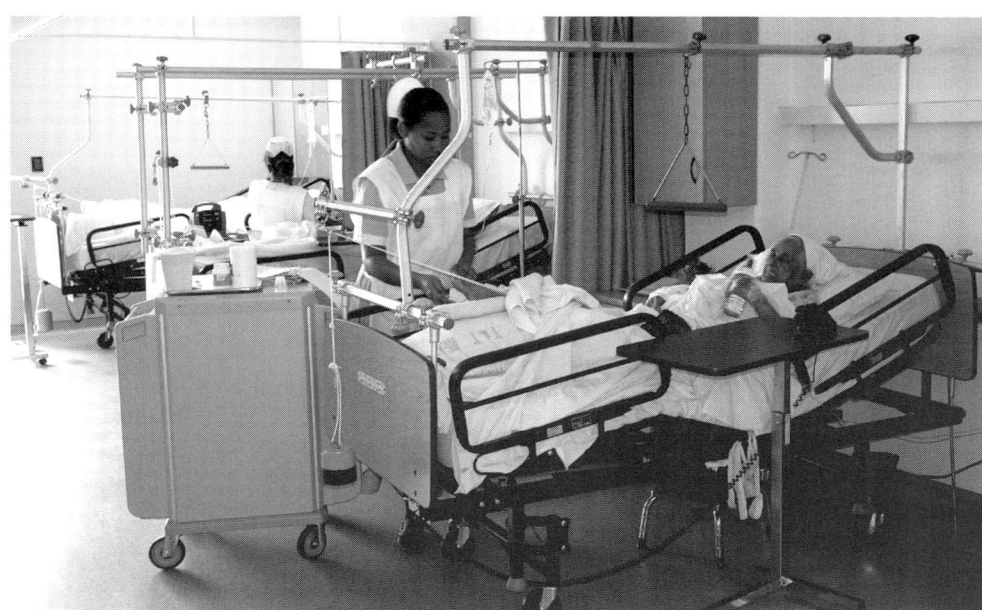

Health is a service industry.

> **Definitions of goods and services**
>
> A good is a tangible item produced by firms and in demand by individuals for consumption or by firms as an input to their production process. Examples of goods include clothing, foodstuffs, minerals, crops and livestock, buildings, machinery and vehicles.
>
> A service is an intangible item produced by firms for the benefit of consumers, not only as individuals but also for society as a whole. Examples of services include catering, hotel accommodation, tourism, transport, health, education, banking and insurance.

Goods

Economists distinguish between many types of goods so it is important to be clear about each of them.

Free goods and economic goods

> **Definitions of free goods and economic goods**
>
> A free good does not have scarcity.
>
> An economic good does have scarcity.

To some economists, there is only one free good – air. Air does not have scarcity. One person breathing air does not deprive others of it. We could say that in the case of a free good, its consumption by one person does not reduce its supply to others. However, we shall be using that as a definition for public goods later on.

Other economists will also allow water in the middle of the ocean to be classed as a free good. Otherwise, water is not a free good. Do you turn off the tap when brushing your teeth? If you are an economist, you should do. It is not because economists are mean! Tap water has scarcity.

All other goods are economic goods. They use up scarce resources in their production. When one person eats a loaf of bread, he is reducing the supply to others. An economic good has opportunity costs. The resources going into an economic good could have been used for something else.

Consumer goods and capital goods

> **Definitions of consumer goods and capital goods**
>
> Consumer goods confer utility or satisfaction. Examples include foodstuffs, clothing and sports equipment.
>
> Capital goods are goods used to make other goods. They do not confer utility directly but they produce consumer goods which do give utility. Alternatively, they produce other capital goods which produce consumer goods. Examples include machines and factories.

EXERCISE

Discuss why some goods, such as a bicycle, could be regarded as both a consumer good and a capital good.

A consumer good or a capital good?

Some consumer goods are called consumer durables.

> **Definition of a consumer durable good**
>
> A consumer durable good is one which provides a flow of utility in the future.

A television set will provide hours of entertainment and information for a number of years. The most important consumer durable is a house but economists qualify this because a house provides a flow of services more than any other consumer good. It can also be considered as an investment. The second most important is usually considered to be a car.

Normal goods and inferior goods

> **Definitions of normal good and inferior goods**
>
> A normal good is one more of which is demanded as income rises. Examples include clothes, CDs, furniture and cell phones.
>
> An inferior good is a good less of which is demanded as income rises. Examples include plastic shoes, margarine and black and white televisions.

Examination Tip

> You will need to be careful when discussing examples of inferior goods. Point out to the examiner that you realise it can be a difficult issue as what is regarded as an inferior good in one country may not be regarded as one in another country.

EXERCISE

Can you think of any examples of inferior goods?

Normal good graph

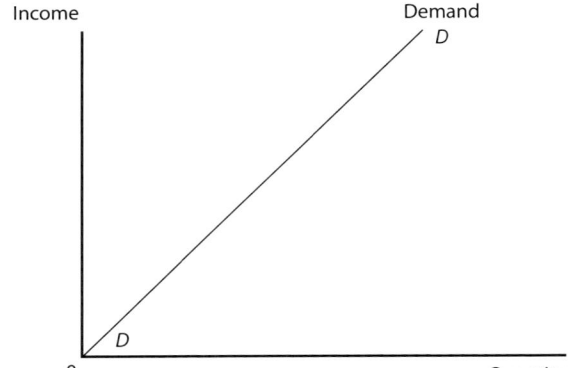

Fig. 6.1
Demand moving directly with income – normal good

Inferior good graph

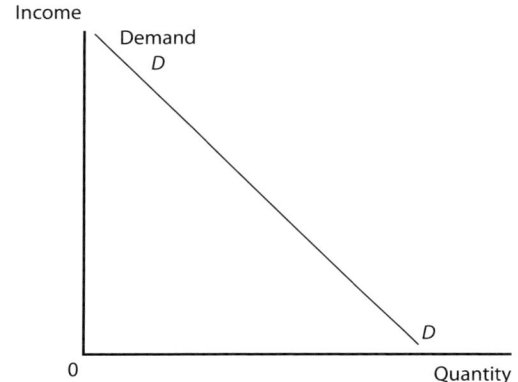

Fig. 6.2
Demand moving inversely with income – inferior good

Demand for a good over ranges of income

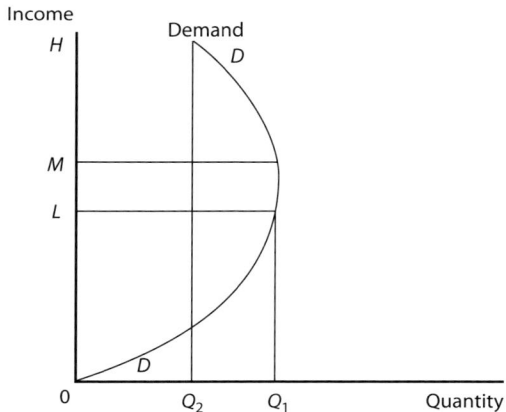

Fig. 6.3
Graph showing the importance of the range of income

Over the range of income from 0 to L, the good behaves like a normal good, i.e. demand increases as income rises. Over the range of income from L to M, demand does not change as income rises but remains at Q_1. Over the high range of income from L to H, demand for the good falls from Q_1 to Q_2 as income rises and the good is behaving as an inferior good.

Giffen goods and Veblen goods

Definition of a Giffen good
A Giffen good is a type of inferior good the demand for which rises as the price increases.

A Giffen good was named after Sir Robert Giffen who claimed that in the Irish Potato Famine of the 1840s, the poor demanded more potatoes when their price rose. He explained that the Irish poor had little income left for other goods such as fish when the price of potatoes rose, so they just bought more potatoes to keep their bellies full.

Definition of a Veblen good
A Veblen good is an example of conspicuous consumption, more of which is demanded as the price rises.

In his book, *The Theory of the Leisured Class* (1899), Veblen argued that rich people bought goods just to be seen in them or with them and that they would even demand more of such goods when the price rose. Such goods were a means of showing off how wealthy you were.

Irish Famine Memorial, Dublin, Ireland.

Source: PA/EMPICS.

The backward-sloping demand curve for Veblen goods

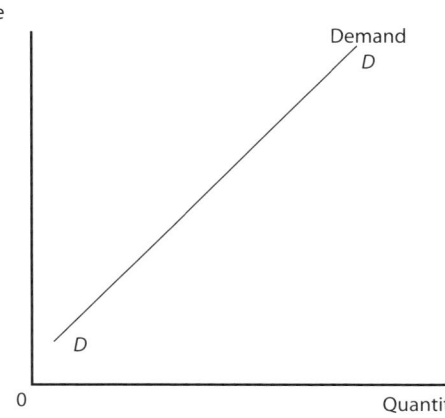

Fig. 6.4
An 'Irrational' demand curve: more is demanded when price rises

These goods involve 'snob buying'. Designer labels and ostentatious gold jewellery are examples of Veblen goods.

Private goods and public goods

> **Definitions of private goods and public goods**
>
> A private good is one the consumption of which by one individual reduces its availability to others.
>
> A public good is one the consumption of which by one individual does not reduce its availability to others.

Most goods are private goods. They are consumed by some individuals and when so consumed, cannot be consumed by others.

Examples of public goods include street lighting, lighthouses, defence and dams for flood control.

The free market would not provide public goods as there could be no charge for them. If one person paid for street lighting, others would be using it free. They are called 'free riders' and this is known as the free rider problem. Another way of looking at this is that public goods are provided by the government and paid for out of tax revenue. Some people do not pay taxes but they still consume the public goods. Non-taxpayers are free riders.

The Pelgre hydro-electric dam, Haiti. Deforestation and subsequent erosion have caused the reservoir to fill up with topsoil.

Source: Stillpictures.

A public good has *non-excludability*. No one can be excluded from using a public good. It can also be described as 'non-diminishing', i.e. it does not become smaller when it is consumed by one person or many persons.

A public good has *non-rivalry*. People do not compete for a public good because you do not have to pay a price for it; you do not have to bid for it as in the market. It can also be described as 'collectively consumed', i.e. many people are consuming it together.

Merit goods and demerit goods

Merit and demerit goods have been mentioned before in an earlier chapter but we shall refer to them again here.

> **Definitions of merit goods and demerit goods**
>
> A merit good has both a private benefit and a public benefit and would be under-consumed in a free market.
>
> A demerit good has a private benefit but a public cost and would be over-consumed in a free market.

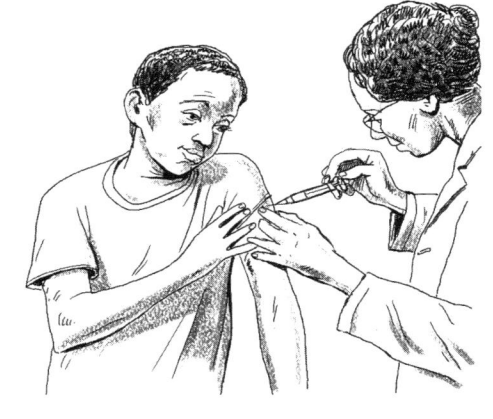

Inoculation is an example of a merit good.

Education and health services are examples of merit goods. We have seen that education confers private benefit because it brings greater earning power. It also brings public benefit because it increases productivity. An everyday health example is cleaning one's teeth. The private benefit is white teeth, healthy gums etc. The public benefit is good breath for those near to you.

Cigarettes and alcohol consumption are a demerit good. They bring private benefit as consumers enjoy them. However, they have costs to society as a whole in terms of the loss of productivity, possible violence and the drain on the health service. An everyday example of a demerit good could be eating garlic-prepared food. It obviously gives pleasure to the consumer but offends those catching a smell of the breath!

Cigarettes are an example of a demerit good.

EXERCISE Consider why governments provide merit goods.

Services

We can divide services into private sector and public sector services. The type of economy, to a certain extent, influences which services are in the private and public sectors. Of course, in Cuba, there are very few in the private sector because it is a command economy. In Cayman, it is the other way round with few services in the public sector. Therefore, we shall be drawing examples mainly from mixed economies in the Caribbean.

Some examples of services

Catering, tourism and transport

Catering is the provision of food, drink and entertainment for others. It is usually a private sector service. Even in Cuba, the government allows some private catering, mainly for tourists. In Barbados, 78% of the Gross Domestic Product comes from services and it employs 75% of the labour force. Catering services in Barbados are mostly in the private sector and are thriving; Barbados has so much expertise in it that it can export catering services. On the other hand, because catering is in the free market part of the economy, Barbados caterers have had to face competition from foreign suppliers in the domestic market.

Tourism is a very important service throughout the Caribbean. In Jamaica, tourism is the largest foreign exchange earner, accounting for over 50% of foreign exchange earnings. It employs 75,000 directly and another 90,000 indirectly. It is a private sector service but, as it is so important to the economy, the government assists the tourism industry. One way it does so is through the Tourism Product Development Company, a government agency to promote tourism.

Lastly, we can take transport. Transport is a service which is divided into two parts: the infrastructure, which consists of the fixed assets, such as the terminals (the ports, airports, stations) and the track and road network on the one hand and the carriers (the ships, airplanes, trains and road vehicles) on the other. As a simplification we can say that the public sector provides the infrastructure and the private sector provides the carriers.

For example, in Trinidad, the ports, such as Port-of-Spain, are in the public sector. The port facilities include handling equipment, warehousing, refrigeration areas, bunkering and freshwater facilities. Other major ports are Point Lisas, Point-à-Pierre, Chaguaramas, Point Fortin and Brighton. There is a privately-owned port, Tembladora. However, the shipping lines using these ports are in the private sector. Similarly, the airports are in the public sector but the airlines are in the private sector.

The roads in Trinidad are in the public sector and maintained by the public sector even when the public sector hires private contractors. However, the carriers are in the private sector to a much greater extent in Trinidad than in other parts of the Caribbean. The public transportation system in Trinidad on the roads is overshadowed by the private sector where the private car is the most common means of transportation. Trinidad and Tobago are estimated to have one of the highest number of cars per capita in the Western Hemisphere.

Education and health services

Even in free market economies, education and health are considered too important for the public good to be left to the private sector. This is because they are *merit goods* (they confer private benefit and social benefit). In the Cayman Islands, probably the most free market economy in the Caribbean, the government has taken a firmer grip on education since 2004 because it wants 'one university graduate in every household in the Cayman Islands by 2020'. Therefore, it is turning its attention to tertiary education and giving the Community College university status. It will offer four-year degree programmes accredited to the University of Tampa, Florida. In Trinidad and Tobago, tertiary education is now free at the University of the West Indies and at other centres.

In 1966, Jamaica established a national health service. The Ministry of Health is responsible for public hospitals, health centres, dispensaries, family planning and public health services. It controls 22 hospitals, 7 specialised hospitals and a teaching hospital at the University of the West Indies. It also controls 150 health centres, clinics and dispensaries. However, Jamaica is a 'mixed economy' and there are some private hospitals generally affiliated to religious organisations.

Examination questions

1. Distinguish, with the aid of examples, between a public good and a merit good. *(10 marks)*

2. Distinguish, with the aid of examples, between a consumer good and a capital good. *(10 marks)*

3. Explain what economists mean by a free good. *(5 marks)*

4. Compare and contrast, with the aid of examples, normal and inferior goods. *(10 marks)*

5. Explain the characteristics of **(a)** a Giffen good and **(b)** a Veblen good. *(6 marks)*

6. Discuss whether services like education or the health service should be provided in the public or the private sector. *(10 marks)*

Part three

Markets and prices

Chapter 7

Economic systems

Although there has been some treatment of the different types of economy earlier in the book, in this chapter you will analyse economic systems in much greater depth than in Chapter 1 and other previous chapters:

- You will learn how different economic systems allocate resources
- You will understand how different systems answer the questions 'What, How and For Whom?'
- You will then analyse the advantages and disadvantages of each type of economic system, starting with the command economy, then dealing with the free market economy and finishing with the mixed economy
- Finally, the traditional economy will be mentioned in relation to the Caribbean

Resource allocation

The economic resources of land, labour, capital and enterprise are scarce and must therefore be divided among competing uses. We have seen in Jamaica that the same land is suitable for arable farming and for the extraction of bauxite. Who decides what use the land is put to? The government? The market? If the government makes the economic decisions, the government will allocate the resources as in a command economy. If the market decides, the land will go to the highest bidder. The degree of government control over the economy determines the economic system.

Take the resource, labour. In a free market economy households, the owners of labour, decide how much labour to supply and where to supply it. They will probably supply it to the firm offering the highest wages and best conditions, other things being equal. In a command economy, the state will direct labour into the sectors the state chooses. In a free market economy, there may be insufficient demand for labour and some people will find themselves unemployed. In a command economy, there will be no unemployment as the state will put all the labour force to work whether it is producing what is wanted or not.

Similarly with capital. Market forces will attract capital (factories, machinery, tools) into those areas of production where it yields the greatest return. In a command economy, the state, as owners of capital, will allocate it where it thinks it is needed.

What, how and for whom?

These are the choices that all economies have to make because there are not enough resources to produce all things for all people. How many televisions, how many cricket bats, how many books, how many patties, how many restaurants and how many bus services will be produced or provided? In a free market economy, the question will be answered by the 'invisible hand'. The consumer exercises his or her choice by spending money in the market. When the consumer chooses a cricket bat, and not a book, resources – land, labour, capital and enterprise – will be diverted from books into cricket bats. The government has no part in it.

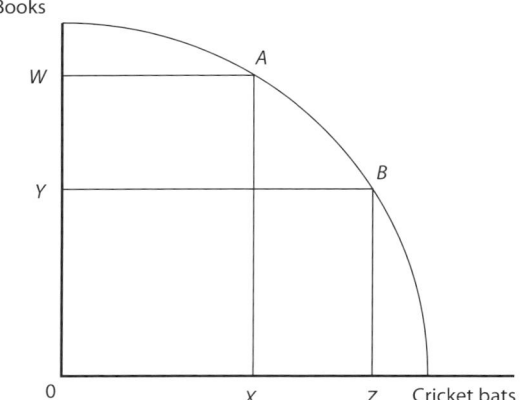

Fig. 7.1
Production possibility to illustrate the allocation of resources

If countries *A* and *B* respond to market forces, they will direct their resources as follows. In country *A*, consumers have chosen 0*W* books and 0*X* cricket bats. The consumers are avid readers and not so enthusiastic about sport. In country *B*, consumers have chosen 0*Y* books and 0*Z* cricket bats. The consumers are not so bookish but keen sports enthusiasts. The economies are being told how to allocate their resources between books and cricket bats. The economies have not enough resources to produce 0*W* books and 0*Z* cricket bats. The consumers have decided the allocation of resources in a free market by their demand.

How will the televisions, cricket bats etc. be produced when there are many ways of producing things? Will they use more machines or more labour? This will be a question of cost. Other things being equal, the least-cost method of production will be chosen. When cheap labour is abundant, more labour will be used and less machines if capital is expensive. In the United States, furniture would be produced by machines and in China it would be produced by hand because machines are relatively low-cost and wage rates are high in the United States, whereas in China it is the other way round.

These first two questions can be answered by Economics, but the third question – for whom will it be produced? – is only partly an economic question. Who has the money in an economic society to buy the goods is a political question. The distribution of income depends on many things, such as the tax system, land tenure, sex discrimination, race discrimination and so on. In a progressive tax system, the government takes a higher proportion of a rich man's income in tax than a poor man's. In a flat rate system, everyone pays the same rate of tax so the rich will have a larger share of goods and services than the poor.

> **Definition of a progressive tax**
>
> A progressive tax is one where the higher the income of the taxpayer, the larger the percentage of total income paid in tax.

> **Definition of a regressive tax**
>
> A regressive tax is one where higher income earners pay a lower proportion of their income in tax compared to lower income earners.

> **Definition of a proportional tax**
>
> A proportional tax is one where the percentage of total income paid in tax remains the same at different income levels.

EXERCISE Which type of taxation do you think is best? Explain your reasoning.

The circular flow of goods and services

The circular flow diagram can be used to show the relative positions of consumers and producers in a free market:

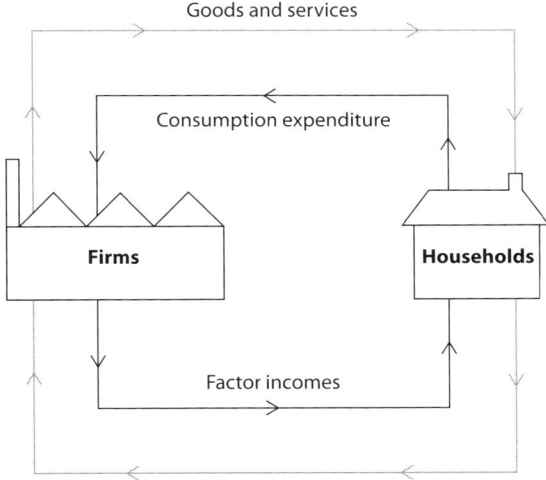

Fig. 7.2
The circular flow of goods and services diagram

Households are the owners of the factors of production, land, labour, capital and enterprise. They provide these factor services to firms in return for factor incomes: rent to land, wages to labour, interest to capital and profit to the entrepreneur. The households supply and the firms demand in the factor market.

Firms produce the goods and services that households demand. In return the households part with their factor incomes in their consumption expenditure. This time the households are demanding and the firms are supplying. In a market economy, demand and supply are the 'rulers'.

The circular flow diagram in Fig. 7.2 has no role for the government. It also assumes that there are no leakages or injections so the economy would be static.

The sectors of the economy

Fishing is in the primary sector.

Source: Stillpictures.

An economy can be divided into three sectors depending upon which resources are being used. These sectors are *primary, secondary and tertiary*.

The primary sector

The primary sector is based on the factor land and 'all that is therein'. Agriculture is a primary sector industry and so is fishing, one producing goods from the soil and the other from the sea, lakes and rivers. Forestry is another primary sector industry. The extraction industries like mining of minerals and oil are in the primary sector. Apart from Cayman, agriculture is a large employer of labour in Caribbean countries but not a big contributor in percentage terms to Gross Domestic Product. Times have changed! Much greater emphasis is placed on the secondary and tertiary sectors in the Caribbean today.

Table 7.1 Agriculture in selected Caribbean countries		
Country	%-age of labour force	%-age of GDP
Cayman	1.4	1.4
Cuba	24	6.6
Grenada	24	9.7
Guyana	N/A	38.3
Jamaica	21	7.4
St Lucia	43	10.7
St Vincent	26	10.6
Trinidad and Tobago	9.5	2

We can see from this that if agriculture contributes so little to GDP in percentage terms, the secondary and tertiary sectors must be far bigger contributors to GDP in Caribbean countries. For example, 41% of St Lucia's and 39% of St Vincent's exports are bananas, but banana prices in the world market have fallen relative to the prices of products from the secondary and tertiary sectors.

The secondary sector

In the secondary sector, raw materials are taken from the primary sector and turned into semi-finished and finished products. This is the industrial sector: the manufacturing and construction industries. For example, in the Jamaican economy, bauxite is the ore extracted from rocks which is refined into aluminium. The extraction is in the primary sector, the refining in the secondary sector. The refined product is semi-finished. It is shipped to other countries to be made into everything from car parts to drink cans. In many Caribbean countries, industry does go right through to the finished product: sugar cane is the primary product and rum is the finished product.

Table 7.2 Industry in selected Caribbean countries

Country	%-age of labour force	%-age of GDP
Antigua	11.0	19.2
Barbados	15.0	16.0
Cayman	12.6	3.2
Cuba	25.0	25.5
Grenada	14.0	15.0
Guyana	N/A	19.9
Jamaica	19.0	42.1
St Lucia	17.7	32.3
St Vincent	17.0	17.5
Trinidad and Tobago	17.0 (approx)	44.0

Many of the industries in these Caribbean countries are in their infancy (known as infant industries) but they are already making a significant contribution to GDP, especially in Jamaica and Trinidad and Tobago. An interesting industry is the manufacture of tennis racquets in St Vincent!

The tertiary sector

The tertiary sector involves *services*. The service industry supplies banking, law, insurance, administration, transport, communications, hotels and catering and tourism to other industries and to individual consumers. Services in Caribbean economies are dominant throughout nearly every country. This is because of tourism. Tourism is a big employer and a big contributor to GDP. The figures speak for themselves!

Air services are an example of the tertiary sector.

Table 7.3 Services in selected Caribbean countries		
Country	%-age of labour force	%-age of GDP
Antigua	82.0	76.8
Bahamas	90.0*	90.0
Barbados	75.0	78.0
Cayman	86.0	95.4**
Cuba	51.0	67.9
Dominica	28.0	63.0
Grenada	62.0	75.3
Jamaica	60.0	50.5
St Kitts	N/A	72.0
Trinidad and Tobago	64.1	54.0

Notes:
Recent figures for St Lucia and St Vincent are unavailable.
* 90% of the Bahamas labour force is made up of 50% employment in tourism and 40% in other services, such as banking and casinos.
** 95.4% of Cayman's GDP is made up of banking, insurance and finance as well as tourism. Hurricane Ivan (September, 2004) hit all the services, not just tourism, very hard.

Apart from the Bahamas and Cayman, services are dominated by tourism. Tourism seems to be doing very well for Caribbean economies but it must be mentioned that tourism is subject to external shocks like hurricanes, terrorism and political instability outside the country.

Definition of an external shock

An external shock is a damaging impact on an economy originating outside its economic system.

 **EXERCISE** See if you can find out how the percentage of GDP from each of the three sectors in your country has changed over the last hundred years.

Economic systems

All economies are mixed economies. However, economists do make classifications into which they can slot countries: free market, command or mixed. In its 'Index of Economic Freedom Rankings', the Heritage Foundation has four categories:

Free: Score 1–1.99
Mostly free: Score 2–2.99
Mostly unfree: Score 3–3.99
Repressed: Score 4–5

In the 2005 edition 151 countries are listed.
The lowest score shows the most free market and the highest score, the most command economy.
Hong Kong (1: Score 1.35) is the most free market, North Korea (151: Score 5.0) the most command economy.

Major Caribbean economies in economic freedom index

Table 7.4 Categorising Caribbean economies			
Free	**Mostly free**	**Mostly unfree**	**Repressed**
	25 Bahamas 2.25	79 Guyana 3.08	145 Haiti 4.04
	32 Barbados 2.35	121 Dominican Republic 3.54	149 Cuba 4.29
	40 Trinidad 2.49		
	47 Belize 2.66		
	54 Costa Rica 2.76		
	60 Jamaica 2.81		

Source: *Heritage Foundation; Economic Freedom Index.*

1 The criteria used by the Heritage Foundation are: trade policy, fiscal burden of government, government intervention in the economy, monetary policy, capital flows and foreign investment, banking and finance, wages and prices, property rights, regulation and informal market activity.

2 Hong Kong is still listed as the most free market economy although it has been taken over by the People's Republic of China as a Special Administrative Region (China is ranked 121).

3 The Cayman Islands are not listed as they are not an independent country.

4 The eight states in the Organisation of Eastern Caribbean States are not listed although six are independent because they are under one bank, the Eastern Caribbean Central Bank and so have no independent control over their money

supply, interest rates and exchange rates. Thus the important criteria used to judge economic systems are lacking, e.g. monetary policy, banking and finance and capital flows and foreign investment.

The three category classification of economic systems

1	2	3
Command economy	Free market economy	Mixed economy
Aka communism	Capitalism	Part capitalist, part socialist.
Totalitarianism	Laissez-faire economy	Some state control, some free market.
Socialism	'Invisible Hand' deciding allocation of resources.	(Mostly free)
Centrally planned economy	(Free)	
State controlled economy		
(Repressed)		
(Mostly unfree)		

Definition of a command economy
A command economy is one where resources are allocated by the state or government through a system of planning.

Definition of a free market economy
A free market economy is one where resources are allocated through the market mechanism with no government intervention.

Definition of a mixed economy
A mixed economy is one where some resources are allocated through the market mechanism and some by the state.

The command economy

A command economy is practised by socialist or communist countries such as North Korea and Cuba. The government owns all the land and capital, but not the human factor of production, labour. However, even if it does not own labour, it directs it into whatever production the state wishes. The government allocates these resources through some central planning authority. Thus there is a vast bureaucracy involved in collecting data about the factors of production and planning how best they can be used for the good of the state and its citizens.

It allocates resources at the macroeconomic level between consumer goods and capital goods. Resources are scarce and there is a trade off between current consumption and future consumption. The government decides what should be invested for the economy to grow and enjoy future consumption.

The government also intervenes at the microeconomic level. It decides which resources will be allocated to each industry for the output targets it has set. Within each industry, the government decides what goods each firm will produce. It also decides which factors of production will be used in each industry and firm.

Tourism is state controlled in Cuba.

The central planning authority must co-ordinate the output of the primary sector with the needs of the secondary sector. If the authority has decided that 10,000 tractors are needed, it must make sure that the land will yield the minerals required and that the population will supply the labour required. The tertiary sector, i.e. the services, also has to be planned. The education system must be directed into producing enough engineers and mechanics to build the tractors.

What shall be produced and how it shall be produced have been dealt with. Now we must deal with 'for whom'?

The government can answer 'for whom' in two different ways. It can distribute goods and services itself directly to consumers. For example, it can have its own stores from which the consumers can obtain their food and other consumer goods. It can run its own schools and other services. Alternatively, it can let distribution take place indirectly through distributing incomes which consumers can spend by their own decisions.

The advantages and disadvantages of the command economy

Advantages
1. The government concentrates on economic growth by investing in capital goods. Future generations should be better off. The state believes that the sacrifice of the present generation is worth it.

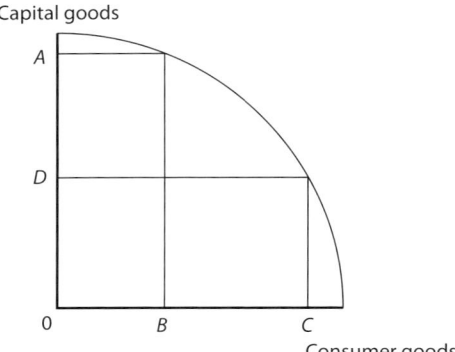

Fig. 7.3
Production possibility in a command economy

The government has put its resources into 0A capital goods and has sacrificed BC consumer goods. The present generation is consuming only 0B goods but future generations should be able to consume more.

2 The government looks after the needs of the people by providing food and clothing and other essentials at low prices. Education and health services will also be provided for all the people without discrimination.

3 The government will ensure equality in the distribution of goods and services. There will not be 'haves' and 'have-nots'.

4 There will be no unemployment of labour. All will have jobs guaranteed. Each person will contribute to the labour force from his or her ability.

5 There will be no demerit goods like drugs and pornography because the government will not put resources into their production. However, there will be merit goods like education and health. For example, the Cuban government has delivered excellent health and education services free to all the population without favour.

6 Prices are controlled to make essentials (and other goods) affordable for all people.

Disadvantages

1 There is likely to be excessive bureaucracy. The state planning agency will be a huge body employing thousands to collect data and make decisions as to what is to be produced and how it is to be distributed. Others in the bureaucracy will need to check that orders have been carried out. Such bureaucracy makes for very slow decision-making. Months, even years, can go by before the decisions have been carried out in full.

2 There can be a wastage of resources. Goods are produced which are not wanted or in quantities in excess of what is wanted. Take the example of tractors again. 10,000 tractors were ordered to be produced but only 5,000 are needed. Resources put into 5,000 tractors have been wasted.

3 It is unfair to make one generation sacrifice for the next. 'No jam today, more jam tomorrow' is not fair. It is 'inter-generational theft'. The next generation is stealing from the present generation.

4 Distribution by a non-price system leads to queuing for bread, potatoes and staple foods. It also leads to black markets. The appearance of black markets in the Dominican Republic, Cuba and Haiti was taken as a sign of government intervention in markets in those countries by the Heritage Foundation. Also, smuggling is a likely result in the absence of many consumer goods.

The free market economy

Self interest operates in the free market economy. If everyone seeks to satisfy their own self interest, there will be no need for government intervention in the economy. Consumers will spend their money in the free market with the aim of maximising utility or satisfaction. Firms will respond to consumer needs by providing the goods and services demanded. In this way, firms will maximise their profits, acting in their own self-interest. Workers will offer their labour where they will maximise their wages as well as giving themselves the leisure and other conditions they want. The whole system should function as if guided by 'an invisible hand'.

The factors of production are owned by private individuals. Land is privately owned. Machines and factories are owned by private firms. Of course, labour is individually owned.

Demand and supply interact to see that the goods and services the economy wants are provided. When there is excess demand for a good, prices will rise. When prices rise, firms will supply more of that good and demand and supply will be in equilibrium again. This is called the price mechanism.

Let's look at it the other way round. When there is a deficiency of demand for a good, prices will fall. Firms will reduce the supply of that good in response to falling prices. Demand and supply will be in equilibrium once more. The price mechanism is at work again.

Boom in digital photography.

When supply needs to be increased in response to increased demand for a good, the factor markets will respond. Firms will demand more of the factors that go into the production of the good for which demand has risen. The price of that factor will rise and the owners of the factor will supply more of it. For example, if the demand for computers rises, firms will supply more computers in response to the price rise. These firms will need more skilled labour in the micro-electronics market and wages for computer specialists will rise. In response to higher wages, the labour market will provide more of them.

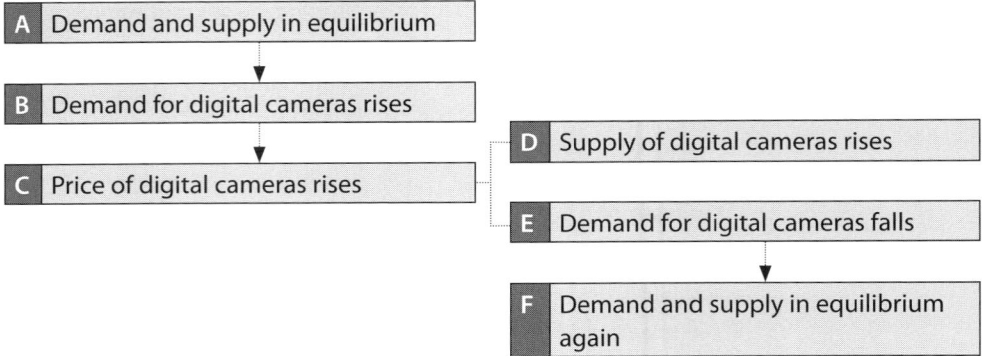

Fig. 7.4 *Flow diagram to show price mechanism at work in a market for goods*

Now we shall see the response of the factor market.

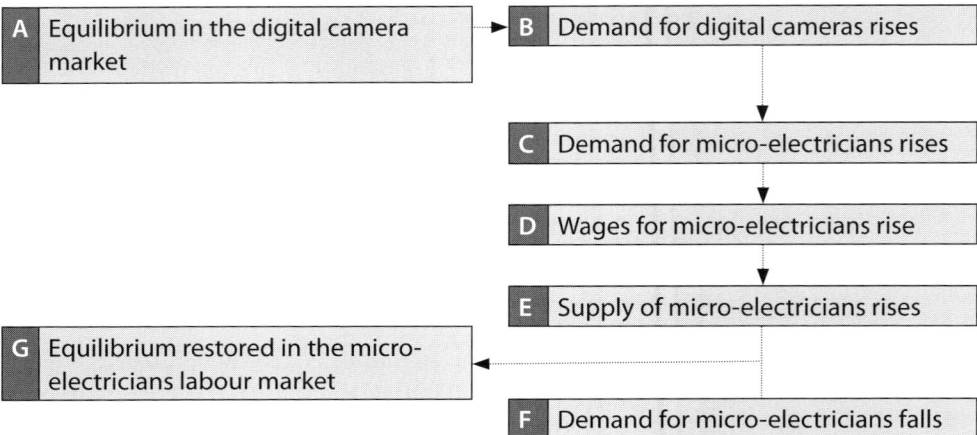

Fig. 7.5 *Flow diagram to show the price mechanism at work in a related factor market*

The advantages and disadvantages of the free market economy

Advantages

1. The free market economy works by itself and needs no government intervention.

2. The market responds quickly to changes in demand and supply conditions.

3. There is no need for any bureaucracy or central planning authority.

4. The more competitive the markets, the better it is. The more firms, the more competition between them to cut prices and improve quality. Firms will undertake research and development (R & D) to come up with even better products.

5. The free market system is efficient. Firms seek to maximise profit. To maximise profit, they minimise cost. Firms will seek the least cost method of production. This makes for 'productive efficiency'.

6. Allocative efficiency is also achieved when the right amount of resources are allocated to the right products. Competing firms in the free market will bring this about.

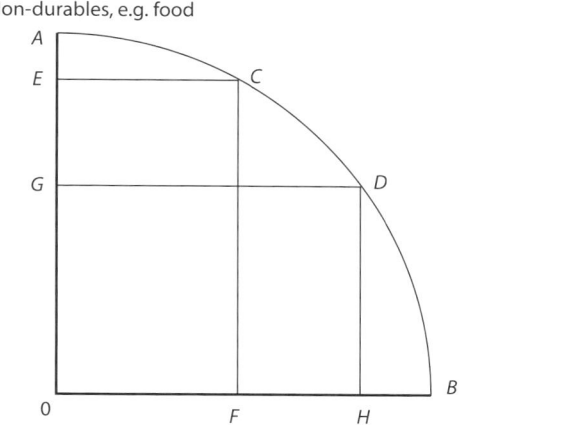

Fig. 7.6
Production possibility curve illustrating efficiency

Productive efficiency is achieved at *C* and *D* because all resources are fully employed at both points (both points are on the production possibility curve).

Allocative efficiency would be achieved at *C* if consumers are satisfied with the combination of 0*E* non-durable goods and 0*F* durable goods rather than the combination at *D*. However, it could be the other way round. It depends on the consumers in that society.

7 If everyone acts in his or her self-interest, society benefits. This is a controversial statement held to be true by supporters of the free market economy.

8 There is freedom of choice throughout the economy.

Examination Tip

> It would be useful to make the link to Pareto efficiency. All points on the curve are Pareto efficient. If you move from a point on the curve, someone will be better off and someone else worse off.

Disadvantages

1 There are 'haves' and 'have-nots' in free market economies. For example, the private ownership of land could cause social tensions.

'Haves' and 'have-nots'.
Source: ABACA/EMPICS.

2. Goods go to the highest bidders. The rich gain at the expense of the poor. The gap between rich and poor grows.

3. The rich can afford better services. They have better education and better health services. In fact the poor may have to go without certain services.

4. Competition can lead to monopoly because a firm which gains cost advantages can lower prices and cut out competitors. Then the monopolist can exploit the monopoly by raising prices and reducing output. Also, there is a loss of efficiency as the monopolist has no need to be efficient.

5. The free market leads to the under-production of merit goods like education and health services.

6. The free market leads to the over-production of demerit goods like drugs and pornography. Where there is demand, there will be supply.

7. The free market fails to supply public goods like street lighting.

8. The free market leads to social costs like pollution, e.g. the chemical factory pours out effluent into the nearby river.

9. There are booms but there are also slumps at the macroeconomic level. Slumps are characterised by falling output and the unemployment of labour and other factors.

10. Directly contrary to point (7) in the advantages, the pursuit of self-interest can lead to selfishness and greed, sometimes known as the survival of the fittest.

11. Advertising, 'The Hidden Persuader', impacts on consumer sovereignty in that consumers do not always have control over what they are buying.

The mixed economy

In reality, all economies are mixed. All command economies have features of the free market and all free market economies have features of command economies. We have seen before that in Cuba, a command economy, small scale catering services are in the free market. In the Bahamas, a free market economy, the government provides a state education system. By looking at the long lists of disadvantages in both command and free market economies, we can see that there must be a combination of the two systems for the good of society.

Mixed economies feel that it is desirable to let consumers exercise choice over the goods they purchase and to let firms choose what goods they will produce and what inputs they will use and in what combination. Workers are given the choice of where they will work. Mixed economies believe that incentives must be allowed to increase productivity. Workers must be rewarded for their skills and hard work with higher wages and managers for their enterprise with profits.

However, governments realise that in the free market, public goods like street lighting will not be produced and merit goods like education and health services will be under-supplied. Demerit goods like cigarettes and alcohol, on the other hand, will be over-supplied. Therefore, the government rectifies these deficiencies but, in doing so, it is intervening in the free market. So, in mixed economies, governments provide public goods, education and health services and regulate the supply of demerit goods with prohibitions and taxes.

Even in the most free market economies, the government has a role to play. The government must provide defence and law and order so that individuals and firms can go about their daily lives and occupations in peace, without fear of losing what they are working for.

The government must provide a stable currency to give consumers and entrepreneurs confidence in the value of money. Therefore, the government must be able to use the money supply and interest rates to control inflation. It must support the currency in foreign exchange markets to stabilise the exchange rate.

In a free market economy the government is expected to be able to smooth out the booms and slumps in the business cycle by the use of taxation and government expenditure. For example, unemployment in a slump can possibly be reduced through lower taxes and increased government expenditure to boost demand.

In the diagram below, the undulating line is the business cycle, the ups and downs of national income. Consumers and firms lose confidence when the future level of economic activity is so uncertain and expect the government to regulate the economy with fiscal (tax and government expenditure) and monetary (money supply and interest rate) policies.

Whether a government can have any success in regulating the economy is debatable but at least the mixed economy gives the government the power and the tools with which to intervene.

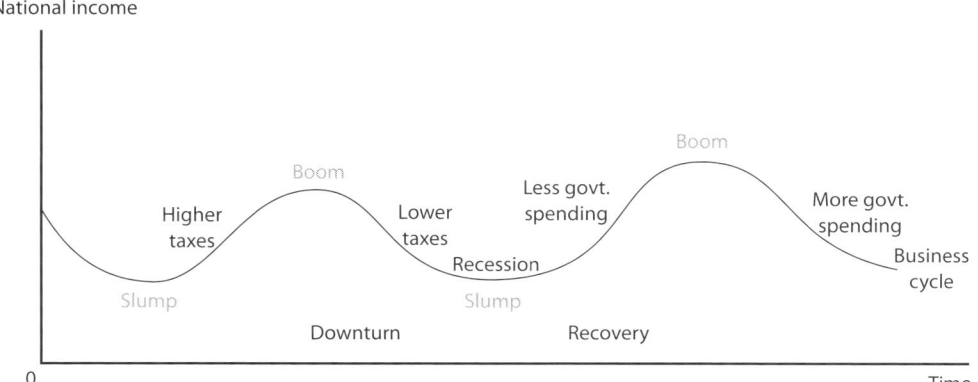

Fig. 7.7
The business cycle

We began this section on 'economic systems' by referring to the Heritage Foundation's Index of Economic Freedom and we conclude by asking why most Caribbean economies are in the 'mostly free' category. The price mechanism seems to be operating in most Caribbean economies so what is stopping these economies moving into the 'free' category? The generalisations to be made are that state-owned enterprises still exist. Privatisation is moving too slowly. The agricultural sectors, chiefly sugar and bananas, are in decline and the governments are 'bailing out' these sectors, sometimes with subsidies. There is the unemployment problem which leads governments to provide welfare.

EXERCISE

The class is divided into three groups and each of these has to consider the advantages of one of the three types of economic system. Two or three people from each group then present their ideas to the rest of the class, leading on to a debate about the relative merits of each system.

The traditional economy

A traditional economy is one which is based on communal ownership of land and subsistence agriculture and fishing. In the Caribbean, traditional economies existed before the coming of Europeans, i.e. amongst Amerindian societies. It is difficult for a completely traditional economy to exist nowadays in the Caribbean but in pockets of land in Guyana and among the Meskito Indians in Central America, there are people living the traditional way of life.

Traditional economies are non-cash economies. Households grow enough food to feed themselves and they subsist on what they produce. Usually there is no surplus. However, if there is a surplus, it can be used in barter which is the exchange of goods for goods or services – non-cash transactions.

> **Definition of barter**
>
> The direct exchange of goods and services for other goods and services without using money.

Nowadays, there are aspects of the traditional economy in most countries of the Caribbean and many students will be acquainted with them. Most people in the Caribbean now have title deeds for land, so that aspect of the traditional economy has gone except amongst some Amerindian tribes in Guyana. However, many people in Caribbean countries grow crops and fruit for subsistence and subsistence fishing is very common in all countries. It goes further than that when a good catch brings in more fish than the fisherman and his family can consume and the surplus is passed on to friends.

Fishing – a traditional economy.

The traditional economy exists side-by-side with the cash economy. Governments came and imposed taxes; taxes required cash and people had to work for wages or produce surpluses to sell in the market place and so purely traditional economies disappeared.

Examination questions

1. Discuss the three fundamental questions involved in the allocation of resources. *(10 marks)*

2. Explain what is meant by a Circular Flow of Goods and Services in an economy. *(10 marks)*

3. Distinguish, with the aid of examples, between the primary, secondary and tertiary sectors of an economy. *(10 marks)*

4. Compare and contrast the advantages and disadvantages of command and free market economies. *(10 marks)*

5. Explain whether you think it would ever be possible to have an economy without any government intervention. *(10 marks)*

CHAPTER 8

The price mechanism

In this chapter you will be working with demand and supply diagrams. The importance of this chapter for your future study of Economics must be stressed. It is the core theory of Economics:

- You will learn that there are many more markets than the street market
- You will be introduced to the market forces of demand and supply
- The demand and supply curves will be carefully analysed
- The concept of the equilibrium price will then be introduced
- The determinants of demand and supply will explained as will the ways in which these influence demand and supply curves

Markets

A market is any place where a buyer interacts with a seller. It does not have to be a physical place like an area of land but, of course, there are such market places in every Caribbean city, town or village. A market can be over the telephone as happens in the bauxite market. It can be by mail order. The fastest growing market today is through the Internet.

The vegetable market is very likely to be a street market. The French term 'market ouvert' (one word is English, the other French! It means 'open market') is applied to a street market. Here a buyer meets a seller 'in the flesh' and the goods are probably passed from hand to hand physically.

A street market is not the only kind of market.

Source: Stillpictures.

The housing market is likely to be controlled by agents. Agents are people who put a buyer into contact with a seller. The goods, i.e. houses, are not moved! The seller puts the house in the hands of the agent. The buyer visits the agent's office or calls him or her on the telephone. The buyer and seller may never meet face to face but it is still a market.

A commodity market is usually an international market for raw materials like bauxite. A thousand tons of the mineral are in a stockpile somewhere and the buyer is told that it is available, as well as the market price, over the telephone. After the sale has been agreed, the mineral is moved by rail within a country or by bulk tanker if it is an international transaction. The buyers and sellers never have the goods in their hands.

A stock exchange is a market where stocks and shares are sold. The exchange is negotiated over the telephone between 'stock brokers'. Stock markets are national and there is a physical place, e.g. The Jamaica Stock Exchange, located at 40 Harbour Street, Kingston, Jamaica, or international, e.g. The New York Stock Exchange in Wall Street. The goods exchanged between sellers and buyers are pieces of paper.

There is also the foreign exchange market (Forex). Here we must think of a currency as a good or commodity that can be bought and sold and which has a market price, e.g. if you want to buy US dollars, you do so on the foreign exchange market (even if you go to your local bank, the transaction is being made in the foreign exchange market) and the $ has a market price in the local currency. You are buying US dollars and someone else is selling them.

'Black' or 'underground' markets are markets that operate outside the law. They usually deal in scarce goods that cannot be obtained easily or legally. The goods themselves may be illegal, e.g. drugs. Alternatively, in the labour market, when there are minimum wages, employers can find workers who are willing to work below the minimum wage through a black market.

The above are examples of some of the markets in goods. There are also markets in services. We can speak of the transport market, the tourist market, the hotel market and the restaurant market. Again, the list is not exhaustive by any means. For example, transport, the moving of people and goods from A to B, is a service. The transport companies, e.g. Caribbean Freight Handlers in Jamaica, supply the service of moving goods internationally and from the ports to destinations within Jamaica.

EXERCISE Choose any one of these various markets and find out as much as possible about it. You can then give a presentation to the class.

Finally, there are factor markets. In a market economy, households are the owners of the factors of production. Individuals supply their land, labour, capital and enterprise. The buyers are the firms. These firms have the demand. We speak of the labour market. Labour is exchanged in the labour market between households and firms for wages. In another market, land is exchanged for rent and, in yet another market, capital for interest. Let us look at the circular flow diagram again.

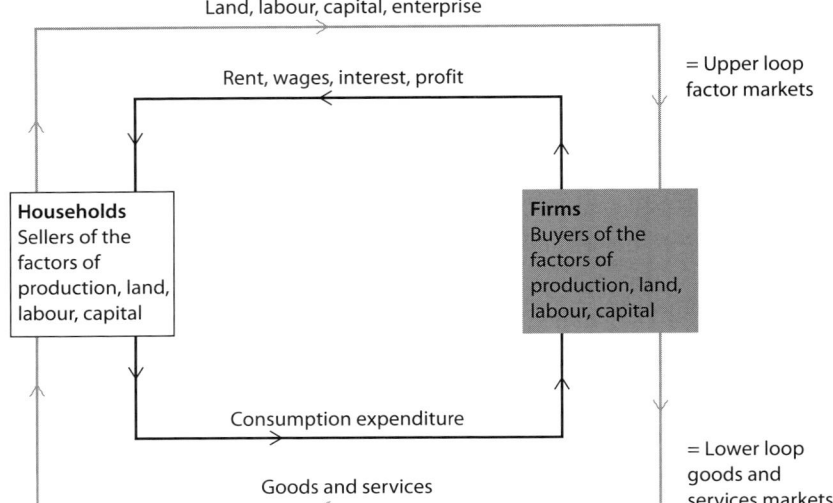

Fig. 8.1
Circular flow diagram showing factor markets and goods and services markets

Definition of a market
A market is where buyers and sellers meet to exchange money for goods and services.

Market forces

The market forces are those of demand and supply. They are the influences which determine price and what shall be produced in a free market. Demand is in the hands of households in the goods and services markets but in the hands of firms in the factor markets. Supply is in the hands of firms in the goods and services markets but in the hands of households in the factor markets.

Definition of market forces
The market forces are those of demand and supply.

Demand

Demand in Economics means the expression of a wish for something. It does not have to be backed by money but it usually is shown by the willingness of the consumer to buy something. Strictly speaking, demand backed by money is 'effective demand'.

Definition of demand
Demand is the quantity of something that a buyer is willing and able to buy over a period of time.

The first law of demand states that the higher the price, the less will be demanded and the lower the price, the more will be demanded, other things being equal ('ceteris paribus'). This law gives rise to the *demand schedule* and the *demand curve*.

> **Examination Tip**
>
> Don't forget to let the examiner know that you are aware of the situation of 'ceteris paribus', i.e. the fact that other things do not change.

Demand schedule

A demand schedule is a table which shows the quantity of a good a consumer demands at each price in a given period of time. For example, an individual's demand schedule for compact discs in a year.

Price in EC$	Quantity CDs
10	64
20	36
30	26
40	18
50	14
60	10

Notes:
(a) The first law of demand is satisfied – the higher the price, the lower the quantity demanded. Price and quantity demanded have an **inverse relationship**. When one is high the other is low.
(b) The demand schedule can be plotted on a **demand curve**.
(c) The demand curve slopes downwards from left to right.

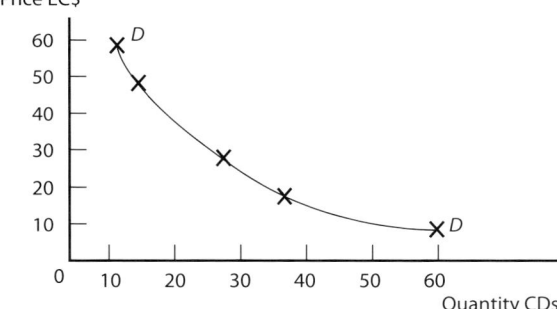

Fig. 8.2
Demand curve for CDs

The most difficult question to deal with is the shape of the demand curve. If we look carefully at the diagram above, we can see that to obtain ten more CDs, we have to give less and less money. The value of the CDs diminishes as we gain more of them. So, if the price falls from EC$60 to $50, we gain only four CDs; if the price falls from $40 to $30, we gain eight CDs; finally, if the price falls from $20 to $10, we gain 28 CDs. For each fall of $10 we are gaining more and more CDs, or CDs in terms of money are falling in value. Economists have an expression for this: there is a *diminishing marginal rate of substitution* of money for CDs. Another way of saying this is by using the word 'utility' (or 'satisfaction'). Every additional CD provides less and less utility.

EXERCISE Choose another example, apart from CDs, such as DVDs or items of clothing. Do you think that the demand curve will be the same shape as for CDs?

> **Examination Tip**
> You need to be able to explain why the demand curve is convex when viewed from the origin. It is because there is a diminishing marginal rate of utility as you go down the curve.

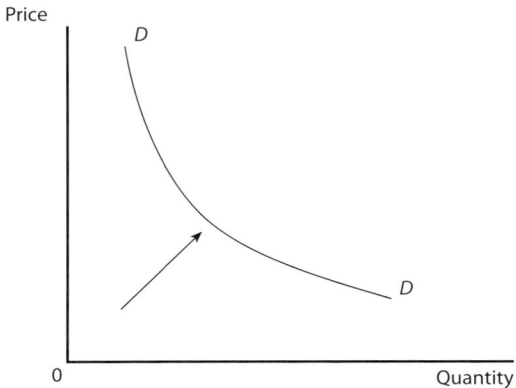

Fig. 8.3 The convex shape of the demand curve

Economics teachers and students often draw straight line demand curves for convenience and, in most cases, they are perfectly acceptable, except when dealing with the precise question above.

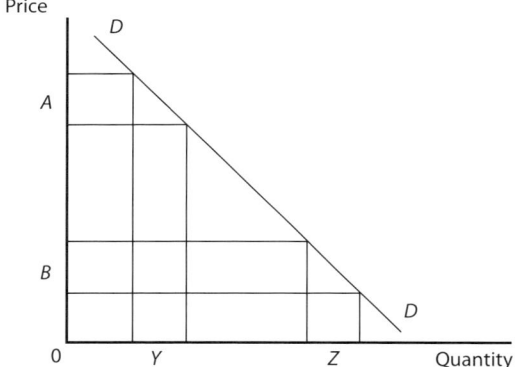

Fig. 8.4 A constant rate of substitution between money and goods

The demand curve slopes downwards from left to right but in a straight line. There is a *constant marginal rate of substitution* between money and goods. The same amount of money yields the same amount of goods at any part of the curve (we still call it a 'curve' even when it is a straight line!). $A = B$ on the price axis and $Y = Z$ on the quantity axis.

The individual and the market demand curve

Take the market for CDs above. An individual has a demand for CDs and all the individual demands added together make the total demand for CDs in the market. This is simply what the 'market demand' means.

> **Definition of market demand**
>
> The market demand is the sum of all the individual demands in that market.

However, sometimes an economist speaks of the market demand being the 'horizontal sum' of all the individual demands. This is set out below.

Individual demand

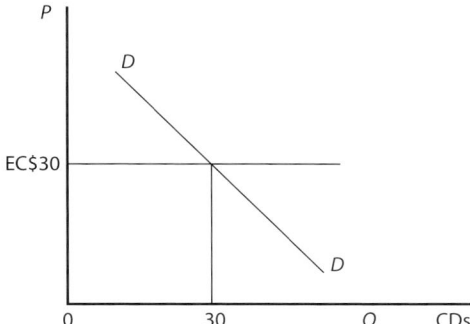

Fig. 8.5
One person's demand for CDs

Market demand (horizontal sum view)

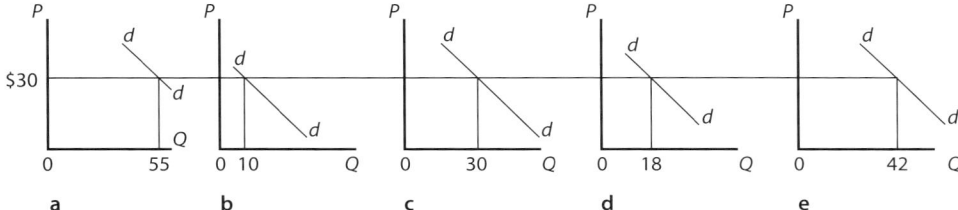

Fig. 8.6
The demand for CDs in the whole market

At the price of $30, **a** demands 55 CDs, **b** demands 10, **c** demands 30, **d** demands 18 and **e** demands 42.

55 + 10 + 30 + 18 + 42 = Total … 155 (horizontal sum because we have placed the graphs in parallel and added across the page). Therefore, the market demand for CDs is 155.

The market demand curve is shown in Figure 8.7.

Fig. 8.7
The horizontal sum of all the individual demand curves

Supply

Supply is the amount or quantity of a good that producers (suppliers) would like to supply at given prices. The first law of supply states that the higher the price, the more will be supplied (and the lower the price, the less will be supplied). If a farmer can grow maize or tobacco and the price of maize rises, he will supply more maize and less tobacco, other things being equal. There is a *direct relationship* between price and quantity supplied – when one is high, the other is high and when one is low, the other is low.

> **Definition of supply**
>
> Supply is the quantity of a commodity that is offered for sale at a price over a period of time.

Supply schedule

A table can be given which shows the quantity supplied at given prices. This table is called the 'supply schedule'. For example, see below a farmer's supply schedule for maize (corn).

Price in EC$	Quantity supplied corn (kilos)
10	5
20	25
30	37
40	47
50	55
60	60

Notes:
(a) The first law of supply is satisfied – the higher the price, the more will be supplied. There is a **direct relationship** between price and quantity supplied: when one is high, the other is high.
(b) The schedule can be plotted on a **supply curve**.
(c) The supply curve slopes upwards from left to right.

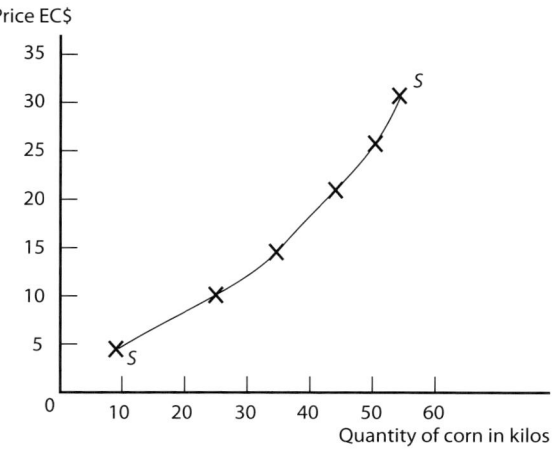

Fig. 8.8
The supply curve for corn plotted from the table above

The supply curve shown in Fig. 8.8 is positively sloped. This signifies that when price goes up (+), quantity supplied goes up (+). The supply curve above becomes steeper because it costs more to produce an extra unit. The one illustrated is just a 'typical' supply curve.

The individual and market supply curve

Again, we shall calculate the 'horizontal sum' from the supply curves below. There are five farmers in the market growing corn. Their total supply at each and every price is the market supply at that price.

> **Definition of market supply curve**
> The market supply curve is the sum of all the individual supply curves.

Individual supply

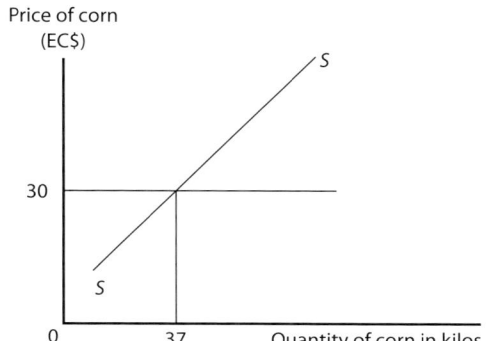

Fig. 8.9
A straight-line supply curve

Market supply (the horizontal sum view)

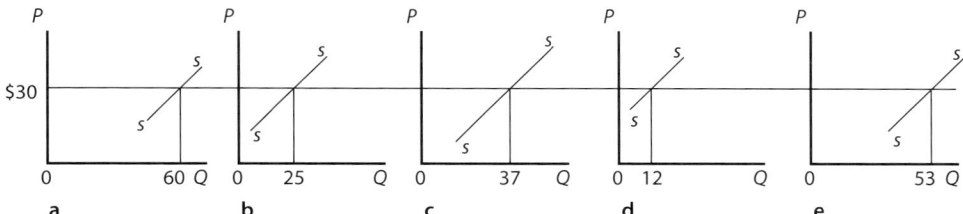

Fig. 8.10
Individual supply curves in a market

At the price of $30 per kilo **a** supplies 60 kilos, **b** 25 k, **c** 37 k, **d** 12 k and **e** 53 k.
60 + 25 + 37 + 12 + 53 = 187 kilos is the market supply (horizontal sum).

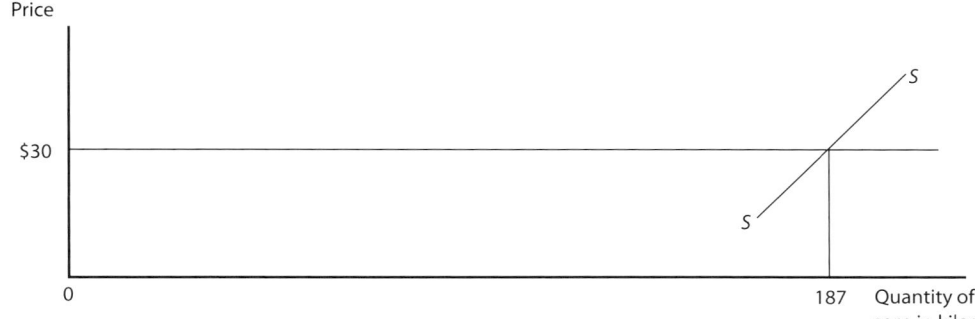

Fig. 8.11
The Market supply curve from the horizontal sum of five supply curves

The equilibrium price

The interaction of demand and supply determine the equilibrium price. The equilibrium price is the free market price. It is the price that prevails when there is no interference in the free market by government or any other agencies, such as when there is collusion between buyers to force down the price, or, more commonly, when there is a 'cartel' which is collusion between suppliers to force up the price.

> **Definition of a cartel**
>
> A cartel is a formal, collusive agreement between suppliers to set a price above the free market price.

The most well known cartel is probably the *Organisation of Petroleum Exporting Countries, OPEC*. (Trinidad and Tobago is not a member, but Venezuela is.)

OPEC controls the price of oil by limiting the supply. It limits the supply by setting a quota for each member state. Each member state agrees not to exceed that quota in production. (This will be shown later in a graph.)

> **Definition of a quota**
>
> A quota is a limit on the quantity of a commodity that can be produced.

The demand curve slopes downwards from left to right and the supply curve slopes upwards from left to right. At some point the two curves must intersect. At that point, demand is equal to supply, i.e. there is an *equilibrium*. The equilibrium point is that point at which consumers wish to buy exactly the quantity that suppliers wish to supply. In general the market is in 'equilibrium' when the market shows no tendency to change the price and the quantity demanded at that price. The market is in a state of rest.

> **Definition of equilibrium**
>
> The equilibrium price and quantity is where the demand of consumers is exactly equal to the supply of producers.

There can be no other price at which buyers can meet sellers in a free market. If a seller tries to sell above the equilibrium price, he or she will sell nothing because a buyer can find a lower price. If a buyer tries to buy at a price below the equilibrium price, he or she will not find a seller because a seller can obtain a higher price.

Of course, certain conditions must be present. These are called the conditions for perfect competition:

1. There must be an infinite number of (very many) independent buyers (no collusion between buyers).

2 There must be an infinite number of (very many) independent sellers (no collusion between sellers – no cartels).

3 There must be an homogeneous product, i.e. all products must be the same in size, weight, appearance, texture etc.

4 There must be perfect knowledge of the market, i.e. the consumer must know where and when the goods are available and at what price.

5 There must be free access to the market.

6 There must be no advertising.

These are the usual six conditions given for perfect competition. You might say they could never exist and that is probably true. The usual example given for perfect competition is a stock exchange. However, open markets in agriculture come very close to fulfilling some of these conditions. For example, there are very many mango sellers, very many buyers and one mango of the same variety is much like another (this is debatable!). Buyers know the price. There is no advertising.

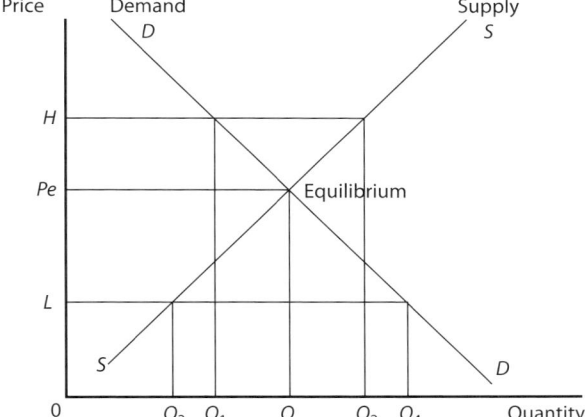

Fig. 8.12
To prove that the equilibrium price is the only price in a free market

P is the equilibrium price and Q is the equilibrium quantity. To prove that only the equilibrium price can obtain in the free market, we take other prices and see what would happen.

Let us take H, a higher price than the equilibrium. At that price, sellers would want to sell more than consumers would want to buy. There would be **excess supply, $Q_2 - Q_1$**. Suppliers would have to lower the price to sell the excess. If not, goods would be left 'on the shelf'. How far would they have to lower the price? At P, the free market price, they would find buyers.

Let us now take L, a lower price than the equilibrium. At that price, buyers would want to buy more than sellers would want to sell. There would be **excess demand, $Q_4 - Q_3$**. Buyers would compete for the scarce goods and they would 'bid up the price'. How far would the price rise? At P, the free market price, buyers would find sellers.

The equilibrium price from schedule and graph

Example

The equilibrium price of tomatoes per kilo			
Price (cents)	Quantity demanded (kilos)	Quantity supplied (kilos)	
150	5	25	
125	10	20	
100	**15**	**15**	Equilibrium price
75	20	10	
50	25	5	

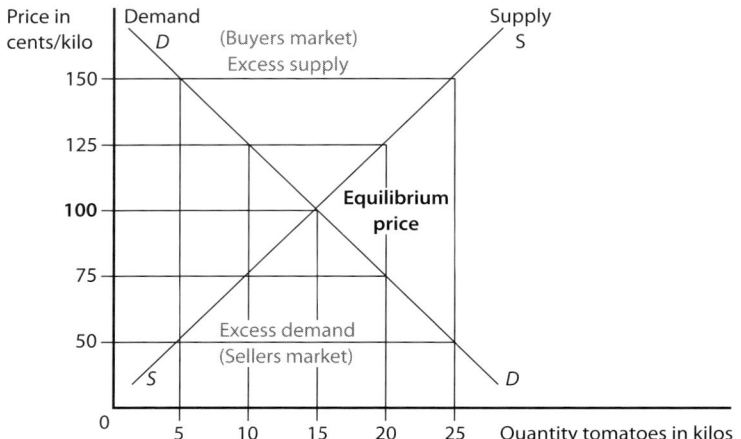

Fig. 8.13
Graph plotted from the table above

At 150 cents only 5 kilos are demanded but 25 supplied. There is an excess supply of 20 kilos and the suppliers will have to drop the price. At 125 cents 10 kilos are demanded but 20 are supplied. There is an excess supply of 10 kilos and suppliers will have to drop their price still further. **At 100 cents, exactly the same number of kilos, 15, are demanded and supplied. This is the equilibrium price, the** *market price.*

At 75 cents only 10 kilos are supplied but 20 are demanded. There is an excess demand of 10 kilos. Tomatoes are scarce and consumers will compete and bid up the price. At 50 cents only 5 kilos are supplied but 25 are demanded. There is an excess demand of 20 kilos. Tomatoes are very scarce and consumers will bid up the price.

EXERCISE Explain why only the equilibrium price and quantity are possible in a free market.

The determinants of demand

The determinants of demand are:

1 The price of the good itself.
2 The prices of all other goods.

3 The income of the consumer.
4 Taste.

Let us look more closely at these four determinants.

The price of the good itself

The higher the price, the less will be demanded and the lower the price, the more will be demanded, other things being equal. It is important to grasp that this is only a movement along the same demand curve.

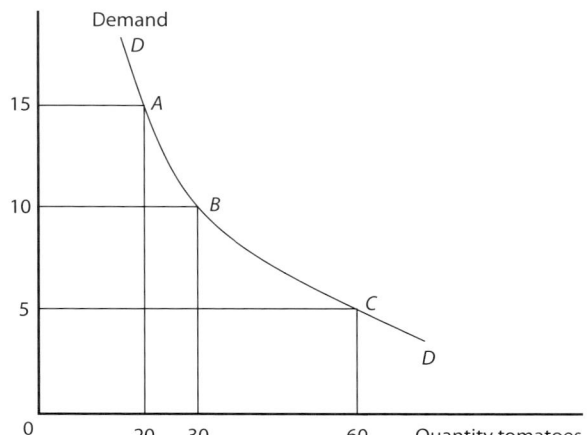

Fig. 8.14
*Movement along the **same** demand curve*

If the price of tomatoes falls from 15 cents to 10 cents, the consumer moves from *A* to *B* **along the same demand curve** and his or her demand rises from 20 to 30 tomatoes.

If the price of tomatoes rises from 5 cents to 10 cents, the consumer moves from *C* to *B* **along the same demand curve** and his or her demand falls from 60 to 30 tomatoes.

Shifting the demand curve

A change in any of the other determinants of demand leads to a **shift of the whole curve**. The other determinants are a change in the prices of all other goods, income and taste.

Changes in the prices of all other goods

Complements

Suppose the price of cheese rises and tomatoes and cheese go together in pizzas and other dishes (they are **complements**), then, other things being equal, the demand for tomatoes will fall but it will fall at each and every price. The whole demand curve for tomatoes will shift inwards. The reasoning is that, if the price of cheese rises, the demand for cheese will fall and cheese is a complement to tomatoes, so the demand for tomatoes will fall at each and every price.

> **Definition of a complementary good**
>
> A complement is a good which is bought and used with another good; it is therefore said to be in 'joint demand' with that other good.

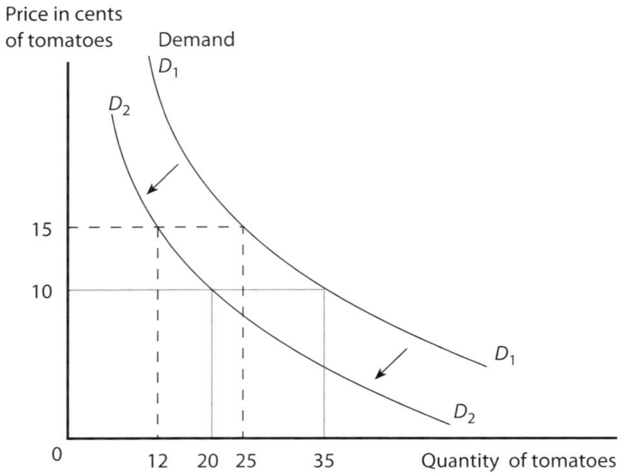

Fig. 8.15
Shifting inwards of demand curve for tomatoes brought about by the rise in the price of cheese which is a complement to tomatoes

At 15 cents the demand for tomatoes has fallen from 25 to 12 tomatoes because of a rise in the price of cheese. At 10 cents the demand for tomatoes has fallen from 35 to 20 tomatoes. At each and every price, the demand for tomatoes has fallen because the price of the complementary good has risen. **The whole demand curve for tomatoes has shifted 'inwards to the origin', parallel to itself.**

EXERCISE — Try and think of some other examples of goods that are complements in joint demand.

Substitutes

Suppose the price of red peppers rises, and red peppers can be used instead of tomatoes (they are **substitutes**), the demand for red peppers will fall and the demand for tomatoes will rise at each and every price, other things being equal. The whole demand curve for tomatoes will shift outwards. The reasoning is that if the price of red peppers rises, less red peppers will be demanded and because red peppers and tomatoes are substitute goods, more tomatoes will be demanded at each and every price.

Definition of a substitute good
A substitute is an alternative good which is in competitive demand.

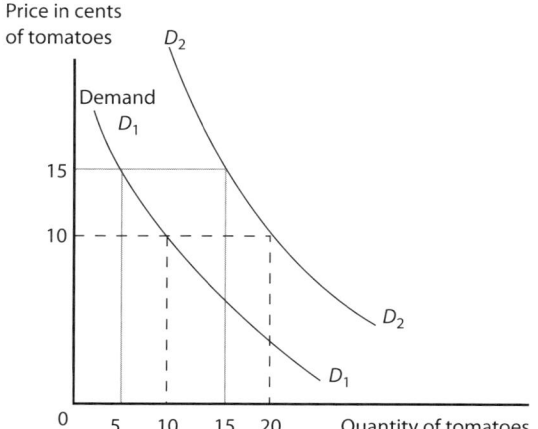

Fig. 8.16
Shifting outwards of the demand curve for tomatoes brought about by the rise in the price of red peppers which are substitutes for tomatoes

At 15 cents the demand for tomatoes has risen from 5 to 15 tomatoes. At 10 cents the demand for tomatoes has risen from 10 to 20 tomatoes. At each and every price the demand for tomatoes has risen because the price of a substitute has risen. The whole demand curve for tomatoes has **shifted outwards from the origin parallel to itself**.

We can now see why 'other things being equal' ('ceteris paribus') is so important. The demand for tomatoes will fall when the price of cheese rises because they are complements but what if the price of tomatoes falls at the same time? We cannot predict what will happen then, so we must say 'other things being equal'. Alternatively, the demand for tomatoes will rise when the price of red peppers rises, but what if the consumer's income falls at the same time? Again we cannot predict what will happen and must state 'ceteris paribus'.

Changes in the income of the consumer

Assuming that the good is a **normal good**, if income rises a consumer's demand will rise and if income falls a consumer's demand will fall at each and every price, other things being equal. Usually incomes are rising but when there is unemployment, incomes are falling. Let us take the case of rising incomes. The consumer's demand curve, and the market demand curve, will shift outwards from the origin, parallel to itself, as in Fig. 8.16 above. For example, a cell phone is a normal good where demand increases as incomes rise.

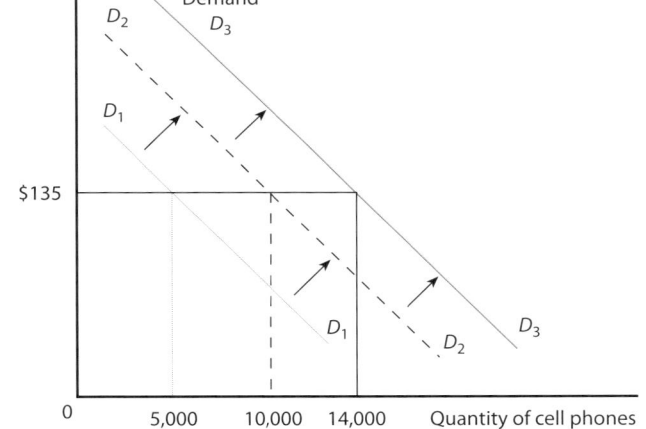

Fig. 8.17
Market demand for cell phones with rising incomes

As incomes rise and cell phones remain at $135, the market demand curve shifts upwards to the right (another way of saying outwards from the origin) parallel to itself. At D_1D_1 5,000 cell phones are demanded, at D_2D_2 10,000, and at D_3D_3 14,000 are demanded.

EXERCISE

If your income rose, how do you think that might affect your choice of products or services to buy?

Change in taste

In Economics, 'taste' is used to cover many things like fashion, crazes, trends, fads etc. If taste moves in favour of a product, demand for that product will increase and if it moves against that product, demand will decrease, other things being equal. Tastes are always changing. Therefore, demand is always changing. A change in taste shifts the demand curve outwards or inwards, parallel to itself. For example, bling (conspicuous gold jewellery) is in fashion at the moment among certain social groups but in a few year's time it may have fallen out of fashion. We can depict this on a graph.

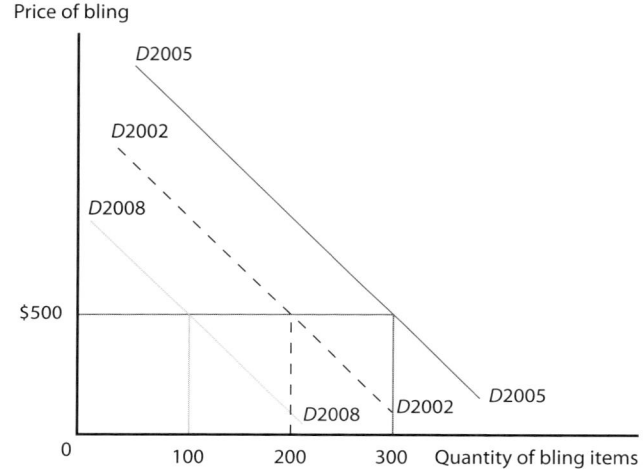

Fig. 8.18
Diagram to show fashion changes on demand for bling

In 2002, the market demand for bling items costing $500 was 200 items. A change in taste (fashion) in 2005 swung in favour of bling and market demand rose to 300 items at the same price. Then there was a dramatic change in taste against bling and in 2008 the market demand dropped to only 100 items.

Of course, if suppliers can predict taste, they can receive large amounts of money. On the other hand, if they get it wrong, they can go out of business.

EXERCISE Can you think of another example of something that is in fashion at the moment, perhaps as a result of an advertising campaign?

Examination Tip

You need to be absolutely certain that you understand the difference between a move along a demand curve (caused by a change in the price of the good itself) and a shift of the demand curve (caused by a change in any of the other determinants).

The determinants of supply

The determinants of supply are:

1. A change in the price of the good itself.
2. Changes in the prices of all other goods.
3. Changes in the costs of the factors of production.
4. The level of technology.
5. The goals of the producer.

(In agriculture we must also consider the forces of nature, hurricane, tsunami and drought.)

Let us look at these five determinants more closely.

A change in the price of the good itself

The first law of supply states that the higher the price, the more will be supplied and the lower the price, the less will be supplied, other things being equal. This will bring about a movement along the same supply curve.

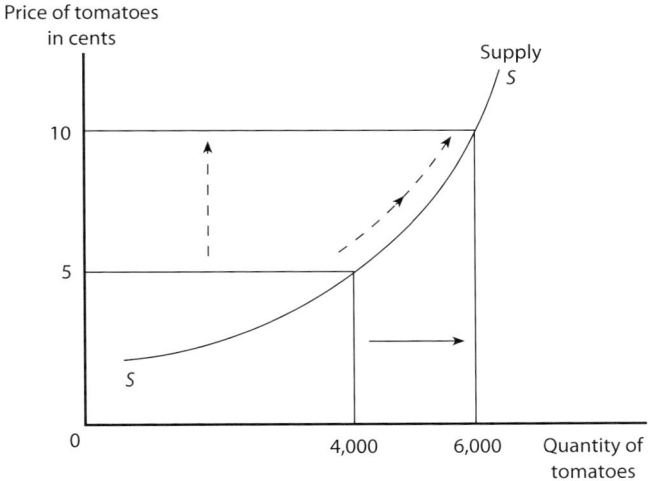

Fig. 8.19
A movement along the same supply curve

A rise in the price of tomatoes from 5 cents to 10 cents has caused a movement **up the same supply curve** and an increase in quantity supplied from 4,000 to 6,000 tomatoes. If a farmer is growing tomatoes and red peppers and the price of tomatoes rises, he or she will supply more tomatoes and less red peppers, other things being equal, i.e. there is no change in the price of red peppers.

Changes in the prices of all other goods

(Strictly speaking this should apply to goods that are related to the good in question. The price of postage stamps will have little impact on the supply of tomatoes!) If the price of red peppers rises, the farmer will switch production from tomatoes to red peppers. At each and every price, he or she will supply less tomatoes. **There will be a shift in the whole supply curve.**

Fig. 8.20
A shift in the whole supply curve

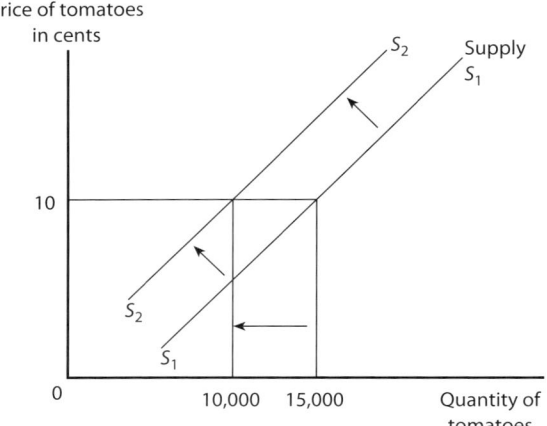

When the price of red peppers rises, the farmer will switch from tomatoes to red peppers. The whole supply curve for tomatoes will **shift upwards to the left**. At 10 cents, supply will fall from 15,000 tomatoes to 10,000 tomatoes, other things being equal (provided that there are no changes in the other determinants at the same time).

Changes in the costs of the factors of production

This refers to changes in the costs of land, labour, capital and enterprise. Keeping to the same example of the farmer and tomatoes, if the cost of fertiliser falls, the farmer will buy more fertiliser and the supply of tomatoes will rise, other things being equal. The whole supply curve will **shift downwards to the right** as shown in the graph below.

Fig. 8.21
A shift in the supply curve for tomatoes downwards to the right

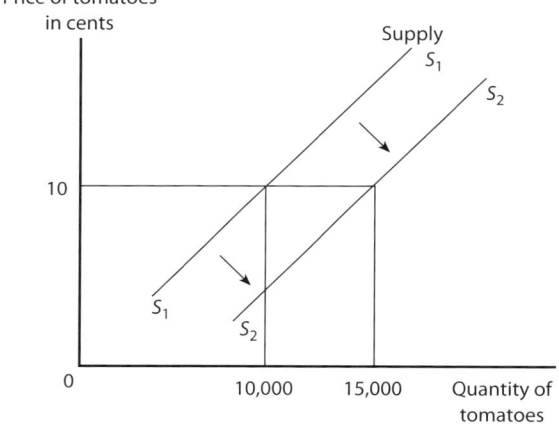

At 10 cents the farmer was supplying 10,000 tomatoes. When the price of fertiliser falls, the farmer applies more fertiliser and the **whole supply curve** of tomatoes shifts outwards (downwards to the right) and 15,000 tomatoes will now be supplied.

Before we leave changes in the costs of the factors of production, it is important to note that tax (like Value Added Tax – VAT) shifts the whole supply curve as if it were a cost of a factor of production. This is because tax must be paid by the supplier to the government. If tax increases the whole of the supply curve shifts upwards to the left and if tax decreases, the whole of the supply curve shifts downwards to the right.

The level of technology

Technology is always improving so that at each and every price, more and more can be supplied. Fertilisers, machines and production techniques are always improving so more and more tomatoes can be produced, other things being equal. The supply curve only moves one way with this determinant – outwards (downwards to the right).

New technology will shift supply curve outwards

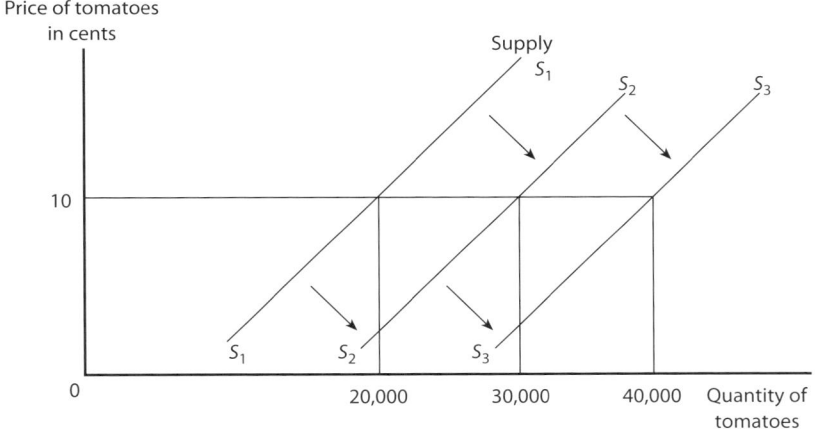

Fig. 8.22
The outward shift in the supply curve due to improved technology

At 10 cents the farmer is able to increase his output from 20,000 tomatoes to 30,000 tomatoes and then to 40,000 tomatoes as technology is continually improving. The **whole supply curve** shifts outwards (downwards to the right).

EXERCISE Research the production of one particular product and see if you can find out what have been the main technological changes in this production.

The goals of the producer

This determinant is not very important. The goal of the producer is profit maximisation. Sometimes a producer will flood the market at a low price to eliminate a competitor (price war) but this is rare and is often illegal in many countries as it is a restrictive trade practice. The supply curve and the amount supplied will be determined by profit maximisation.

The government as a producer in the public sector may not be motivated by profit maximisation but by welfare maximisation. However, in this analysis of the market system, we are considering the 'free market' without government interference.

Movements of both the demand and the supply curves

In the diagram below, we shall shift both the demand and supply curves and observe what happens to the price and quantity demanded.

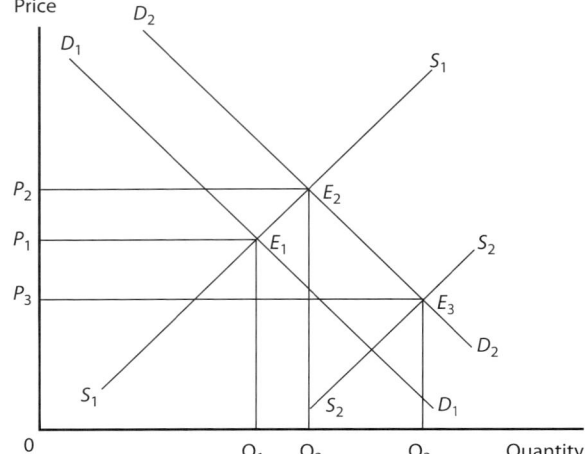

Fig. 8.23
Equilibrium prices and quantities after shifts in both demand and supply

1 The market is in equilibrium at E_1. **Incomes rise** and the demand curve shifts upwards to the right from D_1D_1 to D_2D_2 (the supply curve stays at S_1S_1). The new equilibrium is at E_2. The market price rises from P_1 to P_2. The equilibrium quantity increases from Q_1 to Q_2.

2 The market is now in equilibrium at E_2. **There is an improvement in technology** and the supply curve shifts downwards to the right from S_1S_1 to S_2S_2 (the demand curve is D_2D_2). The new equilibrium is at E_3. The market price falls from P_2 to P_3. The equilibrium quantity increases from Q_2 to Q_3.

The effect of a cartel on the price mechanism

The diagram shows how a cartel, such as OPEC, works.

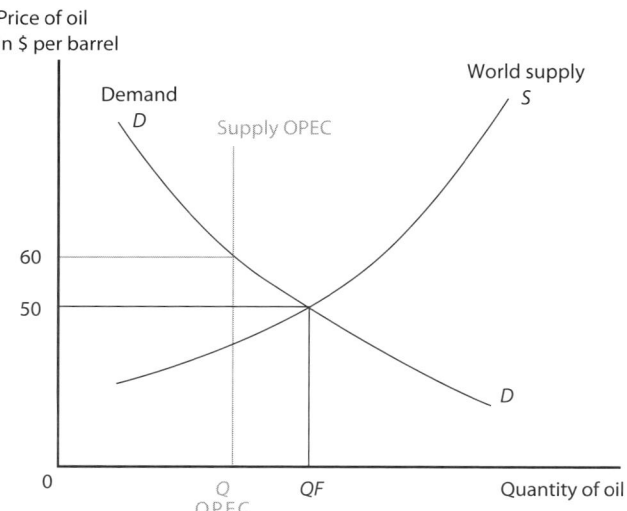

Fig. 8.24
Diagram to show how OPEC fixes the price of oil

The free market price of oil is determined by demand and supply at $50 per barrel and the free market quantity is *QF* barrels. OPEC imposes a quota on the oil production of all its members so that the supply of oil is at a fixed quantity. The supply curve can therefore be drawn as a vertical straight line. This raises the price of oil to $60 per barrel and reduces the quantity supplied from *QF* to *Q*.

EXERCISE

Do you think it is right that a cartel, such as OPEC, can fix prices in this way?

Examination questions

1. **a** What is meant by a market in Economics? *(5 marks)*
   b Distinguish between a goods or services market and a factor market. *(5 marks)*

2. Explain why a demand curve normally slopes downwards and a supply curve upwards. *(10 marks)*

3. Explain why there is sometimes a movement along a demand curve and sometimes a shift of the whole curve. *(10 marks)*

4. Explain what can cause a supply curve to shift to the right. *(10 marks)*

5. Distinguish between a quota and a subsidy. *(5 marks)*

6. Explain what is meant by a market system. *(10 marks)*

Elasticity

In this chapter you will be looking at the concept of elasticity:

- First you will learn the basic form of elasticity, price elasticity of demand or PED
- You will be shown the calculation of PED from a table and from a diagram
- You will learn the different degrees of PED from perfectly inelastic to perfectly elastic
- Some applications of PED will then be given
- The determinants of PED will be explained
- You will then move on to Income elasticity of demand or YED
- The next form of elasticity to be dealt with will be Cross elasticity of demand, CED or XED
- Finally, you will encounter price elasticity of supply or PES

What is elasticity?

We know that demand changes when price changes. It also changes when income changes and when the prices of other goods change. By how much does it change? How much does demand '**stretch**' when one of these variables changes? Economists apply the word '**elasticity**' for this 'stretching' of demand or supply.

Definition of elasticity
Elasticity is the responsiveness of something to a change in another variable.

The price elasticity of demand

Definition of price elasticity of demand
Price elasticity of demand is the responsiveness of the quantity demanded to a change in price.

Price elasticity of demand is the:

$$\frac{\text{percentage change in quantity demanded of the good}}{\text{percentage change in price of the good}}$$

It is given as a mathematical formula:

$$\text{PED} = \frac{\%\Delta qdX}{\%\Delta pX}$$

where X is the good.
% is percentage.
Δ (the Greek letter delta) is change in.
qd is quantity demanded.
p is price.

Examination Tip: If there is a question on elasticity in the examination, define the concept in terms of both words and the formula.

The calculation of price elasticity of demand from a schedule

You may be asked to calculate elasticities. There can be a calculation from a demand schedule or from a graph. Calculation from a schedule is easier so we shall start with that.

Demand schedule for tomatoes

Price in cents	No. of tomatoes
5	28
10	22
15	17
20	14
25	12
30	11

Example 1

Calculate the price elasticity of demand (**PED**) for a rise in price from 20 to 25 cents.

Remember that when there is a rise in price, there is a fall in quantity demanded. When there is a fall in price, there is a rise in quantity demanded.

In a calculation, you must use a + **sign for a rise** and a − **sign for a fall**. **The sign is very important!**

When price rises from 20 to 25 cents, there is a 25% rise in price $\left(\dfrac{5}{20} \times 100\right)$.

When quantity demanded falls from 14 tomatoes to 12 tomatoes, there is a 14.3% fall in quantity demanded $\left(\frac{2}{14} \times 100\right)$.

Applying the formula:

$$\text{PED} = \frac{\%\Delta qdX}{\%\Delta pX} = \frac{-14.3\%}{+25\%} = -0.6$$

Examination Tips

1. Always write out the formula before doing the calculation.
2. The sign is always negative in PED because price and quantity demanded are inversely related – when one goes up, the other goes down.
3. Be careful not to put the equation upside down; the change in the quantity demanded is always on top and the change in the price underneath.
4. Calculate percentages by the formula: $\frac{\text{change}}{\text{original}}$

Example 2
Calculate PED for a fall in price from 15 cents to 10 cents.

The price has fallen by 5 cents from 15, $\frac{5}{15}$ = 33% fall, = –33%

The quantity demanded has risen from 17 tomatoes to 22 tomatoes, $\frac{5}{17}$ = +29%

$$\text{PED} = \frac{\%\Delta qdX}{\%\Delta pX} = \frac{+29\%}{-33\%} = -0.9$$

Note that PED changes throughout the schedule. It is a very special case when PED is unity throughout the schedule and we shall deal with this later in the chapter.

The calculation of price elasticity of demand from a diagram

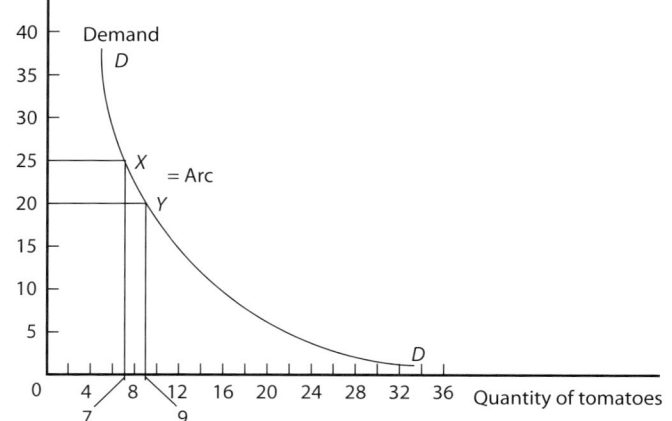

Fig. 9.1
Arc elasticity

XY is an arc on the demand curve *DD*. We are calculating **arc elasticity** or elasticity between two points, *X* and *Y*, on a curve.

Calculation

If we move from *X* to *Y* down the demand curve *DD*, the price of tomatoes falls from 25 to 20 cents. This is a fall of $\frac{5}{25} = -20\%$

For the same move the quantity demanded of tomatoes rises from 7 to 9. This is a rise of $\frac{2}{7} = +29\%$

Applying the formula:

$$\text{PED} = \frac{\%\Delta qdX}{\%\Delta pX} = \frac{+29\%}{-20\%} = -1.45$$

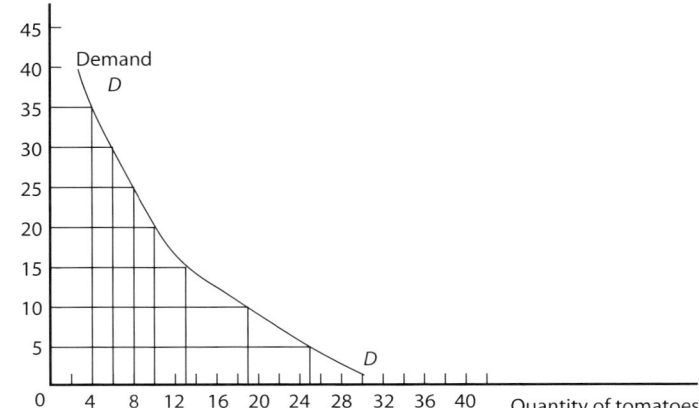

Fig. 9.2
Elasticity decreases as we descend the curve

It is sometimes useful to know that elasticity decreases as price decreases or that elasticity decreases as we descend the demand curve. Let us take three calculations to show this.

1

From 35 to 30 cents: $\text{PED} = \frac{\%\Delta qd \text{ tomatoes}}{\%\Delta p \text{ tomatoes}} = \frac{qd \text{ from 4 to 6}}{p \text{ from 35 to 30}} = \frac{+50\%}{-14.3\%} = -3.5$

2

From 20 to 15 cents: $\text{PED} = \frac{\%\Delta qdT}{\%\Delta pT} = \frac{qd \text{ from 10 to 13}}{p \text{ from 20 to 15}} = \frac{+30\%}{-25\%} = -1.2$

3

From 10 to 5 cents: $\text{PED} = \frac{\%\Delta qdT}{\%\Delta pT} = \frac{qd \text{ from 19 to 25}}{p \text{ from 10 to 5}} = \frac{+32\%}{-50\%} = -0.6$

The value of PED has fallen from 3.5 near the top of the curve to 0.6 near the bottom of the curve. PED elasticity decreases as we descend the curve. This is important for the manager of a store to know, as we shall see later. If PED is 3.5 at the top and 0.6 at the bottom, somewhere in between must be unity (= 1).

'Elastic', 'inelastic' and 'unitary elasticity'

If PED is greater than 1 (> 1), it is said to be **'elastic'**.
If PED is less than 1 (< 1), it is said to be **'inelastic'**.
If PED is exactly 1, it is said to be of **'unitary elasticity'**.

There are five degrees of elasticity:

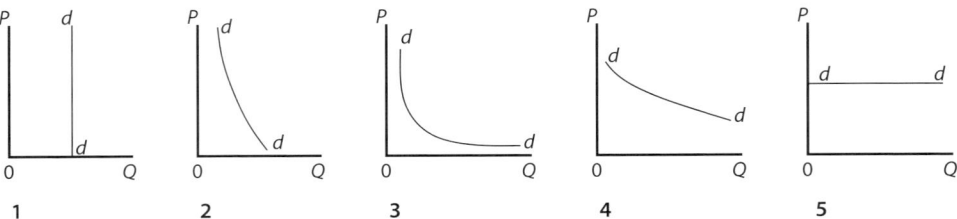

Fig. 9.3
The five degrees of PED

1 Perfectly inelastic. Whatever the price, quantity demanded stays the same. PED is 0.

2 Inelastic. PED is between 0 and 1. It is less than 1 (< 1).

3 Unitary elasticity. PED = 1. PED is unity (= 1) throughout the curve. (The demand curve is called a 'rectangular hyperbola' – see later.)

4 Elastic. PED is greater than 1 (> 1).

5 Infinity, or infinitely elastic. PED = ∞. At a certain price demand is unending. The seller can sell all he or she can put on the market. Above that price he or she will sell nothing.

Can these demand curves be related to real markets or are they just theoretical?

Man working in salt fields, Thailand.

Source: Stillpictures.

Diagram 1 above: salt is a commodity which may have a perfectly inelastic PED because it is an essential good and forms such a small proportion of total expenditure that a consumer may demand the same quantity whatever the price.

Diagram 3 above: processed cheese has a PED of about 0.98 (which is very close to unity) in some markets. Whatever the price, revenue (price × quantity) will remain the same. However, in markets where incomes are high, processed cheese may find no demand. It is a special taste or, in some cases, it may qualify as an inferior good.

Diagram 5 above: this application is important for the seller. At the market price the seller can sell all he or she can put on the market. It is likely in agricultural goods like bananas.

EXERCISE Can you think of other examples of each of these five degrees of elasticity?

Further applications of price elasticity of demand

Revenue maximisation

Price in cents	Quantity of tomatoes	Revenue (p × q) in cents	
5	25	125	elastic
10	19	190	elastic
15	13	195	elastic
20	10	200}	unitary elasticity
25	8	200}	unitary elasticity
30	6	180	inelastic

(This schedule has been taken from the graph in Fig. 9.2.)

Revenue is the total sales and is calculated from the number of goods sold multiplied by the price at which they are sold. The formula is: $r = p \times q$

Examination Tip

> Make sure that you do not confuse revenue with profit. In order to calculate profit, you need to know the costs of production but there is no mention of costs in the above schedule.

A seller can use elasticity to **maximise revenue**. In the schedule above, revenue is maximised at between 20 and 25 cents. (It looks as if it is maximised at either 20 or 25 cents. In fact it will be maximised at 22 or 23 cents.)

What a firm needs to do to increase revenue

1. When demand is elastic, the seller should **lower** the price to increase revenue. This is because the percentage increase in quantity sold will be greater than the percentage decrease in price, i.e. quantity goes up more than price goes down proportionately.

2. When demand is of unitary elasticity, the seller is maximising revenue.

3. When demand is inelastic, the seller should **raise** the price to increase revenue. This is because the percentage decrease in quantity sold is less than the percentage increase in price, i.e. quantity goes down less than price goes up proportionately.

Therefore, a knowledge of PED is of great use to the manager of a retail outlet. How does he or she find PED? The manager can use trial and error, i.e. experiencing sales at different prices but there can be costly mistakes in this method. Sometimes he or she can consult head office but elasticity figures for the same product can vary from market to market. In some countries it is possible to consult the relevant government department which keeps elasticity figures for certain retail goods, e.g. the PED figure for processed cheese is a government figure in the UK.

EXERCISE Consider how a seller can use a knowledge of price elasticity of demand to his or her advantage.

A special application of the price elasticity of demand

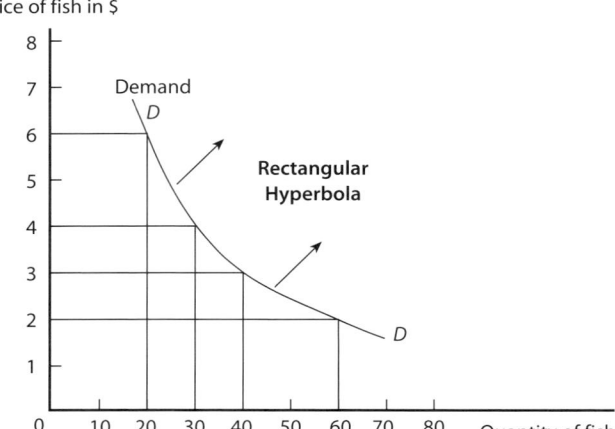

Fig. 9.4
Demand curve is a rectangular hyperbola (Note: The rectangles between the curve and the axes are equal at any point.)

This is a special case. Whatever the price, total revenue stays the same.

Price in $	Quantity of fish	Total revenue in $
6	20	120
4	30	120
3	40	120
2	60	120

(This schedule has been taken from the graph in Fig. 9.4.)

If a seller faces a rectangular hyperbola, what should he or she do? Revenue stays the same at any price. In the case of a shop, perhaps the seller should set a low price on this good to attract customers who may buy other goods once inside the shop.

Another special application of price elasticity of demand

Suppose a local council has spaces for stalls in a local market and there is strong demand for these spaces. The demand curve is shown below. What should the council charge prospective stallholders to maximise its revenue?

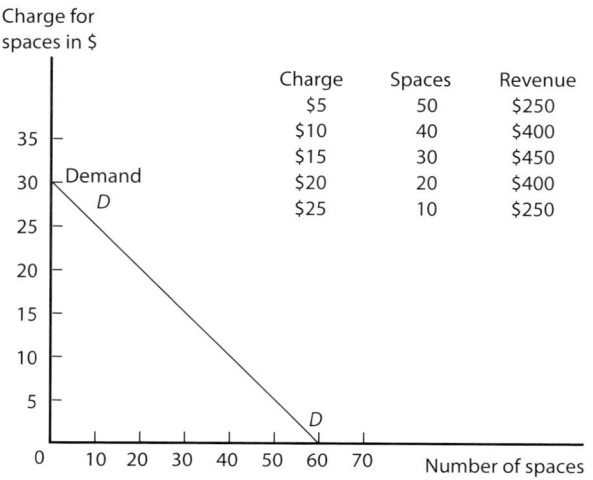

Fig. 9.5
A straight line demand curve

A knowledge of PED is very helpful here. At the mid-point of a straight line demand curve, PED is unity. Revenue is maximised where PED = 1. Therefore, the council will maximise revenue at the market by charging $15 per space.

The determinants of price elasticity of demand

1. How the good is defined determines the elasticity, e.g. if we define the good as 'food' demand is inelastic (we must eat to live!) but if we define it as 'cheese', demand is very much more elastic.

2. The number of substitutes available. The more substitutes, the more elastic the demand for a good, e.g. there are many brands of trainers so demand for a certain trainer will be elastic, other things being equal.

3. The closeness of a substitute. The closer the substitute, the more elastic the demand for a good. Red Stripe is a close substitute for Labatts lager. Demand for Red Stripe will be highly elastic.

4. The time period. Roughly the longer the time the consumer has to buy the good, the more elastic the demand. If an office worker rushes out from the office at lunchtime to do his or her shopping, demand is inelastic. If you have several months to make a purchase, demand can be highly elastic.

5. We have noted before that the demand for salt is highly inelastic. This is because it is such a small proportion of total expenditure that it will be demanded whatever its price. A box of matches falls into the same category of goods. Therefore the proportion of income or expenditure is a very important determinant of PED.

The income elasticity of demand

> **Definition of income elasticity of demand**
> Income elasticity of demand is the responsiveness of quantity demanded to a change in income.

Income elasticity of demand is the: $\dfrac{\text{percentage change in quantity demanded}}{\text{percentage change in income}}$

It is given as a mathematical formula: $\text{YED} = \dfrac{\%\Delta qdX}{\%\Delta Y}$

where X is the good,
where Y is the symbol for income. ('I' in Economics is the symbol for investment so it cannot be used for income.)

The calculation of income elasticity of demand from a schedule

Income in TT $ per week	Quantity demanded of restaurant meals
250	1
350	2
450	4
550	7
650	10
750	15

Examination Tips

1. In YED, the sign (+ or –) is very important. A + sign indicates that it is a normal good, i.e. one more of which is demanded as income rises. Restaurant meals would be an example.
2. A – sign indicates that it is an inferior good, i.e. one less of which is demanded as income rises. Plastic shoes might be considered an example.

Restaurant meals are an example of a normal good.

Calculate YED for meals in restaurants for a change in income from $450 to $550 per week:

$$YED = \frac{\%\Delta qdX}{\%\Delta Y} = \text{From 4 to 7 meals} = \frac{3}{4} = +75\%$$

$$\text{From 450 to 550} = \frac{100}{450} = +22\%$$

$$YED = \frac{+75\%}{+22\%} = +3.4 \text{ (Again, the + sign indicates a normal good.)}$$

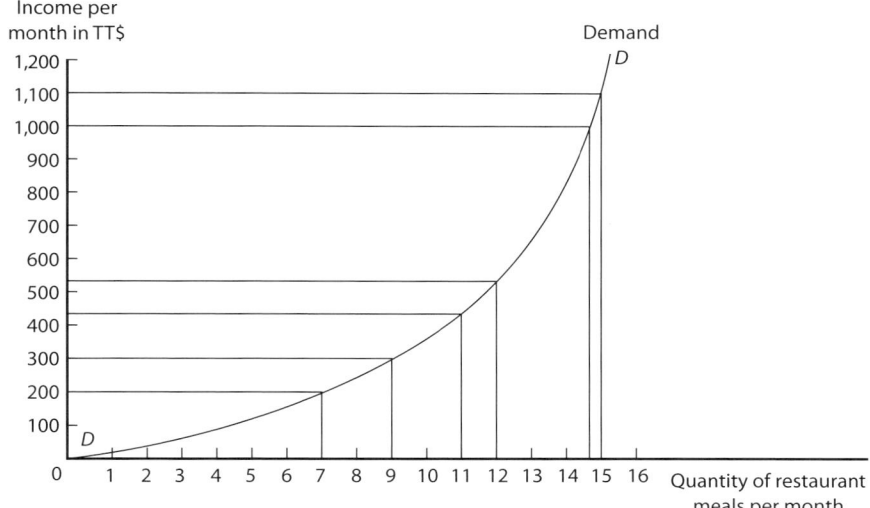

Fig. 9.6 *Income elasticity of demand by graph*

When a person's income rises from TT$200 to $300, he or she increases the consumption of restaurant meals from 7 to 9 per month. The income elasticity of demand is:

$$\text{YED} = \frac{\%\Delta qdX}{\%\Delta Y} = \text{From 7 to 9} = \frac{2}{7} = +29\% = \frac{+29\%}{+50\%} = +0.6$$

$$\text{From \$200 to \$300} = +50\%$$

The + sign indicates that restaurant meals are a normal good.

We can see at a glance that a person on a high income of $1,100 does demand more restaurant meals than a person on a low income of $200. However, when income rises above $1,100, it would make little difference to the restaurant meals consumed because the demand curve is very steep at that point – income elasticity of demand would be very low.

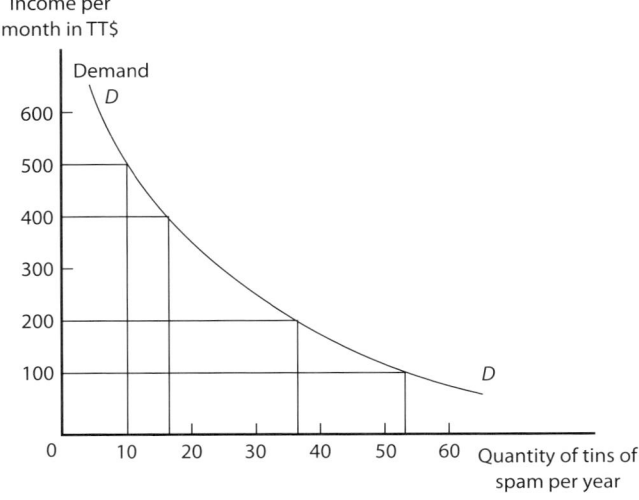

Fig. 9.7 *Income elasticity of demand – inferior good*

To some people, spam is an inferior good, but to others it is not. It is a matter of taste but we are presuming that as income rises, people will switch from spam to ham or other better quality meat.

Perhaps spam is an example of an inferior good, perhaps not.

EXERCISE Why might a good be regarded as an inferior good by one person and a normal good by another?

Example 1
To calculate YED for a change of income from $100 to $200 per month:

$$\text{YED} = \frac{\%\Delta qd \text{ spam}}{\%\Delta Y} = \text{From 53 tins to 37 tins} = \frac{16}{53} = -30\% = \frac{-30\%}{+100\%} = -0.33$$

$$\text{From \$100 to \$200} = \frac{100}{100} = +100\%$$

Example 2
To calculate YED for a change in income from $400 to $500 per month:

$$\text{YED} = \frac{\%\Delta qd \text{ spam}}{\%\Delta Y} = \text{From 17 tins to 10 tins} = \frac{7}{17} = -41\% = \frac{-41\%}{+25\%} = -1.6$$

$$\text{From \$400 to \$500} = \frac{100}{400} = +25\%$$

The – sign indicates that spam is an inferior good, less of which is demanded as income rises. For an inferior good, YED decreases as we descend the demand curve, i.e. there will be little change in the quantity of spam demanded when incomes are low.

The cross elasticity of demand

Definition of cross elasticity of demand

Cross elasticity of demand measures the responsiveness of the quantity demanded of one product to the change in price of another product.

$$\text{XED (or CED) is the: } \frac{\text{percentage change in quantity demanded of good } A}{\text{percentage change in price of good } B}$$

It is given as a mathematical formula:

$$\text{XED} = \frac{\%\Delta qdA}{\%\Delta pB}$$

where X is the symbol for cross (or C with some economists).
where A is one good and B is another good.

Note that the sign, + or – , is very important as it indicates whether the goods are **substitutes** or **complements**.

When the price of one good rises, and the quantity demanded of another good rises, those goods are **substitutes** and the sign will be +. For example, chicken and fish may be substitutes; when the price of chicken rises, less chicken is demanded and more of the substitute, fish, is demanded.

Coffee and tea are substitutes.

When the price of one good rises and the quantity demanded of another good falls, those goods are **complements** and the sign will be – . For example, bread and butter may be complements; when the price of bread rises, less bread is demanded and less of the complement, butter, is demanded.

The closeness of the substitutes and complements to each other is very important in XED. Two brands of coffee are very close substitutes and a small increase in the price of one brand will lead to a big change in the quantity demanded of the other; the coefficient for XED will be very high. Coffee and tea are substitutes but they are not close substitutes. A rise in the price of coffee will lead to an increase in demand for tea, but it will not be a very big increase; the coefficient for XED will be low.

Cameras and film are complements.

Cameras and film are complements (albeit film cameras are almost out of date!). They are very close complements, almost in joint demand. A rise in the price of cameras will lead to a big fall in quantity demanded of film; the XED coefficient will be very high. Holidays and cameras are complements, but they are not close complements. A rise in the price of holidays will lead to a fall in the quantity demanded of cameras but not a big fall; the coefficient for XED will be low.

EXERCISE Can you think of other examples of substitutes and complements?

What about an increase in the price of postage stamps and the quantity demanded of holidays? They are **unrelated products**. A rise in the price of one will have no impact on the quantity demanded of the other. XED will be irrelevant.

Graphical representation of substitutes and complements

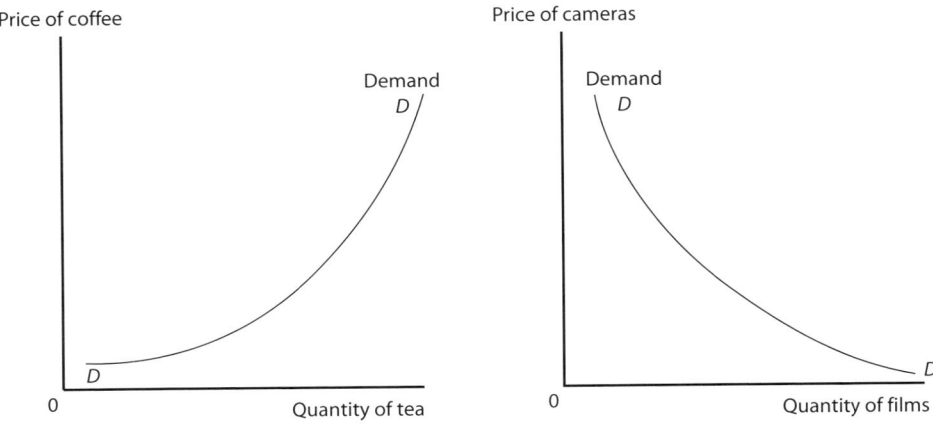

Fig. 9.8 *Demand curve for substitutes*   **Fig. 9.9** *Demand curve for complements*

Schedules for substitutes and complements

Substitutes		Complements	
Price of coffee $	Quantity of tea (bags)	Price of cameras $	Quantity of film (rolls)
5	100	200	1,000
6	150	400	900
7	225	600	800
8	350	800	700
9	500	1,000	600
10	700	1,200	500

Example 1
To calculate XED for tea brought about by a rise in the price of coffee from $8 to $9.

$$\text{XED} = \frac{\%\Delta qd \text{ tea}}{\%\Delta p \text{ coffee}} = \text{From 350 to 500 bags} = \frac{150}{350} = +43\% = \frac{+43\%}{+12.5\%} = +3.4$$

$$\text{From } \$8 \text{ to } \$9 = \frac{1}{8} = +12.5\%$$

The + sign shows that the goods are substitutes and the XED coefficient of 3.4 shows that tea and coffee are highly substitutable between those prices.

Example 2
To calculate XED for rolls of film brought about by the rise in the price of cameras from $600 to $800:

$$\text{XED} = \frac{\%\Delta qd \text{ film}}{\%\Delta p \text{ cameras}} = \text{From 800 to 700 rolls} = \frac{100}{800} = -12.5\% = \frac{-12.5\%}{+33.3\%} = -0.4$$

$$\text{From } \$600 \text{ to } \$800 = \frac{200}{600} = +33.3\%$$

The – sign shows that the goods are complements but, at XED – 0.4, not close complements.

The application of cross elasticity of demand

When two firms are selling a similar product, the price that one firm charges will have an impact on the demand for the other firm's product. Therefore, managers will watch closely the pricing decisions of other firms in the same market. They will be in competition as their products are substitutes. They will see what a reduction in the price by a competitor will do to demand for their own product.

A price war using **predatory pricing** (hunting a competitor to death and destruction!) is the ultimate stage in the application of XED. One firm, often to gain a monopoly, will lower its price so that there will be no demand for the competitor's product which will be forced out of the market.

However, there is non-price competition, e.g. in advertising, after-sales-service etc. which can make XED less critical.

The price elasticity of supply

> **Definition of price elasticity of supply**
> Price elasticity of supply measures the responsiveness of quantity supplied to a change in price.

Price elasticity of supply is the: $\dfrac{\text{percentage change in quantity supplied}}{\text{percentage change in price}}$

It is given as a mathematical formula:

$$\text{PES} = \frac{\%\Delta qsX}{\%\Delta pX}$$

Where PES is price elasticity of supply.
Where X is the good in question.

The calculation of price elasticity of supply from a schedule

Price of tomatoes in $	Quantity of tomatoes supplied in kilos
5	100
10	1,000
15	2,000
20	5,000
25	10,000

To calculate PES for a rise in price from $10 to $15:

$$\text{PES} = \frac{\%\Delta qs \text{ tomatoes}}{\%\Delta s \text{ tomatoes}} = \text{From 1,000 to 2,000 kilos} = \frac{1{,}000}{1{,}000} = 100\% = \frac{100\%}{50\%} = 2$$

$$\text{From \$10 to \$15} = \frac{5}{10} = 50\%$$

The sign will always be positive (+) as price and quantity supplied always move in the same direction.

The calculation of price elasticity of supply from a diagram

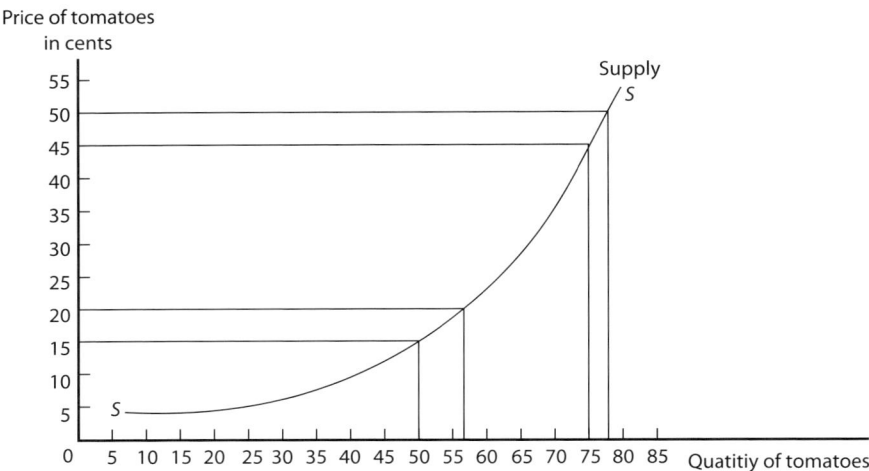

Fig. 9.10 Supply curve for tomatoes

Example 1
To calculate PES for a rise in price of tomatoes from 15 to 20 cents:

$$\text{PES} = \frac{\%\Delta qs \text{ tomatoes}}{\%\Delta s \text{ tomatoes}} = \text{From 50 to 57 tomatoes} = \frac{7}{50} = 14\% = \frac{+14\%}{+33.3\%} = +0.4$$

$$\text{From 15 to 20 cents} = \frac{5}{15} = 33.3\%$$

Example 2
To calculate PES for a *fall* in price from 50 to 45 cents:

$$\text{PES} = \frac{\%\Delta qs \text{ tomatoes}}{\%\Delta s \text{ tomatoes}} = \text{From 78 to 75 tomatoes} = \frac{3}{78} = -4\% = \frac{-4\%}{-10\%} = +0.4$$

$$\text{From 50 to 45 cents} = \frac{5}{50} = -10\%$$

We have just used the + and − signs to show that the PES answer is always positive.

The determinants of price elasticity of supply

Time is the greatest and most obvious determinant of supply. The longer the time, the more elastic the supply; the shorter the time, the less elastic the supply. For example, farmers cannot change their supplies at short notice. Usually, once the crop has been sown, the supply for the year has been determined. It takes two years to fatten calves for beef. It takes twenty years or more to grow trees for timber!

Another determinant of supply is the elasticity of supply of resources (inputs such as raw materials). If the inputs are inelastic in supply, the final product will be inelastic in supply. Note that this applies to labour as an input. If there is full employment, it will be difficult for a producer to increase his or her labour force quickly, except, perhaps, at great cost. Also if the labour needs to be highly skilled, it will probably increase the inelasticity of its supply.

Examination questions

1. a Explain what is meant by price elasticity of demand. *(4 marks)*
   b Compare and contrast the five degrees of PED. *(6 marks)*

2. Discuss the potential usefulness of price elasticity of demand for a business. *(10 marks)*

3. Distinguish between income elasticity of demand and cross elasticity of demand. *(10 marks)*

4. Discuss whether **(a)** soap and **(b)** foreign holidays were likely to have a high or low price elasticity of demand. *(10 marks)*

Chapter 10

Market structures

In this chapter we shall be examining how the four market structures are determined by the degree of competition in each. You will study:

- Perfect competition, an ideal market structure that is hard to find in an economy
- Monopolistic competition, the market structure we find most commonly in everyday life
- Monopoly and the arguments for and against
- Oligopoly and its special characteristics

Perfect competition

In discussing the price mechanism in Chapter 8, we outlined the six conditions necessary for perfect competition to exist so here is a reminder of what they are:

1. A large number of independent sellers.
2. A large number of independent buyers.
3. An homogeneous product (every product must be the same).
4. Perfect knowledge of the market.
5. Free and easy access to the market.
6. No advertising.

Pfizer's Building

In 1 and 2 above, we say 'independent' because there must be no collusion between sellers (remember OPEC!) and no collusion between buyers.

In this chapter we are not thinking of how the market price is set in a free market. We are concentrating on the position of the firm in an industry. By 'firm', we mean any business enterprise from the sole trader, such as the holder of a market stall, to a large multinational corporation. It is likely that a sole trader is more able to fulfil the conditions of perfect competition than a multinational corporation.

In a place like Port-of-Spain, there will be hundreds, even thousands, of electricians in the market, offering the same service, to thousands of customers who can look up electricians in the telephone directory. On the other hand, a multinational like the pharmaceutical giant, Pfizer, operates in a market with very few sellers, certainly not homogeneous products, probably selling to very few outlets like the health service, requiring highly specialised knowledge and advertising extensively.

> **Definition of perfect competition**
> Perfect competition is a market structure where there is a large number of buyers and sellers, the sellers offering identical products and with no one firm able to influence the price.

In perfect competition, each firm is a **price taker**, i.e. each firm must accept the market price.

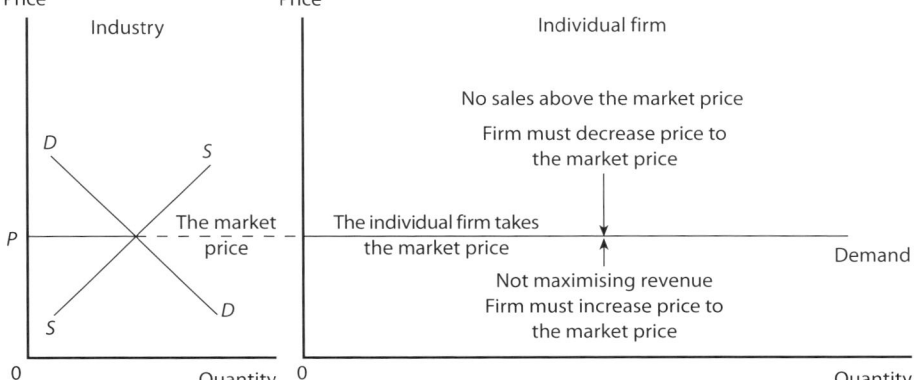

Fig. 10.1
The firm as a price taker in perfect competition

In perfect competition, each firm faces a perfectly horizontal demand curve at the market price as seen in the graph above. The firm can sell all it can supply at that price but if it tried to set a price above the market price, it would sell nothing. Of course, below the market price, it could sell all its supply but it would not be rational to sell at a lower price when it can find a higher price.

Does perfect competition ever exist? In our example of the electricians in Port-of-Spain, we can see that there is not an identical product (service); one electrician may well be better than another. There is not perfect knowledge of the market on the part of the buyers. There is not free and easy access to the market and there is certainly advertising because electricians promote themselves in local newspapers and trade journals. Perhaps the local fruit and vegetable market provides a better example of perfect competition.

Freedom of entry to the market is often given as another condition for perfect competition. Certainly anyone is free to set up a market stall provided he or she can pay the charge. There is a homogeneous product: one carrot is much the same as another. The sellers are price takers; if one seller tries to sell above the market price, he or she will sell nothing because the buyer will go to the next stall. There is perfect knowledge because buyers can walk around the market finding out where the goods are and what the price is. There is no advertising except by the stallholders calling out their goods. However, free and easy access is debatable. The fruit and vegetable market is not always nearby.

In Chapter 8 we concluded that the Stock Exchange was the closest market to perfect competition because:

1. there are very many stockbrokers, an infinite number of buyers (the whole world on an international stock market);

2. there is a homogeneous product (e.g. a share certificate in a firm);

3. there is perfect knowledge of the market (share prices are quoted in daily newspapers, on the internet and on television and radio in some countries);

4. there is free and easy access to the market (by picking up a telephone);

5. there is no advertising (in some stock exchanges it is illegal for brokers to advertise their services).

Perfect competition is the ideal of the free market or capitalist economy. In such an economy there should be no interference in the market. Let the market forces work ('laissez-faire') and consumers will find the goods they demand and resources will be allocated efficiently. However, there are failures as we shall see at the end of the chapter.

'**Consumer sovereignty**' (the consumer rules) exists in perfect competition and that is what free market supporters believe in. If a consumer demands a product, that product will be produced. If the consumer finds the price too high, he or she will not demand that product. Suppliers will try to find a way of reducing costs so that they can bring the price of the product into the range that the consumer can afford. Therefore, the consumer can drive down costs and contribute to more efficient production. If consumer tastes change, the suppliers must make their supply reflect this change, e.g. consumers increasingly want tea bags instead of tea leaves.

EXERCISE To what extent do you think that perfect competition is a theoretical idea without any real examples?

Profit

In free market or capitalist economies, the profit motive is justified. Firms enter business to make profit and the system would not work if profit making was denied. Firms pursue their selfish interest, i.e. they make profit. It is their reward for risk-taking and free market economists say that it is a just reward.

In perfect competition firms make profit, but there is a special term for this profit – **'normal profit'**.

> **Definition of normal profit**
>
> Normal profit is the profit that could be earned in the next best alternative business. It is what keeps a firm in that business and it is thus the opportunity cost of being in business.

If a firm could make more profit in another industry, then it would change industry. The opportunity cost would attract the firm into other areas of business. Therefore, in perfect competition, there are hundreds or thousands of firms making normal profit. If one firm finds that revenue – costs < normal profit, then it will go out of business and put the capital elsewhere.

This is the incentive to keep costs down and to be efficient. If a firm in perfect competition cannot keep costs below revenue, it will make losses and go out of business. If a business in perfect competition is making in excess of normal profit, it will attract other businesses to enter the industry and competition will drive down profits to the level of normal profit once again. Again, notice that this is a virtue of a free market economy.

Here we must distinguish between the **short run** and the **long run**. In perfect competition, in the short run, supernormal profits are possible but they are not possible in the long run because the long run is a period of time long enough for other firms to enter the market attracted by the supernormal profits made by some firms. The entry of these other firms will bring the firm back to normal profits.

> **Definitions of short run and long run in perfect competition**
>
> The short run is a period of time short enough for some firms to make supernormal profits.
>
> The long run is a period of time long enough for new firms to enter the market so that supernormal profits disappear.

EXERCISE Consider the differences between normal and supernormal profits.

Monopolistic competition

This is the most common form of market structure in that we come across it most often in our everyday lives. Monopolistic competition can occur in any sort of market, e.g. in markets where we find big firms like the camera corporations (e.g. Canon) and the toilet soap producers (e.g. Unilever), as well as in local markets

Locals at a small bar talk and drink beer. A bar is an example of monopolistic competition.

Source: AP/EMPICS.

where we have the bars and restaurants. Most of the goods we buy are produced by firms in monopolistic competition. There are many firms in competition but each firm has a **differentiated product** and each firm has some control over price. While firms in monopolistic competition are not price takers, they are not completely free to be price setters.

> **Definition of monopolistic competition**
>
> Monopolistic competition is a market structure where firms compete through differentiated products as well as through price and non-price competition, such as quality of service, advertising and other forms of promotion.

For example, the camera market is monopolistically competitive. There are many large firms – Canon, Nikon, Pentax, Minolta, Olympus, Fuji, Sony, to name just the major Japanese players in the market. There are thousands of independent buyers. Thus there is competition. However, there is a **differentiated product**. Each firm will claim something unique about its brand and its model of camera, competing to gain an edge over its competitors. For roughly the same performance of camera, each firm will charge a different price. How different depends on the firm's estimation of its own strength in the market.

In monopolistic competition, such as the camera market, price competition is so keen that the consumer can benefit considerably by researching the market and finding the lowest price for a model of similar performance. However, there is also very strong non-price competition. Advertising costs are very high and firms in monopolistic competition feel that they must advertise to compete.

In monopolistic competition, a firm faces a downward sloping demand curve. If it sets a higher price, it will lose sales and if it sets a lower price, it will gain sales.

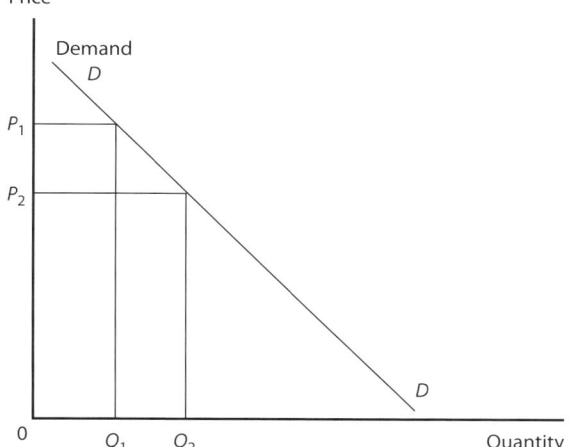

Fig. 10.2
Downward-sloping demand curve in monopolistic competition

The monopolistically competitive firm can set the price at P_1 but it will only sell Q_1 goods. If it lowers the price to P_2, it will sell more goods, Q_2, but the change in revenue depends upon the price elasticity of demand for the good between those two points.

'Me-too' is also a feature of this structure. The great German camera producer, Leica, rested on its reputation for the high quality of its single lens reflex cameras (SLRs) but found its sales dropping in competition from the Japanese producers, especially when digital cameras were introduced and Leica did not produce a digital camera, thinking that their SLR cameras would still dominate the top end of the market. However, Leica has now entered the digital camera market, in collaboration with Panasonic, with 'Me-too' products, producing a digital camera range to ensure the very survival of the firm.

Cameras are expensive and not an everyday item in shopping, especially amongst students, so let us take an everyday item which is in monopolistic competition – toilet soap. There are many big and famous brands in this market – Camay, Lux, Palmolive, Dove, Cussons – to name but a few. They are in keen competition through differentiated products. Some may say that one toilet soap is like another in that it performs the function of cleaning the skin and leaving a fragrant smell. However, the firms compete through product differentiation such as the size and shape of the bars, the texture, the colour and the fragrance. The producers claim the benefits to the skin conferred by their products. They compete in price. Finally, they compete in non-price competition. Advertising is prominent in this market and a firm would lose sales immediately if it failed to put its product before the public everyday on billboards, in newspapers and glossy magazines, on the radio and on television. The advertisements are trying to persuade the public that their product is different to their rival's, and superior – product differentiation.

In monopolistic competition, there is very good knowledge of the market because of the media of advertising. However, the public can be deceived by the mass of technical data with cameras and the unproven claims of the toilet soaps. There is free and easy access to the markets in the two examples we have considered: cameras (through internet shopping) and toilet soaps through shops and even street vendors. Therefore, monopolistic competition does lean more to perfect competition than it does to monopoly.

However, it is not necessary that firms have to be big in monopolistic competition. There are markets where units are small but they are in monopolistic competition because there is a differentiated product and sellers are not price takers. The local catering market is an example of monopolistic competition. It leans more to perfect competition than to monopoly. Each local bar or restaurant has a differentiated product, e.g. the premises are different, they may offer a 'Happy Hour' or they may have a pool table or a dart board. One restaurant may specialise in sea food and another in curries. The landlord and bar staff may concentrate on giving excellent service. The opening hours can be different. In all these ways we can say there is a differentiated product. There can be differences in prices in drinks and meals – price competition is keen. The businesses are small, however, and there is only a little scope for economies of scale. Such markets are still monopolistically competitive. They also advertise, but on a small scale, e.g. in the local press.

EXERCISE Discuss why monopolistic competition is closer to perfect competition than it is to monopoly.

Profit

Definition of supernormal profit

This is a surplus above the profit needed to keep a firm in business, i.e. it is the excess over the opportunity cost of the profit.

Supernormal profits would attract other firms to enter the industry in monopolistic competition just as in perfect competition. They can exist in the short run but they will be competed away in the long run.

The size of firms

We tend to think of firms in monopolistic competition as being giants and in the camera market and the toilet soap market they are. This is likely to be the case because such firms can achieve **economies of scale**. However, there are many sorts of monopolistically competitive markets and markets with very small businesses, like local bars and restaurants, which cannot achieve economies of scale.

Definition of economies of scale

Economies of scale occur when increasing levels of production lead to lower unit costs; in other words, output increases at a faster rate than costs.

The economies of scale can be shown in a simple table.

Table 10.1 The economies of scale: falling average costs		
Output in units	Total costs in $	Average (unit) costs in $
1,000	1,000,000	1,000
2,000	1,600,000	800
3,000	2,000,000	667
4,000	2,200,000	550

As the firm increases in size (here measured by output), its unit costs fall. Small firms are often unable to achieve these economies. Thus we find large firms in some markets in monopolistic competition. With lower costs they can lower prices.

Monopoly

As mentioned earlier, monopoly in Economics is strictly a market where there is only one seller in the market. However, in Business Studies it can be defined as one firm having 25% or 30% share of the market. For example, The Trinidad and Tobago Electricity Commission provides 95% of the nation's electricity, but private companies produce the other 5%.

> **Definition of monopoly**
>
> A monopoly is a market structure where there is only one firm in the market and so a monopoly can be a price-setter.

A monopolist faces a downward-sloping demand curve. A monopolist can set price and quantity but he cannot set both at the same time. This is a common misconception about monopoly. A monopolist is constrained by the demand curve like any other supplier in imperfect competition.

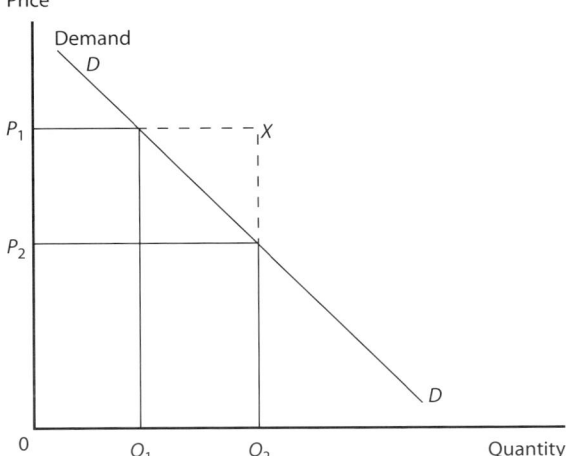

Fig. 10.3
The constraint of the demand curve

A monopolist can set the price at P_1 or can set the quantity at Q_2 but he or she cannot set P_1 price together with Q_2 quantity. This would take the monopolist to point X which is beyond the demand curve. P_1 price must go with Q_1 quantity and P_2 price must go with Q_2 quantity. If the monopolist chooses to supply Q_2, he or she must accept price P_2.

Barriers to entry

A monopoly can exist only because new firms can be prevented from entering the market. They can be prevented by various 'barriers to entry'.

> **Definition of barriers to entry**
> Barriers to entry are restrictions preventing firms from entering a market.

Legal barriers

A government can pass a law which gives the sole right to a firm to produce and sell a good or service. The East Caribbean Central Bank has been given the sole right to issue notes and coins in the Organisation of Eastern Caribbean States. One authority must have control over the money supply, therefore the government confers a legal monopoly.

Another legal barrier is a patent. A patent is a legal document which gives the exclusive right (monopoly) to the proceeds of an invention. This is considered necessary as inventors would not be prepared to put their time, money and intellectual talent into a product if someone could immediately copy it and reap the benefits. Consider the intellectual property rights that composers have over their music.

> **Definition of a patent**
> A patent is a legal document that gives exclusive rights to the proceeds of an invention.

Natural monopoly

> **Definition of a natural monopoly**
> A natural monopoly exists when one firm achieves long run average costs so low that other firms cannot compete.

Gas, water and electricity are commonly given as examples of a natural monopoly. Let us take electricity as an example. Suppose many firms were generating electricity in the past. Then one firm gained more customers by some means or other and grew bigger than its rivals and was able to achieve economies of scale and lower costs. It then passed on these lower costs to its customers in the form of lower prices and forced other firms out of the market. The firm took over more customers, achieved more economies of scale, lowered prices and squeezed yet other firms out of the market. Eventually that firm would become the only provider of electricity in the market – a monopoly.

New firms cannot enter such a market because they would have to start at the same size as the monopolist to have the necessary economies of scale and clearly that is not possible so the natural monopoly remains.

Restrictive trade practices

Illegal monopolies may exist because of a lack of ability or will on the part of a government to track them down. For example, a major supplier of electrical goods may try to force retail outlets to stock only its goods by offering huge supplies at discounted prices. This is known as a **'restrictive trade practice'** and is hard for a government to track down.

Cartels are restrictive trade practices. Cartels are associations of sellers which restrict supply in order to fix prices. If a cartel succeeds in bringing in 100% of suppliers, it has monopoly power. OPEC is not a monopoly but in its control over the major oil producers it is powerful enough to have a strong influence on the price of oil.

Mergers

The approach to mergers in any particular country will depend on the government's stance. The problem is that if there are only two firms in a market and they merge, they become a monopoly.

> **Definition of a merger**
>
> A merger is when two or more firms in a market join together to give them more market power.
>
> A horizontal merger occurs when two firms in the same stage of production merge, e.g. two shoe manufacturers.
>
> A vertical merger occurs when two firms in different stages of production merge, e.g. a shoe manufacturer merges with a shoe retail outlet.

State monopolies

State monopolies occur in command economies, e.g. the state's ownership of land and other natural resources in Cuba. However, in mixed economies state monopolies are also common. Nuclear power is considered so strategically important that it really needs to be completely under the control of the government.

Profit

A monopolist can enjoy supernormal profits in the long run because, by definition, no other firms exist in the market and no new firms can enter the market. In other markets, supernormal profits would attract new firms but they cannot enter in monopoly.

Some common misconceptions about monopoly

We have seen already that it is mistakenly thought that a monopolist can set both price and quantity whereas only one or the other can be set.

1. A monopoly must make a profit. A monopoly can make supernormal profits but it does not have to make any profits at all. A monopoly can make losses just like any other business if it is run badly.

2. A monopoly is inefficient. This is also not true. A monopolist has the incentive to

make the business as efficient as possible. If he lowers his costs, he makes more profit, other things being equal.

3   A monopolist is anti-social. Not true, again. A monopolist who enjoys the economies of scale and passes on these lower costs in lower prices to the public is a benefit to society. On the other hand, monopolists who exploit their monopoly power to raise prices greatly to make higher profits can be anti-social. Monopolists who restrict output to keep prices high are depriving the public of supplies and this is anti-social.

4   Monopoly holds back innovation. There is no incentive for monopolists to introduce new technology and bring in fresh ideas. This can be true. However, on the other hand, monopolists can be the leaders in technological innovation. Microsoft is not a monopoly, but it is in a very commanding position in the software market. Bill Gates certainly uses Microsoft's profits to innovate and introduce new technology. You could argue that innovation is more likely under monopoly.

Price discrimination

Price discrimination is associated with monopoly. If a consumer could buy the good elsewhere, there could be no price discrimination. Price discrimination is more common in services than goods as we shall see later.

> **Definition of price discrimination**
> Price discrimination is the charging of different prices to different consumers for the same good or service for reasons not associated with costs.

Conditions necessary for price discrimination

1   There must be monopoly power. The monopolist is a price setter and can therefore set different prices for different consumers or markets.

2   There must be the ability to prevent resale. If one person can buy a good at a lower price than another, the person who is being charged the higher price can arrange for the other person to buy the good for him. This is why price discrimination is more effective in services. A cosmetic surgeon can price discriminate because no one can have another person's operation for them! Successful surgeons and lawyers can price discriminate.

3   The price discriminating monopolist must be able to divide the market up by its different price elasticities of demand. The more inelastic the demand, the higher the price that can be charged.

Price discrimination is not usually illegal. The airlines price discriminate by first class, business class and tourist (economy) class. You may say that each class provides a different service but the differences in costs have little or no relation to the differences in prices. They also discriminate by season of the year, time of the week and time of booking. Two people can be sitting next to each other on an aircraft and have paid vastly different prices for their tickets! (Transport is a service. Airlines can prevent resale.)

Monopolists justify price discrimination by arguing that it benefits the public. By being able to charge high prices in one market, low prices can be charged in another market.

EXERCISE

Do you think it is right that many people on one air journey may have paid very different prices for their seats?

Oligopoly

> **Definition of oligopoly**
> An oligopoly occurs when a few firms dominate a market.

It can be as few as two firms although there is a word 'duopoly' for a market with only two sellers. An oligopoly can easily behave like a monopoly when the firms collude, as in a cartel. When oligopolists agree to limit competition between themselves it is called 'collusive oligopoly'. OPEC formally became a collusive oligopoly in 1960 and enjoyed its exploitation of market power most in the 1970s, 1973–74 and 1978–79 in particular.

It has since become weaker as some oil producers have stayed out of the cartel and others within it have broken ranks and not kept to their quotas.

The opposite of collusion is competition. Sometimes oligopolists choose to compete and this can be just as good for consumers as perfect competition as they drive down prices. In this case, monopolists are in a price war with each other as they seek to eliminate the competitor from the market. A price war between oligopolists is risky and damaging to profits and usually oligopolists prefer to compete in non-price competition. Their actions can be explained by the '**kinked demand curve**'.

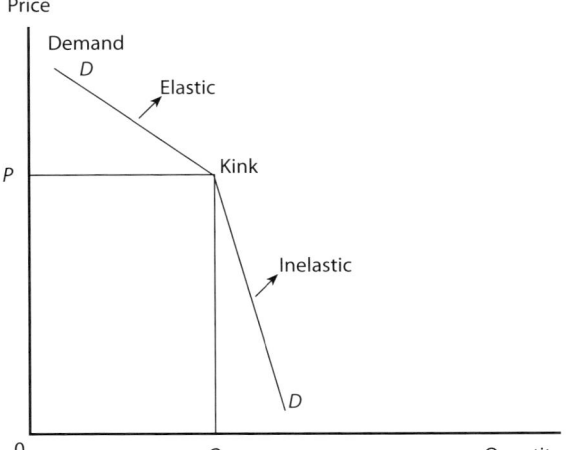

Fig. 10.4
The kinked demand curve under oligopoly

An oligopolist faces a kinked demand curve. If he or she raises price above P, he or she will choke off much demand (sales) because above P, PED is highly elastic and revenue will fall. If a rival did raise price above *P*, the other firms would hold their price at *P* and reap the benefit in the form of increased revenue as they would win the rival's customers. If he or she lowers price below *P*, he or she will gain little demand (sales) because PED is inelastic and revenue will again fall. Once again, the other firms would hold their prices at *P* and lose very few customers to the rival who had lowered the price.

The kinked demand curve explains why prices are stable under oligopoly.

Therefore, oligopolists tend not to compete with each other in price but compete in non-price competition such as promotions and service.

Interdependence

In oligopoly, there are only a few firms in the market. Consequently they have to watch the others very carefully and follow their moves. This is referred to as **'interdependence'**. The kinked demand curve explains how they are interdependent in price.

Oligopolists are also interdependent in products. If one produces a new product, the others have to follow. This is well shown in the washing powder market. When one firm produced a tablet instead of powder, the other firms had to follow. 'Me-too' is certainly true.

Oligopolists also watch each other's advertising campaigns (non-price competition is very important). This leads to very high advertising costs in some oligopoly markets, e.g. toilet soaps and washing powders. Interdependence means that one oligopolist cannot ignore the actions of another.

Barriers to entry

In oligopoly, there are barriers to entry which are similar to the barriers to entry in monopoly. Oligopolists tend to be large firms which can benefit from economies of scale. Cost barriers are significant. Also, it is difficult for a new firm to break into a market where there has to be so much product innovation and where there are such high advertising costs.

Example: The cruise line market and the Caribbean
We can use the cruise line market as an example of oligopoly in the Caribbean and as a link to the next chapter, 'Market failure'.

Two cruise lines, Carnival Cruise Line and Royal Caribbean International, between them held a 61.7% market share of the Caribbean Cruise Line market in 2003 (they are both US listed corporations). They bring external benefits to Caribbean countries in the spin offs from tourist expenditure but they also bring external costs in terms of the damage they do to the ecosystem with discharges (Market failure).

They are very powerful in the market, almost wielding domination over local governments. For example, one way of dealing with external costs like pollution is to **make the polluter pay** for the pollution through tax. When the Caribbean Tourism Organisation, backed by certain governments, proposed a US $20 tax per passenger,

The Jewel of the Seas, the cruise liner belonging to the Royal Caribbean International shipping company, is the world's largest cruise ship.

Source: DPA/EMPICS.

the Carnival Cruise Lines executive opposed it. There was collusion between the cruise lines in opposing the tax, exploitation of monopoly power. The hidden threat was to take the cruises out of the Caribbean or away from those countries supporting the tax and the Caribbean governments backed down. When oligopolists compete they make the market like perfect competition but when they collude they make the market like monopoly.

Examination questions

1 a Explain the characteristics of perfect competition. *(5 marks)*
   b To what extent do you think perfect competition exists in reality? *(5 marks)*

2 Distinguish clearly between normal and supernormal profits. *(10 marks)*

3 Explain the conditions which are necessary for price discrimination to occur. *(5 marks)*

4 a What is meant by an oligopolistic market structure? *(5 marks)*
   b Examine how the kinked demand curve can be used to explain the interdependence of firms in oligopoly. *(5 marks)*

5 Is it inevitable that all monopolies will be bad and against the public interest? *(10 marks)*

Market failure

In this chapter we shall examine where and how inefficiency occurs in markets.
- You will first examine market failure in relation to efficiency or inefficiency
- You will learn the concept of marginal cost in relation to allocative efficiency
- You will examine market failure under monopoly
- Information failure is explained and applied to the labour market
- You will learn about positive and negative externalities and social benefits and social costs
- You will be made aware of the consequences of market failure in the forms of: (a) unemployment, (b) the gap between rich and poor, including the Lorenz Curve, (c) poverty and (d) economic depression in the business cycle

Allocative efficiency

Resources are allocated efficiently where the value placed on the good, in other words, the price that consumers are willing to pay for it, exactly matches the cost of producing that good. If consumers were willing to pay more for the good than it cost, the good would be **undersupplied**, meaning that not enough resources were being put into the good. This is the same as saying that the public want more resources allocated to that good. The implication is that elsewhere in the market, resources were being allocated to goods that the public did not want – those goods were being **oversupplied**. Undersupply and oversupply both express allocative inefficiency.

This situation can be illustrated by a simple demand and supply diagram.

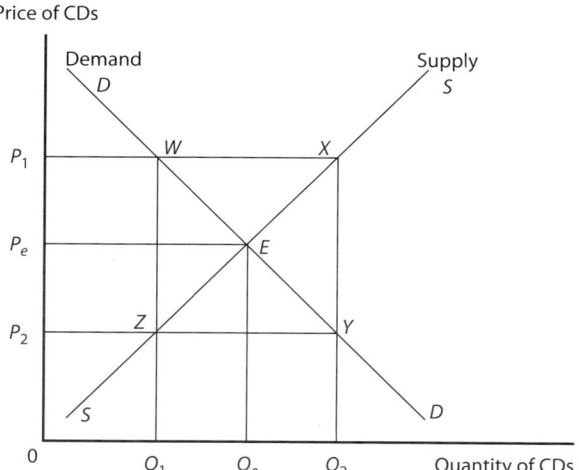

Fig. 11.1
Allocative efficiency and inefficiency

The demand curve shows the value consumers place on CDs. The supply curve shows how many CDs suppliers are willing to supply at certain prices. At the equilibrium price, the value that consumers place on CDs is equal to the cost of producing the CDs, i.e. the suppliers are getting back exactly what they have laid out in producing those CDs.

Allocative inefficiency occurs away from the equilibrium position. At point W, $Q_2 - Q_1$ resources have been wasted because suppliers have oversupplied the CDs and consumers do not want Q_2 but only Q_1 (W–X measures the excess supply). The resources being put into CDs could have been allocated more efficiently in some other market. The price mechanism gets resource allocation right!

At point Z, there is a shortfall in output. Suppliers are only supplying Q_1 CDs but consumers want Q_2 CDs (Y–Z measures the excess of demand over supply, the shortfall). Suppliers are not putting enough resources into CDs. The public want more resources allocated to CDs. Presumably, if the economy is on its production possibility frontier, those resources are going into other goods which the public do not want; there is allocative inefficiency.

Marginal cost

> **Definition of marginal cost**
> Marginal cost is the addition to total cost from producing one more unit.

The cost to the supplier of producing another unit (in this case, another CD) is known as the **marginal cost**. Only in perfect competition does the marginal cost curve equal the supply curve. **Therefore, allocative efficiency only occurs under perfect competition.** The implication is that there is allocative inefficiency in other markets.

Let's look at that another way. In imperfectly competitive markets, firms price above marginal cost ($P > MC$) because they want to make supernormal profit. P_1 is the value that consumers place on the good, so suppliers are not supplying enough of that good. In other words, suppliers are not allocating enough resources to that good. There is allocative inefficiency. We can see this on a simply demand curve graph.

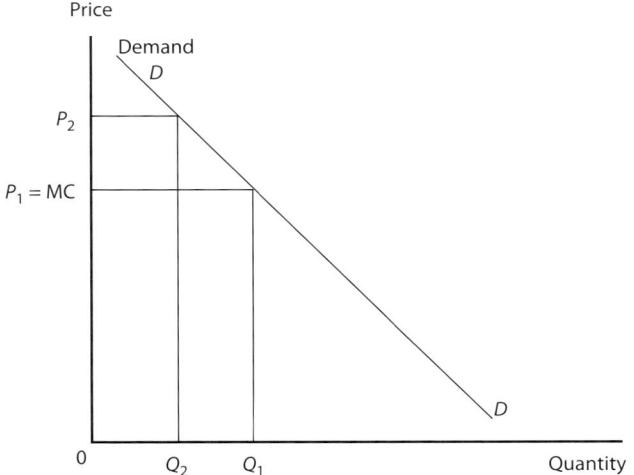

Fig. 11.2
Allocative inefficiency

In imperfect competition, such as monopolistic competition, firms will price at P_2, above the marginal cost price, P_1. They will not be supplying enough (shortfall $Q_1 - Q_2$). They will be holding back supply to keep the price high. They will not be putting enough resources into the good. There will be allocative inefficiency.

An exception in imperfect competition

In a state monopoly, e.g. a public transport system, the government may instruct the managers to set the price (the 'fare' in the case of transport) at the marginal cost as in perfect competition. This policy is called **'marginal cost pricing'**. The idea is that the state should not make a profit out of its own citizens. As a state monopoly is owned by the citizens, the citizens should not be making a profit out of themselves! Therefore, marginal cost pricing can lead to resources being allocated efficiently in a monopoly.

Market failure under monopoly

Many countries legislate against monopolies because they are seen to be against the public interest. Cable and Wireless (C&W) held a monopoly in the telecommunications market in many Caribbean territories. Recently, however, C&W has been surrendering its exclusive licences following the lead given by Jamaica. There are four companies operating in the Jamaica telecommunications market. Grenada, St Lucia, St Vincent, the Grenadines and St Kitts & Nevis have also liberalised the market and the Cayman Islands are planning to end C&W's monopoly. You may say that with the mobile phone market and the internet, it was inevitable that C&W had no case for continuing its monopoly, but there was also impending government anti-monopoly legislation against C&W, as in Barbados.

Why do countries legislate against monopolies such as C&W?

Monopolists charge higher prices than firms in perfect competition. The public suffer from these higher prices. When mobile phone companies entered Caribbean markets, C&W had to drop its prices by as much as 40% and they are still dropping. In Barbados, C&W said that if it had to lose its monopoly, and thereby monopoly profits, it would have to lay off workers.

1 Monopolists produce lower output than firms in perfect competition. This is a welfare loss on the part of the public which is deprived of the quantity of goods it demands.

2 Monopolists have no incentive to innovate, introduce new products and new production techniques. Again, this is against the public interest. A monopolist can make supernormal profits without introducing new products and production techniques.

3 Monopoly leads to a bigger gap between the rich and the poor. It encourages an uneven distribution of income. In a national monopoly there are a limited number of owners of shares in the monopoly so the fact that these shareholders are becoming richer may not have any significance for the rest of the population. Local monopolies, however, can make the gap between rich and poor more apparent and more socially divisive.

Examination Tip

> You need to remember that monopolies can be beneficial and that all of the four points above can be contradicted. For example, economies of scale can allow monopolists to charge lower prices and they may be able to undertake more research, development and innovation because they can use their supernormal profits to these ends.
>
> However, on balance, monopolies are generally taken to be against the public interest and are seen as the opposite of perfect competition.

EXERCISE Consider the relative advantages and disadvantages of monopoly. Focus on one in your own country if there is a suitable example. On the whole, would you say monopolies are generally good or bad for an economy?

Information failure

One of the necessary conditions for perfect competition is 'perfect knowledge of the market'. There is market failure when this condition is lacking. It is called 'information failure'.

Information failure occurs when:

1. The public does not know where the goods are available.
2. The public does not know when the goods are available.
3. The public does not know the price of the goods.
4. The public does not know the specifications of the goods or their quality.
5. The public is persuaded (or deceived) by advertising.

When the market fails to inform the public, goods can be unsold, leading to a wastage of resources. This is a big failure in the market.

Consumers may frequently pay higher prices than they need to because of information failure. This is common when consumers do not have the time and other resources to 'shop around'. In some markets the internet has helped to remove this problem by providing information which is easily accessible.

When the public is persuaded by advertising (**'persuasive advertising'** is one of the types of advertising), it may buy goods which it does not want. The 'before and after' advertising that persuades young men that they will win over a girl if they wear a certain aftershave lotion is usually giving false information and leads to the purchase of goods not really wanted (and which cause great disappointment!)

EXERCISE Look at some of the current advertising campaigns. Do you think that advertising is a good or bad feature of economies today?

For many years the public was unaware of the dangers of smoking. This information failure was probably the most serious there has ever been because it has led to countless deaths from lung cancer. Tobacco advertising has now been banned in many countries. In other cases it is allowed but tobacco products must carry the warning 'Smoking Kills'.

Packaged food products are now required to list the ingredients in great detail because in the past the failure to provide such information has led to poor diets, ill health and obesity. Even when the information is provided, it may be in such a form that the public does not understand it.

In this technological age, the public may be more and more confused by the mass of data which is provided by the suppliers. In this case, the information is being given but the public cannot understand it. The failure here is the lack of explanation about the technical terms and performance.

Information failure in the labour market

There are very common cases of information failure as indicated in the examples below:

1 Unemployment can exist when jobs are available. This can be because of information failure. The unemployed do not know where the jobs are available because the jobs are not advertised sufficiently.

2 Many workers remain in low-paid jobs when higher paid jobs, which they are capable of performing, are available. The workers are either misinformed about wage rates or about the qualifications necessary for the jobs.

3 Even within the same firm, a vacancy can be available in another department or in a higher tier job but workers do not know about it because of information failure. The job has not been well advertised.

Education is an example of a merit good.

These cases of information failure have very serious results. Of course, the most significant is unemployment. However, there is the consequent failure of not having the best workers in the jobs and the inefficiency that results.

Positive externalities

Goods which bring positive externalities are called **'merit goods'**.

A positive externality is also known as an 'external benefit'.

Sometimes actions in the market affect only the consumer and supplier. However, market actions can also effect others. When they do, an externality arises.

Definition of positive externalities

A positive externality exists when there is both private and public benefit, such as with a merit good. An external benefit occurs when a member of society (the third party) gains utility or satisfaction from the actions of others.

External benefits are obviously desirable. For example, education brings a private benefit in that it increases the earning power (as well as other benefits) of the person being educated, but it also benefits society by increasing productivity (as well as other benefits).

There is market failure in that the market undersupplies positive externalities. This can be shown on a graph.

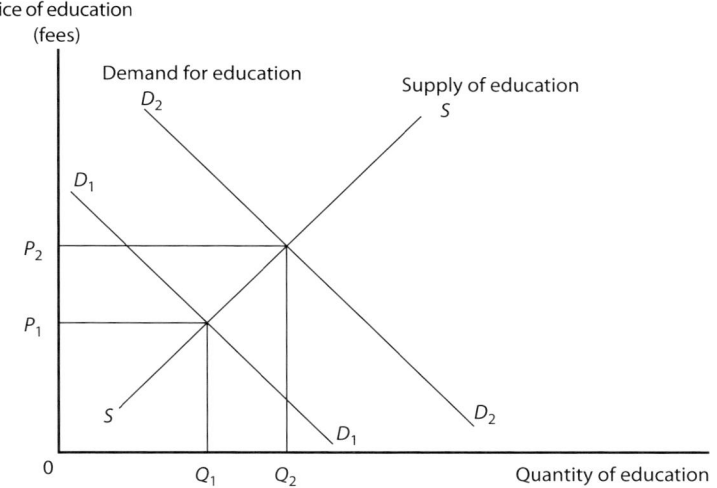

Fig. 11.3
The market undersupplying education

The demand curve shows the value that an individual places on education. The supply curve shows the quantity of education that suppliers would supply at any price.

$D_1 D_1$ is the individual's demand curve for education considering only the private benefit. $D_2 D_2$ is society's demand curve for education considering both private and public benefits (external benefits). The market **undersupplies** education by $Q_2 - Q_1$. There is market failure in the case of positive externalities. This diagram can be applied to any positive externality, e.g. an inoculation. The conclusion is that merit goods are undersupplied by the market.

Negative externalities

Goods which bring negative externalities are called **'demerit goods'**.

A negative externality is known as an external cost or a social cost.

> **Definition of negative externalities**
>
> A negative externality exists when there is private benefit but social cost, as with a demerit good. Social cost occurs when a third party in society suffers from the actions of others.

Social costs are obviously undesirable but without government intervention, social costs (negative externalities) arise. A negative externality which we have already considered is the damage to the sea water and the reefs which cruise liners cause.

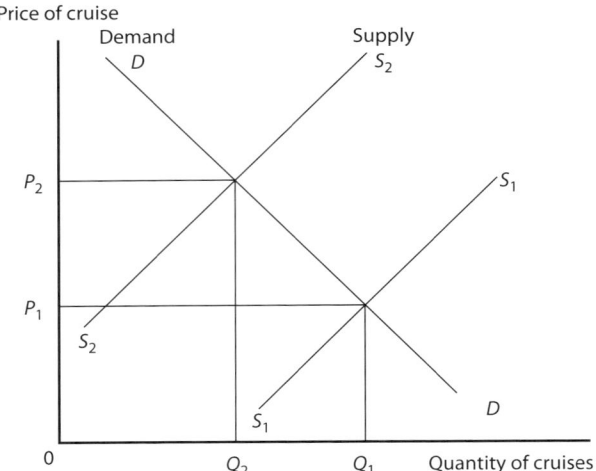

Fig. 11.4
The market oversupplying cruises

DD is the demand curve for cruises. S_1S_1 is the market supply for cruises at P_1. If the cruise lines had to pay their for social costs (the negative externalities which they cause), the supply curve would shift to S_2S_2. (Remember that under the 'Determinants of Supply', we saw that an increase in the costs of production shifts the supply curve upwards to the left.) This would raise the price of cruises to P_2 and cut back the quantity to Q_2. Cruises have been oversupplied by $Q_1 - Q_2$. There has been market failure.

Another way of looking at it is that cruise line passengers are getting their cruises too cheaply. If they had to pay for the damage to the sea and reefs, they would have to pay much more for their pleasure. That is why some Caribbean governments wanted passengers to pay a tax of US$20 per cruise.

Cigarette smoking causes a negative externality but does the market fail in allowing smoking to continue? Smokers are taxed a lot for their pleasure so do they not pay for their social costs? Governments are still unsure what the external costs of smoking are. They can assess the costs to the health services, and the loss of production, but have they yet assessed the costs of passive smoking? In the cases of smoking, does the polluter pay the price? Probably not in most countries.

EXERCISE

Do you think that governments should ban smoking?

The conclusion is that demerit goods are oversupplied by the market.

Public goods

The market fails to supply public goods.

> **Definition of public goods**
>
> A public good is one the consumption of which by one individual does not reduce its supply to others.

Elbow Reef Lighthouse, Hope Town harbour, Bahamas. A lighthouse is an example of a public good.

Source: Stillpictures.

Examples of public goods:

1. Street lighting.
2. A lighthouse.
3. Radio waves.
4. Defence.
5. Flood barriers.

Public parks and pavements are more controversial so keep clear of them (not literally!). Enjoy them, but do not list them under 'public goods'. The police force is also debatable. You can pay for policing at sporting and social events in some countries. The police are allowed to charge for their services in such cases.

EXERCISE

Why is it sometimes quite difficult to be certain what is a public good in particular countries?

The characteristics of public goods:

Public goods have three characteristics.

1. *Non-excludability*. It is impossible to stop one consumer consuming the good once it has been provided for others. Street lighting is available to all and nobody can be prevented from using it. Radio waves provide another excellent example of non-excludability.

   Consider a pavement again. There is limited space on a pavement and the consumption of it by one individual does reduce its supply to others. One person excludes another sometimes. Those who would include pavements on the list of public goods would say that the supplier cannot exclude anyone from using the pavement.

2. *Non-rivalry.* When one person consumes a public good, they are not competing with another person for it. There is enough for everybody. Consider a lighthouse. When one ship is using the light to keep off the rocks, it is not competing with other ships who are using the same light. Again, radio waves provide another excellent example of non-rivalry.

Consider a public park. Two people may want to sunbathe in the same spot in a public park. There is rivalry.

3. The 'free rider' problem. If one person pays for a public good, another person can use it without paying. That second person is called a 'free rider'. This is the case for flood barriers. One householder may pay for a flood barrier but he or she cannot stop others benefiting without paying.

Consider that public goods are provided by the government out of taxes. Some people do not pay taxes yet they consume public goods. They are free riders in a broad sense.

The market fails to provide public goods but the government considers that they confer so much social benefit that it provides them free of charge. However, a public good must not be defined as a good provided by the government.

The main consequences of market failure

The wastage of resources/unemployment

In economic theory, resources are allocated efficiently in perfect competition but in other forms of competition, such as monopolistic competition, monopoly and oligopoly, they are allocated inefficiently. The market fails when there is not perfect competition. This is an over-simplification. In perfect competition, there can still be wasted resources. Unemployment, not just of labour, but also of other resources can and does occur under the market system.

Sir John Compton, leader of the opposition United Workers Party, is carried by supporters during celebrations after winning the parliamentary elections on 12 December 2006 in Castries, St Lucia. He promised to reduce crime and unemployment. Unemployment is an example of market failure.

Source: AP/EMPICS.

Demand deficient unemployment

In the market system, if consumers demand a good, resources will be put into the supply of that good and it will be produced in sufficient quantities to meet the demand. However, what if the good is not demanded? Resources will not be put into that good and, unless they can be put into an alternative good, the resources will be idle. For example, if there is a demand for cars, resources will be put into cars. Steel will be demanded and there will be employment for car workers. However, if there is a lack of demand for cars, what will happen to the steel industry and what will happen to the jobs for the car workers? These resources will try to find alternative employment but what if there is no alternative employment? The steel will lie idle and the car workers will be unemployed.

Cars are expensive and require high incomes in the economy. What if incomes are low? There will be no, or very little, demand for cars. The demand for cars is income elastic. In free market economies, some will become rich while others can remain poor. Certain goods are demanded when incomes are high and certain other goods are demanded when incomes are low but overall, when incomes are low, there will be a deficiency of demand for income elastic goods. Such unemployment is called **'demand deficient unemployment'**.

Therefore, there can be wasted resources even when the market system is working and countries can be inside their Production Possibility Frontiers. The market can fail to produce full employment and in an earlier chapter we saw that unemployment is what drew Karl Marx towards communism and the command economy. Under the command economy there is no unemployment of labour.

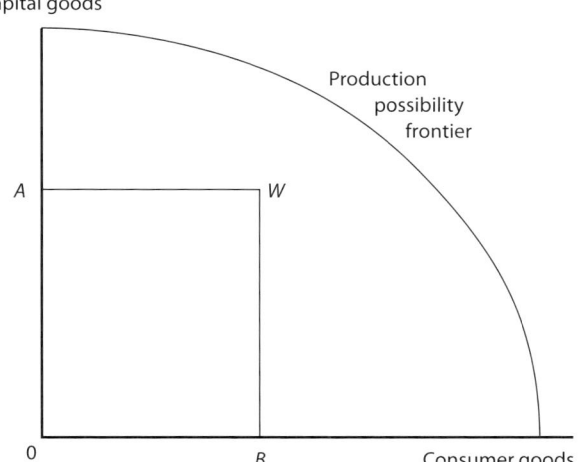

Fig. 11.5
Unemployed resources

The country is at point *W*, well inside its production possibility frontier, because of insufficient demand. This can happen when the market system fails due to the deficiency of demand.

Structural unemployment

Structural unemployment is similar to demand deficient unemployment but it occurs when demand falls drastically in one particular industry in the economy and

Sugar plantation.
Source: Stillpictures.

employment cannot respond to the changes. In the Caribbean demand for sugar has fallen because of the subsidies paid to European beet sugar producers under the Common Agricultural Policy of the European Union. This has caused structural unemployment in the sugar industry in the Caribbean. The market fails to respond to the change. Sugar workers cannot find alternative employment quickly and remain unemployed, sometimes for a long time.

Technological unemployment

This is a special case of structural unemployment. As firms seek to profit-maximise, they are always looking for the least-cost method of production and this leads to the introduction of new technology. Most of this new technology is labour-saving and thus profit maximising leads to unemployment. This has been most apparent in computerisation. There has been widespread unemployment created in the service industries such as banking. There is the argument that computerisation has created employment in its own related industries but it has probably caused more unemployment in the whole economy.

Frictional unemployment

Frictional unemployment occurs when workers are between jobs. They have left one job and are looking for another. Therefore, it is not really to be classed as market failure because it is often a healthy sign when workers are trying to find better jobs or are retraining to qualify for better jobs. In a boom, there will be a high demand for labour, higher wages will be offered and there may well be a high level of frictional unemployment.

When workers stay unemployed between jobs, and do not take available jobs, they are classified as being in *'Search unemployment'* which is a type of frictional unemployment.

Unskilled, low-paid labour usually take the first job on offer and do not stay frictionally unemployed for long. However, in a slump, there may not be the jobs available and then this category of labour will experience long frictional unemployment.

Highly qualified, well paid labour may stay frictionally unemployed for a long time. Such people are waiting for the 'right' job to be offered. They often have savings that allow them to stay unemployed without hardship.

Carnival celebrations in Trinidad.

Seasonal unemployment

This is very common in the Caribbean. Many jobs are seasonal and when the season is over the workers become unemployed. In the Caribbean, the tourists tend to come throughout the year and so employment in tourist-related industries is fairly steady. However, if hurricanes occur more and more frequently, demand will dip for employment in these industries during the hurricane season.

'Crop Over' is a festival in Barbados that lasts approximately five weeks starting in July. It is a period of high demand and high employment in costume making, music and retailing as well as in street markets. After 'Crop Over', there is an immediate decline in jobs and therefore 'seasonal unemployment' goes up.

The end of the Carnival period in Trinidad and Tobago also brings seasonal unemployment. It has become such a big festival that it attracts high demand for jobs from October of the year before when Carnival preparation starts. However, after the Carnival is over, there is seasonal unemployment, e.g. for Calypsonians.

Real wage, or classical, unemployment

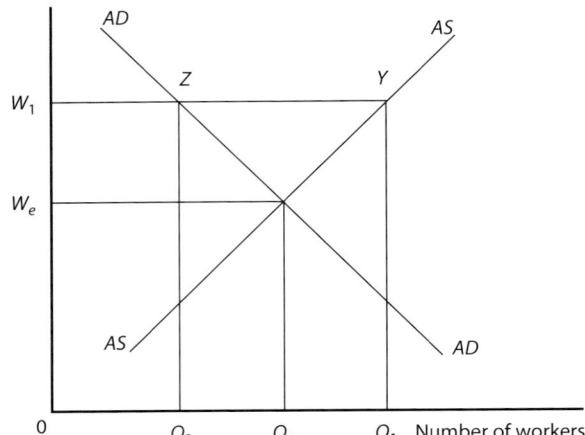

Fig. 11.6 *Real wage unemployment*

Real wage unemployment occurs mainly in two cases: (a) where trade unions have driven up wages above the equilibrium level or (b) where governments have introduced minimum wage legislation and set the level too high.

The labour market was in equilibrium at W_e and Q_e. When the wage is pushed up to W_1, workers would like to offer Q_1 labour (more people would join the labour force as seen by point Y on the aggregate supply of labour). However, employers would be willing to employ only Q_2 workers at this wage, W_1, shown by point Z on the aggregate demand for labour. Disequilibrium unemployment is $Q_1 - Q_2$ (Y – Z). However, Q_1 were not employed before the wage was pushed up so only $Q_e - Q_2$ will actually lose their jobs.

International unemployment

This is a relatively new term to explain the unemployment of local workers due to changes in international demand. The Caribbean, and the Eastern Caribbean in particular, is suffering from this type of unemployment in the banana industry. The European Union has outlawed the preference by the UK in favour of Caribbean banana suppliers. Demand has fallen drastically for Caribbean bananas and there is large scale unemployment.

EXERCISE Find out how many people are unemployed in your country. Try and discover the reasons for the different types of unemployment there.

The gap between rich and poor

In the free market economy, everyone pursues their own self-interest. When there is private ownership of land and other factors of production, some people are wealth holders and others are not. There is a gap between rich and poor at the heart of the system. In Cayman, the owners of the factors of production are very few, perhaps only four or five families. The gap between rich and poor is pronounced. Cayman is a free market economy. Contrast this with Cuba where the state owns all of the factors of production (except labour). There are no rich people but there are no poor people either. Cuba is a command economy.

In business transactions, the sellers make money from the buyers. This is another way by which the rich become richer and the poor become poorer. The gap between rich and poor is very pronounced in the United States, a free market economy. On the other hand, in the Scandinavian economies there are 'no Rolls Royces, but no Minis either', meaning that there are no very wealthy people and no poor people. In these economies, the governments redistribute wealth from the rich to the poor by very high progressive taxation. Scandinavian governments have decided to put right the inequalities of income which result from the free market system.

The **'distribution of income'** is shown by the Lorenz curve below.

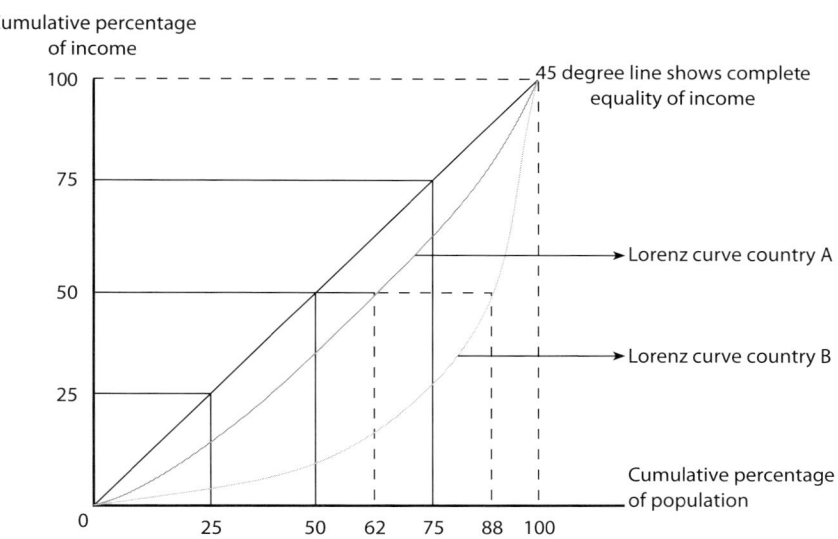

Fig. 11.7
The Lorenz curve

On the 45 degree line 25% of the population hold 25% of income
                      50% 50%
                      75% 75%

There is a perfectly even distribution of income.

On the Lorenz curve for country A, 62% of the population hold 50% of the income. Looking at this inversely, 38% of the population hold 50% of the income. Income is unevenly distributed but not as much as in country B.

In country B, 88% of the population hold 50% of the income or, inversely, 12% of the population hold 50% of the income. Income is very unevenly distributed. This is likely to be the case in free market economies where the pursuit of wealth is built into the system. There is a gap between rich and poor which the system will make steadily worse without government intervention.

EXERCISE Do you think that governments should intervene to try and reduce the inequality of income distribution in an economy?

Poverty

There is relative and absolute poverty.

> **Definitions of relative and absolute poverty**
>
> Relative poverty occurs when one person is poor in comparison with another.
>
> Absolute poverty occurs when a person cannot afford the basic necessities of life.

The free market fails to prevent poverty. Relative poverty is built into the system as there will always be 'haves' and 'have-nots' in the free market system as private ownership of the factors of production is the rule.

However, the free market system fails when absolute poverty occurs. If there can be unemployment in a free market economy, and there is no government assistance for the unemployed (no social security or welfare state), there can be absolute poverty. This could be said to be the biggest condemnation of the market system. Countries set a **'poverty line'** below which is absolute poverty. Where that line is set varies from country to country according to the prices of the basic necessities of food, shelter and clothing. So the level of the poverty line depends on the level of national income.

The United Nations Development Programme (UNDP) sets the poverty line at US $1 per day. People below that line are living in extreme poverty, reflecting a lack of income and basic services. It is estimated that 45% of the population of Jamaica fell below the poverty line in 1991 and 16% were still below it in 1997. The Government of Jamaica regarded this as unacceptable and started a National Poverty Eradication Programme which the UNDP is collaborating with. Market failure such as this is not being met by handouts but by creating market-based schemes like the creation of small and medium sized entrepreneurs in manufacturing and the service industry, particularly tourism – market solutions for market failure.

Slums. Haiti. Poverty is an example of market failure.

Source: Stillpictures.

Economic recession

Aggregate demand, *AD*, is the total of all demand in the economy. It is made up of four components: consumption expenditure by households (*C*), investment (*I*), government expenditure (*G*) and net exports (*X* – *M*).

Formula:
$AD = C + I + G + X - M$

Before we analyse this further, we can simply state that if *AD* falls, the economy can go into recession. If any one of the components of *AD* falls, the economy can go into recession. For example, many Caribbean countries are heavily dependent on tourism (exports because it is the selling of services to foreigners). If tourist demand for the region or a country falls, there will be economic recession, other things being equal. Tourist expenditure falls so local governments receive less in airport taxes and duties; the incomes of citizens fall without tourist expenditure and there is unemployment in the tourist industry; the fall in local incomes leads to a fall in consumption expenditure, *C*; the fall in consumption leads to a fall in the incomes of suppliers and so on. This is called the **'multiplier effect'**. The fall in tourist demand has led to a fall in aggregate demand, not just by the initial fall in tourist expenditure, but by a multiplied amount as it works through the whole economy. The market system is operating and it can lead to economic recession.

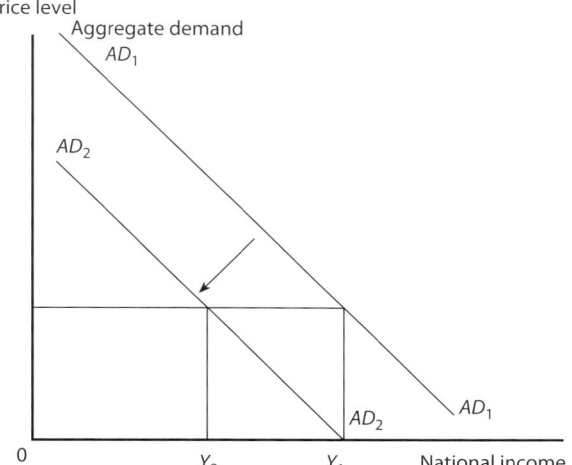

Fig. 11.8
The aggregate demand curve

The aggregate demand curve slopes downwards from left to right. At higher prices, individuals, firms, foreigners and the government are likely to demand less goods. The whole curve will shift inwards to the origin if all, or one of the components of *AD*, decrease. The inward shift will reduce the level of national income from Y_1 to Y_2, indicating an economic recession. Thus a fall in tourist demand (a fall in exports) will lead to a fall in the level of national income and possibly to economic recession.

A free market economy is subject to a series of booms and slumps as we have seen before. Governments have tried to 'fine tune' their economies to stop these booms and slumps occurring but it is now accepted that fine tuning is too difficult and often fails in any case. The business cycle is inevitable.

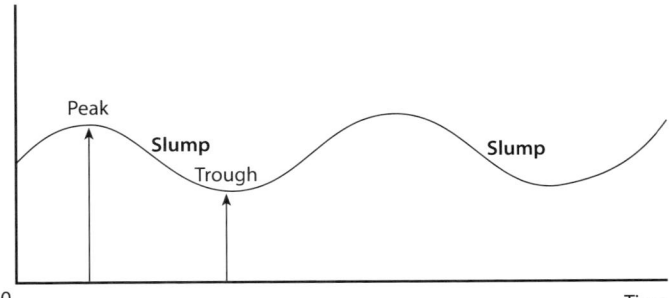

Fig. 11.9
The business cycle

'Economic depression' is rather a strong term to apply to the slumps and troughs of the business cycle but the economy is depressed in a slump. There is a fall in the components of aggregate demand, e.g. businesses are not investing as investment opportunities seem to be lacking. Incomes are falling as firms are not investing. Consumption expenditure is falling because incomes are falling. All of these are characteristics of a slump. However, the graph of the business cycle shows the economy pulling out of the trough. This would not be the case in a fully fledged economic depression. Free market economies can be subject to depressions and so they can be considered the most serious market failure.

Conclusion: The decline in the welfare of society

If we summarise all the aspects of market failure which we have just gone through, we conclude that market failure can lead to a general decline in the welfare of society. Welfare here implies prosperity, good living conditions, employment, availability of goods and services including health services and education and the absence of calamity. However, the market system can give rise to:

- Welfare loss from the misallocation of resources.
- High prices under imperfect competition, especially monopoly.
- Information failure leading to welfare loss in goods and services.
- Information failure leading to unemployment.
- Lack of merit goods, e.g. education and health.
- Consumption of demerit goods.
- Lack of public goods.
- Unemployment.
- A gap between rich and poor.
- Poverty.
- Economic depression.

Examination questions

1 What is meant by allocative efficiency? *(5 marks)*

2 **a** Outline the main features of monopoly. *(4 marks)*
   b Explain the possible advantages and disadvantages of a monopoly. *(6 marks)*

3 Distinguish, with the use of examples, between positive and negative externalities. *(10 marks)*

4 Outline the main features of a public good, a merit good and a demerit good. *(10 marks)*

5 Distinguish between the different types of unemployment that can occur in an economy. *(10 marks)*

6 Distinguish between absolute and relative poverty. *(5 marks)*

7 Explain what is meant by a business cycle. *(5 marks)*

8 Discuss the economic consequences of unemployment. *(10 marks)*

9 Why might a government wish to create jobs? *(10 marks)*

10 What is meant by a 'multiplier effect' in an economy? *(10 marks)*

Part four

The financial sector

CHAPTER 12

Money

In this chapter you will be making a fairly detailed study of money and the part it plays in the economy.

- You will learn about the origins of money and its displacement of barter
- You will learn the functions of money
- You will learn the characteristics of money
- You will be introduced to inflation, a very important topic in Economics

Money

Before money existed, there was **barter** which is the exchange of goods for goods (or goods for services, services for goods or services for services). Barter allowed trade to take place but it was very limited, chiefly being confined to local markets. Barter requires a 'double coincidence of wants', i.e. you must want what I have and I must want what you have. One person may have a chicken and the other a bag of flour. Perhaps these wants will coincide but often they will not and trade cannot take place. Another hindrance to trade through barter is 'divisibility' or, more precisely, 'indivisibility'. Some goods are not divisible, e.g. a cow, and therefore cannot be exchanged for something of less value like a goatskin of wine. Therefore, barter broke down all too frequently and trade could not take place.

EXERCISE Consider the various problems and disadvantages of barter. Imagine what would happen if all money disappeared and we went back to a situation of barter.

> **Definition of barter**
>
> Barter is the direct exchange of goods or services for other goods and services without the use of money.

People sought something which everyone wanted – a precious metal. The first money was therefore precious metal, such as gold or silver. Precious metal had 'intrinsic value', i.e. value within itself because it was used for ornaments, jewellery, goblets and plates, etc. Gold and silver were also rare so they had 'scarcity value'. Soon coins of specific weights were minted and they were trusted because the prince put his head on one side as if guaranteeing the value of the coin – the 'face' value. Soon confidence in money became widespread, trade increased and markets became more extensive. Therefore, money is at the heart of the development of economies.

The functions of money

1 Money is a medium of exchange.
2 Money is a measure of value.
3 Money is a store of value.
4 Money is a standard of deferred payment.

Let us now examine how well money performs these functions. It performs the first one very well. There is no better medium of exchange. Money is acceptable by everyone; indeed, it must be accepted when it is legal tender. Money is divisible into low values so that it can be used in small transactions like buying a newspaper.

> **Definition of legal tender**
> Legal tender is money which must be accepted by law in a transaction or in the settlement of a debt.

There is less certainty about money's performance in the second function as a measure of value. It is something that everyone knows and it is acceptable in the short term. Comparisons can be made by using money values, e.g. a lobster tail is EC $15 and a chicken is EC $10; the lobster tail is worth more than the chicken. However, 'you do not use a piece of elastic to measure a length'! The value of money can be affected by inflation.

Inflation

> **Definition of inflation**
> Inflation can be defined as the persistent tendency for the general level of prices to rise over a period of time.

When prices rise, money falls in value. It takes more money to buy the same amount of goods and services as before so money in comparison with goods and services has fallen in value. So money can be used as a measure of value in the short term, when its own value has not had time to change, but in the long term, with inflation, its value is likely to have changed. Something that costs J$10,000 in 2007 will not be worth, **in real terms**, as much as something worth J$10,000 in 1997. The Jamaican dollar has fallen considerably in value in the past ten years. The rate of inflation in Jamaica in 1994 was 33.2% which is very high. It fell to 6.3% in 1999 and has been kept carefully under control since then except for the period between September 2004 and September 2005 when it rose to 19%.

> **Definition of the real value of money**
> Real terms are money values when inflation has been taken into account.

For example, assuming the rate of inflation to have been 10% per year, a painting which cost $10,000 in 1995 would have fallen in value:

1996	$9,091	the formula being used is:
1997	$8,264	$n \times \dfrac{100}{110}$ where n is the dollar figure.
1998	$7,513	
1999	$6,830	

The painting has fallen in value in real terms.

Examination Tip

Remember to make sure that you show the examiner that you are aware of the distinction between money in real and in nominal terms. When it is in real terms, it means that the effect of inflation has been taken into account.

EXERCISE Consider why inflation is considered to be such a bad situation for many people.

As for the third function, money as a store of value, it performs this function very badly. A rational person does not store something which is falling in value. It is better to turn money into some other asset, such as a stamp collection, which is likely to go up in value in money terms, and probably in real terms, over the years. Money can be used as a store of value if it earns interest in a bank account but the rate of interest must exceed the rate of inflation for the value of the deposit to be maintained or even increase. Gold is a better store of value but the International Monetary Fund (IMF) discourages the reliance on gold. Of course, a person is foolish if he stores value in something that is perishable like rubber!

The fourth function is money as a standard of deferred payment. This means that money can be used to settle a debt at a future date. It performs this function well because, even if there is inflation, the fall in the value of money can be covered by a rate of interest. If the rate of inflation was 5% per year and the debt was to be paid at the end of the year, the creditor could negotiate a rate of interest of 5%, or more, to make sure he or she would not lose on the transaction.

Definitions of debtors and creditors

A debtor is a person who owes money.

A creditor is a person who has made a loan and to whom a debt is due.

Today much business is conducted on credit and while this would be possible under barter, whereby one person would promise to hand over goods in the future settlement of the debt, it is so much easier with money acting as the standard of the debt. If the creditor wanted certain goods in the future, he could use the money given to him by the debtor to buy those goods.

In conclusion we must realise that the rate of inflation must be very high before money can fail to perform the four functions above. People have confidence in money, especially when the monetary authorities keep inflation under control, and we expect them to!

The characteristics of money

Acceptability

Money must have 'acceptability'. It cannot perform its functions unless a party in a transaction knows that he or she can take money from one person and use it for another transaction with another person. Legal tender reinforces acceptability.

Divisibility

Money must have 'divisibility'. Money must be able to be broken down into small values so that it can be used for small transactions or transactions that are not round figures. Therefore money is divided into denominations.

> **Definition of denominations**
>
> Denominations are the given values of money that a country adopts. For example, the Eastern Caribbean dollar is divisible into the following denominations:
>
> Banknotes – $5, $10, $20, $50 and $100.
>
> Coins – 1 cent, 2 cents, 5 cents, 10 cents, 25 cents and $1.

Portability

Money must have 'portability', i.e. it must be easy to carry around. Gold is portable but it is very heavy. Notes and coins are very portable. A transaction of relatively high value, say EC $10,000, could be settled by carrying 100 × $100 notes in the pocket.

Paper money.

Durability

Money must have 'durability'. Money does not deteriorate. This must be examined critically. Notes are not durable, especially small denomination notes. Small denomination notes go from hand to hand quickly ('circulation of money') and become dirty or torn. Some people do not keep notes carefully but stuff them into all parts of their clothing. Small denomination notes have to be recalled and reissued. Coins are durable, but it is surprising how often coins are lost and the coinage has to be reissued regularly.

Non-forgeability

Money must have 'non-forgeability', i.e. it cannot be forged or counterfeited. If money could be made by a forger, money would no longer be scarce: it would lose its value and its acceptability. 'Gresham's Law', from the sixteenth century, states that 'bad money chases out good'. Obviously if you have a coin which you suspect is forged you will spend it first and keep hold of your good coins. Banknotes are 'security' printed, i.e. they are printed very carefully with intricate designs, very special inks and watermarks. It is very difficult to forge banknotes but sometimes they are passed in dark corners and in the middle of bundles of notes. Coins are minted at secure mints. Coins are less likely to be forged because (a) they are of less value than notes and (b) the metal that goes into making them has value.

Note that a coin has an 'intrinsic' value, which is the value of the metal it is made of, and it also has 'face' value, which is the value stamped on it. The intrinsic value must be less than the face value. If not, it would be profitable to melt down the coin and sell the metal.

Scarcity

Money must have scarcity. The amount of notes and coins in circulation is kept closely under control by the monetary authorities to maintain the scarcity value.

Liquidity

> **Definition of liquidity**
> Liquidity is the ease by which an asset can be turned into cash without loss.

Money, of course, is the most liquid of all assets. We can go further and say that money is **the only perfectly liquid asset**. There is no point in changing one dollar for another dollar. It will not make your assets more liquid!

Near money

> **Definition of near money**
> Near money refers to highly liquid assets other than money.

Postal orders and postage stamps are near money. They have face value. Postal orders can be accepted in payment of a debt at their face value but they do not have to be. They are not legal tender. Postal orders are held because they are felt to be safer than cash in that they can be made out in someone's name and have to be written on for encashment (not always). However, the speed with which they can be redeemed ('redeem' = 'buy back') for cash makes them illiquid, e.g. a post office has to be open.

Postage stamps are not cash. They can be exchanged at their face value in some outlets but many post offices will not redeem postage stamps which they have already sold or, if they do, they will redeem them at a discounted value.

Money substitutes

These are usually ranked in order of liquidity.

Plastic

Bank deposits are not liquid but they can be turned into cash very quickly and easily so they are fairly liquid. It used to be the case that they could be turned into cash when banks were open, often only five days a week during banking hours, not usually an 8-hour day. However, ATMs (Automated Teller Machines) are accessible at all times of the day or night for withdrawals of cash up to a specified amount so they have made bank deposits much more liquid than they used to be. A bank card, a debit card or a credit card is needed. Bank cards are made of plastic so 'plastic' is a money substitute.

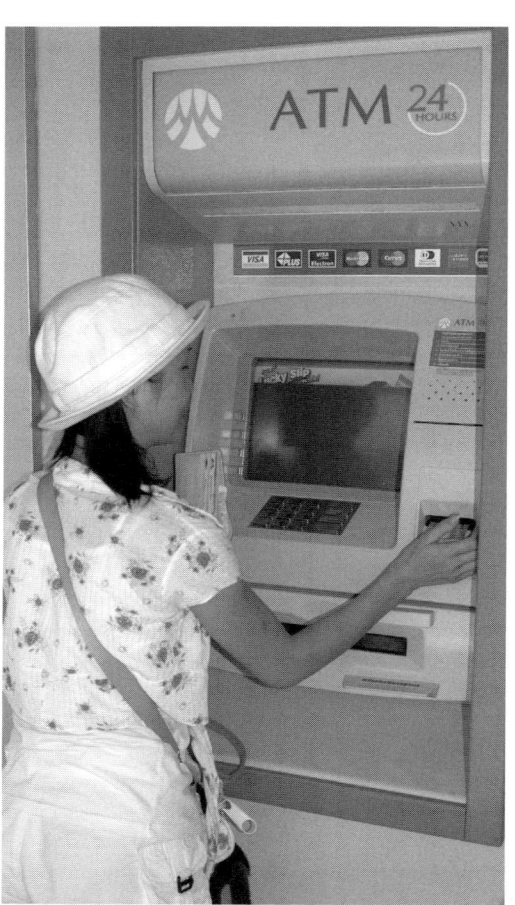

Plastic gives access to money.

In other transactions, such as paying for goods and services, plastic can be used but it can also be refused. The payer's account will be debited very quickly (within 24 or 48 hours) but the payee may insist on cash. Plastic is not legal tender.

The difference between a debit card and a credit card is that a debit card is issued by the holder's own bank and when presented in payment, the holder's account will be debited.

A credit card is issued by a credit card company. When presented in payment by a holder, the credit card company settles the debt immediately and the holder's account **with the credit card company** is debited for that amount. The holder has to settle this debt at some time in the future, usually within 56 or 59 days, either in full or in part. The holder is being given 'credit' by the credit card company.

Examination Tip: Debit cards and credit cards can easily be confused; make sure that you understand the key difference between them

Cheques

A cheque is a piece of paper instructing a bank to pay someone (the 'payee') by the person who writes the cheque (the 'payer' or 'drawer'). If the account holder wants to

Cheques are not legal tender.

draw cash, he or she makes the cheque out to 'Cash' or to himself or herself. Debit cards have made this a rare practice. When the payee presents the cheque, he or she will be paid and the drawer's account will be debited. Cheques are fairly liquid. They are redeemed at their face value. They are not legal tender. A person can refuse to accept a cheque in payment of a transaction.

Deposit accounts

Deposit accounts in banks and building societies are much less liquid. They are money but before they can be made liquid, they have to be transferred to another account and that can take time, according to the length of the 'time' deposit. The minimum time can be only 48 hours but is usually seven days and there is no real upper limit for the maximum. Money may be held in a time deposit of three or five years.

EXERCISE Draw a line across a page and call it the 'liquidity spectrum'. Make the left end the most liquid and the right end the least liquid. Place all of the items mentioned on the line, placing them in terms of their liquidity.

The money supply

The money supply (M) is a measure of the total amount of money in the economy. However, the total depends on how the money supply is defined, 'narrow' or 'broad'.

> ### Definitions of narrow and broad money
>
> Narrow money concentrates on the first function of money, i.e. money as a medium of exchange. It consists of notes and coins in circulation and in the tills of banks and also the operational balances that commercial banks hold with the central bank.
>
> Broad money brings in another function of money as a store of value. It consists of notes and coins in circulation, plus sight deposits at banks, plus operational balances that commercial banks hold with the central bank plus time deposits at banks.

The control of the money supply is extremely important and in Caribbean economies it is in the hands of the central banks, e.g. the Bank of Jamaica or the Central Bank of Barbados. An increase in the money supply, without a corresponding increase in goods and services, can lead to inflation. A decrease in the money supply can lead to deflation and recession.

Appendix to Chapter 12: The measurement of inflation

It is important for every country to know what is happening to prices. In the Caribbean, the statistics on prices are usually monitored by the central banks but they can be kept by a bureau of statistics. In Jamaica, this body is called the Statistical Institute of Jamaica and another body which uses the data is the Planning Institute of Jamaica. This body is most interested in prices when it investigates where the poverty line is to be set (recently set at J$137,000 per year for a family of five) and then how many families are below this poverty line. However, all groups in the economy are interested in what is happening to prices: the business world, the government, the trade unions (in negotiating for wage increases) and, of course, the consumers.

Barbados National Bank.

The rate of inflation is measured by the **Consumer Price Index (CPI)**. This is a measure of prices in the **'basket'** of shopping that a family of five faces each week. In Jamaica, the basket consists of the following categories of expenditure:

Food and drink.
Fuels and other household supplies.
Housing.
Household furnishings and other furniture.
Healthcare and personal expenses.
Personal clothing and accessories.
Transportation.
Miscellaneous expenses.

The CPI must be updated to reflect changes in consumer tastes, e.g. in 'food and drink', very few consumers use tea in the form of tea leaves any longer; they use tea bags. Tea leaves must be removed from the index and be replaced by tea bags. In 'miscellaneous expenses', many Caribbean indices do not yet include CDs and DVDs.

Some categories are more important than others. If more than 50% of the weekly expenditure goes on food and drink, what happens to food and drink prices is more important to the family than what happens to household furnishings and furniture prices.

Therefore, in calculating the rate of inflation, the relative importance of the categories in the basket is reflected by a system of **weights ('weighting')**. The Planning Institute of Jamaica weights food and drink at 56 points, the most important category.

> **Definition of weighting**
> Weighting is the awarding of points to each item in the basket to reflect its relative importance in the basket of household expenditure.

In Jamaica 100 points are distributed throughout the categories. Some countries have a base of 1,000 points.

Within each category there are many items. Let us take 'food and drink'. It can be sub-divided into four items: cereals, vegetables and tubers, fish and meat, dairy.

How the rate of inflation is calculated from a price index

(The example below is a simple model and is in no way representative of true prices and weights. The imaginary prices are in dollars.)

Table 12.1 How a consumer price index is calculated

Example of a consumer price index

Basket	Prices year 1	Base 100	Prices year 2	Index	No. of units n	Total spent $n \times p$	Weights $\frac{n \times p}{2{,}500}$	Weighted index weights × index
fish and meat	400		560	140	1	560	22	12,320
dairy	300		390	130	2	780	31	12,090
cereals	200		240	120	3	720	29	6,960
vegetables and tubers	100		110	110	4	440	18	1,980
totals	1,000			500		2,500	100	$\frac{33{,}350}{100}$
rate of inflation				500/4 25%				33.3%

Notes:
1 An Index is the base year, 100 points + the rate of inflation.
2 The total expenditure by the household is the number of units bought × the price at which they were bought (year 2 prices).
3 The weights are calculated by the proportion of total expenditure on each item to the total expenditure by the household, $\frac{N \times P}{\text{Total spent}}$.
4 The rate of inflation from the weighted price index is found by the formula: $\frac{\Sigma W \text{ index}}{\Sigma \text{ weights}}$.

Where the Greek letter sigma, Σ = 'sum of', and W = weights.

The cost of living for this household at first appears to have gone up by 25% but that does not reflect the relative importance of the items in the basket. This household has spent $1,340 on items which have gone up by an average of 35% but only $1,160 on items which have gone up by an average of 15%. The items must be weighted to give their true impact on the cost of living. Therefore the true cost of living for this family has gone up by 33.3%.

> **Definition of rate of inflation**
> The rate of inflation is the percentage increase in prices in an economy over a period of one year.

EXERCISE Try and find out the current rate of inflation in your country.

Examination questions

1 a What is meant by barter? *(3 marks)*
   b Explain the main disadvantages of barter. *(7 marks)*

2 a Outline the main functions of money. *(5 marks)*
   b Explain the main characteristics of money. *(5 marks)*

3 a Define inflation. *(3 marks)*
   b Explain how the rate of inflation can be measured. *(7 marks)*

4 Explain what is meant by the 'real' value of a sum of money. *(5 marks)*

5 Explain, with the aid of examples, what is meant by liquidity. *(5 marks)*

CHAPTER 13

The financial sector

In this chapter you will learn about the various bodies which make up the financial sector and what their roles and functions are.

- You will learn what the money market consists of
- You will then see the part played by the money market in the economy through an expanded circular flow diagram
- There will then be an examination of the financial sector in the Eastern Caribbean
- You will learn the role of central banks in the economy
- The types of financial intermediaries will be explained
- Finally, financial instruments in the public sector, e.g. bonds, and in the private sector, e.g. stocks and shares, will be examined

The money market

The 'money market' is like any other market in Economics except that the 'good' is money in its various forms, vary rarely cash, but money in the form of deposits in banks and other financial institutions. Demand comes from borrowers and supply comes from lenders. The borrowers can be individuals, firms or governments and the lenders are the financial institutions who are lending money deposited by individuals, firms, governments or foreign banks or governments. It is a service industry in that the financial institutions are providing a service of lending money. Their return for this service is interest in all its forms.

Economic development would not have been possible without the development of the money market. Governments could not have developed an infrastructure, firms could not have expanded, individuals could not have set up businesses or bought houses without being able to borrow money. However, money was not lent as if the financial institution was a charity. It had to be paid for in the form of interest. The economic world as we know it, therefore, is only possible because there is a money market.

Financial intermediaries

> **Definition of financial intermediaries**
>
> Financial intermediaries are institutions like banks which channel funds from depositors to borrowers. The depositors become lenders because it is their funds which the financial institutions lend to their customers.

The common function which these institutions perform is to introduce lenders to borrowers or borrowers to lenders. Therefore, we are dealing with the following institutions in the Caribbean:

Central banks
Commercial banks
Development banks
The Stock Exchange and stock brokers
Credit unions
Insurance companies

EXERCISE Try and find out the names of the different financial intermediaries in your country.

Examination Tip

When these intermediaries channel funds, they rarely do so in the form of cash. They do so in the form of **money substitutes** (see Chapter 10) such as cheques, debit cards, credit cards, direct debits and standing orders.

Financial intermediaries are in the tertiary sector of the economy. They provide services.

One of the services provided is advice. There are experts in the financial sector who advise customers where to invest their funds or how to borrow funds. They can advise their investors on which investments will yield the highest rate of interest. They can advise borrowers on where they can borrow at the lowest rate of interest.

Many people with funds want their funds to earn a high rate of interest but they also want quick and easy access to these funds. People who want to borrow often want to borrow a large sum of money for a long time, e.g. to buy a house when the loan is usually for 25 years. Obviously a person with funds which he or she wants quick access to will not lend for 25 years! The financial intermediary performs the function of collecting deposits from thousands of people and then lending to people who want long-term loans. A large number of depositors are not likely to be demanding

People often borrow money to buy a house.

Source: Stillpictures.

withdrawals at the same time so the Credit Union is able to lend for a long time. Another way of looking at this steady availability of funds is that as some people are withdrawing money, new customers are depositing some. Therefore there are always funds available for long-term loans. This service is called **'maturity transformation'**. 'Lending short and borrowing long' do not go together outside the financial sector! When you lend a friend EC$10 you are lending for a short time. You would not lend if you were not going to be paid back for twenty five years!

> **Definition of maturity transformation**
>
> Maturity transformation is the process of changing short-term deposits into long-term loans.

Lending money involves the risk of not being paid back. An individual may not be prepared to take this chance but he or she trusts that his or her money is safe in the hands of a financial intermediary like a credit union. Therefore, financial intermediaries are taking the risk away from individuals. This is called **'risk transformation'**. The financial intermediary may suffer a loss if a customer defaults on repayment but it can cover the loss with the interest it is earning on other loans.

> **Definition of risk transformation**
>
> Risk transformation is the process of transferring the risk of a loss from a depositor to the financial intermediary.

Financial intermediaries enjoy 'economies of scale' because they are so large that their costs are low. Bad debts, i.e. debts that are not repaid, are like costs. In the above case, they can spread their costs over the huge funds which they have received in deposits so that they became proportionally smaller.

The circular flow of income

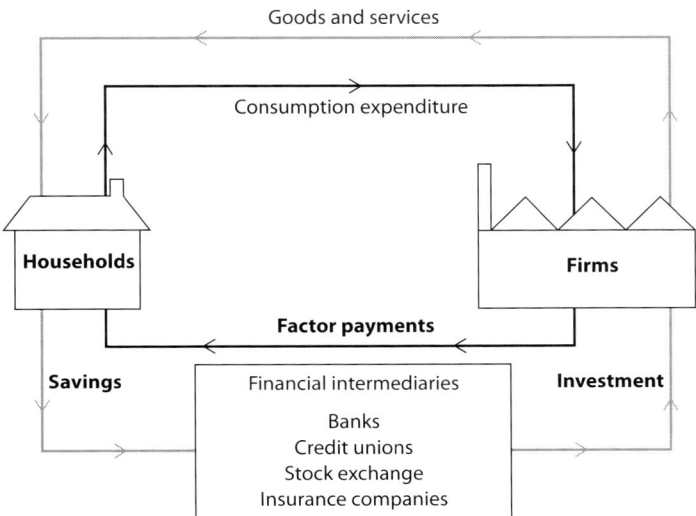

Fig. 13.1
A simplified circular flow diagram

Firms make factor payments to households in the form of wages, dividends on profits, interest and rent. Households spend some of these factor incomes on goods and services but they do not spend all of these factor incomes. Some is left over for savings. They channel these savings through financial intermediaries, like banks, into investments which they hope will bring returns. Firms are looking for funds from these financial intermediaries and hence investment in firms takes place.

An example: The financial sector in the Eastern Caribbean

The following is a chart of financial intermediaries which make up the financial sector under the **Eastern Caribbean Central Bank** as of November 2005.

Table 13.1 Financial institutions under the Eastern Caribbean Central Bank								
Financial institutions	Banks	Offshore banks	Develop. banks	Credit unions	Insurance companies	Nat. devel. foundations	Finance companies	Building assocs.
Anguilla	4	3	1	1	20	0	0	0
Antigua Barbuda	8	16	1	5	24	1	3	0
Dominica	4	1	1	16	20	1	1	1
Grenada	5	0	1	18	25	1	1	1
M'serrat	2	13	0	21	25	1	6	0
St Kitts Nevis	6	1	1	4	12	1	1	0
St Lucia	6	4	0	21	25	1	6	0
St Vincent and Grenada	4	9	1	9	13	1	2	1
Total	39	47	6	95	164	7	20	3

Source: *Eastern Caribbean Central Bank.*
Notes:
1 Banks refers to clearing banks or commercial banks. They may be locally owned (21) or a subsidiary of a foreign bank (18).
2 Offshore banks are banks that are regulated by the Offshore Banking Acts in the respective countries, but they have tax concessions.
3 A credit union is a non-profit-making co-operative savings association which makes loans to members at low interest.
4 An insurance company covers a person or business against risk, loss or damage in return for a premium or payment.
5 Development finance institutions are set up to finance regional development and their performance is closely monitored by the ECCB.
6 Building associations make loans for the purchase of housing.

The major financial institutions in the Caribbean

The central banks

To name a few:

>The Central Bank of The Bahamas.
>The Central Bank of Belize.
>The Central Bank of Barbados.
>The Eastern Caribbean Central Bank.
>The Cayman Islands Monetary Authority.
>The Bank of Guyana.
>The Bank of Jamaica.
>The Central Bank of Trinidad and Tobago.

How closely a central bank works with the government varies from country to country. In some countries, the central bank is independent of the government but, in others, it is like a government department, e.g. part of the Ministry of Finance.

The functions of a central bank in general are:

i   To be responsible for the whole monetary system and see that banks and other financial institutions are doing their jobs properly and efficiently.

ii To act as banker to the government, i.e. keeping the bank accounts of government departments and carrying out the government's monetary policy.

The functions of a central bank in more detail are:

To issue notes and coins
Legal tender is the notes and coins issued by the central bank. When the Eastern Caribbean Central Bank succeeded the Eastern Caribbean Currency Authority in 1983, the West Indies dollar was withdrawn and a new currency, the East Caribbean dollar, was issued. When the public demands more notes and coins from their bank accounts, the commercial banks have to withdraw more notes and coins from their own accounts at the central bank. The central bank then knows that it has to issue more notes and coins. This will not cause inflation because the demand for more notes and coins in the first place was to keep up with the increased number of transactions the public wishes to perform. Also, notes become dirty and torn and coins are lost and they must be replaced (this was referred to in the previous chapter).

To act as a bank
A central bank is:

1 banker to the government. Tax revenue must be deposited in the central bank. Also each government department will keep an account at the central bank into which it can deposit money and on which it can write cheques.

2 A central bank is banker to the commercial banks. Commercial banks keep **operational balances** at the central bank. They can deposit cash in these accounts and draw cash from them. When commercial banks have to make payments between themselves (called 'clearing') they use these accounts to transfer balances, e.g. if a customer of The Royal Bank of Trinidad and Tobago writes a cheque in favour of a customer of First Citizens Bank, First Citizens Bank will present this cheque to The Royal Bank of Trinidad and Tobago at the clearing meeting and ask for payment. The Royal Bank of Trinidad and Tobago can transfer the correct amount from its account at the Central Bank of Trinidad and Tobago to the account of First Citizens Bank, both banks keeping accounts at the central bank.

3 A central bank is banker to foreign banks which keep balances of the home currency to support the exchange rate of their own currency.

To organise borrowing arrangements for the government
When the government wants to borrow money, the central bank will issue bills or bonds for the public to buy. The public subscribes and the government has raised its

loan. When the bills and bonds reach maturity, the central bank must repay the public. It can do this by using tax revenue, thus reducing the national debt, or it can issue new bills and bonds and, with the income from them, pay off the maturing bills and bonds.

> **Definition of the national debt**
> The national debt is the total of government borrowing.

To give advice to the banks and other financial institutions
It advises them on what government policy is and it hopes for co-operation from the banking system. For example, it advises the banks to keep a safe cash ratio to meet withdrawals (and not to lend out too much money). This will stop the banks from 'crashing', i.e. being unable to meet their customers' withdrawals. Therefore, the central bank asks banks periodically to make reports. If the commercial banks do find themselves in trouble in meeting withdrawals they can go to the central bank for help. This function of the central bank is called the 'lender of last resort'.

To operate the government's monetary policy
This will be dealt with in the next chapter. The government must keep a stable currency and avoid inflation and the central bank is responsible for this.

To operate the exchange rate policy
The central bank must keep balances of its own currencies and of the currencies of all countries with which it trades. If the policy is to keep the exchange rate stable, and other countries are increasing demand for the local currency, its exchange value will rise. The central bank can bring the exchange value down again by buying the foreign currencies out of its fund, i.e. increasing the supply of the local currency. (Again, this will be dealt with more fully in a later chapter.)

In the diagram below, the exchange rate between the J$ and the US$ is floating. This means that the value of the J$, in terms of US$, is determined by the forces of supply and demand. If US tourists wish to take more holidays in Jamaica, they will demand more J$s and the demand curve for the J$ will shift upward to the right. The value of the J$ will rise to US$75.

The Bank of Jamaica, fearing that at this exchange rate Jamaican exports will lose competitiveness, will want to stabilise the exchange rate at US$1: J$65. Therefore, it will supply more J$s out of its fund. It will supply exactly that amount which will bring the exchange rate back to US$65. The supply curve for J$s will shift downwards to the right and the new equilibrium will be at Q_3. The exchange rate will be back at US$1 : J$65.

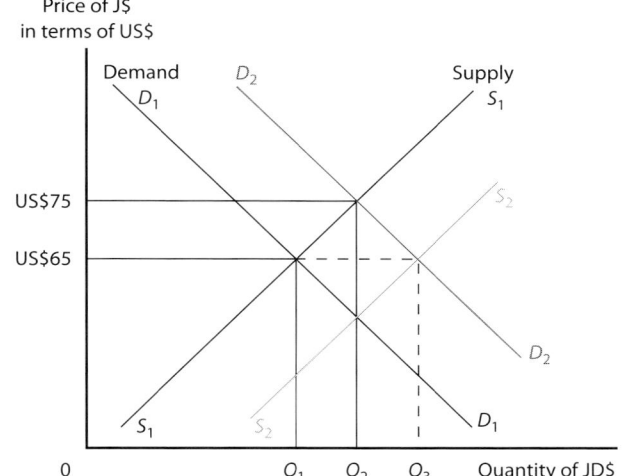

Fig. 13.2
Floating exchange rate: a central bank keeping a stable exchange rate

---

EXERCISE Consider the importance of the central bank in your country.

The stock exchanges

To name a few:

> Barbados Securities Exchange.
> Cayman Islands Stock Exchange.
> Eastern Caribbean Securities Exchange.
> Jamaica Stock Exchange.
> Trinidad and Tobago Stock Exchange.

A stock exchange is part of the capital market which is the market in long-term loans. These are loans for the financing, the raising of capital, of companies. The capital is raised by selling shares in the company. These can be a new issue of shares to raise new capital. On the other hand, the Stock Exchange is usually trading second-hand shares, i.e. shares already in existence which a shareholder wishes to sell. Shares in companies are permanent loans to the company. The company never buys back its shares. A shareholder can only get his or her money back by selling the share to another buyer and there may be a capital gain or loss in this transaction depending on how the company has been performing.

Shares would be very illiquid assets (very difficult to turn into cash) if it were not for the Stock Exchange. The Stock Exchange is a market which is usually open five days a week during trading hours, say 9.00 a.m. to 4.00 p.m. Therefore, the Stock Exchange provides **'maturity transformation'** in that companies have funds for a long time while the providers of these funds (the lenders) can obtain cash in 24 hours – they can obtain liquidity through the Stock Exchange.

Stock brokers

Stock brokers are special types of financial intermediaries. Companies raise some of their funds in the form of share capital. A share is a piece of paper which confirms ownership of part of the company. An investor may want to invest by buying shares in a company rather than depositing in a bank or credit union because the returns (the 'dividends') from stocks and shares can be greater, or the capital growth can be greater. The investor may just want the excitement of watching the performance of the company in the Stock Market which is given in the daily newspapers.

EXERCISE Choose one or two firms that are listed on a stock exchange and follow the change in the price of the shares over a one or two week period.

The investor goes to a stock broker. A stock broker does not own the shares but puts the client in touch with the company which wants to raise capital funds or someone who is selling the shares in the company. The stock broker charges a fee for this service. The stock broker is an expert who can give advice to clients. Stock brokers give advice on which companies are performing well and whose shares will yield the greatest dividends. They also advise on which shares to buy for quick returns and which to buy for capital growth.

Definitions of some terms used in a stock exchange
Capital is the money used for carrying on a business.
A share is a part of the capital of a company.
A broker is a 'go-between' between a seller and a buyer; he or she is a person who buys and sells for others without having the goods in his or her possession.
A dividend is a sum of money paid out of the profits of a company to a shareholder.

Development banks

To name a few:

> Caribbean Development Bank (CDB), Bridgetown, Barbados.
> Inter-American Development Bank, Bahamas.
> Agricultural Development Bank of Trinidad and Tobago.

Development banks, as the name suggests, assist development. For example, the Caribbean Development Bank is dedicated to the economic growth and development of the countries of the Caribbean. It provides loans to member countries to develop, e.g. in 2002, its loans to members totalled US$115,100,000 (in that year, with the exception of Belize, 83% of its loans went to the Eastern Caribbean).

Examples of the sort of projects that the loans were directed to are shown below.

Table 13.2 Direction of CDB loans in 2002	
Development projects	2002 percentage of loans
Transport, communications and sea defences	19
Agriculture, forestry and fisheries	11
Power, energy and water	2
Social services	9
Financing and distribution	18
Multisector and others	41

Source: Caribbean Development Bank.

Procedure

Note:
The procedure outlined below is for the Caribbean Development Bank but other development banks have roughly the same aims and will follow a similar procedure.

A member country is invited to bid for a loan for a project. The project is evaluated by the CDB by a sort of 'cost–benefit analysis', i.e. how much would the project cost and what benefits would it bring to the country and its people. The CDB staff make an appraisal of each project called the 'Appraisal Report'. It is not available to the public. There are many countries bidding for loans. The successful bid will be the one with the lowest cost–benefit ratio.

The proposals must be advertised so that firms that are interested in bidding for the projects are made aware. The borrowing country then asks for tenders. The borrowing country will then look at (a) the technical quality of the bid and (b) the price. Suppose two bids are evaluated the same. The rule is that the tender will go to the local bidder. This is because the local firm can bring in local expertise. It will also ensure that spin-offs from the project, like job creation, go to the country.

Then the progress of the project is monitored by portfolio managers from the CDB to see that the project is keeping within the budget and is technically sound.

The CDB is a Canadian Development Bank with Caribbean countries in joint ownership. Therefore, Canadian firms frequently bid for the contracts and Canadian consultants frequently monitor the projects. These consultants gain experience in different sectors of Caribbean economies and also local knowledge.

EXERCISE Try and find out something about a development project in your country. Where does the finance come from?

Commercial banks

These are also known as 'joint stock banks' because they are owned by shareholders and they aim to make profit for their shareholders by lending out their customers' deposits to gain interest. However, they also have to pay interest to their customers on their time deposit accounts. Therefore, the commercial banks must receive higher interest rates than they pay out. For example, if they pay 4% on a savings account and they make a loan at 6%, they are making 2%. Let us simplify the balance sheet of a bank.

Liabilities	Assets
Customers' deposits	Cash
Sight deposits	Loans
Time deposits	Bills
	Investments

Fig. 13.3 *A simplified balance sheet of a commercial bank*

A commercial bank is in an unusual position: it takes its liabilities (what it owes, i.e. its customers' deposits) and turns them into its assets (what it owns)! It uses those assets to make profit for the shareholders. It will certainly pay interest on the time deposits. It must make sure that the interest it receives from its assets, other than cash, is higher.

The composition of a commercial bank's assets is very important. A proportion of the assets must be liquid, i.e. cash, so that it can meet its customers' demands for withdrawals (usually about 12.5%). Then it needs to hold some assets which are not so liquid but which can be turned into cash quickly, e.g. bills which can be sold in the money markets five days a week. Some loans are fairly liquid, others not so liquid. The bank's investments are likely to be the least liquid of its assets in that they cannot be turned into cash for a few years in some cases. However, it is the least liquid assets, loans and investments, which will make the most profit. **Therefore a commercial bank has a clash between liquidity and profitability.**

Definitions of two terms used in accounting
A liability is what is owed.
An asset is what is owned.

EXERCISE

Consider the conflict between liquidity and profitability for a bank.

They are also known as 'clearing banks' because they clear their net indebtedness to each other in a process called 'clearing'. The customers of one bank make payments to the customers of other banks by cheque. At the same time, the customers of the latter bank are also making payments to customers of the former bank. All of these payments are collected together at the clearing process and the payments of one bank are subtracted from the payments of the other bank to find the 'net indebtedness', i.e. one bank must be in debt to the other. This debt is then settled or 'cleared'. For example:

Total payments of bank A customers to bank B customers	$ 15,349,455
Total payments of bank B customers to bank A customers	$ 12,433,207
Net indebtedness of bank A to bank B	$ 2,916,248

Bank A must pay bank B $2,916,248 to clear the debt.

Thirdly, and rarely, they are known as 'retail banks' because they take deposits from, and make loans to, their customers at known interest rates.

To name some commercial banks in the Caribbean:

>The National Bank of Anguilla.
>Provident Bank and Trust (Belize).
>National Commerce Bank Group (Jamaica).
>First Citizens Bank (Trinidad and Tobago).

These banks operate current accounts. With these accounts, customers can withdraw money or make payments to other people or to shops and other businesses. Commercial banks sometimes pay interest on balances in these accounts but the interest rate is usually very low. Sometimes the bank charges a fee to hold such an account.

They also offer deposit accounts ('time' deposits) from which no payments are made and consequently there are no cheque books with such accounts. However, they offer a higher rate of interest. Usually, the greater the deposit, the higher the rate and, the longer the deposit, the higher the rate.

They offer their customers services on current accounts. We have seen the checking service. A 'standing order' service is provided: if a regular payment of the same amount has to be paid, e.g. monthly or yearly, from the current account, the bank will see that it is made. A 'direct debit' service is also provided: if a regular payment of varying amount, e.g. an electricity bill, has to be paid, the bank will see that it is made.

A commercial bank will also give advice. Not only will they give advice on the different accounts available but also on interest rates.

Commercial banks make loans to their customers. As they are loaning their customers' money they have to be very careful that these loans are secure. They used to believe that they were only in a position to make short-term loans but today some commercial banks go in for long-term loans, e.g. repayment in 20–25 years, provided they are secure. In this respect the commercial banks are now competing with credit unions and building societies. They are seeking new ways in which to make profits for their shareholders. Therefore they are extending their services.

Credit unions

Credit unions are very popular in the Caribbean. Trinidad and Tobago has over 75 credit unions and Jamaica over 65, but even the smaller countries have many.

To name the five leading credit unions in St Lucia:

>St Lucia Civil Service Co-operative Credit Union.
>The Laborie Co-operative Credit Union.
>The St Lucia Teachers' Co-operative Credit Union.
>The Royal St Lucia Police Co-operative Credit Union.
>Choiseul Co-operative Credit Union.

A credit union is owned by its members who wish to benefit from its services. These are to provide savings and to make loans and provide other financial services at rates which are generally lower than those of other financial institutions. They are 'co-operatives' and 'mutual' organisations, i.e. working together and owned by the members, in that they are formed by people who have some common bond like living in the same neighbourhood or going to the same church.

They are non-profit making institutions because the members are not intending to make a profit out of themselves! If their revenue turns out to be greater than their costs, they return this 'profit' to their members in the form of increased interest on their savings or lower rates on loans. Sometimes, they do provide the same services as banks like operating current accounts but they also branch out into insurance services.

They hold annual general meetings (AGMs) at which they elect their directors on the basis of one member, one vote, not according to how much money a member has put into the credit union. They can reject directors whom they consider are not administering the credit union well.

EXERCISE

Why do you think credit unions are so popular in the Caribbean? Find out as much as you can about he ones which operate in your country.

Insurance companies

Insurance companies can be included in the financial sector because they hold huge sums of money which they can inject into the circular flow of income.

To name some insurance companies in the Caribbean:

> The Beacon Insurance Company.
> Barbados Mutual Life Assurance.
> British Caribbean Insurance Company.
> Guardian Life of the Caribbean Limited.
> Trinidad and Tobago Insurance Limited.

An insurance company takes away the risk. For example, if you are a car owner and driver, you risk having an accident which may damage your car, another car, cause injury to yourself or to a third party. Without insurance, you would be risking having to pay damages which could be huge. Therefore, you pay an insurance company to cover that risk. Such a payment to an insurance company is called a **'premium'**. However, an insurance company will make a profit because the total premiums paid will exceed the amount it pays out. Also the premium income is invested, often through the Stock Exchange. Insurance companies are amongst the biggest shareholders. They are called **'institutional shareholders'**.

In the insurance world are people called **'actuaries'**. An actuary is a mathematician who assesses insurance risks using statistical techniques. The more cars an actuary can have data on, the more accurate can be the assessment of the risk. This is called **'the law of large numbers'**. It is unpredictable whether you will have a car crash or not, but the predictability of car crashes from a million drivers will be very accurate. Therefore insurance companies do not make losses. They are very profitable! They are **'spreading the risk'** of you having an accident over thousands of motorists who are all paying premiums in the event that one of you will have an accident.

> **Definitions of two insurance terms**
>
> A premium is a sum of money paid for insurance.
>
> An actuary assesses insurance risks and calculates premiums.

Financial instruments

Financial instruments are the securities by which central governments, local governments, businesses and individuals raise money.

> **Definition of a security**
>
> A security is a certificate in evidence of debt or property.

Government securities

Governments raise money by taxes and by borrowing. Government borrowing is called the 'National Debt'. Governments borrow from the public for new undertakings but they also borrow to pay back old debt. The public will always lend to the government because it is absolutely risk-free. The government will always pay back at the date of redemption. Meanwhile, the public know that it can always sell the security on the market if it wants money before the redemption date. Government securities should provide a higher return than rates on time deposits offered by commercial banks.

Earlier in this chapter we saw that it is one of the functions of the central bank to raise money for the government. We shall examine in more detail how the Eastern Caribbean Central Bank raises money by issuing securities and take this example as typical of how other Caribbean governments borrow.

Treasury bills

These are issued for short-term borrowing of up to a year. A treasury bill has a purchase price and a redemption price (the price paid when the debt is repaid). The difference is the interest the government pays. For example, a $20 treasury bill redeemed at $20.50 after six months is earning interest at the rate of 5% per year.

Treasury notes

These are for longer-term borrowing, i.e. longer than a year but under ten years. A typical treasury note would be for three years. It carries a stated interest rate which is paid half-yearly. For example, a $100 treasury note at 7.5% per year would pay $3.75 twice yearly. If the holder kept it until maturity, he or she would earn $22.50.

Treasury bonds

These are for long-term borrowing, i.e. more than ten years. A treasury bond carries a stated rate of interest.

When a government wishes to raise money by borrowing, it announces the **issue** so that the public is prepared and can decide whether to make a bid. For example, the government of St Kitts and Nevis may announce that it will be offering treasury bonds to the total value of $5,000,000, in denominations of $20, bearing an interest rate of 6.5% at auction on 20 January 2007, and a deadline for submitting bids. It reconfirms these details three weeks before the auction in the government gazettes, regional newspapers and on the ECCB website. An interested bidder would take note and decide how many bonds to bid for. The bonds are usually sold at face value, $20 in our example, but occasionally at premium when a bidder would have to bid above face value.

A successful bidder can hold the bonds until maturity if he or she is going for a long-term savings option, or can sell before maturity on the Eastern Caribbean Securities Exchange.

In the original bidding, buying and selling of securities, the public must use a licensed intermediary, i.e. the public do not go to the market. The ownership of bonds is recorded in a confirmation notice. Interest is paid into the owner's bank account of which details have been given.

Post office savings accounts are a form of lending to the government. The Post Office is a government department. Many small investors cannot think of taking up treasury bills, notes and bonds because they only have a small amount of savings. There is always a local Post Office and it is easy to open a savings account. The savings are risk-free but the interest is relatively low.

Local government bonds

These are also called 'municipal bonds'. Cities, towns and local government agencies raise money by issuing bonds. It is more risky to lend to a local government than it is to the central government. Even so, local government bonds pay lower interest rates than central government bonds. They attract lenders because they can be bought at a discount, i.e. at less than the face value.

Companies and corporations

Shares

The usual way for a public limited company, a PLC, to raise money externally (from the public) is by selling shares through the Stock Exchange. The commonest share is the ordinary share or 'equity'. The share will never be redeemed by the company but can be sold again and again on the Stock Exchange. It pays a dividend (the equivalent of interest) as the return on the investment. The amount of the dividend depends on the profit that the company has made and how much of the profit the directors decide to distribute to shareholders. Investing in ordinary shares carries great risk so a) the dividends can be high to compensate and b) ordinary shareholders can have a say in the running of the company by voting at the Annual General Meeting.

Corporate bonds

These are also called debentures. Corporate bonds are issued by companies which do not want to issue new shares, perhaps because new shares dilute the ownership of the company or are a drain on the profits. Corporate bonds are riskier than government bonds because companies can go under more easily than governments! Therefore corporate bonds pay higher rates of interest than government bonds. They carry a maturity date at which the bond will be redeemed. Five years is a common length for a corporate bond.

The public is attracted to corporate bonds because of the higher interest rates and because they will be paid back before shareholders in the event of the company going bankrupt.

Examination questions

1 Distinguish between maturity transformation and risk transformation *(10 marks)*

2 Explain the functions of a central bank. *(10 marks)*

3 a What is a share? *(3 marks)*
   b Discuss the role of a stock exchange in an economy. *(7 marks)*

4 Explain why commercial banks always have to achieve a balance between liquidity and profitability? *(10 marks)*

5 a What is a credit union? *(3 marks)*
   b Why are credit unions so popular in the Caribbean? *(7 marks)*

Part five

Economic management: policies and goals

Public finance: national income

In this chapter you will be introduced to national income accounting.

- You will learn that national income accounting measures the total wealth of a country and you will learn what methods are used to measure this wealth
- You will study the difference between Gross National Product (GNP), Gross Domestic Product (GDP) and National Income (NI)
- You will be shown the usefulness of these figures in making comparisons over time and between countries
- You will see that the measure over time brings in economic growth
- You will then learn how to discuss standard of living and quality of life
- You will be given a much-expanded circular flow diagram to illustrate how National income is measured by the income, output and expenditure methods

What public finance involves

'Public finance' is a term favoured by the United Nations and taken up by Caribbean countries to cover:

National income accounting
National budget
Taxation
Balance of payments

National income accounting

National income is a loose term for either Gross National Product (GNP), Gross Domestic Product (GDP) or National Income (NI) (which to an Economist means 'net national income at factor cost'). They are three different ways of measuring the same thing: the total wealth of a country at a given time. Knowing the total wealth of a country is not going to help the country become wealthier, but it is useful in comparisons – comparisons over time and between countries. What is being compared is **economic growth**. (See 'More on economic growth' later in this chapter.)

> **Definition of economic growth**
>
> Economic growth is the percentage increase in national income, usually measured by GDP, over a period of time.

Over time

A country wants to know if its Gross Domestic Product has grown over the past five years, e.g. is Jamaica wealthier than it was five years ago? This will give an idea about whether it has been pursuing the right policies. Of course, this is of great importance to 'developing' countries but 'developed' countries also keep these accounts. Imagine the total wealth of the United States measured in dollars.

Here it is estimated in 2004: US$11,750,000,000,000.

China is second at US$7,262,000,000,000 but China is growing fast and some economists estimate that it will overtake the United States by the middle of this century. We are therefore interested in the growth of China's GDP between 2004 and 2050. China has had amazing economic growth as measured by GDP, in some years in excess of 10%.

Shanghai, China.

Between countries

Caribbean countries' GDPs are compared with each other but there is not much to be gained if their economies are entirely different. When they were plantation economies, perhaps there was something to be gained by comparisons and if their economies are tourism based, there still may be some value in comparisons. The point is that you must compare 'like with like' and in reality no two economies are the same. However, students will be interested in these estimates for 2004:

Trinidad and Tobago
US$11,480,000,000.
Jamaica
US$11,130,000,000.

Source: *CIA The World Fact Book. (Figures are given in 'purchasing power parity' whereby exchange rates are adjusted to equalise prices of goods and services between countries.)*

Examination Tip

It is important to stress the use of purchasing power parity when comparing countries as this takes into account the price of goods and services in different countries.

But, you will say, Trinidad and Tobago has oil so the comparison is not valid!

Some other GDP figures for Caribbean countries (2004 estimates in PPP $):

Table 14.1 GDP in US$ for selected Caribbean countries at PPP	
Barbados	5,295,000,000
Guyana	4,569,000,000
British Virgin Islands	2,899,000,000
Belize	2,498,000,000
Cayman Islands	1,778,000,000
St Lucia	1,391,000,000
Antigua and Barbuda	750,000,000
Grenada	440,000,000
Dominica	384,000,000
St Vincent and the Grenadines	342,000,000
St Kitts and Nevis	339,000,000
Turks and Caicos	216,000,000
Anguilla	112,000,000

Source: *CIA The World Fact Book.*

EXERCISE Why do you think economists want to compare GDP figures over time and between countries?

Gross Domestic Product

This is the measure of national income most favoured by the United Nations. It measures the total output (product) of all the resources within the economy.

There are three ways of measuring GDP: the output method, the income method and the expenditure method. As they are three ways of measuring the same thing, they must necessarily be equal.

The output method measures the value of all the output in the country. Double counting is a problem. The output of one firm is the input of another firm and must not be counted twice. For example, the making of rum.

	Value of output $	Intermediate goods $	Value added $
Sugar cane grower	100	0	100
Refiner	150	100	50
Rum distiller	250	150	100
Rum retailer	300	250	50
			300

The easiest way of dealing with double counting is to go straight to the value of the final good, in this case rum, $300. However, the same result is achieved by adding up the values added, again $300. If you added the cost of all the intermediate goods you would be double counting because the output of the refiner includes the output of the sugar cane grower and the output of the distiller includes the output of the refiner, etc.

Inflation must also be taken into account. This is the difference between 'monetary GDP' and 'real GDP'. Real GDP is monetary GDP taking inflation into account. Monetary GDP must be deflated (reduced) by the **GDP deflator**.

Note that the GDP deflator is not the same as the price index because in national income all prices have risen, not just those in a shopping basket. The Consumer Price Index does not include items like defence expenditure!

For example:

	Year 1	Year 2
Monetary GDP	$500 million	$650 million

GDP deflator 125

Real GDP in Year 2 $\quad\quad\quad\quad\quad\quad\quad\quad \dfrac{\$650 \times 100}{125} = \$520$

The formula is:

$$\dfrac{\text{monetary GDP}}{\text{GDP deflator}} \times 100$$

Therefore, in real terms GDP has only risen by $20 million, not $150 million because inflation has risen by 25%.

EXERCISE Why do you think it is important to take inflation into account when studying GDP figures?

The income method is the addition of all incomes earned in the economy over the year. These incomes must be matched by some output. **Transfer payments** are not counted.

> **Definition of a transfer payment**
> A transfer payment, such as a state pension, is one for which there is no corresponding good or service.

A state pension is a transfer payment. A pensioner is making no contribution to output when he or she receives the pension.

The income method consists of the addition of all incomes earned in the production of goods and services.

Factor incomes = wages + rent + interest + profit

Another issue to consider are the services of a housewife. The washing, cleaning, cooking, ironing and bringing up the children are very valuable to the economy but they are not counted. If the family had to pay a maid, a cook and a laundryperson, those incomes would be counted.

The expenditure method is the addition of all final expenditures. Once again the expenditure on intermediate goods must not be double counted. Remember also not to include government expenditure on transfer payments. In another part of the book we saw that Aggregate Expenditure is made up of Consumption Expenditure, Government Expenditure, Investment and Expenditure on Exports less Expenditure on Imports:

$$AE = C + I + G + X - M$$

Output Method ≡ Income Method ≡ Expenditure Method
(≡ necessarily equal to.)

Gross National Product

Gross National Product is Gross Domestic Product plus Net Property Income from Abroad. Some of the output of a country's citizens is made abroad. Some of the output of foreigners is made in your country. The difference is Net Property Income from Abroad. Such property income comes from investments in land, property, business and banks. For example, many Jamaicans have businesses in the United States. There is one which makes Jamaican foods, notably Jamaica patties. At the same time, many citizens of the United States have businesses in Jamaica, e.g. hotels. The income from the Jamaican business in the United States less the income from the United States business in Jamaica is the Net Property Income from Abroad. It can be positive or negative in the GNP accounts depending on whether your citizens are making more money abroad than foreigners are making in your country.

$$GNP = GDP + NPIA$$

Gross Domestic Product focuses on what is produced at home whereas GNP focuses on what is produced at home or anywhere in the world by your citizens.

Market prices and factor cost

Market prices contain indirect taxes and subsidies. Taxes make the goods and services more expensive than the value of the inputs in them and subsidies make them cheaper. Taxes must be subtracted and subsidies added to turn market prices into factor cost.

(Indirect taxes are taxes on goods and services.)

Definition of market prices and factor cost

GDP or GNP at market prices less indirect taxes plus subsidies equals GDP or GNP at factor cost.

GDP – Indirect tax + subsidies = GDP at factor cost.

National income

This is a loose expression for Net National Income at Factor Cost. Capital goods depreciate with use and age. The country's capital depreciates. Depreciation must be subtracted. Depreciation is called 'Capital Consumption' in national income accounting. Depreciation is notoriously difficult to calculate in huge items like dams and hydro-electric plants but it must be done.

Net investment = gross investment – depreciation.

'At factor cost'. Again, taxes must be subtracted and subsidies added.

> **Definition of depreciation**
> Depreciation means the fall in the value of capital goods through age and wear and tear.

The relationship of the three measures of national income:

Gross Domestic Product
Plus net property income from abroad equals
Gross National Product
Less capital consumption (depreciation) equals
Net National Product
Less taxes plus subsidies equals
Net national income at factor cost

Economists and the United Nations prefer **'Gross'** because of the difficulty of calculating depreciation and they prefer **'Domestic'** because they want to concentrate on what is produced in the country.

The United Nations monitors the GDP figures of all countries.

An example

The Gross Domestic Product of Jamaica in 2004:

Services	US$7,260,000,000
plus	
Manufacturing and Mining	US$3,100,000,000
plus	
Agriculture	US$770,000,000
equals	
Gross Domestic Product	US$11,130,000,000

(These figures are approximations and only a rough guide to a breakdown of a country's GDP.)

More on economic growth

Comparisons over time tell us about 'economic growth'. Developed countries grow but they cannot be expected to grow at a fast rate because they are already developed and no major structural changes can be made to their economies. A growth rate of 3% is relatively good for a developed country. The United States is expected to achieve a 3% growth rate or better in 2007. A 2% growth rate is satisfactory for most governments in developed countries.

Developing countries are looking for much higher growth rates. A 5% growth rate is good, 7% very good and over 10 %, as we have seen in China, is spectacular. It is hard to sustain such high growth rates but China's growth rate at present shows no sign of slowing down.

Table 14.2 Real GDP growth rates in five Caribbean countries for 2006 (%)	
Bahamas	3.0
Barbados	2.3
Belize	3.5
Cuba	3.0
Guyana	1.9

Source: *CIA Fact File.*

None of these growth rates is spectacular. At least none are negative. A negative growth rate is possible and could be due to a natural disaster, like Hurricane Ivan in Cayman.

Per capita GDP

This is a figure of very great interest to the United Nations as it is used to measure the 'standard of living'. 'Standard of living' is, to some extent, going out of fashion and economists prefer to use the expression 'quality of life'. The per capita GDP figure is the usual measure taken when discussing **economic development**.

> **Definition of economic development**
> Economic development is the improvement of human welfare which tended to be called the 'standard of living' but is now more commonly referred to as 'quality of life'.

Per capita GDP is found by dividing real GDP by the population. This gives the amount of goods and services each individual in the country has at his or her disposal. Standard of living is measured in material things only; 'quality of life' brings in other non-material things which contribute to well-being.

$$\text{Real per capita GDP} = \frac{\text{Real GDP}}{\text{Population}}$$

Trinidad and Tobago:

$$\text{Real GDP} = \frac{\text{US\$11,480,000,000}}{\text{Pop.: 1,088,644}} = \text{real per cap. GDP US\$10,532}$$

Table 14.3 Real per capita GDP in selected Caribbean countries estimated for 2004/05 in US$		
Bahamas	$5,295,000,000/301,790	16,300
Barbados	$4,569,000,000/279,254	6,350
Cayman Islands	$1,778,000,000/279,457	31,613
Cuba	$33,920,000,000/11,346,670	3,000
Guyana	$2,899,000,000/765,283	3,814

Source: Adapted from CIA World Fact Book.

If we are comparing standards of living from purely real GDP per capita figures, it would appear that the Cayman Islands have the highest standard of living and Cuba has the lowest out of the countries in Table 14.3.

Criticism of real GDP per capita as a measure of living standards

To start with, we must say that in spite of all the weaknesses of the real per capita GDP measure, it is probably the best one we have at the moment. It is relatively easy to calculate. The United Nations uses it.

Two American economists, W. Nordhaus and J. Tobin, produced '*A Measure of Economic Welfare*' (MEW) in 1972. This measure is undoubtedly good, but it is complicated and the values which they place on items like 'leisure' are rather subjective, i.e. they reflect their own personal opinions. Therefore we still retain real GDP per capita.

Is a person in Cayman really ten times better off than a person in Cuba? We must doubt that. First of all, there is an uneven distribution of income in Cayman but a more even distribution in Cuba. Distribution of income is very important (remember the Lorenz curve from Chapter 11). In Cayman, there are some very rich people, but others are relatively poor. In Cuba, there are no rich and poor. Therefore, a Cuban may be enjoying a better standard of living than a Caymanian. Therefore, we must know how income is distributed before we can comment on the standard of living.

Per capita GDP only takes into account those goods and services which reach the market place. We have already seen that the services of a housewife (apologies for this sexism!) are not counted. There are many other goods and services which do not reach the market place. Subsistence crops do not reach the market place but are a very important contribution to the standard of living. These are the crops which you grow on your own land and consume yourself. They are important in Caribbean countries. The value of subsistence can be calculated and it is included in the GDPs of many Third World countries but it is not included in those of western industrialised countries. Subsistence crops are not counted in most economies, even developing economies, so the omission of subsistence is a big weakness of per capita GDP.

DIY (Do-it-Yourself) is not calculated in GDP.

'Do-it-yourself' (DIY) flourishes in some economies, e.g. painting your own house or servicing your own car. If you had to pay someone else to do these jobs, that would be recorded in GDP, but they are not when they are done under DIY. Charity work done by church groups is very strong in some Caribbean countries. The goods and services produced in these sectors should be measured, but they are not.

Per capita GDP is a material measure and does not include such things as freedom, justice, security, leisure and even happiness. They are very important in our quality of life. In the Caribbean, leisure is very highly valued. We are not 'workaholics'. Just sitting in the sun contributes to our quality of life. What is the point of having all the goods and services if you do not have the freedom to enjoy them or if there is no security from internal or external attack? Caribbean countries may be low in per capita GDP but they are very high in non-material benefits.

Leisure contributes to the quality of life.

'Regrettables', according to Nordhaus and Tobin, are those things which we have to buy but we wish we did not have to. They inflate the GDPs of countries considerably. Think of the insulated, heated house which is required in Northern European countries which

Commuting to work could be regarded as an example of a 'regrettable'.

adds billions of dollars to GDP in those countries. They are not needed in Caribbean climates.

Another interesting regrettable is commuting to work. In western industrialised countries, relatively few people work in the place in which they live and they have to spend billions on transport. In Caribbean countries, it is much more common to work where you live and there is not so much commuting. Therefore, regrettables should be subtracted from GDP and should not be included in measures of the standard of living.

Education is called an 'intermediate' and should be subtracted from GDP services because it is counted in the increased productivity it brings. You must not 'double count'. However, this would apply to all economies because education is a service in all of them and would not affect international comparisons of living standards.

Lastly, Nordhaus and Tobin refer to 'disamenities', such as pollution. The expenditure on pollution control and elimination occurs in some economies, but not in others where there is much less pollution. Disamenities inflate some countries' GDPs much more than others. Therefore, it is simpler to remove them from GDP calculations so that fair comparisons of standards of living can be made.

'Quality of life' is a better expression because it embraces not just goods and services but also freedom, security, justice, leisure and happiness; in fact, all of the things that make life enjoyable. We must conclude that the quality of life in most Caribbean countries is much higher than the per capita GDP figures would suggest at first sight because of all the uncalculated benefits which are present in the Caribbean way of life.

EXERCISE What do you think ought to be included in a definition of 'quality of life'?

The circular flow of national income

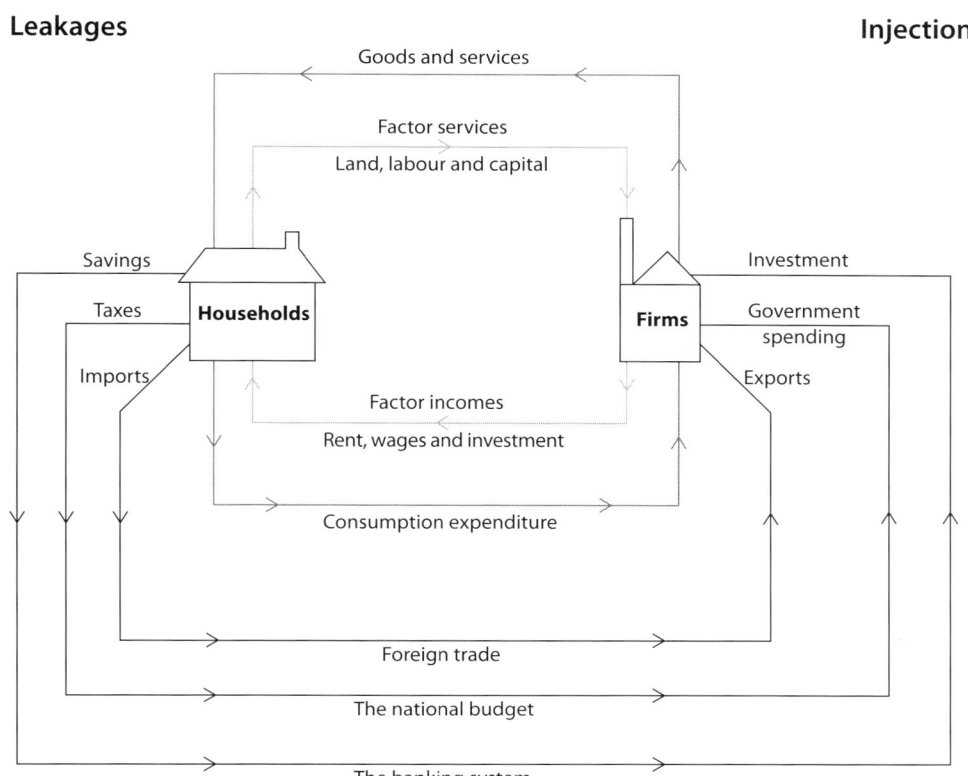

Fig. 14.1
The circular flow of the national income

We should be familiar with the circular flow diagram by now. This time we have added **leakages and injections.** Without leakages and injections, the circular flow economy would be static. It would experience neither economic growth nor economic decline. Consumption expenditure by households would exactly match the goods and services produced by firms. The factor incomes paid out by firms would exactly match the factor services supplied by households. In fact this economy would wind down as there would be depreciation (**capital consumption**). The buildings would need repair and the machines would break down or become worn out and need replacement. Without leakages and injections, therefore, the circular flow diagram is unrealistic.

> **Definition of capital consumption**
> Capital consumption is the depreciation of capital goods during production.

Leakages or withdrawals

Another unrealistic aspect of the circular flow diagram without leakages is its assumption that households spend all their incomes. They do not. Some income is leaked into savings ('what is not spent is saved'). Some income is taken by the government in taxes and some income is spent on imported goods. With leakages out of the circular flow, the economy would certainly wind down.

Injections

Injections go into firms. Some investments replace the capital goods that have depreciated to maintain the output of goods and services. Other investments are the building of new factories and the purchase of new machines which will increase the output of goods and services. The government spends its tax revenue which becomes another injection into the circular flow. The last injection is by foreigners who buy the exports of this economy and their spending goes into firms in this economy.

Equilibrium

The economy will be in equilibrium if the leakages are equal to the withdrawals. In Economics, leakages are symbolised by W (= withdrawals) and injections are symbolised by J (= injections). Therefore the economy is in equilibrium when $W = J$.

However, W embraces savings, taxes and imports:

$W = S + T + M$ (M stands for Imports).

On the other side, J embraces investment, government expenditure and exports:

$J = I + G + X$ (X stands for exports)

Therefore the economy is in equilibrium when:

$S + T + M = I + G + X$

> **Examination Tip**: The various injections into the circular flow and withdrawals or leakages from it are very important and you need to make sure that you fully understand these.

Disequilibrium

If the leakages from the circular flow exceed the injections, the economy will wind down or deflate. There will be negative economic growth (which can be experienced in the real world, e.g. by Ethiopia in its civil war). This is symbolised thus:

$S + T + M > I + G + X$

If the injections into the circular flow exceed the leakages, the economy will grow or inflate. There will be economic growth (which is what all countries are seeking to achieve). This is symbolised thus:

$S + T + M < I + G + X$

Using the circular flow diagram to show the three ways of measuring national income

The **output method** (adding up the values of all the goods and services produced in the economy) can be shown on the upper loop in our diagram. If we cut the upper loop, and added all that was flowing out of firms into households, we would have GDP by the output method.

The **income method** (adding up all the factor incomes in the economy) can be shown on one of the lower loops (labelled 'factor incomes'). If we cut this loop, and added all the incomes that were flowing out of firms and into households for rents, wages and interest, we would have GDP by the income method.

The **expenditure method** (adding up all the expenditure by households on the goods and services produced in the economy) can be shown on the other lower loop (labelled 'consumption expenditure'). If we cut this loop, and added all the expenditures on goods and services that were flowing from households into firms, we would have GDP by the expenditure method.

Aspects of public finance in the three lowest loops

Savings by households reach firms by being channelled through **the banking system**. We already have seen that households make deposits which banks, credit unions and insurance companies are able to lend to firms seeking loans. The banking system is an essential part of the economy without which the economy could not operate.

Taxes are set out in **the national budget**. The Minister of Finance decides what taxes will be levied and they are received by the Treasury (or 'The Exchequer'). He or she also decides government expenditure in the budget and thus the taxes are channelled back into the circular flow.

Imports are part of **foreign trade**. Households' expenditure on foreign goods and services are part of the **balance of payments** (discussed further in a later chapter). If the balance of payments balances, expenditure by our households will be matched by foreign households' expenditure on our goods and services. Foreigners' expenditure on our exports comes into our economy through foreign trade.

Examination questions

1 Explain the differences between GDP, GNP and NI. *(10 marks)*

2 Discuss the differences between the output, income and expenditure methods of measuring GDP. *(10 marks)*

3 **a** Explain what is meant by real GDP. *(3 marks)*
   b Why is it important to use real GDP figures when comparing countries? *(7 marks)*

4 **a** What is meant by the circular flow of income in an economy? *(4 marks)*
   b Compare and contrast the injections into and the leakages or withdrawals out of the circular flow. *(6 marks)*

5 Why do GDP figures not always give an accurate indication of the standard of living in a country? *(10 marks)*

6 Distinguish between the standard of living and the quality of life in a country. *(10 marks)*

Public finance: the national budget

In this chapter you will study the national budget and the national debt.

- You will learn that the national budget lays out the revenue and expenditure of the government for the year
- You will go into detail about items on both the revenue and the expenditure side
- You will make a close examination of Jamaica's revenue and expenditure estimates for a year
- You will then be introduced to fiscal policy, the government's decisions over taxation and government expenditure
- You will study the different types of tax
- Finally, you will learn about the national debt

The national budget

The Minister of Finance, Mr Owen Arthur, presents the budget for Barbados.

The Minister of Finance will announce his expenditure plans every year in a budget: how much the government will be spending and what it will be spent on. He will also announce his revenue plans: how much money he proposes to raise and from where it will be raised. A government raises most of its money through taxation. Taxation and expenditure plans are called the **'fiscal policy'** of the government.

Definition of fiscal policy
Fiscal policy refers to the government's plans for taxation, expenditure and the national debt.

In most countries, the 'fiscal year' runs from April to March or, to be precise, from 1st April to 31 March in the following year, as in Jamaica. (The Bahamas is exceptional in that the fiscal year runs from 1 July to 30 June.) The Minister of Finance announces his budget early in the fiscal year. In Jamaica in 2005, 'Budget Day' was 14 April.

In broad terms fiscal policy is the decision whether to have:

a a balanced budget where revenue is equal to expenditure, $R = G$ ('G' for government spending).

b a budget surplus where revenue exceeds expenditure, $R > G$.

c a budget deficit where expenditure exceeds revenue, $R < G$.

A budget does not have to balance. It is not irresponsible for the Minister of Finance not to balance the budget. It depends on his fiscal policy, which should be geared to the needs of the country. A government may want to boost the economy by spending more than it takes in taxes. It can do this by borrowing. So, in a deficit budget, the Minister also has to state the government's borrowing requirement, known as 'the public sector borrowing requirement' (PSBR). A budget deficit is inflationary, other things being equal, because the government will be 'pumping' money into the economy by spending more than it is taking out.

The Minister may decide to run a budget surplus. His or her aim may be to slow down the economy because it is 'overheating', i.e. facing inflationary pressures. Alternatively, he or she may want to use the surplus to reduce the government debt. A budget surplus is deflationary because the government is taking out more money from the economy than it is putting in.

In the long run, i.e. over a number of years, a government's fiscal policy would be to balance the budget but in any one year there is likely to be either a deficit or a surplus.

Table 15.1 A balanced budget			
Revenue		**Expenditure**	
Direct taxation	$100m	National security	$15m
Indirect taxation	$30m	Education	$25m
Borrowing	$20m	Health	$40m
		Social security	$50m
		Transport	$20m
	$150m		$150m

Suppose there is a high level of inflation, e.g. 25% per year. Prices are rising by 25% in the year. The Minister of Finance finds that the government's expenditure is greater than planned and there is not the revenue to meet it. It is possible to have a 'mini' budget during the fiscal year to raise additional revenue but it is uncommon.

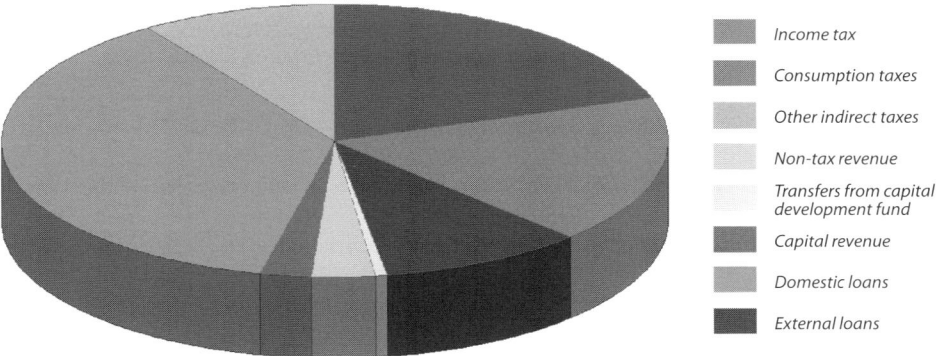

Fig. 15.1
Pie chart of Jamaica's budget revenue 2004–05

Where the money comes from

Source	Amount J$
Income tax	66,066,100
Consumption taxes	56,765,900
Other indirect taxes	32,803,000
Non-tax revenue	9,788,592
Transfers from Capital Development Fund	2,354,700
Capital revenue	7,945,800
Domestic loans	121,699,400
External loans	30,730,500
Grand total	328,153,992

Notes:
1 Consumption taxes are general consumption tax and special consumption tax.
2 Non-tax revenue comes from such sources as the Post Office.
3 Transfers from capital development fund refers to revenues taken from this fund in the current year.
4 Capital revenue comes from such as land sales, loan repayments, etc.
5 Domestic loans refers to the national debt (see later in the chapter).
6 External loans come from the World Bank (multilateral) and Britain (bilateral).

Fig. 15.2
Pie chart of Jamaica's budget expenditure estimates, 2004–05

Where the money goes to

Source	Amount J$
Ministry of Finance and Planning	243,959,004
Ministry of Education, Youth and Culture	30,213,600
Ministry of Health and Departments	15,620,270
Ministry of National Security	15,197,481
Ministry of Local Government, Youth and Community Development	4,774,927
Other Government Departments	18,388,130
Grand Total	328,153,412

Not quite a balanced budget!
Source: *Ministry of Finance and Planning, Jamaica*
Notes:
Expenditure to the government ministries and departments goes under '**recurrent**' and '**capital**' expenditure. Recurrent is the expenditure for the running expenses of the ministry while capital is for the creation of infrastructure, buildings, machinery, etc. The two have been added together in the table.

EXERCISE The principle of trying to balance revenue and expenditure is essentially the same for a government as it is for an individual. Draw up your own personal budget of income and expenditure over the period of a week or a month.

Fiscal policy: taxation

There are two sorts of taxes, direct and indirect taxes. Direct taxes are taxes on income and indirect taxes are taxes on expenditure. Income can come from three main sources: wages, capital gains and profits. The tax on wages, often called 'income tax', raises the most revenue in many countries. Capital gains tax is a tax on the increased revenue from investment. In some countries there is a capital gains tax on deposit accounts in banks. Usually there is no capital gains tax on the gain made from buying and selling a house, but there is on most other capital gains. Tax on the profits of companies is a direct tax because distributed profits are 'income' to shareholders.

> **Definitions of direct and indirect taxes**
>
> A direct tax is one levied on the income of an individual or an organisation.
>
> An indirect tax is one levied on the expenditure on goods and services.

Progressive, proportional and regressive taxation

One of the guiding principles of a tax system is **equity**, i.e. fairness or justice. The **sacrifice principle** implies that each taxpayer ought to make equal sacrifice. Therefore, a rich person ought to pay more in tax than a poor person. The sacrifice principle can be applied to **progressive taxation** and to **proportional taxation**.

Progressive taxation

In progressive taxation, the rate of tax increases as income rises. In other words, the percentage of income taken in tax rises as income rises. It can lead to very complicated tax systems. However, most countries using progressive income tax systems have simplified them in recent years into three or four tax 'bands' or 'brackets'. Very low incomes are not taxed at all. Then when income reaches a 'threshold', it becomes taxable. As income rises thereafter, it passes into higher tax rates. Below is a simple example.

Table 15.2 Progressive tax		
Income $	Tax rate %	Tax paid $
1 to 1,000	0	0
1,001 to 5,000	10	400
5,001 to 10,000	20	1,000
10,000 and above	30	($12,000) Tax paid $10,000 to $50,000
		$13,400 Total tax paid on income of $50,000

EXERCISE Do you agree with the principle of a progressive tax?

Proportional taxation

In proportional taxation, a flat rate is levied, say 25%. A low income is taxed at 25% but so is a high income. However, the high income pays more in tax because 25% of $50,000 ($12,500) is more than 25% of $10,000 ($2,500). A proportional tax (a flat rate tax) is very simple in application and is favoured by Jamaica.

Regressive taxation

Properly speaking, in regressive taxation, the tax rate would fall as income rises (or increase as income falls). A lump sum tax is a regressive tax. The same amount of money is taken in tax whatever the income. Therefore, it forms a bigger percentage of a low income than a high income. Poll taxes are regressive; a poll tax is one of a fixed amount per head of the population.

> **Definitions of different taxation principles**
>
> A progressive tax is one where the higher the income of the person, the larger the percentage of total income paid in tax.
>
> A proportional tax is one where the percentage of total income paid in tax remains the same at different income levels.
>
> A regressive tax is one where higher income earners pay a lower proportion of their income in tax compared to lower income earners.

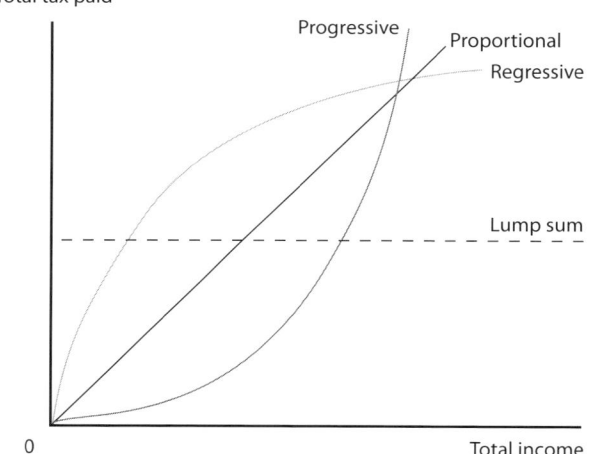

Fig. 15.3
Total tax paid under four tax systems

The two direct taxes which bring most revenue in Jamaica are: PIT (personal income tax), at a flat rate of 25%, and CIT (Company/Corporation Income Tax) at 33.3%.

The disincentive of steep progressivity

In the 1980s, fiscal policy was under review in many countries. Some countries had steeply progressive tax rates rising through eight brackets to a top bracket in which incomes were taxed at over 80%. Thus, some tax systems were very complicated and the 'super tax' bracket was certainly a **disincentive** to work harder and earn more.

Why enter the top bracket when the government took 80 cents and you were left with only 20 cents!

So, early in the 1980s, economists, such as Professor Art Laffer in the United States, questioned whether such high tax rates yielded more **or less** revenue for the government. They argued that steeply progressive tax rates were a disincentive to increase income and that lower tax rates would actually yield more tax revenue. President Reagan of the United States and Margaret Thatcher, the British Prime Minister, were persuaded to cut tax rates, certainly to lower the rate in the top bracket, and to simplify tax systems. Also, many Caribbean countries decided to change their fiscal policies at that time. The UK income tax was simplified to three brackets and the top tax rate was 40%.

The Laffer curve

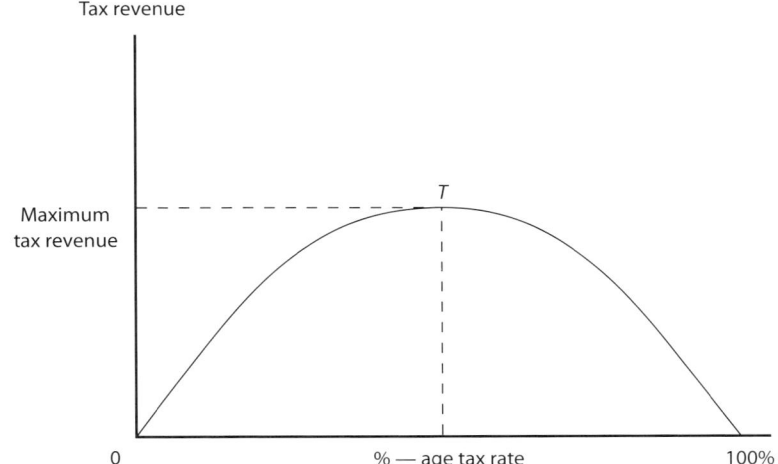

Fig. 15.4
The Laffer curve showing that tax revenue falls when the tax rate passes a certain rate

This curve had a great influence over a number of Ministers of Finance.

At a zero tax rate, there is no tax revenue. As the tax rate rises, tax revenue increases but at a slower and slower rate showing that there is a disincentive resulting from increasing tax rates. There comes a point, T, where, if the minister increases tax rates further, tax revenue will actually fall. After T, disincentives have become stronger and stronger. When the tax rate reaches 100% all income would be taken in tax and no one would bother to work and the government would have no tax revenue!

Where is T? Is it 40%, 50% or 60%? Does the Minister of Finance have to use trial and error? The United Kingdom chose 40% as its top tax rate.

EXERCISE What do you think the top rate of income tax should be in an economy?

Indirect taxation

Indirect taxes are taxes on expenditure on goods and services. If you do not want to pay these taxes, you do not buy the goods! However, some goods are essential and these are usually exempt from tax or are 'zero-rated', e.g. basic foods, children's clothes and sometimes books. The most common indirect tax is VAT (value added tax). In Jamaica it is known as GCT (general consumption tax) and is levied at 15%.

Indirect taxes are regressive because they take more of a low income than a high income. If you have to pay 15% VAT on a television set priced at EC$1,000, you will pay $150 in tax. $150 is a bigger proportion of an income of $3,000 than it is of an income $6,000, 5% as against 2.5%.

EXERCISE Explain why VAT is a regressive tax.

In Jamaica there is also SCT (special consumption tax) which is levied on petroleum products, alcoholic beverages and tobacco products. (Taxes on alcohol and tobacco are sometimes known as 'sin taxes'!)

Indirect taxes are usually proportional taxes, e.g. VAT, but they can be lump sum also, e.g. a tax of EC$2 on a ticket to a pop concert whatever the price of the seat.

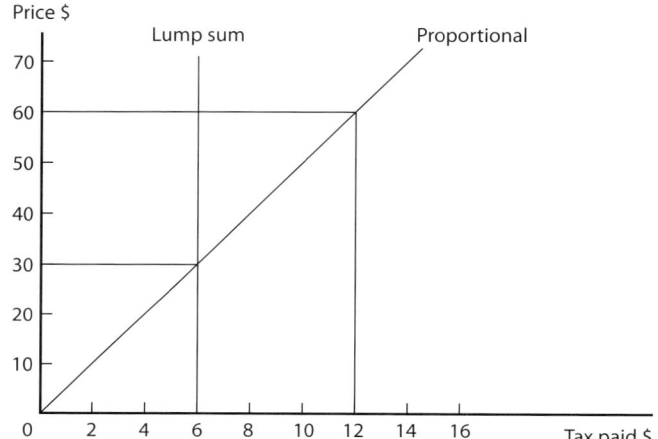

Fig. 15.5
Indirect taxes

The proportional tax is 20%. However, a tax of $12 is a bigger proportion of a low income than a high income. In the case of indirect taxes, a proportional tax is regressive. The lump sum tax above is $6 whatever the price of the good.

Some economists argue that indirect taxes are not regressive because the rich consume more expensive goods than the poor, e.g. a rich man drinks champagne at EC$100 a bottle and a poor man drinks beer at $2 a bottle. Therefore, at 15% VAT, a rich man is paying $15 for his drink and a poor man is paying only 30 cents for his. This is being too clever! If rich and poor consume the same goods, VAT is regressive!

Fiscal policy and indirect tax

Indirect taxes are taxes on goods. These taxes will raise the most revenue for the government in relation to the price of the good when the **price elasticity of demand is inelastic** (see Chapter 9). That is the basis for the special consumption taxes in Jamaica. They are levied on petroleum products, alcoholic drinks and tobacco

Taxes on cigarettes are sometimes known as 'sin taxes'.

Source: Stillpictures.

products. All these are highly inelastic in demand, i.e. if you raise the price, demand falls very little.

'Sin taxes' are put on alcohol and tobacco. These two goods are addictive which means demand is highly inelastic. A rise in the price of cigarettes is not likely to reduce demand by very much. The first reaction of consumers is to cut back but very soon demand is back to its former level. The Minister of Finance knows that raising taxes on cigarettes is certain to increase tax revenue.

EXERCISE Do you think it is right that such a high proportion of the price of alcohol or cigarettes should be in the form of taxation?

In Chapter 6, we looked at the **determinants of supply**. One of them was **'the costs of the factors of production'**. We said then that an indirect tax is like a cost of a factor of production. **An indirect tax shifts the supply curve upwards to the left by the vertical amount of the tax.** The diagram below illustrates this.

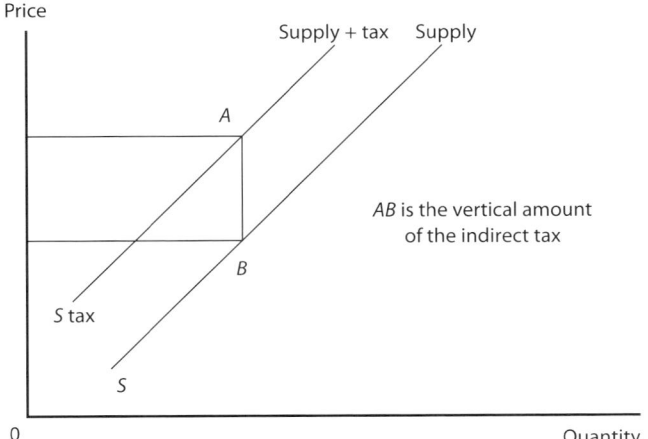

Fig. 15.6
The effect of an indirect tax on the supply curve

However, we need the demand curve to know what will happen to price and government revenue. The demand curve will be drawn steeply to show that demand is inelastic. The effect on price and revenue can be read from the diagram.

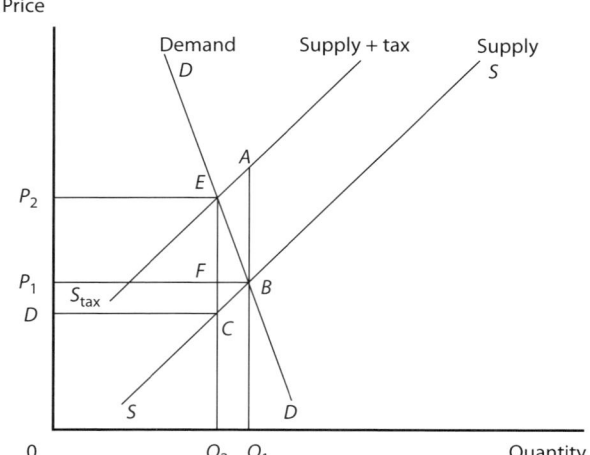

Fig. 15.7
Graph showing the effect on price and revenue of an indirect tax with an inelastic demand curve

AB is the vertical amount of the tax. It has shifted the supply curve upwards to the left from S to S tax. The equilibrium between demand and supply has moved from point B to point E and the price has risen from P_1 to P_2.

a The consumer has to pay a higher price.

Revenue is the price of the good multiplied by the quantity bought, $R = P \times Q$. Before the tax, the revenue was the rectangle $P_1 \, B \, Q_1 \, O$. After the tax, the revenue is $P_2 \, E \, Q_2 \, O$. However, the supplier has to give some of this revenue to the government in tax. The government's tax revenue is measured by the rectangle $P_2 \, E \, C \, D$. The supplier is left with the rectangle $D \, C \, Q_2 \, O$.

b The government has done very well out of the tax. Quantity demanded has fallen very little because demand is inelastic but price has risen very much from P_1 to P_2. (Not by the vertical amount of the tax because the demand curve is not vertical.)

Examination Tip

> The link between the imposition of a tax and the price elasticity of demand is very important. Make sure you fully understand what is involved.

The incidence of the tax

Definition of the incidence of a tax

The incidence of a tax means on whom the tax falls, i.e. who pays the tax.

The supplier must hand over the tax to the government, but he can recover some of it from the consumer. The supplier hands over $P_2 \, E \, C \, D$ to the government, but can recover $P_2 \, E \, F \, P_1$ from the consumer. In fact, the supplier has only paid $P_1 \, F \, C \, D$ and the consumer has paid most of the tax. In our example, the incidence of the tax is mainly on the consumer. This is the case with 'sin taxes'. Consumers are made to pay for their sins!

Therefore, it is common fiscal policy to increase indirect taxes on goods with inelastic demand.

Subsidies

Subsidies are payments or grants by the government to the supplier in order to lower the costs to the supplier and to increase supplies. They are the opposite of taxes and have the opposite effect to taxes on the supply curve. A subsidy shifts the supply curve downwards to the right by the vertical amount of the subsidy. Subsidies are part of national budget plans and are therefore part of fiscal policy.

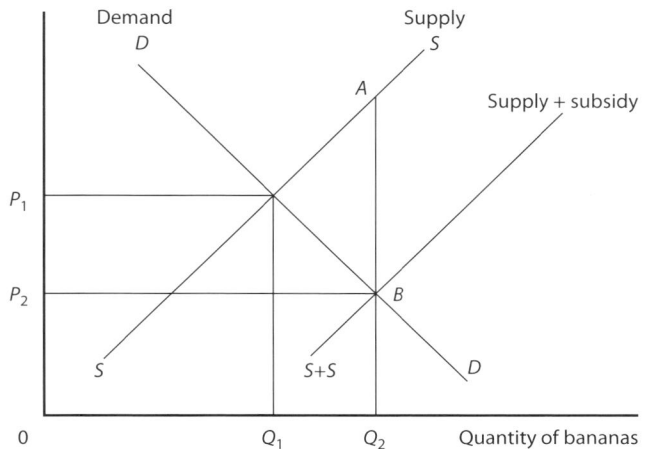

Fig. 15.8
The effect of a subsidy

The subsidy is measured by AB. It shifts the supply curve downwards to the right by AB, the vertical distance between the supply curves. This increases supply from Q_1 to Q_2 and lowers the price from P_1 to P_2. It has the same effect of lowering the cost of production.

Dr Ralph Gonsalves, the Prime Minister of St Vincent and the Grenadines, who is also Minister of Finance, decided to continue to subsidise the banana growers through 2005 with a subsidy of more than EC$1,750,000. He had two main reasons for doing this:

a   to assist producers after Hurricane Ivan which damaged 25% of the crop and;

b   to enable banana farmers to improve their farms and farming techniques to face new competition in the industry.

Prime Minister Gonsalves subsidised banana growers in St Vincent and the Grenadines in 2005.

Subsidies are not common and they are discouraged by the World Trade Organisation in its pursuit of **free trade**. For example, the fishing industry in the Caribbean has been heavily subsidised over the past twenty five years because fish and fish products are such an important part of the food consumption of Caribbean countries. There are still some fish subsidies but they have been removed or reduced by many Caribbean countries.

EXERCISE Consider whether it is right to subsidise some types of production.

The national debt

The national debt belongs to fiscal policy because managing the national debt is part of the budget each year. The Minister of Finance decides in the budget whether to run a budget deficit, i.e. whether expenditure will exceed revenue from taxation and other sources. If there is a deficit, the difference must be made up by borrowing from the public, hence the national debt.

Students often worry about the national debt because it seems that the country 'cannot make ends meet'. There are, however, ways of looking at the national debt which will remove the causes of concern.

1. It is a debt to oneself. The citizens lend their own government money. They are lending it to themselves in a way.

2. It is always there. There is no need to repay the debt. If some citizens who have lent the government money want to be repaid, they can cash in their loans and not lend again. Meanwhile, other citizens will make new loans.

3. If the government did not borrow, it would have to raise taxes which is not usually very popular.

4. Having the national debt gives the government another tool of fiscal policy. It can use this tool to stimulate the economy or to calm it down, i.e. to make injections into, or withdrawals from, the circular flow of the economy.

However, there are some real concerns about the national debt.

1. Financing a budget deficit by borrowing and spending (**deficit financing**) is inflationary. (see 'The causes of inflation' in the next chapter). It is an injection of money into the economy.

2. Increasing the size of the national debt to keep taxes lower is popular with the present generation who have low taxes but repaying the national debt by raising taxes later is not popular with the next generation of tax payers. That is called **'intergenerational theft'**, i.e. stealing from one generation to pay for another generation's benefits.

3. If the government borrows from the public through the public sector borrowing requirement (PSBR), there are less loans from the public available to the private sector. This is called **'crowding out'**. The government does not have first call on the public's money, but the public will always lend to the government because it is safe to do so. Also the government can always make the loan attractive.

> **Definitions of finance terms**
>
> Deficit financing is where the government borrows money.
>
> Intergenerational theft is making a later generation pay the debts of a previous generation.
>
> Crowding out is the diverting by the government of money away from the private sector.

External debt

This is also part of the budget and therefore plays a part in fiscal policy. Nearly all Caribbean countries have external debt, sometimes called 'foreign debt'.

> **Definition of an external debt**
>
> External debt is money owed to foreign countries or foreign institutions, such as banks. It can be divided into multilateral and bilateral debt.

When a country borrows from international lenders like the International Bank for Reconstruction and Development (the World Bank), the Caribbean Development Bank and the European Union, there are very many lender countries so the debt is to many parties, i.e. it is multilateral.

When a country borrows from an individual country, it is entering bilateral debt, i.e. debt between two parties, the lender and the borrower. Many Commonwealth Caribbean countries borrow from Britain with which they had historical links but Jamaica, for example, also borrows from Germany, Kuwait and the Netherlands.

External debt is more of a cause for concern because it is a debt to a foreigner and must be repaid. Caribbean Ministers of Finance tend to keep foreign borrowing low, especially in comparison with domestic borrowing.

EXERCISE

Should we be worried about the size of a country's national debt?

Examination questions

1 Distinguish, with the aid of examples, between direct and indirect taxes. *(10 marks)*

2 Distinguish between progressive, regressive and proportional taxation. *(10 marks)*

3 Draw a demand and a supply diagram. Show and explain the effects of introducing **(a)** an indirect tax and **(b)** a subsidy. *(10 marks)*

4 Explain why a budget may not always balance. *(10 marks)*

5 Distinguish between multilateral and bilateral debt. *(5 marks)*

Inflation and causes and consequences of inflation

In this chapter you will be studying inflation in all its aspects: what inflation is, the causes and consequences of inflation and government policies to deal with it.

- You will start with the definition of inflation and the implication of the two key phrases in the definition
- You may be surprised to learn that inflation is not always 'a bad thing' and that the **rates of inflation** are what matter
- Then come the causes of inflation: the monetarist explanation and explanations of demand–pull and cost–push inflation
- Finally, you will deal with the consequences of inflation and come back again to the realisation that inflation is not always 'a bad thing'

Inflation and deflation

> **Definition of inflation**
>
> Inflation is the persistent tendency for the general level of prices to rise over a period of time.

It must be 'persistent' because prices rise and fall, especially seasonal prices in fruit and vegetables. The price rise must be going on over time, i.e. 'persisting'. It must be the 'general level of prices' because some prices are rising while others are falling, e.g. the prices of micro-electrical goods are tending to fall in the present day while fuel prices are tending to rise. In Chapter 12 on Money, we examined the calculation of inflation through the Consumer Price Index. A comprehensive Consumer Price Index includes every good or service that is purchased by the average household over a time period and it is updated from time to time as consumer tastes change. Therefore there is balance between falling prices and rising prices in this index.

EXERCISE Find out the current rate of inflation in your country. Is the trend over the last few months upwards or downwards?

> **Definition of deflation**
>
> Deflation is the persistent tendency for the general level of prices to fall over a period of time.

In the first instance students will probably think that deflation is 'a good thing' –

falling prices – fantastic! However, falling prices are not usually desirable in the broad view of the economy, as we shall see. They may be desirable in a particular case at a particular time, but not for the economy as a whole.

EXERCISE Try to think why falling prices might not be good for an economy.

Acceptable and unacceptable rates of inflation

(Later in the chapter we shall be studying the **consequences of inflation** so here we are just taking an overall view.)

Governments aim to have inflation under control. They recognise that a low rate of inflation, a target rate, is good for the economy and that a 'creeping' inflation may be tolerable. A high rate of inflation, however, is seen as bad for the economy and a 'runaway' inflation or 'galloping' (inflation out of control) and hyperinflation (the most famous example is Germany's hyperinflation of 1923) are viewed as disastrous. So what are the levels we are talking about?

An inflation rate of 0–1% would be considered too low, probably signalling too little activity in the economy in the form of a lack of demand. Rising demand shows rising incomes, a sign of economic growth.

An inflation rate of 2% is often a target rate of inflation. The general level of prices is rising, but it is under control. There is a healthy increase in demand and the economy is growing. So a government may be aiming at an inflation rate of between 1–2%. If the rate exceeds 2%, the government may consider deflationary policies are needed in order to check demand.

However, some governments would accept higher inflation rates, even up to 5%. This is the case with developing economies where there is faster growth and increasing demand, pushing up prices beyond 2%. Therefore, these countries are targeting rates between 2–5%. These governments would only act to stop the 'overheating' of the economy if the rate went above 5%.

Therefore, rates above 5% are above the target and deflationary action may need to be taken. Inflation still may not be out of control, but it must be monitored very carefully. If prices were rising faster than 5%, incomes would need to be rising above 5% for living standards to be maintained. If trade unions push for wage increases of above 5%, because workers always expect their living standards to improve, this may make firms raise prices even more and the economy will enter an inflationary spiral → higher prices → higher wages → higher prices → higher wages … The brakes must be put on!

Remember that inflation = rising prices = fall in the value of money. When your grandfather says 'I can remember when a bottle of beer was 20 cents in 1960' (and it is now $2), he is implying a 'golden age' of his youth when money was worth ten times more than today. Money has fallen in value. (You should reply: 'But grandfather, would you like the wages of those days?' and then run away quickly! Everyone would like the prices of 45 years ago and the wages of today!)

Therefore, governments must be concerned about the fall in the value of money. If your country's money (its 'currency') is falling in value, investors will not want to invest as their investments would fall in value. Your country's exchange rate would depreciate (fall in value) and you would have to pay more for your imports. Foreigners would be put off your goods because your prices are rising. Therefore, when inflation rates are approaching 10%, something must be done or the economy could be heading for trouble. For the year September 2004 to September 2005, Jamaica's rate of inflation was 19% (Statistical Institute of Jamaica). Inflation is a recurring cause of concern in Jamaica.

Economists do not give a precise figure for hyperinflation but when Brazil's inflation in 1989 reached 1,765% (yes, 1,765%!), it was on the brink of hyperinflation. Hyperinflation is disastrous because money loses all value. People try to get rid of their money as quickly as possible and turn it into other assets which might protect their savings. Barter becomes the means of exchange. Foreign currencies are used if possible. Investment does not take place. Trade stops. Eventually the currency has to be reissued. In 1994 Brazil issued the Real. In July 1994, price increases dropped dramatically and hyperinflation was over.

The causes of inflation

Milton Friedman, the US economist, and winner of the Nobel Prize for Economics in 1976, said: '**Inflation is always and everywhere a monetary phenomenon.**' Therefore let us start with the monetarist cause. Some economists and governments have been influenced by Friedman and have come back to the idea that inflation is caused by 'too much money chasing too few goods'.

In 1906, the economist Irving Fisher put forward the idea of the quantity theory of money which relates the level of prices to the amount of money in the economy.

The quantity theory of money

Professor Fisher produced a simple equation to explain this theory. Many economists have elaborated on this equation since 1906, but the basic 'Fisher equation' is one that is behind today's thinking on the causes of inflation.

The Fisher equation: $MV = PT$

Where M is the amount of money, the stock of money or the money supply.
Where V is the velocity of circulation, the rate at which money changes hands. Money can finance many different transactions as it goes from hand to hand.

If $5 finances transactions worth $20, the velocity of circulation is $\frac{\$20}{\$5} = 4$

In the economy as a whole the formula for V is $\frac{\text{Gross Domestic Product}}{\text{Money supply}}$

where P is the price level,
where T is the number of transactions taking place in the economy.

The left-hand side of the equation, MV, is the money supply multiplied by the number of times it goes round in the economy. The right-hand side, PT, is the number of transactions multiplied by the price at which they take place.

The right-hand side of the equation is the national income. The left-hand side is the money supply. The right-hand side of the equation must be equal to the left-hand side, because the total expenditure in the economy, the national income, must be financed with the amount of money in the economy, i.e. the money supply times the velocity of circulation. Therefore, the Fisher equation can be re-written:

$$MV \equiv PT$$

where $\equiv$ is 'necessarily equal to'.

The next step was for Fisher to recognise V and T as constants, i.e. quantities which remained the same while the variables, M and P, may change. We re-write the equation to show this:

$$M\bar{V} \equiv P\bar{T}$$

If V and T are constants, P must vary with M.

Let us work through an example:

$M = \$1,000; V = 4: P = \$8; T + 500$

Thus: $\$1,000 \times 4 = \$8 \times 500$.
Therefore: $\$4,000 = \$4,000$, the right-hand side is financed by the left-hand side.

Suppose the money supply increased to $1,500. Remember V and T are constants. What would happen to P?

$\$1,500 \times 4 = P \times 500$. Turn the equation round to find P.

$$P = \frac{\$1,500 \times 4}{500} \quad P = \frac{\$6,000}{500} \quad \text{Therefore } P = \$12$$

The money supply increased by 50% and the price level increased by 50%. The price level varies in direct proportion to the money supply. When the money supply increases, the price level increases. The money supply depends on the price level. **Therefore inflation is caused by increases in the money supply.**

As I said before, the quantity theory of money as explained by the Fisher equation has had a great influence on governments (and economic advisers to governments) in the last thirty years. Governments realised that to control inflation, they had to control the money supply. Control of the money supply is through **monetary policy**.

> **Definition of monetary policy**
> Monetary policy is concerned with the money supply and/or the rate of interest.

John Maynard Keynes and his wife. Keynes concentrated on aggregate demand in terms of demand–pull inflation.

Demand–pull inflation

This explanation for the cause of inflation is from the economic theory of John Maynard Keynes, a UK economist of great influence in the 1930s and throughout the Second World War and its aftermath. In 1936, he wrote his most famous work, *General Theory of Employment, Interest and Money*. His followers are called 'Keynesians' and there is supposed to be a great conflict in Economics between Keynesians and Monetarists.

We shall return to monetary policy later in the book.

> **Definition of aggregate demand**
>
> Aggregate demand is the total expenditure on goods and services in the economy.

Aggregate demand is made up of consumption expenditure, investment, government expenditure and net exports (exports – imports). (You may remember that these are the injections into the circular flow.)

$$AD = C + I + G + X - M$$

Where AD is aggregate demand, C is consumption expenditure, I is investment, G is government expenditure, X is exports, M is imports and $X - M$ is net exports.

If aggregate demand increases, there will be economic growth because suppliers will respond to increased demand by supplying more goods and services. To supply more goods and services, more factors of production will have to be employed. So far, so good for the economy.

The problem arises when supply cannot respond to an increase in aggregate demand because all resources are fully employed. Then an increase in aggregate demand will drive up prices. This is the **demand–pull inflation** explanation for the cause of inflation. Keynes put this explanation in a graph of which a simplified version is given below.

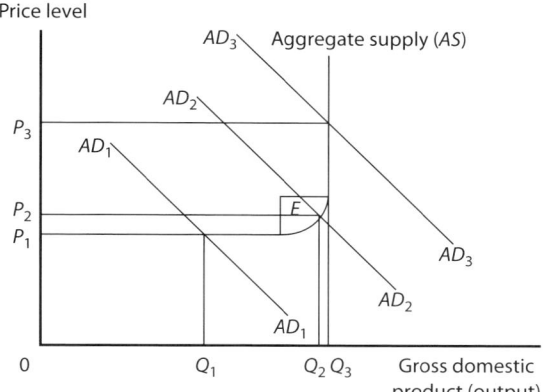

Fig. 16.1 Demand–pull inflation

The aggregate supply curve, AS, shows the total supply in the economy with the available factors of production. At AD_1, the price level is at P_1 and there is no inflationary pressure as the AS curve is perfectly elastic (horizontal straight line). At AD_2, the 'elbow', E, has been reached and the full employment level is near. There is the beginning of inflationary pressure as more supply is squeezed out of the factors of production, but the price level has had to rise to P_2. After the elbow, the AS curve is completely inelastic (vertical straight line). Supply cannot be increased and with increased demand to AD_3, prices shoot up to P_3. Between AD_2 and AD_3 there is **demand–pull inflation**.

Governments faced with demand–pull inflation would tackle the components of aggregate demand by **monetary or fiscal policy**, e.g. raising direct or indirect taxes would choke off consumption expenditure by households. Again, we shall be dealing with policy later.

Cost–push inflation

Cost–push inflation occurs because of a rise in the costs of production. Firms try to pass on their increased costs in the form of higher prices to the consumer.

> **Definition of aggregate supply**
>
> Aggregate supply, AS, is the total output of all the firms in the economy at any given price level.

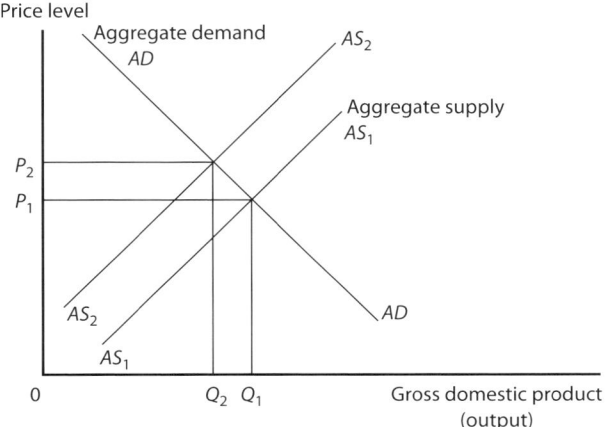

Fig. 16.2 Cost–push inflation

The AS curve shifts upwards to the left with a rise in the costs of the factors of production. The level of output shrinks from Q_1 to Q_2 and the price level rises from P_1 to P_2.

Increased wage demands by trade unions drive up costs. Firms will try to pass these costs on in the form of higher prices but they may also be forced to cut back on production if the costs of production rise. **Elasticity is very important**. If demand is inelastic, firms have more chance of passing on the higher costs in higher prices without cutting back on production. If, on the other hand, demand is elastic, raising prices will choke off demand and the firm will have to cut back on production drastically. For example, if oil prices rise and oil is a big cost in production, there will be cost–push inflation certainly because firms will pass on the higher costs in higher prices of petroleum products facing inelastic demand–transport costs will rise, but demand for transport will hardly fall at all. The 1973–74 oil crisis, when oil prices rose fourfold, led to worldwide inflation.

Cost–push inflation is often called **'imported inflation'**. You can think of oil again. If the costs of imports rise and demand for imports is inelastic, the costs of firms will rise and will be passed on to consumers in higher prices.

Note that if a rise in wages is accompanied by an increase in productivity, there will not be cost–push inflation. That is why trade unions are always being told by firms that there must be increased productivity before wage demands can be met.

The inflationary spiral

When demand–pull and cost–push inflation interact, we have the phenomenon called the inflationary spiral. It is difficult to know what starts the spiral, whether it is cost–push or demand–pull.

Suppose that trade unions succeed in forcing up wages across the board: cost–push inflation. Firms raise prices: cost–push inflation. Workers demand higher wages because of inflation. They succeed in winning higher wages and demand more goods and services: demand–pull inflation. One firm's prices are another firm's costs: cost–push inflation. Prices rise → workers demand higher wages → costs rise → prices rise, and so on. The economy has entered an inflationary spiral.

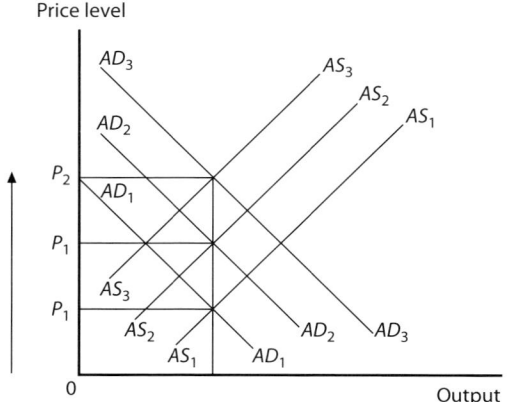

Fig. 16.3
The inflationary spiral

EXERCISE Try and find out what have been the main causes of inflation in your country.

The consequences of inflation

Inflation is the persistent tendency for the general level of prices to rise and provided that the rate of inflation is low, anticipated and under control, it can be good for the economy. Conversely, inflation of a high rate, unanticipated and out of control, is very bad for the economy.

The beneficial consequences of inflation

A redistribution of income

While the general level of prices is rising, some prices are rising and others are not and some prices are rising faster than others. There will be a **redistribution of income** from those whose incomes are not rising to those whose incomes are rising. In demand–pull inflation, goods in shops will probably rise in price while their costs of the factors of production may not be rising in price. There will be a redistribution of income from suppliers to retailers.

Harrison's Department Store, Bridgetown. Retail outlets can benefit from inflation.

Rising prices signal rising profits for those whose costs are not rising. This is very important in the economy as it leads to a redistribution of resources into those parts of the economy where profits are rising and out of those parts of the economy where profits are falling, or not rising as fast. Some industries are booming and others are declining and inflation can speed up this process. Economics teaches hard lessons. This one is that there is often no point in trying to save declining industries. If the industry is sick, let it die quickly, so that resources can be diverted into the flourishing industries.

In inflation there is a redistribution of income from **lenders to borrowers**. In inflation, the value of money is falling. Therefore, a borrower has to pay back less **in real terms** than he or she borrowed. If a person borrowed $1,000 for a year and the yearly rate of inflation was 5%, he or she would be paying back approximately $950.

Definition of real monetary values

Real terms are money values corrected for the effects of inflation. They are monetary terms deflated by the consumer price index.

A lender can allow for the rate of inflation in setting the interest rate. A lender will set an interest rate plus the rate of inflation. The rate of inflation will be built into the interest rate. If the lender wants 5% interest and the rate of inflation is 5%, he or she will set the rate of interest at 10%.

However, there will still be a redistribution of income from lenders to borrowers if the correct rate of inflation is not anticipated. This happens when the rate of inflation is not forecast accurately.

Taking out a mortgage to buy a house in inflation is a very good step, other things being equal, especially if it is taken out at a low fixed rate of interest. This is because house price inflation is often higher than the consumer price index and the lender has based the rate of interest on the latter inflation rate. Over twenty five years the borrower can do very well.

If the cause of inflation is cost–push, wage earners may benefit because the firm may not be able to pass on the rising costs in the form of higher prices, or it can raise prices, but not by as much as wages rise. Therefore workers with higher incomes face prices which have not risen or not risen as fast as their wages.

Finally, taxpayers can benefit because the government sets tax rates in the budget for the whole year. If inflation throughout the year is greater than anticipated and taxpayers' incomes have risen in line with inflation, taxpayers are paying less tax in real terms. There is a redistribution of income from the government to taxpayers. However, taxpayers may not benefit if wage inflation takes them into a higher tax bracket.

Unfavourable consequences of inflation

People on fixed incomes can suffer in inflation. Pensioners are often sufferers because their pensions are fixed, and in an inflationary situation, prices are rising. Even if the pensions are **index linked**, they can suffer relative to other income earners in society because their pensions do not rise as fast as other incomes.

> **Definition of index linking**
>
> Index linking or indexation is the system by which wages are directly linked to the consumer price index.

Pensioners are in a weak position because they do not usually have a trade union to argue their case. It could be argued that pensioners should have their pensions linked not to prices but to other incomes. Then they would not become poorer relative to other groups in society as they have become in most countries in the last fifty years.

Everyone suffers in demand–pull inflation when firms are enjoying rising prices and increasing profits and they become careless about efficiency. Firms do not have to worry about cutting costs or even the quality of the products when they are selling more and more goods at higher and higher prices in inflation.

On the other hand, firms themselves can suffer in demand–pull inflation. They are enjoying rising prices but to have to keep changing their price lists adds to their costs. Such costs are called **'menu costs'**.

Definition of menu costs
Menu costs are the costs of changing prices in an inflationary situation.

Menu costs vary according to (a) the rate of the inflation and (b) the nature of the business. If the rate of inflation is low, menu costs may not be a factor at all but if the rate inflation is high, especially approaching hyperinflation, menu costs can be considerable. Imagine repricing in a supermarket everyday or even several times a day! Petrol stations can have high menu costs when oil prices are frequently changing. Their pumps sometimes have to be reset almost daily. Vending machine businesses also face steep menu costs. The operator will have to drive around town resetting the vending machines for all increases in prices, again possibly on a daily basis.

Prices have to be changed continually during high levels of inflation.

There can be a redistribution from taxpayers to the government (we have seen the other way round above). This occurs in progressive tax systems when incomes are rising and income earners move into higher tax brackets and have to pay more in taxes. (This does not happen if the government anticipates the rate of inflation accurately and sets the tax brackets accordingly.)

To sum up: in general terms anticipated inflation can be beneficial or it can have no unfavourable consequences. Unanticipated inflation will have benefits to some, but severe hardships to others. Hyperinflation, as explained earlier in the chapter, is disastrous for an economy.

EXERCISE

Think about who is likely to benefit from inflation and who is likely to be badly affected by it.

Examination questions

1 a What is meant by inflation? *(4 marks)*
   b Compare and contrast the possible causes of inflation *(6 marks)*

2 Discuss the beneficial and the unfavourable consequences of inflation. *(10 marks)*

3 Distinguish between inflation and deflation. *(5 marks)*

4 Explain what is meant by the quantity theory of money. *(5 marks)*

CHAPTER 17

Policies to deal with inflation

Monetary stability (keeping prices stable) is most important in an economy. If prices rise, the value of money falls and confidence in the economy is lost so the government must control inflation. In this chapter:

- You will have the difference between monetary and fiscal policy explained in detail
- You will learn how the government controls the money supply through the reserve base
- Interest rates to control the money supply are then dealt with
- In fiscal policy, you will revisit direct and indirect taxation and government spending
- The chapter concludes with supply side policies to deal with inflation

Deflation is not such an important consideration. However, if deflation were to occur, falling prices would act more directly on the economy than rising prices. Producers would not be willing to produce if the prices of the goods they produced were falling. Without production, there would be no employment of the factors of production. Households would have no incomes. The whole economy would quickly grind to a halt.

The government deals with inflation through **monetary and fiscal policies** and **supply-side policies**.

> **Definition of monetary policy**
>
> Monetary Policy deals in the control of the supply of money and/or the rate of interest. It is usually decided by the Minister of Finance in consultation with the Central Bank of the country.

Governments use a combination of monetary, fiscal and supply-side policies to deal with inflation, depending on its causes. As we gave the first cause of inflation as being the monetary cause ('too much money chasing too few goods'), let us deal with monetary policy first.

Monetary policy

As well as being divided into money supply and interest rate policies, it can also be divided into long-term and short-term policies. Roughly speaking, control of the money supply is a long-term policy and use of interest rates is a short-term policy:

Monetary policy	
Money supply	Interest rates
Long-term	Short-term

The definitions of narrow and broad money were given in Chapter 12.

Aggregate demand, especially the consumption, expenditure and investment components of aggregate demand, is financed with this money supply. Commercial banks and other financial institutions enable their customers to write cheques on their accounts, have overdrafts and take out loans. They are private, profit-making institutions and the government cannot interfere with their operations except in a very subtle way. It is in this subtle way that the Minister of Finance through the Central Bank controls the money supply in most Caribbean countries.

There are two operational tools used by Central Banks:

1 The monetary base (reserve base) of the money supply.
2 Open market operations.

How the monetary base works

Commercial banks do not need to keep their customers' deposits in cash at the bank. They only need to keep a percentage in cash, enough to meet withdrawals. The ratio of cash to deposits is very important; a bank must keep enough cash to meet withdrawals. If a customer were to ask to withdraw money from his or her account, and the bank said that it did not have the money, the bank would 'crash'. On the other hand, if the bank were not making profits by lending out customers' deposits at interest, the shareholders would not be happy. Therefore, commercial banks must hold some cash at all times, but must be lending out as much money as possible.

In Jamaica and other Caribbean countries, the central bank (the Bank of Jamaica) *by law* can require the commercial banks to keep deposits *in cash* at the central bank. This is called **'the monetary base'**. Control of the monetary base gives the central bank control over the long-term money supply.

1 To reduce the money supply, the central bank would require the commercial banks to deposit more cash at the central bank. They would have to respect this order by law. Therefore, they would have to reduce their own holdings of cash. This would make their cash ratio unsafe, i.e. they would not have enough cash to meet customers' withdrawals. Therefore, they would have to stop making loans, or call in loans. Thus the money supply is reduced.

2 To increase the money supply, the central bank would require the commercial banks to reduce their cash deposits at the central bank. This would increase the cash they held so that they would be more than safe in meeting customers' withdrawals. Therefore, they would be able to lend out more money to their customers and thus increase the money supply.

If the government felt that inflation needed to be reduced, it could increase the cash base of the money supply. This would reduce aggregate demand and prevent demand-pull inflation.

How open market operations (OMO) work

Open market operations is the method favoured by the Bank of Jamaica to control the money supply and other countries use OMO in varying degrees. Open market operations concern the buying and selling of government bills, bonds and other government securities in the market for securities.

Suppose the bank wishes to reduce the money supply. It will sell securities on the open market. Members of the public will buy these securities. They will pay for them by cheques drawn on their commercial banks. These cheques will be made payable to the central bank. The commercial banks are in debt to the central bank to the amount of these cheques. The central bank settles these debts by reducing the deposits of the commercial banks at the central bank. Therefore, the commercial banks have reduced the monetary (reserve) base of the money supply. They will have to restore this base to the required level. Therefore they will have to curtail their lending or call in loans so that they can top up their deposits at the central bank. Thus, the central bank has reduced the money supply by selling securities on the open market.

How is the central bank sure that the public will buy these securities when offered for sale? The government broker who sells the securities is clever. Apart from the fact that he knows the public always wants to lend to the government because the public is sure the loan will be repaid and it will earn some interest, he can increase the rate of interest to make the loan more attractive. He is 'clever' in that he must adjust the rate of interest so finely that the government's cost of borrowing is not too high, but it must be high enough to attract the public.

If the government felt that inflation needed to be reduced, it could sell government securities on the open market to reduce the money supply and thus reduce aggregate demand.

Suppose the central bank decides to sell a $500 bond on the open market. In the diagram below you can trace the results **from right to left**.

Table 17.1 Open market operations

Central bank		Commercial bank		General public	
Liabilities	Assets	Liabilities	Assets	Liabilities	Assets
− $500 bond	+ $500 cheque deposited by commercial bank	− $500 payable to the Central Bank	− $500 customer's deposit	− $500 cheque drawn from account at commercial bank	+ $500 bond

Monetary policy through interest rates

Interest rates are the **cost of borrowing or the cost of money**. If money is made dearer, less will be borrowed and the money supply will be reduced. The government, through the Minister of Finance in consultation with the central bank, adjusts the rate of interest frequently to control the money supply. It is a short-term policy to deal with inflation.

Let us take the example of Trinidad and Tobago. The Central Bank of Trinidad and Tobago uses a 'Repo' Rate. This is the rate at which the central bank as 'lender of last resort' will lend to the commercial banks of Trinidad and Tobago when they are having liquidity problems, i.e. when they are short of cash. Other countries' central banks call this rate 'Bank Rate', 'Base Rate' or 'Minimum Lending Rate'.

At the end of 2005, the Central Bank of Trinidad and Tobago raised the Repo Rate to 6%. This influenced interest rates throughout the economy. Interest rates are the cost of money. If a commercial bank has to borrow at 6%, it will lend at a higher rate to its customers, say 8% or even higher. Mortgage rates and higher purchase rates will go up as will all other interest rates in the economy. This will choke off the demand for money and ease inflationary pressure.

Consumption

A person can either spend (consume) or save. **Therefore, the rate of interest is the opportunity cost of holding money.** The higher the rate of interest, the greater the cost of holding money for consumption spending. This can be shown on the **liquidity preference curve** which is the demand curve for money.

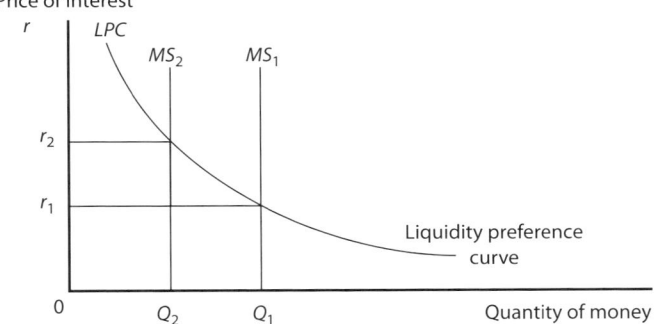

Fig. 17.1
The liquidity preference curve

If the Central Bank raises the rate of interest from r_1 to r_2, the public's demand for money, the money supply, will fall from Q_1 to Q_2. This will reduce inflationary pressure by reducing consumption spending and thus the C component of aggregate demand.

Some consumption expenditure is interest elastic. Buying a car is often done on credit and if interest rates are high, the car becomes more expensive and consumption is choked off. On the other hand, consumption that does not depend on borrowing will hardly be affected by interest rates and will be interest inelastic. Also, if a person strongly wants something he or she will buy it whatever the rate of interest. However, the major purchases in a household, the house itself, the car, the consumer durables like electrical goods, will be interest elastic when they depend on borrowing. A very rich person does not have to borrow so his or her consumption will tend to be interest inelastic.

Investment

Investment is the I component of aggregate demand. Raising interest rates will also choke off investment because it will become more expensive to borrow money for investment purposes. If the rate of interest rises, the efficiency (profitability) of investment, or capital, falls. This is shown by the **marginal efficiency of investment**.

> **Definition of the marginal efficiency of investment**
>
> The marginal efficiency of investment is the return from each additional dollar of investment.

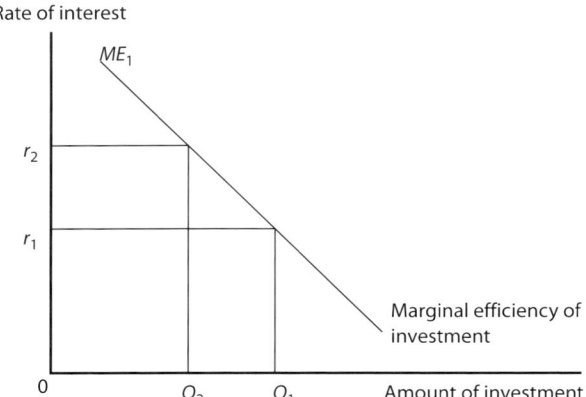

Fig. 17.2 *The marginal efficiency of investment*

If the central bank raises the rate of interest from r_1 to r_2, the amount of investment will fall from Q_1 to Q_2. This will reduce the I component of aggregate demand and reduce inflationary pressure. This is shown in the diagram below.

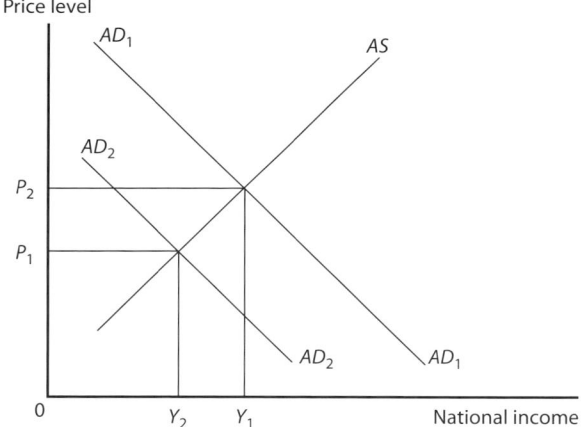

Fig. 17.3 *Controlling inflation by reducing aggregate demand*

Note that elasticity is very important. If investment is interest elastic, the percentage change in interest rates will have a big impact on investment. Conversely, if investment is interest inelastic, interest rate policy will have little effect on investment. If an entrepreneur sees a good investment opportunity, one that will bring in a high rate of return, he will not be so concerned about the cost of borrowing to finance this investment. Many economists tend to believe that investment is, on the whole, **interest inelastic**.

Fiscal policy

> **Definition of fiscal policy**
>
> Fiscal policy controls aggregate demand through taxation and government expenditure. It is usually outlined in the budget.

There are two sorts of taxes, direct and indirect. Direct taxes are taxes on income and indirect taxes are taxes on expenditure. Both can be used to reduce aggregate demand and remove inflationary pressure.

Direct taxation

If the Minister of Finance raises direct taxes in the budget, he or she will reduce disposable income and reduce the consumption component of aggregate demand, other things being equal, e.g. incomes are not rising at the same time.

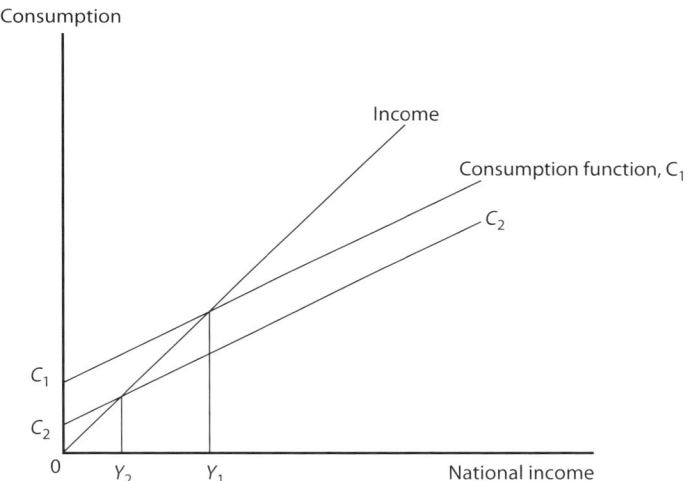

Fig. 17.4
Reducing consumption through Increasing direct taxation

> **Definition of the consumption function**
>
> The consumption function shows how consumption varies with income.

When income rises, consumption rises. The steepness of the rise shows how much consumption varies with income. The consumption function does not start at the origin as there must be some level of consumption to survive.

When consumption is reduced by increasing direct taxes, the consumption function shifts downwards from C_1 to C_2 and national income falls from Y_1 to Y_2. With less income, aggregate demand will fall and inflationary pressure will be reduced. However, lowering aggregate demand and consequently national income in this way is risking unemployment. However, the government is probably sure that there is no danger of bringing about unemployment when using this policy.

Built-in stabilisation

A progressive tax system, whereby the percentage taken in tax by the government rises as income rises, stabilises the level of consumption and thus controls inflationary pressure. It follows that the more steeply progressive, the stronger the built-in stabiliser. In simple terms, the more you earn, the more is taken in tax and the less remains for consumption. The C component of aggregate demand is kept under control automatically.

In the diagram below, as Gross Domestic Product increases, tax revenue increases because people have rising incomes and pay more tax. The rate in TR_1 is not as progressive as the rate in TR_2. Therefore, TR_2 has a greater degree of in-built stabilisation.

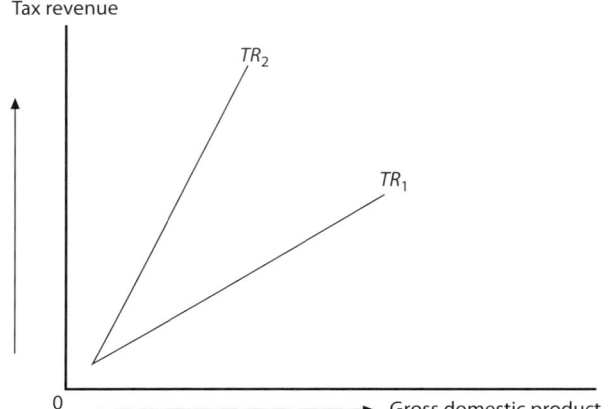

Fig. 17.5
Income tax as a built-in stabiliser

Indirect taxation

Indirect taxes are taxes on goods and services. Value added tax is a percentage of the price of the good (in Jamaica the VAT taxes are general consumption tax and the special consumption tax). Governments use indirect taxes primarily to raise revenue and not to discourage consumption, except in the case of 'sin taxes' (introduced in the previous chapter). This is because a decrease in consumption can lead to a decrease in output. To put it another way, indirect taxes can reduce aggregate demand but they can also reduce aggregate supply and this threatens unemployment.

They act indirectly on demand–pull inflation by reducing supply, raising the price and thereby choking off demand. An indirect tax shifts the supply curve upwards to the left as shown in the diagram.

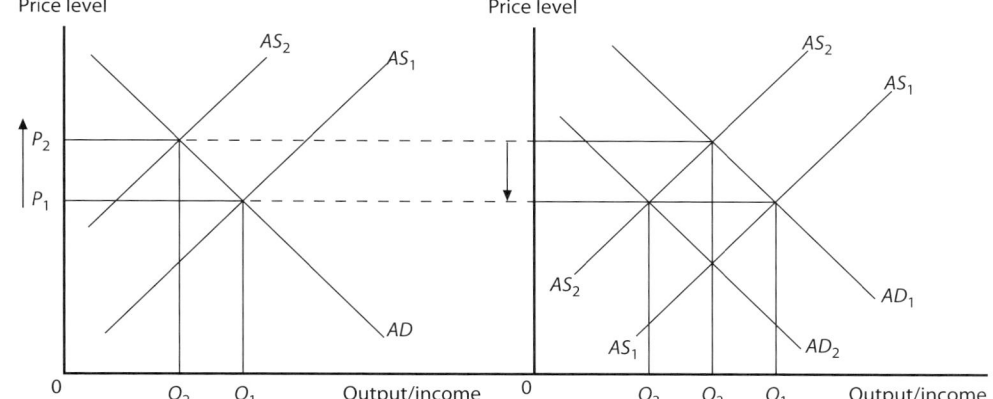

Fig. 17.6
Initial and subsequent effects of an increase in indirect tax

In diagram A, an increase in indirect taxes has shifted the aggregate supply curve upwards to the left and raised the price level from P_1 to P_2. In Diagram B, the initial effect on the same demand curve would be to choke off demand from Q_1 to Q_2, but the subsequent effect would be to lower national income, thereby shifting aggregate demand from AD_1 to AD_2 and bringing the price level back to P_1.

The central bank's policy in raising indirect taxation is to lower the price level by choking off aggregate demand. However, this can have serious effects on unemployment as we see from the output axis where output is reduced from Q_1 to Q_2 and then to Q_3.

Government expenditure

This is the *G* component of aggregate demand. In the budget, the Minister of Finance decides how much money the government is going to spend in the coming year. If he or she increases government expenditure, it could be an inflationary fiscal policy if aggregate supply is not increasing at the same time. If he or she reduces government expenditure, it could be a deflationary fiscal policy. Again, the impact on jobs in operating a deflationary fiscal policy could be severe. However, reducing government expenditure is used to combat inflation. Other measures to protect jobs must be taken at the same time. Such measures could be supply-side policies which we will look at a little later.

Government expenditure can also act as a built-in stabiliser. When Gross Domestic Product is high, government expenditure is low, and when Gross Domestic Product is low, government expenditure is high. In the diagram below, *GG* is government expenditure. It moves inversely with Gross Domestic Product. When there is inflationary pressure, government expenditure is automatically reduced, e.g there is less need to pay unemployment benefits because GDP is increasing.

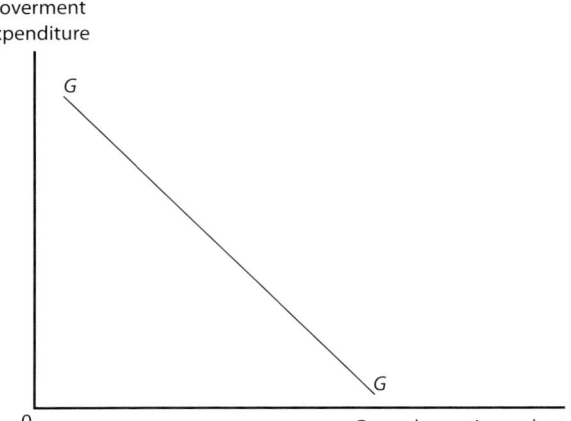

Fig. 17.7
Government expenditure as a built-in stabiliser

Supply-side policies

Definition of supply-side policies

Supply-side policies are those which are designed to influence aggregate supply, such as through the efficiency or costs of production.

Supply-side policies have become very fashionable in Economics over the past thirty years. They are positive policies in dealing with inflation (they seem to have no drawbacks) as they bring down inflation and increase output and employment at the same time.

In the diagram below, the supply-side policies shift the aggregate supply curve downwards to the right from AS_1 to AS_2. This lowers the price level from P_1 to P_2 (reduces inflation) and increases output (and employment) from Y_1 to Y_2.

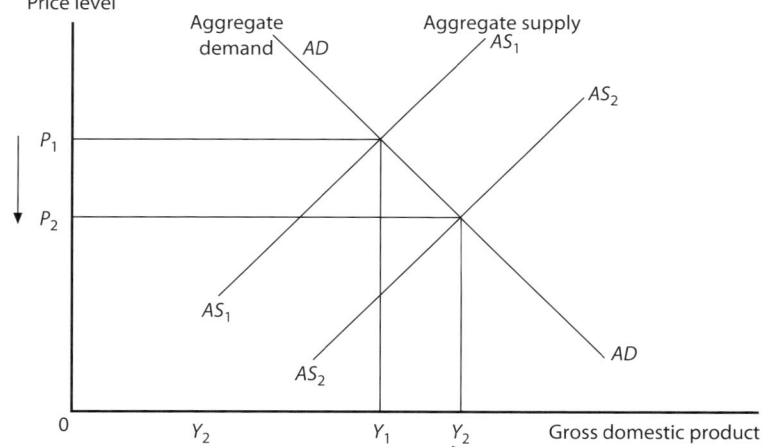

Fig. 17.8
The effect of supply-side policies

Supply-side policies improve efficiency in the use of the factors of production, land, labour, capital and enterprise.

Examples of supply-side policies include the following.

1 Privatisation. This is the selling off of nationalised industries to the private sector. It is expected that the private sector, driven by the profit motive, will cut costs and improve efficiency. The inputs will be made to achieve greater outputs.

EXERCISE Do you think it is better for firms to operate in the private rather than the public sector?

2 Ending or reducing unemployment benefit. This will bring more potential workers into the workforce and increase output. Cutting income tax rates is also an incentive to work harder as we saw when dealing with income tax and incentives in Chapter 15.

3 Introduction and improvement of technology. This is the biggest success in supply-side policies and has greatly increased output. Think of computerisation in banking. Some argue that with the increase in technology, there is the possibility of unemployment, but others argue that technology increases employment in technology-related industries. Workers have to be re-trained which brings us to the next example.

EXERCISE Can you think of any other examples of technological improvements that have increased output and productivity?

4 Re-training of workers increases workers' mobility (their ability to move from one occupation to another) and increases productivity as workers will move from declining industries, sometimes called 'sunset' industries, into new expanding industries, sometimes called 'sunrise' industries. They will be trained to work with new technology and increase output.

5 Education itself is a supply-side policy. The more educated the workforce, the more productive it is. As developing countries move from universal primary education through universal secondary education and into tertiary education, productivity is increasing. That is why Caribbean governments put such an emphasis on education.

6 When trade unions cut down the number of hours their members can work, negotiate higher rates of pay and take industrial action such as strikes, they are reducing output. Curbing the power of trade unions is a supply-side policy to increase output and lower costs.

Supply-side policies, in most cases, are slow to show benefits, but in the long run, they will bring down inflationary pressures even when there are high levels of economic growth.

Examination questions

1 Why do governments want to keep down the rate of inflation? *(10 marks)*

2 Discuss, with the aid of examples, the use of supply-side policies to bring down the rate of inflation. *(10 marks)*

3 Compare and contrast monetary and fiscal policy as methods of controlling inflation. *(10 marks)*

4 Explain, with the aid of a diagram, what is meant by the marginal efficiency of investment. *(10 marks)*

5 Explain what is meant by the consumption function. *(5 marks)*

CHAPTER 18

Unemployment: the role of trade unions

In this chapter types of unemployment will be recalled from Chapter 11 so it will be helpful to go back to that chapter and refresh your memory.

- You will learn about the measurement of unemployment and the difficulties involved in practice
- You will learn of the disadvantages of unemployment to the economy
- In dealing with the causes of unemployment you will be re-acquainted with the types of unemployment
- After a short section on trade unions and unemployment, you will end the chapter looking at the role of trade unions

The International Labour Organisation (ILO) definition of unemployment is adopted in most countries of the Caribbean. It has the advantage of giving a comparison between different countries and is recognised by the United Nations.

> **Definition of unemployment**
> Unemployment is the number of people who are able and willing to work within two weeks if offered a job but who have no job at the time the count is made.

Measurement of unemployment

The ILO's measurement gives an absolute figure, i.e. the number unemployed in the country, and it also gives an unemployment rate. The rate is given as a percentage and is calculated:

$$\frac{\text{Number unemployed}}{\text{Total labour force}} \times 100$$

Let us take Jamaica's figures (very approximate):

$$\frac{177,000}{1,140,000} = 15.5\% \quad \text{Jamaica's unemployment rate.}$$

177,000 is the absolute figure for the number unemployed in Jamaica. 15.5% is the rate of unemployment, i.e. 15.5% of the workforce are unemployed.

EXERCISE Find out the current rate of unemployment in your country. Is the trend over the past few months upwards or downwards?

Are university students unemployed?

Unemployment figures are very difficult to collect and calculate by the ILO method. The working population may be given as all those between the ages of 16 and 60 years who are not so badly physically or mentally disabled that they are incapable of working. However, the working population is not the labour force. Many over the age of 16 are still in education and not seeking work. They are in the working population but not in the workforce. However, if offered work in the next two weeks, many students would take it.

Some people, other than students, are not seeking paid employment in the next two weeks. They are in the working population but not in the labour force. Probably the biggest group of these are married women running the home. They can enter and leave the labour force and make the figures very difficult to collect. There are others who are in the working population, but who are not seeking work. They are living off unearned income from investments or savings. They may enter the workforce when conditions suit them. The people collecting data on unemployment using the ILO method therefore have much difficulty.

Full employment is not 0% unemployment. About 1% of the population are physically or mentally incapable of work. However, full employment is not 1%. 3% unemployment can be accepted as full employment. Why is this? It is because 1% to 2% may be between jobs and this is quite acceptable in determining full employment.

The 'natural rate of unemployment' could be higher than the 2–3% discussed above. It is where the aggregate demand for labour equals the aggregate supply of labour at the current wage rate. This could be at 5% of the workforce. At this wage rate, more workers are not being attracted into the workforce by the wage level and employers have enough workers without having to put wages up to attract more. There is equilibrium in the labour market at that rate of unemployment. The natural rate of unemployment depends on the mobility of labour, both between different locations and between different occupations, the level of training of the workforce, information about jobs, the gap between wages and unemployment benefits and the attitude to being unemployed. Take the mobility of labour as an example. If labour moves between occupations and different areas of the country easily, the natural rate of unemployment will be lower.

The gap between unemployment benefits and wages is interesting. It is shown by the replacement ratio which is the ratio between unemployment and wages in work:

$$\text{Replacement ratio} = \frac{\text{unemployment benefit}}{\text{wages in work}} \times 100$$

Examples:

a $\frac{\$500}{\$1,000} \times 100 = 50\%$ **b** $\frac{\$750}{\$1,000} \times 100 = 75\%$ **c** $\frac{\$1,000}{\$1,000} \times 100 = 100\%$

In (a) the unemployed have a strong incentive to work.

In (b) the incentive to work is stronger than in (a), but the unemployed may chose to stay out of work.

In (c) there is no monetary incentive to work because a person can receive as much from benefit as from work, so the natural rate of unemployment will remain the same.

Governments must not allow unemployment benefits to rise too high if they want to reduce unemployment.

EXERCISE Consider some of the practical difficulties in measuring unemployment.

The disadvantages of unemployment

Unemployment brings disadvantages to the individual who is unemployed and to the country as a whole.

To the individual employed	To the country as a whole
Loss of income	Reduced output
Poverty and hardship	Loss of tax revenue
Loss of self esteem	Unemployment benefits
Depression	Higher crime rates
Idleness and potential for crime	

EXERCISE   Consider the various disadvantages of being unemployed.

The causes of unemployment

Some of the causes of unemployment can be related to the business or trade cycle and some cannot.

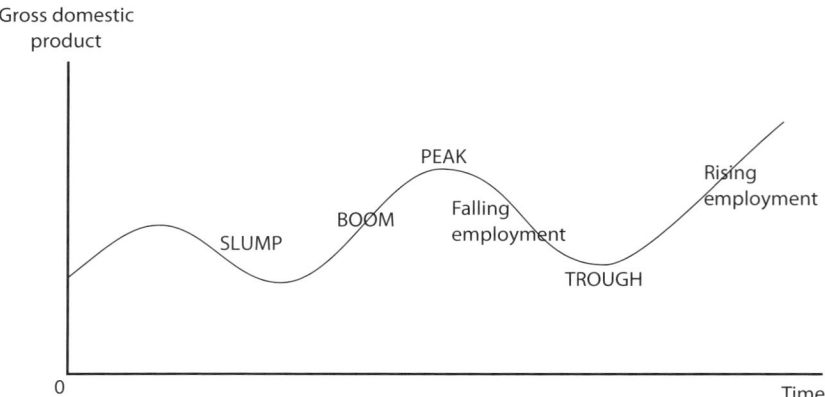

Fig. 18.1
The business cycle

In a boom there is increased demand, production and investment. Therefore, there will be increased employment. In a slump there will be decreased demand, production and investment. Therefore, there will be increased unemployment.

Frictional unemployment

When people are between jobs, they are known as **'frictionally unemployed'**. There is always frictional unemployment in an economy and it is accepted in the natural rate of unemployment, as we have seen. Workers leave one job looking for higher wages or better working conditions. Some are looking for a job nearer home. Others lose their jobs by being sacked. They are in the process of looking for new jobs.

Search unemployment is part of frictional unemployment. It refers to those who are out of work while between jobs and they may not accept the first job on offer, but go on looking for the particular job they want.

There are two interesting points of discussion about frictional unemployment.

1   Is frictional unemployment related to the trade cycle? Some argue that frictional unemployment will be higher in a boom because there is increased employment in a boom and more jobs will become available. Workers will always be chasing higher wages in a boom. Others argue that frictional unemployment will be higher in a slump as more workers will be laid off and looking for jobs. On the other hand, it could be argued that in a slump the sense of job insecurity will be strong and workers will try to hold on to the job they have at all costs. On balance, frictional unemployment is probably higher in a boom, unless the slump is severe.

2 Is the period of frictional unemployment higher among the high paid than among the low paid? Some argue that the low paid have little skill and must accept the next job that is offered. Also they 'will have little put by for a rainy day' and must find work as soon as possible. Therefore, their frictional unemployment lasts one week or two. The highly paid have skill and do not have to take the first job that comes along. There will be many opportunities for their skill and they can search for the best opening. They will also have savings to survive on between jobs. Perhaps the job they have lost paid them a generous redundancy package. They will be frictionally unemployed for longer, perhaps as long as a year. Others argue that low paid workers will find it harder to find work because they lack skill and will be between jobs for a long time. Whereas high paid, high skilled workers will quickly find another job where their skills are needed.

Seasonal unemployment (unemployment which depends on the time of the year) is another form of frictional unemployment. It is common in the Caribbean in the agricultural sector and in the tourist industry. Seasonal workers are waiting for the next season to come round and are temporarily out of work.

Casual unemployment is also part of frictional unemployment. Actors are waiting for their next part in a play.

Structural unemployment

This is unemployment that arises due to changes in the structure of the economy. It can result in long-term unemployment when workers are immobile between occupations. They lose their jobs in declining industries, but cannot take jobs in rising industries because they have not the skills required; they are immobile between occupations. Structural unemployment has occurred in the Caribbean because of the

Structural unemployment in the sugar industry leaves mills derelict.

decline of the sugar and banana industries due to falling European demand for Caribbean agricultural produce. Tourism is a booming industry but agricultural workers cannot easily move to jobs in the tourist industry.

Regional unemployment is structural unemployment as it affects a particular area of the country or the region. The heavily subsidised European beet sugar industry has made the Caribbean cane sugar industry suffer regional unemployment.

Technological unemployment is a form of structural unemployment. Workers lose their jobs because labour-saving technology is introduced. Workers in banking, accounts offices and even in hotel and airline reservations have lost their jobs with computerisation and the Internet.

Technology has made outsourcing possible due to the revolution in telecommunications. Outsourcing involves a firm having production done where costs are lowest. Internet service providers outsource much of their work to Indian call centres and local call centres suffer unemployment.

Cyclical, or demand-deficient unemployment, is certainly related to the business cycle. The word 'cyclical' makes this obvious. In a slump, aggregate demand falls and firms reduce their output and lay off workers.

Examination Tip

> It is important to stress that the demand for labour is 'derived demand', i.e. it is derived from what the labour produces.

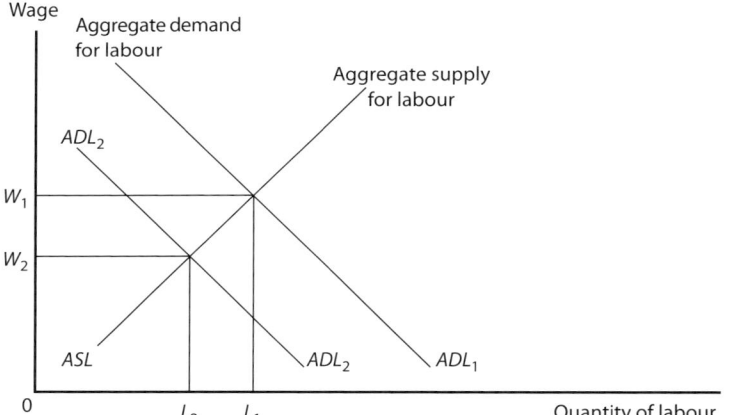

Fig. 18.2 *Demand deficient unemployment*

Aggregate demand falls in the downward slope of the business cycle so the aggregate demand for labour falls from ADL_1 to ADL_2 and the quantity of labour employed falls from L_1 to L_2.

Trade unions and unemployment

In pressing for higher wages, trade unions can cause unemployment. This is an apparent contradiction in the role of trade unions. Instead of improving the lot of the workers, they can actually worsen it. However, the explanation is that trade unions can improve the lot of their members while worsening the lot of non-members. They can improve the lot of those in work while worsening the lot of those out of work. This can be seen in their demands for **minimum wage legislation**. A national minimum wage is the law throughout the country. It is a wage below which an employer cannot pay. A national minimum wage can cause unemployment as shown in the diagram below.

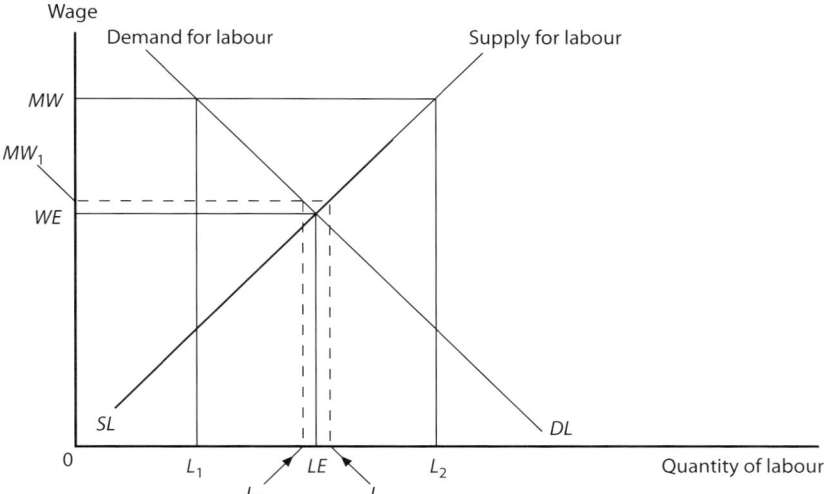

Fig. 18.3
The effect of minimum wage legislation

When trade unions demand a minimum wage of MW, unemployment is likely to result. The equilibrium wage was WE and the equilibrium quantity of labour employed was LE. At a minimum wage of MW, L_2 workers would like to work at such a high wage, but employers would wish to employ only L_1 at this high wage. There will be $LE - L_1$ unemployment created. (Note that unemployment is not $L_2 - L_1$ because $L_2 - LE$ were not employed before the minimum wage; they would just like to join the labour force at that wage.)

Governments, advised by economists, are aware of the dangers of creating unemployment by instituting a minimum wage. Therefore, they go part of the way to meet the wishes of trade unions, and agree to a minimum wage, but they set it at MW_1, just above the equilibrium wage. Employers will probably accept this and not lay off $LE - L_3$ workers. They might even employ L_4, but this is unlikely as they were not employing that quantity of labour before the minimum wage.

If workers cannot be replaced by machines, demand for labour will be inelastic and the minimum wage legislation will not lead to much unemployment. However, if workers can be replaced by machines, employers will substitute machines and there will be severe unemployment.

EXERCISE

Find out if there is a minimum wage in your country and, if so, what it is.

The state-owned Petroleum Company of Trinidad and Tobago. OWTU, which represents the workers at this plant, is a long-established and powerful trade union.

The role of trade unions

To summarise the role of trade unions in the Caribbean, we can use the website of the Oilfields Workers' Trade Union of Trinidad and Tobago which claims to be 'the most respected, progressive, vibrant and independent trade union in the Caribbean Region'. It was founded 65 years ago and now has 9,000 members. It does not just represent those in oil, but other sectors such as gas, chemical, electricity, manufacturing, agriculture and forestry, transport, hotel, catering and hospitality, education and financial services.

In its bulletin, 'About the OWTU', it gives its objects as:

1 To secure the membership of all workers, not just those in the oil industry, who wish to join a union.

2 To obtain just and proper rates of wages, hours of work and working conditions.

3 To regulate the relations and settle disputes between employers and workers.

4 To provide the following benefits for members:
   - Relief in sickness, accidents and disablement in the course of their employment.
   - Death benefits.
   - Legal advice and assistance in connection with employment.
   - Promotion of legislation in the interests of members.

5 To publish a general newspaper.

6 To further the work of any body which promotes the interests of labour.

7 To promote the material, social and educational welfare of members.

8 To give financial assistance to members when on strike.

9 To defend workers' interests against employers who seek to lower the standard of living and dignity of workers.

10 To provide grants and endowments to colleges and institutes which educate the working class.

11 To aid other trade unions or societies which promote the interests of workers.

This is a summary of the aims of the OWTU and is fairly representative of how trade unions see their role in other Caribbean countries.

EXERCISE Find out information about another trade union in the Caribbean. When you go out to work, do you think you would be likely to join a trade union?

Trade unions follow the principle of 'strength in numbers'. One worker has little power, but if he or she joins with other workers in a trade union they have more power in their negotiations. Therefore, trade unions use **'collective bargaining'** in negotiations with employers. Employers are usually represented by the management and they bargain **'across the table'** with the union representatives. This style appears confrontational, and it sometimes is, but it does not have to be. Management wants to cut costs, and that can be wage costs, and unions want to increase wages. Management wants to introduce new machines and new technology and unions may think that they should resist this to safeguard the jobs of their workers. However, it is in the interests of both parties to increase production and productivity, because increased production will bring greater sales, secure jobs and may even increase employment. Increased productivity will bring greater profits to the firm, part of which may be passed on to the workers in higher wages. Then both sides will be working together.

The power of trade unions to a large extent depends on the state of the economy and on the business cycle. If there is a boom in the economy, trade unions will have greater bargaining power, especially if there is full employment. Management will have to yield to wage demands if that is the only way they can increase production to meet the rising demand from consumers. On the other hand, in a slump, when there are thousands of workers unemployed and ready to step into the shoes of workers trying to hold out for higher pay, unions are in a weak position.

A worker wishing to join a union has to pay a fee or union 'due'. This can be deductible from wages. The more members the union has, the more funds it has. The longer a union can go on without having to dip into these funds, e.g. if it does not have to pay out strike pay, the more the funds will grow. These funds give a union power. The OWTU, with 9,000 members and 65 years of existence, must have built up considerable funds. If these funds are invested wisely, they will grow and grow. An individual worker could not manage to pay legal fees in the case of a dispute, e.g. a dispute over wrongful dismissal, but with the union funds to draw on, he or she could hire lawyers to fight his or her case.

Examination questions

1 Discuss the difficulties involved in obtaining an accurate figure for the number of people unemployed at any one time in an economy. *(10 marks)*

2 Compare and contrast the different possible causes of unemployment in an economy. *(10 marks)*

3 Discuss the arguments for and against a minimum wage. *(10 marks)*

4 a Explain what is meant by a trade union. *(4 marks)*
  b Discuss the advantages and disadvantages of trade unions in an economy. *(6 marks)*

5 Discuss the economic consequences of unemployment. *(10 marks)*

6 Describe the various functions of trade unions and say which one you think is the most important and why. *(10 marks)*

Part six

International trade

CHAPTER 19

International trade

In this chapter you will learn about the gains from trade and the theory of comparative advantage which forms the basis of international trade.

- You will start with the difference between closed and open economies and see the difficulties that closed economies experience
- You will then look at Caribbean trade patterns and be given the example of Trinidad and Tobago's
- You will then be introduced to the 'terms of trade' and 'exchange rates'
- You will learn of protectionist measures like tariffs, quotas, exchange controls and subsidies
- The chapter ends with the 'theory of comparative advantage'

Closed and open economies

Definitions of closed and open economies

A closed economy has no foreign trade.

An open economy has foreign trade.

Crowded city street, Haiti.
Source: Stillpictures.

Economic growth in a closed economy will be limited. Population growth will mean more mouths to feed and more goods to be produced, but there are limitations to growth because of the finite resources of the economy. Also, with closed economies, it is difficult to enjoy the economies of scale unless the economy is very big. With closed economies, each economy would be poorer and the world as a whole would be poorer. We can imagine a closed economy gradually using up its finite resources and becoming poorer and poorer. More mouths to feed with finite food resources leads to starvation and death. Thomas Malthus foresaw that population growth would outstrip food supplies. Perhaps a closed economy would be driven to attack its neighbours to gain more land and raw materials when starvation threatened.

The law of diminishing returns

Malthus understood that population increases exponentially or, in simple terms, at an increasing rate: not 1,2,3,4 … but 2,4,8,16 … This growth in population would put increasing pressure on land which does not increase. Land is the **fixed factor**. Population is the **variable factor**.

> **Definition of the law of diminishing returns**
>
> The law of diminishing returns states that if increasing units of a variable factor are applied to a fixed factor, sooner or later diminishing returns would set in, i.e. the output increases but less than proportionately.

Translated to people and land, it means that if more and more people have to live on the same amount of land, they will each have less and less (their returns).

However, in the traditional economy where subsistence agriculture is practised, you can image that a family has its traditional plot of land and the family grows in size. In the extended family system the plot of land has more and more mouths to feed. Each person will have less and less and eventually there will be starvation. The law of diminishing returns will apply.

EXERCISE Is the world population now too large?

Caribbean trade patterns

In the open economies that we have in the Caribbean, we enjoy goods and services from all over the world. In schools we have books and paper produced abroad. In

People wait at the airport. Tourism is an export.

sport we have trainers, boots, cricket bats, golf clubs and balls. In entertainment we have foreign films and DVDs. These are imports.

We also export our bananas, sugar, rum, bauxite and music. Tourism is the biggest export for many of our economies in the Caribbean. It is hard to think of the Caribbean without trade.

Caribbean countries are free to find a range of markets for their exports and imports as we can see with the growth of trade with the United States, South America and the Far East.

The pie charts below show the pattern of the trade of Trinidad and Tobago today.

Trinidad and Tobago's trade pattern 2005

Direction of exports

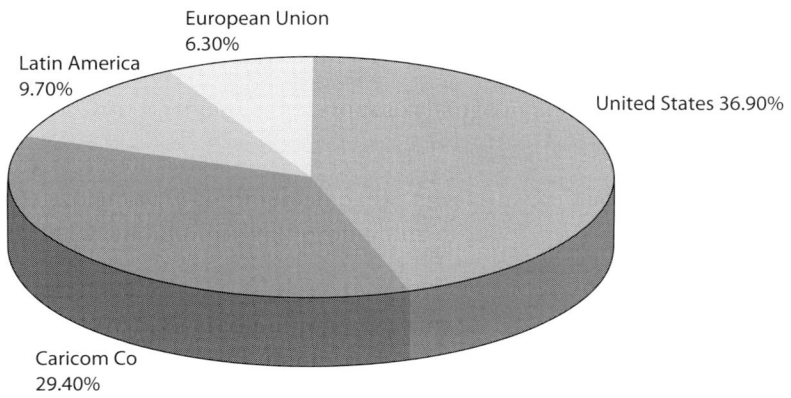

Fig. 19.1
Trinidad and Tobago: direction of exports

Source: *CIA The World Fact Book.*

Source of imports 2005

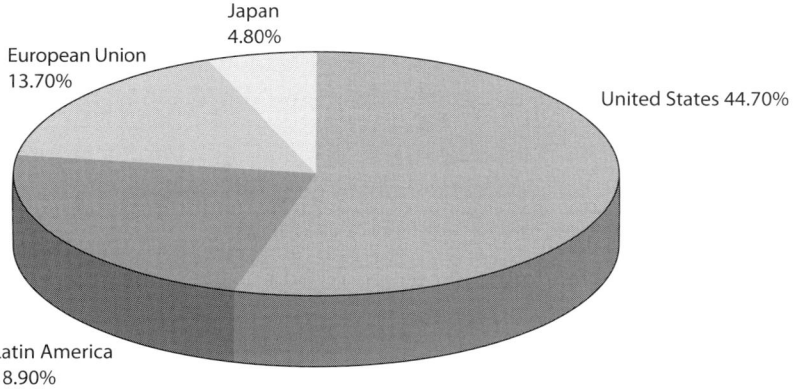

Fig. 19.2
Trinidad and Tobago: source of imports

Source: *CIA The World Fact Book.*

Tourism has been the big growth market in Caribbean trade and has fuelled the growth of many Caribbean economies, e.g. Barbados. Tourism earns foreign exchange with which Caribbean countries can afford more and better imports. The tourists gain with wonderful holidays and the West Indians gain with higher incomes and more goods and services. The gains from trade are obvious.

> **Definitions of exports and imports**
>
> An export is a good or service sold to a foreigner. An import is a good or service bought from a foreigner.
>
> *Note:* By 'foreigner' we mean a person in another country.

Tourism is therefore an export for Caribbean countries even though the tourists are coming into our countries. When a foreigner buys a ticket on British West Indian Airways (BWIA), the national airline of Trinidad and Tobago, Trinidad and Tobago is exporting.

When a Caymanian uses Cable and Wireless as an Internet server, he or she is importing because Cable and Wireless is a foreign company.

However, tourism is very complicated. Caribbean countries export tourism, but when a tourist stays in a foreign-owned hotel, e.g. a Hyatt hotel, there is an import taking place as well. A tourist may drink a Scottish whisky. He or she is paying for it in local currency but some of this price must go on importing the whisky from UK.

EXERCISE Think of as many goods and services as you can that are imported into your country.

The factors that influence international trade

Demand and supply

Resources are not distributed evenly throughout the world. The factors of production and what they are able to produce are vastly different in different parts of the world. Therefore, some countries have large amounts of land, but little labour, e.g. Australia. Other countries have a shortage of land, but abundant labour, e.g. Singapore. This gives rise to differences in demand and supply which influence trade.

Countries with little land will demand agricultural produce from countries with abundant land. Countries with little labour resources will demand labour intensive goods, such as some manufactured goods.

It is difficult to discuss trade without coming back to **oil** again. Oil is vital for production, if only for the transportation of raw materials and finished products. Some countries have oil, others do not. Oil producing countries supply oil and the rest of the world demands oil. This brings us to another factor which influences trade, **price**.

Price

The price of an internationally traded good will be that price which is exactly enough to match the quantity that a country wishes to export with the quantity that the rest of the world wishes to import, ceteris paribus, e.g. if there are no tariffs and no transport costs.

In the diagram below, Country A has an excess of supply of aluminium at the price of aluminium on the international market. Country A will wish to export this excess aluminium. Country B has an excess of demand for aluminium at the international price and would be willing to import at this price what Country A wishes to export. Therefore, the international price for aluminium will be set at PIT.

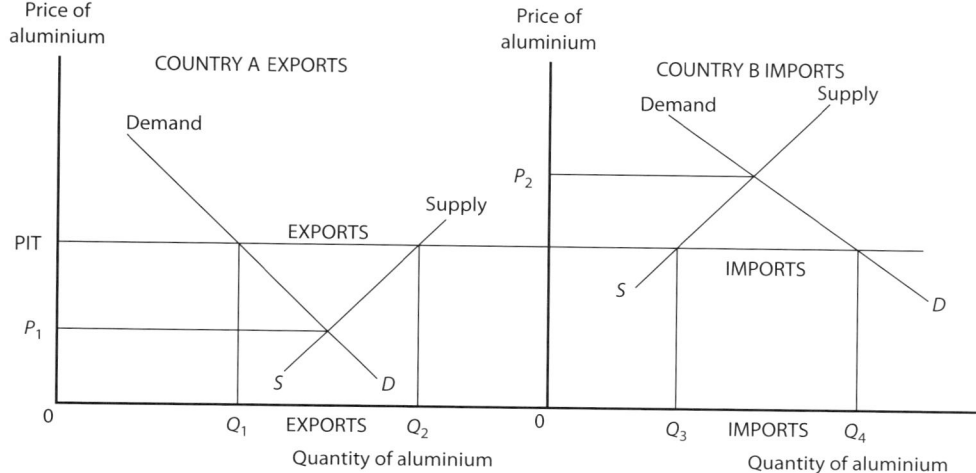

Fig. 19.3 Determination of price in international trade

The terms of trade

Demand and supply determine price in a free market. Even when there is a powerful cartel, OPEC, in the supply of oil, the price is still affected by demand and supply.

How much an importing country has to pay an exporting country for trade goods is called the **terms of trade**. How many bags of coffee does Jamaica have to supply to buy a barrel of oil? This is the explanation of the terms of trade through barter, or **'net barter terms of trade'**.

> **Definition of the terms of trade**
> The terms of trade are the ratio of export prices to import prices. You can think of them either in terms of goods to pay for goods (barter) or in terms of dollars (monetary terms of trade).

The terms of trade influence trade because they will determine the level of exports necessary to import a certain quantity of goods demanded.

The exchange rate

Definition of the exchange rate
The exchange rate is the price of one currency in terms of another.

The exchange rate will obviously have a great influence on international trade. Generally speaking, international trade is conducted in the so-called **'hard currencies'**, such as the US$, the GBP (£) or the Euro (€).

Hard currencies.

Definition of a hard currency
A hard currency is one with a high and stable exchange rate.

In practice, a hard currency is a currency that is accepted by every country in trade and balance of payments settlements.

A country whose currency is weak (of low value in transactions) will find it expensive to import and find that it receives little for its exports in hard currency. It will be restricted in trade by the weakness of the currency. A country with a strong currency will find its imports cheap and will receive a good rate for its exports.

There is no such thing as an 'international currency', but the US$ is acceptable throughout the world. Therefore, the rate between the local currency and the US$ is very important in international trade. If your exports buy many US$, your imports will be easily affordable. It will be easy to conduct international trade.

(Note: Terms of trade and exchange rates will be dealt with at length in the next chapter.)

Non-economic factors

Foreign policy and diplomacy influence international trade. Simply put, you trade with your friends and not with your enemies. In time of war, you do not supply your enemies and they do not supply you. On the other hand, when you have begun diplomatic relations with a country, trade is often used to cement this relationship. When President Nixon visited China in 1972, both countries pledged to work towards the full normalisation of diplomatic relations and to open trade and other contacts. Thus began the so-called 'Ping Pong' diplomacy. This was cemented by the granting of Most Favoured Nation (MFN) Status to China in 1980. MFN is now called 'Normal Trade Relations' (NTR), which clearly shows the importance of trade in US diplomatic relations. The United States now has NTR with all countries except those it has cut diplomatic relations with such as Cuba and North Korea.

An important step in international trade – President Nixon's visit to China in 1972.

Source: AP/EMPICS.

If a country is very friendly with other countries, usually its neighbours, it can enter into preferential trade agreements. Under these agreements, common external tariffs are enforced against countries outside the trade area, and preferential tariffs, or no tariffs at all ('free trade'), are given to the partners in the trade bloc. **CARICOM, The Caribbean Community and Common Market**, also known as **The Caribbean Community**, came into being on 1 August, 1973, replacing **CARIFTA, The Caribbean Free Trade Association**. There are fifteen full members and five associate members. On 1 January 2006, **The Caribbean Single Market Economy** treaty came into effect. This has set up free trade agreements with other CARICOM members and some other countries, such as Costa Rica, and preferential agreements with two South American countries, Venezuela and Colombia.

Protectionist measures or policies

Protectionist measures, i.e. policies imposed by governments to protect domestic industries and producers, are the biggest influences on trade. They affect both imports and exports. They restrict imports coming in to the country and they also affect exporting countries because they add to the costs of exporting to the protectionist countries. However, they are chiefly aimed at restricting imports.

A government will take protectionist measures to restrict imports in order to achieve the following aims.

The protection of infant industries

This is the 'infant-industry argument'. Just as a baby needs its mother to survive its early years, so a new industry needs help in finding markets, achieving lower costs by expanding output, introducing new methods of production and experimenting with new products. These are sometimes called 'sunrise' industries. The government and the infant industry argue that they would be crushed by competition from foreign imports with superior products and lower prices. The argument goes on to say that when the infant industry has grown up, it will not need protection any longer and it will be able to compete against imports and even export its goods.

The protection of declining industries

These are the so-called 'sunset' industries. The government and the declining industry argue that they provide jobs. If competitive imports are not restricted, there will be unemployment and hardship. The argument accepts that the industry is in decline and will eventually cease to exist or 'die', but that it should be allowed to die painlessly. Through protection, the government would allow the industry to find other products to produce or, failing that, the labour force would be given time to find other jobs and be re-trained.

> **EXERCISE** Do you think it is right that governments sometimes protect infant and declining industries?

The strategic industry argument

This argument for protection states that a country needs certain industries for its security in time of war. This argument can be applied directly to the arms industry, the aircraft industry, shipbuilding and even the steel industry, but it is extended to include agriculture as a strategic industry because in time of war, the country must have secure food supplies.

To safeguard jobs

Another reason is to safeguard jobs, not just in sunrise and sunset industries, but in all industries which face foreign competition. This is a powerful argument, especially in the twenty-first century and with the outsourcing of jobs to India and China. Economists, however, would say that local industry must adapt and that local workers must re-train to meet the changing global conditions.

To raise revenue for the government

This really only applies to one protectionist measure and that is the imposition of tariffs. Tariffs are taxes on imports and if the demand for the imports is inelastic, tariffs will raise prices without decreasing supply proportionally, and so bring increased revenue for the government.

Discriminatory measures

Discriminatory measures can be used to favour certain importers over others. For example, Caribbean countries can use protectionist measures to give preference to imports from other Caribbean countries and limit imports from Latin America.

To prevent deficits in the balance of payments

When a country is buying more from foreigners than foreigners are buying from it or, simply, when a country is importing more than it is exporting, it has a deficit in its balance of payments, other things being equal. An obvious way to correct this deficit is to cut down on imports by using protectionist measures like tariffs. Methods to reduce expenditure on consumption which will include consumption of imported goods. These are called **'expenditure-dampening'** measures and they are deflationary. The problem is that not only will they reduce expenditure on imports, but also they will reduce expenditure on domestically-produced goods and this will lead to reduced consumption, unemployment and deflation in general.

To prevent dumping

> **Definition of dumping**
>
> Dumping is the selling of goods at a price that is below the cost of production.

It generally applies to the selling of goods abroad at prices lower than they are sold at home. Dumping can (unfairly) destroy domestic industries and employment. Therefore anti-dumping measures can be justified. On the other hand, anti-dumping measures stop your own citizens enjoying rock-bottom prices. If a foreign exporter is foolish enough to sell below cost, let your citizens enjoy it!

There is 'method-in-the-madness' in dumping on the part of foreign exporters. They may want to crush a domestic industry and then capture the market. When they have captured the market, they will raise prices. This is called **'predatory dumping'** (dumping to hunt out and kill!).

If dumping stops comparative advantage, then protectionist measures can be justified. However, domestic producers sometimes shout 'dumping' when it is not really happening; they are hiding their own inefficiency and the foreigner's efficiency.

EXERCISE If the Grenada government subsidises its banana growers so that they can sell at low prices abroad, is this not dumping? Consider the case for and against this subsidy.

Protectionist measures are disliked by Economists as they interfere with the market mechanism, the forces of demand and supply. They are also under attack from the World Trade Organisation (WTO) in its pursuit of globalisation and the breaking down of barriers to trade so that there can be the free flow of goods, services, technology and ideas. The chief protectionist measures are tariffs, quotas and exchange controls.

Tariffs

> **Definition of a tariff**
>
> A tariff is a tax on imports.

It works like any other tax; it reduces the supply and raises the price. See the diagram below which roughly explains how the Common Agricultural Policy of the European Union operates tariffs against imports from outside the Union.

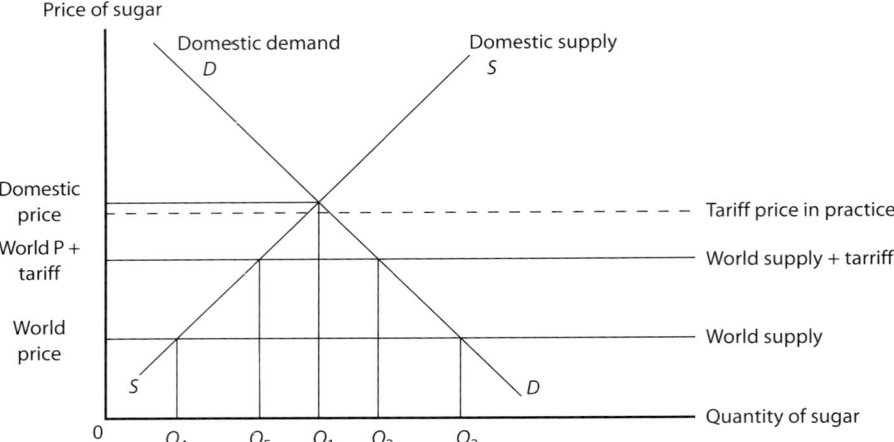

Fig. 19.4 The operation of a tariff

Without trade, the quantity supplied and consumed would be Q_1 and the price would be at the domestic price line where the domestic supply curve intersects the domestic demand curve, well above the world price.

The world supply is a horizontal straight line, perfectly elastic, because the importer can import as much as he or she wishes at that price. Q_2, where the demand curve intersects the world supply line, would be imported and consumed at the world price. At this price, domestic suppliers can only supply Q_4, where the domestic supply curve cuts the world price line. Domestic producers are inefficient in comparison with world producers.

Local producers press the government to introduce protection in the form of a tariff against world suppliers. The government places a tariff on imported sugar which raises its price to world price + tariff. At this price, domestic demand (and consumption) is Q_3. There has been a **welfare loss** on the part of domestic consumers of $Q_2 - Q_3$ because of the tariff and they also have to pay a higher price.

At the world price + tariff, domestic producers can supply Q_5. The tariff has increased their supply from Q_4 to Q_5. The tariff is benefiting inefficient domestic producers.

In practice the tariff is likely to be pushed up to the dotted line, labelled 'tariff price in practice', to make imported sugar enter the market at the same price as locally produced sugar. This increases the welfare loss of domestic consumers and forces them to pay the domestic price. Domestic suppliers have been able to increase their supply to the market from Q_4 to Q_1, further encouraging their inefficiency.

Economists dislike tariffs because of the interference in the free market. Consumers lose both ways – less supply and higher prices. The inefficient local producers are encouraged.

Who gains from the tariff? Local producers, as we have seen. The government also gains revenue from the tariff.

Quotas

Definition of a quota

A quota is a quantitative limit set on imports.

A government may be worried about the number of new cars being imported because they are upsetting the balance of trade and using up so much foreign exchange. Therefore, it decides that only *X* units of cars can be imported (in the case of private cars, some African countries have set quotas of zero units temporarily!).

In the diagram below, a quota has been imposed on the import of cars. The equilibrium price of imported cars was *PE* and the equilibrium quantity was *QE*. The quota reduces the number of cars imported from *QE* to *QQ* and raises the price from *PE* to *PQ*. The local consumers suffer a welfare loss in having less cars to buy and they also have to pay a higher price for a car.

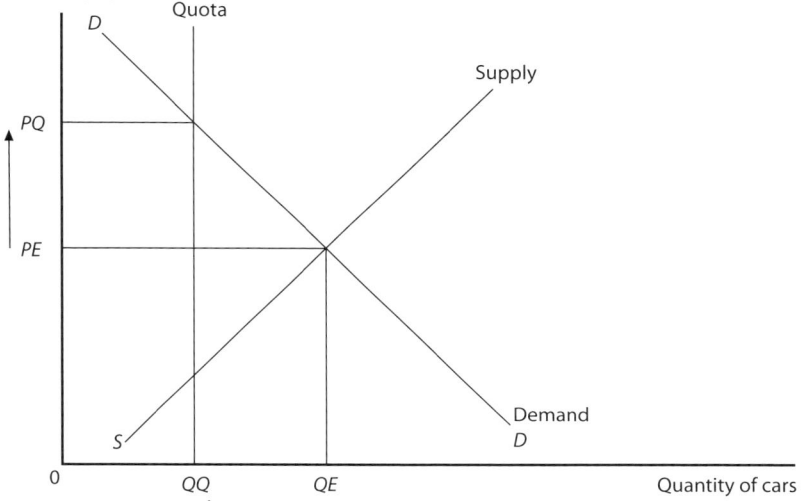

Fig. 19.5
The effect of a quota

There are no local car producers in our example. All cars have to be imported. They are imported by agents or dealers. Unlike with a tariff, the government receives no revenue from a quota. The agents just receive a higher price for their cars. They make higher profits. These profits are called **'contrived profits'** because the entrepreneur has not earned them. They have been presented 'on a plate' by the government to the agents.

Who will be allowed to import the quota? Of course, the agents are very keen to win the quota because of the contrived profits. The government can auction the quota and award it to the highest bidder. This brings revenue to the government and also cuts some of the contrived profit.

However, to sum up, economists dislike quotas because consumers suffer a loss of goods and pay higher prices. There is the possibility of corruption, and usually the government receives no revenue. On the other hand, they are a simple and effective way of reducing imports, stabilising the balance of trade and saving foreign currency.

Exchange controls

The economists at the International Monetary Fund are opposed to tariffs and quotas, but they will sometimes accept exchange control as a method of reducing a deficit in the balance of trade and saving foreign currency.

By the method of exchange control, an importer has to apply to the central bank for the foreign currency needed to pay for the imports. The central bank can either approve the application or reject it. If the application is rejected, the goods cannot be imported. The government, through the central bank, is able to give priority to the import of goods which it considers have priority, like medicines and books, and turn down applications for foreign currency to import luxury items.

Consumers do suffer when they cannot buy the imported goods they want and when they cannot take their foreign holidays. However, exchange control is meant to restrict the items that the economy can do without and allow the imports of the necessities.

The gains from trade

1 Consumers gain from trade

The most obvious gain is the consumption of a good that you would not have without trade. Jamaica does not have oil. Jamaica imports oil that enables the consumption of public and private transport and all the benefits that flow from transport. Europe does not produce coffee. Europe gains coffee from trade. Northern Europe has a cold, wet climate. From tourism Northern Europeans gain the advantages of the Caribbean climate, the warmth, the trade winds, the clear seas and the golden beaches.

2 Producers gain from trade

Producers gain markets for their goods and services. There are risks in supplying overseas markets, but the gains are the rewards for the risks taken. This enables production to expand which brings us to another gain.

3 Economies of scale

The local market is perhaps too small for the increased production of goods and services and without trade, a firm cannot achieve the economies of scale. Trade opens up other markets, some of them very large. The exporting firm can expand production to serve these markets and achieve economies of scale.

4 Greater productive efficiency

Producers will also benefit from improved, imported technology and expertise. This will enable production to expand at lower costs, thus improving efficiency.

5 The world gains from trade

The world gains from international trade. Each country is able to **specialise** in what it does best, what it produces best. This brings the division of labour that increases production and lowers cost. World output increases and the surpluses are traded to the advantage of everyone. Britain could grow coffee, but it would have to be grown in huge, heated, greenhouses yielding small output at great cost. Jamaica can grow the coffee of the highest quality in abundance. Jamaica specialises in coffee growing and Britain specialises in chemicals. Both countries gain from the specialisation.

6 Foreign exchange

An economy gains foreign exchange from international trade. Foreign exchange enables more trade, with more and more trading partners, to take place. Foreign exchange enables a country's citizens to enjoy foreign travel. Travel is an education and so on…

7 Increase in world output

In general, foreign trade increases world output and enables everyone who participates in it to enjoy a higher quality of life.

8 A win–win situation

Trade brings a **'win–win'** situation. There are at least two countries involved in trade. One does not win while the other loses. Both win or gain. This is called 'a win–win' situation. (See the examples of absolute advantage and comparative advantage below.)

The theory of international trade or comparative advantage

Resources are not distributed evenly throughout the world. Some countries, e.g. the United States, have abundant resources while other countries, e.g. Burkina Faso, have very limited resources. Resources are also immobile. Of course, land is immobile and to a large extent what is in the land is immobile too, until it has been processed into products.

Labour is, perhaps surprisingly, immobile too. Students tend to think that people can move from one country to another, but that is not the case when considering labour as a factor of production. There are cultural and language barriers and restrictions on emigration and immigration that stop labour from being mobile. China has abundant labour, but it cannot be moved en masse to Australia. Japan is rich in capital and this is a more mobile factor, but the Japanese keep their capital endowments in Japan first of all and only invest abroad when conditions are right. Enterprise is mobile, but only recently is the mobility being put to great effect in globalisation, bringing a world without borders.

> **Definition of globalisation**
> Globalisation is the extension of free trade throughout the world.

Therefore, if the resources cannot be moved, only the products that they yield are moved in international trade.

Specialisation

Each country must specialise in producing what it is best at. This means what its resources will yield the most of. Australia has abundant land and so produces agricultural products, the wool and the meat from the sheep, the dairy produce and beef from the cattle, etc. China must produce what is best by labour-intensive methods. Japan must produce by capital-intensive methods. These are sweeping generalisations to show what specialisation entails.

Specialisation increases production and leads to surpluses, output over and above the country's own needs. These surpluses can then be traded and all countries gain. It would not be safe for a country to specialise completely (**exclusive specialisation**) so countries practise **partial specialisation** whereby they concentrate in producing what they are best at, but still produce limited amounts of products they are not so good at producing. For example, it would not be wise for a country richly endowed with capital to give up the production of food entirely. What would happen if their supplies of food were cut off in a war?

Comparative advantage

In 1817, David Ricardo, a British economist, wrote his famous work, *Principles of Political Economy and Taxation*, in which he explained the gains from trade by the theory of comparative advantage. This theory still holds good today, nearly two hundred years later!

Assumptions in the theory

In the theory, trade is simplified as **bilateral trade**, i.e. trade between only two countries and there are only two goods. In the real word, of course, there is **multilateral trade**, i.e. trade between many countries and there are thousands of goods. Nevertheless, the theory of comparative advantage holds good however many countries and goods are involved.

Another assumption is that opportunity costs are constant. This is not true. Opportunity costs will inevitably change over time, e.g. as production of one good goes on over time, resources will be used up.

It is also assumed that there are no transport costs or tariffs. Both of these would increase the costs of moving goods from one country to another.

Absolute advantage

Before comparative advantage can be explained, the **theory of absolute advantage** must be understood.

> **Definition of absolute advantage**
> One country has an absolute advantage over another country when it can produce a good using less resources than the other country.

Example 1
Where one country produces one good but not another. The two countries in this bilateral trade are Country A and Country B, and the two goods are oil and wheat. The units are **output per man hour** so the country with the higher number of units is the better producer of that good.

Before trade:

	OIL	WHEAT
Country A	10	0
Country B	0	8

Country A has an absolute advantage in oil and Country B has an absolute advantage in wheat. Both countries will gain from trade. Both will gain the good that they did not have before trade. Trade will take place at an exchange rate decided between the two countries, say 5 units of oil for four units of wheat.

After trade:

	OIL	WHEAT
Country A	5	4
Country B	5	4

Both countries now have 5 units of oil and 4 units of wheat. Both have gained a good that they did not have before. Country A has gained wheat and Country B has gained oil.

Example 2

Still absolute advantage, but where both countries produce both goods, and one country is a better producer of one of the goods and the other country is a better producer of the other. Each country will specialise in the good it has an absolute advantage in; in the case below, Country A in oil and Country B in wheat.

Before trade:

	OIL	WHEAT
Country A	8	4
Country B	3	6
(World output)	11	10

Country A produces both oil and wheat, but it is a better producer of oil than Country B because it can produce 8 units in a man hour whereas Country B can only produce 3 units. Country B can also produce both oil and wheat, but it is a better producer of wheat than Country A because it can produce 6 units of wheat per man hour whereas Country A can only produce 4 units. Each country will specialise in the good in which it has an absolute advange: Country A will produce oil and Country B wheat.

Specialisation:

	OIL	WHEAT
Country A	16	0
Country B	0	12
(World output)	16	12

Each country will specialise in the good that it is best at producing. When Country A switches exclusively to oil it will produce 16 units of oil because for very unit of wheat it gives up it will gain 2 units of oil (the ratio of wheat to oil is 4:8, or 1:2). In practice you can arrive at the right answer by doubling the specialist good. When Country B switches to wheat it will produce 12 units of wheat. It is exclusive specialisation because the product in which there is a disadvantage is not produced at all.

The world has gained 5 units of oil and 2 units of wheat (from 11 to 16 units of oil and from 10 to 12 units of wheat.

After trade:

	OIL	WHEAT
Country A	12	5
Country B	4	7

Both countries know that they can gain from trade so they will set an exchange rate between oil and wheat which will make each gain. A unit of wheat is worth 1/3 units of oil. Country B decides to keep 7 units of wheat and trade the other 5 units. It will receive from A 4 units of oil in return. Country A will have 5 units of wheat imported from Country B and 12 units of oil that it has kept. Both countries have gained from trade. Country A has gained 4 units of oil and 1 unit of wheat. Country B has gained 1 unit of oil and 1 unit of wheat.

Comparative advantage

Ricardo proved that a country that had an **absolute advantage in both goods** could still gain from specialisation and trade as long as it had a **comparative advantage** in one good. This is hard to believe when you have a country very well endowed in natural resources trading with a country very poorly endowed. However, comparative advantage still holds true if the less well endowed country has a comparative advantage in one good. In the following example, Country A has an absolute advantage in the production of both oil and wheat.

> **Definition of comparative advantage**
>
> A country has a comparative advantage in the production of a good if it can produce that good at a lower opportunity cost.

The **theory of comparative advantage** states that trade can benefit all countries if they specialise in producing the goods in which they have a comparative advantage, i.e. if they can produce them at lower opportunity costs.

In the example below, Country A has a lower opportunity cost in wheat because it has to forgo only 1.3 units of oil to produce 1 unit of wheat, whereas Country B has to forgo 1.5 units of oil for 1 unit of wheat.

Example 3 Comparative advantage

Before trade:

	OIL	WHEAT
Country A	4	3
Country B	3	2
(World output)	7	5

Country A has an absolute advantage in the production of both oil and wheat, but its advantage in wheat is greater than its advantage in oil. We say that Country A has an absolute advantage in both goods but a comparative advantage in wheat because a ration of 3:2 is superior to a ratio of 4:3. Country B has an absolute disadvantage in both goods, but a comparative advantage in oil because the ratio of 3:4 is not as unfavourable as the ratio of 2:3.

Specialisation:

	OIL	WHEAT
Country A	0	6
Country B	6	0
(World output)	6	6

World output after specialisation is 6 units of oil and 6 units of wheat. The world has gained 1 unit of wheat but lost 1 unit of oil. However, the gain is greater than the loss because 1 unit of wheat is worth 1.4 units of oil. The net gain is 0.4 units in a common currency.

After trade:

	OIL	WHEAT
Country A	3.5	3.5
Country B	2.5	2.5

Country A decides to keep 3.5 units of wheat and export 2.5 units to Country B. Country B pays 3.5 units of oil for its imports of 2.5 units of wheat. Both countries have net gains because they have each gained 0.5 units of wheat but lost 0.5 units of oil. The gain is greater than the loss because 0.5 units of wheat are worth 0.7 units of oil.

By specialisation and trade the world has gained and both countries have gained.

No trade situation – no comparative advantage:

	OIL	WHEAT
Country A	4	4
Country B	3	3

When both the ratios are the same there can be no trade because there is no comparative advantage. This is the only situation where there can be no gain from trade. (The opportunity cost of a unit of oil is the same in both countries, and the opportunity cost of a unit of wheat is the same in both countries.)

Trade and the production possibility frontier

Example 4 Absolute advantage and trade brings increases in output and goods

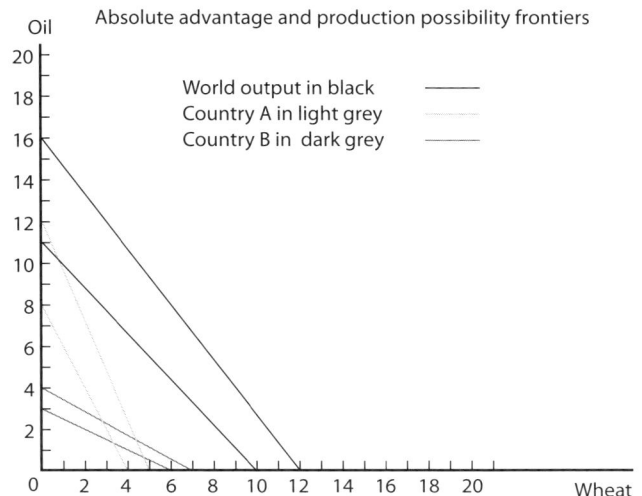

Fig. 19.6
Trade shifts production possibility frontiers outwards

Example 5 Comparative advantage and trade brings increases in output and goods

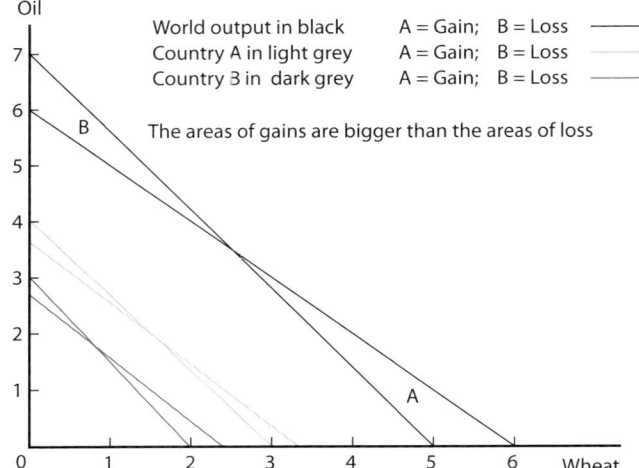

Fig. 19.7 *Comparative advantage: shifts in production possibility frontiers*

Through trade, the world's production possibility frontier shifts outwards and each country's production possibility frontier shifts outwards. This is clear in the first diagram, Figure 19.6 (Example 4), but is not so clear in the second diagram (Example 5) because the production possibility curves swivel. There you must look more closely at Figure 19.7.

Examination questions	
1 Distinguish between an open and a closed economy.	*(5 marks)*
2 Compare and contrast the different types of protectionist policies.	*(10 marks)*
3 Explain what is meant by the theory of comparative advantage.	*(10 marks)*
4 Why do some countries use partial rather than total specialisation?	*(10 marks)*
5 Explain what is meant by the gains from international trade.	*(10 marks)*
6 Discuss why some countries use protectionist policies.	*(10 marks)*

CHAPTER 20

Terms of trade, exchange rates and the balance of payments

In this chapter you will look into the terms of trade and the exchange rate in more detail. The chapter will round off international trade with the balance of payments.

- The terms of trade are examined in detail and the 'Terms of Trade Index' is introduced
- You will be given explanations of the 'devaluation', 'revaluation', 'depreciation' and 'appreciation' of currencies
- You will then learn about the different exchange rate systems, i.e. floating, fixed and managed
- The 'balance of payments' comes next and is a major part of the chapter.
- There is an examination of Jamaica's balance of payments
- The problem of a deficit in the balance of payments is discussed as well as the solutions that are applicable, including devaluation

The terms of trade

Definition of the terms of the trade

The terms of trade are the ratio of export prices to import prices (monetary definition). They can also be seen in terms of the goods that have to be exported to pay for the goods that are imported (barter definition).

Examination Tip: The terms of trade and the balance of trade are very different; make sure you don't get them confused!

Formula

$$\text{Terms of Trade Index} = \frac{\text{The price index of exports}}{\text{The price index of imports}} \times 100$$

In the previous chapter we concentrated on the **net barter terms of trade (NBTT)** in a very simplified way, e.g. how many bags of coffee have to be exported to pay for a barrel of oil. If the price of oil rises, more bags of coffee will have to be exported to pay for the barrel of oil, ceteris paribus. If the price of coffee rises, less bags of coffee will have to be exported to pay for the barrel of oil, ceteris paribus. (Ceteris paribus – other things being equal – because we are assuming that the price of the other good stays the same.)

Terms of trade: how much coffee buys a barrel of oil?

However, international trade involves thousands of goods being exported and imported and the net barter terms of trade would be inadequate to deal with the terms of trade as a whole. The net barter terms of trade is a particularly good way of considering a developing country's position when it is relying particularly on the export of one crop, e.g. Malawi and tobacco. How much tobacco does Malawi have to export to buy a tractor? This example illustrates a Third World problem, i.e. the reliance on agricultural exports that are tending to fall in price relative to the prices of manufactured goods that they have to import.

Therefore, when dealing with international trade in a broad sense, i.e. not concentrating on just one good for another, we have to use prices. These prices have to be weighted to reflect their importance and then averaged out over thousands of goods and so the terms of trade are a complicated calculation for a country, a little bit like the Consumer Price Index!

Examination Tip

> If the terms of trade improve, they are said to move in favour of a country. If the terms of trade worsen, they are said to move against a country.

An example of the movement in the terms of trade is the oil crisis of 1973–74. The price of oil quadrupled (went up by four times). The terms of trade moved massively in favour of the OPEC countries and the 'Oil Sheikhs' could buy their Rolls Royces and racehorses. It was called a crisis because oil importers at one stroke had their terms of trade deteriorate massively. The United States, the world's biggest oil importer, was almost in a panic. However, economists, in particular Alan Greenspan, Chief Economic Adviser to Presidents Nixon, Ford and Reagan during the crisis, 'played it cool' and told the US Administration not to worry. They knew that the terms of trade would move back in favour of the United States and the other Western industrialised countries as the years went by because the manufactured goods they exported would rise in price relative to the oil they imported. Also, the increased demand from the oil producing countries spending their 'petro-dollars' would hasten this process (petro-dollars refers to the currency surplus that oil-producing countries enjoyed after 1973). The economists were right: oil prices fell relative to manufactured goods and the terms of trade moved back in favour of Western industrialised countries relatively quickly.

EXERCISE

Consider what happened to the terms of trade when oil prices quadrupled in 1973–74 from the point of view of (a) oil exporting and (b) oil importing countries.

The Terms of Trade Index

A base year is selected and given the value of 100. If export prices rise by 2%, the index of export prices will be 102. If import prices rise in the same period by 5%, the index of import prices will be 105.

Examples

1. Terms of Trade Index $= \dfrac{102}{105} \times 100 = 97.1$

   The terms of trade have deteriorated.

2. Export Price Index = 97; import price index = 101.

   Terms of Trade Index $= \dfrac{97}{101} \times 100 = 96$

   The terms of trade have deteriorated again.

3. Export Price Index = 108; import price index = 102.

   Terms of Trade Index $= \dfrac{108}{102} \times 100 = 106$

   The terms of trade have improved (always compare with the base year = 100).

EXERCISE Calculate the Terms of Trade Index when the Export Price Index is 103 and the Import Price Index is 87.

Other influences on the terms of trade

1. If one country's rate of inflation rises relative to its trading partners' rates of inflation, there will be a favourable movement in its terms of trade. This is surprising at first because a rise in prices chokes off demand. Therefore, it is a short-term effect on the terms of trade. A rise in export prices, not brought about by increased demand but by inflation, is usually a cause for concern.

2. A rise in the value of a country's currency (an 'appreciation') will also bring about a favourable movement in its terms of trade. This leads to a fall in the price of imports. Less of its currency will be needed to buy a unit of the foreign currency; imports will therefore fall in price.

The terms of trade and Caribbean countries

Rising tourist prices are good news for Caribbean countries. They are likely to rise with:

1. Higher inflation in Caribbean countries relative to the United States and European inflation rates. The Terms of Trade Indices will be moving in favour of Caribbean countries like Jamaica, other things being equal.

2. Increased demand for tourism. If the United States and European countries are experiencing rising incomes, tourism is likely to increase in demand because it is a normal good.

Rising prices of manufactured goods are bad news for Caribbean countries. Caribbean countries are net importers of manufactured goods. This would mean a rise in the price of goods they tend to import relative to the prices of goods they export, ceteris paribus.

A fall in the prices of agricultural exports like bananas, coffee and sugar will move the terms of trade against some Caribbean countries.

High rates of inflation in countries like Jamaica in the short run will improve the terms of trade.

Rising oil prices will help Trinidad and Tobago's terms of trade, but what will they do to the other Caribbean countries' terms of trade?

EXERCISE Consider the good and bad aspects of changes in the terms of trade for Caribbean countries.

Exchange rates

The exchange rate of a country is also known as the foreign exchange rate.

> **Definition of an exchange rate**
> The exchange rate is the price at which one currency is bought and sold for another currency.

Examples
Here are some recent examples of selected exchange rates in the Caribbean.

US$1: BBD 1.99	or	BBD 1: US$0.50
US$1: XCD 2.69	or	XCD 1: US$0.37
US$1: JMD 64.68	or	JMD 1: US$0.015
US$1: TTD 6.25	or	TTD 1: US$0.16

Notes
1 BBD, XCD, JMD and TTD are abbreviations used for the Barbadian, East Caribbean, Jamaican and Trinidad and Tobago dollars by the Forex Market. (Forex = Foreign Exchange.)

2 Students are tempted to say that the Jamaican $ is weak because there are J$65 to US$1, and the Trinidad and Tobago dollar is strong because there are TTD$6.25 to US$1. This is the wrong use of 'weak' and 'strong'. These words are used to show the exchange rate movements. If the Jamaican $ keeps the same rate or improves, i.e. if less J$s are needed to buy US$1, you could say that the Jamaican $ was 'strong' against the US$. If more Trinidad and Tobago $s are needed to buy US$1, and that was the trend, you would say that the Trinidad and Tobago $ was 'weak' against the US$. In other words, 'strong' or 'weak' are relative terms.

The Barbadian $ and the East Caribbean $ have **fixed exchange rates**

The Jamaican $ and the Trinidad and Tobago $ have **floating exchange rates**

In practice, to a greater or lesser degree, all exchange rates are **managed**

EXERCISE Find out the rate of exchange of your country's currency against the U.S. dollar.

Devaluation, revaluation, depreciation and appreciation

Before you go any further with exchange rates, you must make sure that you use the following terms correctly.

a Devaluation

Devaluation occurs when a currency falls in value **against all other currencies**. It used to be a fall in value against gold, but there is no longer a gold standard. If the Jamaican $ is devalued, it falls in value against the US $, the £ Sterling, the Euro, the Trinidad and Tobago $, the Brazilian Real … and all other currencies.

Countries can devalue deliberately to make their exports cheaper and their imports dearer, but devaluation is monitored by the International Monetary Fund (IMF) and the IMF must give approval for large devaluations, e.g. above 10%. The IMF has stated that countries should 'avoid manipulating exchange rates to gain an unfair competitive advantage over other members'.

b Revaluation

Revaluation means that a currency increases in value **against all other currencies**. It is very rare. There have been three major revaluations since the Second World War: the Swiss Franc, the German Mark and the Japanese Yen. Why should a country revalue? It might revalue in response to positive economic conditions, i.e. it is doing very well in its balance of payments, in order to lower inflation, i.e. to choke off demand or to please investors or trading partners.

In 1985, under the 'Plaza Agreement', the Japanese revalued the yen. It did so under pressure from the United States. The trade balance between the United States and Japan was very much in Japan's favour and had been for years. Americans were buying Japanese cars, cameras, watches, etc and the Japanese were not buying American goods to anywhere near the same extent. The Japanese agreed to revalue.

Japanese vehicles waiting to be exported.

Western countries and Japan are trying to put pressure on China to revalue the Yuan Renminbi (CNY) (current rate US$1 = CNY 8.01) because Chinese exports are so attractive at the current exchange rate.

The reissuing of a currency is not the same as a revaluation. Currencies are reissued in hyperinflation or when the central bank loses control over its notes and coins and transactions become unwieldy, e.g. the Turkish Lira was reissued in 2005 with 1 new lira equal to 1,000,000 old lira.

c Depreciation

Depreciation occurs when a currency falls in value **against another currency**, i.e. against the currency of its chief trading partner. When the Jamaican $ falls in value against the US$, it 'depreciates' against the US$. Under a floating exchange rate system, currencies are depreciating and appreciating all the time.

d Appreciation

Appreciation occurs when a currency rises in value **against another currency**.

Exchange rate systems

We will be dealing with three exchange rate systems: floating, fixed and managed. In the examples we chose earlier in the chapter, we have two floating exchange rates, Jamaica's and Trinidad and Tobago's, and two fixed, Barbados and the Eastern Caribbean Dollar.

History

Under its liberalisation policies, the government and the Bank of Jamaica allowed the Jamaica $ to float in 1991. In 1993 the Central Bank of Trinidad abolished its fixed Exchange Rate system and adopted a floating Exchange Rate system.

Barbados adopted a fixed exchange rate of BBD 2: US$1 in 1972. The Eastern Caribbean $ was fixed against the US$ from 1976 at XCD 2.7: US$1.

Floating exchange rate

A floating exchange rate means that the exchange rate is responsive to changes in demand and supply conditions in the market, i.e. it is 'market-determined'. This is explained in the diagram below.

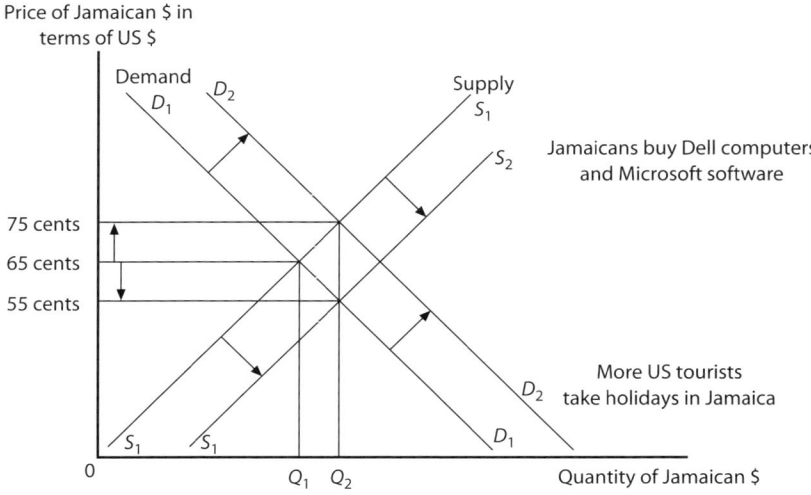

Fig. 20.1
Determination of the exchange rate by market forces (demand and supply)

When US tourists demand more holidays in Jamaica, they will be increasing the demand for Jamaica $s. This will shift the demand curve for Jamaican $s upwards to the right from $D_1 D_1$ to $D_2 D_2$ and raise the price of the Jamaica $ from 65 US cents to 75 US cents. The Jamaica $ will **appreciate** against the US$.

When Jamaicans buy more computers and software from the United States, they will be supplying more Jamaica $s. This will shift the supply curve downwards to the right from $S_1 S_1$ to $S_2 S_2$ and the price of the Jamaica $ will fall from 65 US cents to 55 US cents. The Jamaica $ will **depreciate** against the US$.

Of course thousands of goods and services are being traded between Jamaica and the United States daily and the determination of the exchange rate will be very complicated. It will **fluctuate** (go up and down) daily.

Fluctuations in the exchange rate are not good for foreign trade. Traders lose confidence because they are not sure how much they will receive for the exports and how much they will pay for their imports. Wide fluctuations could bring heavy losses in foreign trade. Therefore, central banks **intervene** in the foreign exchange market and the system becomes one of **managed floating**. Such intervention is given the name **'dirty floating'** because it is not a **'freely floating exchange rate'** once the central bank has intervened.

> **Definition of dirty floating**
>
> Dirty floating is a system of flexible exchange rates where the central bank intervenes to prevent wide fluctuations in the exchange rate.

In fact, the central bank probably has a **target exchange rate** which it is aiming at. Suppose the Bank of Jamaica has a target rate of J$65: US$1. If there is strong demand for the Jamaica $ and the rate is heading towards J$60: US$1, the Bank of Jamaica will supply Jamaica $s (by buying US$s) and drive the rate down again to the target.

EXERCISE If there was a target rate, what action would the Bank of Jamaica take if the Jamaica $ was falling in value?

Fixed exchange rate

The Central Bank of Barbados and the Eastern Caribbean Central Bank operate **fixed exchange rate systems**. Both their currencies are **tied** to the US$, i.e. they are fixed against the US$. The advantage of tying the exchange rate to the currency of the leading trading partner is the confidence it brings in transactions between the two partners and the simplicity of calculation. Also, the US$ is one of the strongest currencies in the world and will give stability to the local currency tied to it.

What happens when market forces, i.e. demand and supply, put pressure on the fixed exchange rate? The answer is simple: the central bank must administer exactly the correct counter-weight. If increased demand is driving up the price of the currency, the Central Bank must increase supply in exactly the same measure.

A fixed exchange rate is often illustrated by **'the snake in the tunnel'**. (This expression was first used in the European Monetary Union in 1972. The 'snake' was the European currencies and the 'tunnel' was the US$. It is an amusing illustration of how a fixed exchange rate system works even if it is stretching it a bit to apply it to Barbados and the Eastern Caribbean exchange rates!)

Barbados $ fixed exchange rate against US $ — theoretical explanation

Fig. 20.2
A fixed exchange rate system

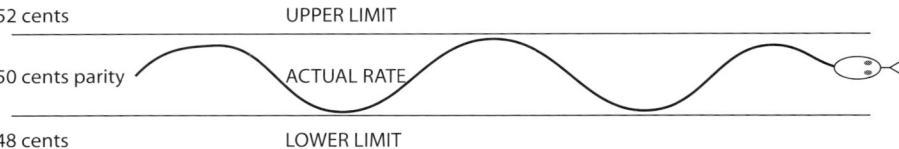

The Barbados $ is fixed at the rate of B$2: US$1, or B$1: US 50 cents. Sometimes this rate is called its **'par value'** or **'parity'**.

> **Definition of parity**
> Parity is the standard equivalence in currency. For example, B$2 : US$1.

Suppose the Bank of Barbados set upper and lower limits at 4% on either side of parity. It would then intervene whenever the Barbados $ was approaching an upper limit of 52 US cents. It would sell Barbados $s to lower the exchange rate. Suppose the Barbados $ was reaching the lower limit of 48 US cents. It would buy Barbados $s to raise the exchange rate.

Such a fixed exchange rate system needs to be monitored constantly by the central bank and intervention must be frequent. Therefore, it is a **managed exchange rate** in another form, albeit a much stricter managed system.

To intervene in exchange rate markets, central banks must keep **funds** of foreign currencies, e.g. the Bank of Barbados must keep a fund of its own currency, Barbados $s, and a fund of US$s.

The disadvantage of a fixed exchange rate system is that your currency rises and falls with the currency it is tied to, e.g. the US$. If the US$ depreciates, the Barbados $ and the Eastern Caribbean $ depreciate and Barbados's imports from outside the US$ bloc become more expensive. On the other hand, if the US$ appreciates, imports become cheaper.

Managed exchange rate

Strictly speaking a managed exchange rate system should be applied to managed floating exchange rates. When central banks 'manage' exchange rates, they intervene in the exchange rate markets by buying and selling currencies to counter the depreciation or appreciation of a currency.

The rate of interest can also be used to manage the exchange rate. A high rate of interest would attract inflows of capital which would increase demand for the currency and make it appreciate. However, the huge capital flows which chase high interest rates (**'hot money'**) are usually confined to the banks in the capital cities of developed countries and are not a feature of Caribbean countries.

The balance of payments

A country records its transactions with the rest of the world. They are put together in a balance sheet which is known as the **balance of payments**.

> **Definition of the balance of payments**
> The balance of payments is a record of all financial transactions with the rest of the world; it shows a country's payments to and receipts from foreign countries.

The balance of payments is divided into four headings:

1. The current account.
2. The capital account.
3. The financial account.
4. Net errors and omissions (the balancing item).

The current account

The current account is itself divided into four parts:

1. The trade in goods.
2. The trade in services.
3. Income.
4. Current transfers.

1. The trade in goods refers to the trade in **visibles** which are items which can be seen and touched. A banana is a good which, when exported from a Caribbean country, is a credit item. Oil is a good which, when imported by Caribbean country, is a debit item. There is a balance on this account between exports and imports, or debits and credits.

   If exports exceed imports, there is a **surplus** and if imports exceed exports, there is a **deficit** in the **balance of trade**.

2. Services involve the trade in **invisibles**. They include transport, banking, insurance, tourism and other services. If an American takes a holiday in Jamaica, Jamaica is selling a service to the United States and it is recorded as a credit in the current account. If a Jamaican flies by British Airways, it is recorded as a debit in the current account. If credits exceed debits there is a surplus, and if debits exceed credits, there is a deficit in the **invisible balance of the current account**.

3. Income can also be referred to as **net property income from abroad**. When a Jamaican sets up a business in the United States, the profits are income to Jamaica. If a Jamaican works abroad and sends some of his salary back to Jamaica, that is also a credit item under Income. Dividends on shares held in foreign companies,

interest on foreign bank accounts and rent received from foreign properties also come under Income. However, at the same time as your citizens are receiving income from abroad, foreigners are earning income from your country. Therefore, there are credits and debits in this section of the current account as in the other sections. That is why it is known as **net** property income from abroad, i.e. the difference between your citizens' incomes abroad and foreigners' incomes in your country.

4 Current transfers are money sent back to your country by private individuals, often to their families as gifts. Jamaicans abroad make huge gifts to families back home. Also governments make transfers which are recorded in this section of the current account when they make their payments to international bodies like the United Nations.

The capital account

If one of your citizens sells land which he or she held in a foreign country, it is classed as a credit of a non-financial asset in the capital account. If your government makes a grant to another country for a project, it would be classed as a debit of a financial asset in the capital account.

The financial account

The financial account records investments by your citizens abroad which are debits and investments by foreigners in your country which are credits. Just think of whether the money is going out or coming in (investments in your country by foreigners are called **'inward investment'**, but the term 'outward investment' is not often heard).

Since the 1973 oil crisis, there has been reference to **'Hot money'** in the balance of payments financial account. Oil producing countries, chiefly in the Middle East, built up huge financial balances (the **'petro-dollars'** that we have mentioned earlier in this chapter) from the sale of oil after 1973–74. This period coincided with the revolution in electronic telecommunications so these balances could be transferred round the world almost instantaneously. The word 'hot' was used because the money moved so fast. This money chases high interest rates and does not usually feature in the financial accounts of developing countries.

Errors and omissions

Mistakes inevitably occur when there are millions of entries to be made. A balance sheet must balance but a balance of payments account fails to balance and it must be made to balance by the recording of net errors and omissions. When net errors and omissions are included, the balance of payments balances. (It used to be called the 'balancing item'.)

Balance of Payments Standard Presentation (In millions of US dollars)			
	Cr	Dr	Net
Current Account	4401.2	4617.5	−216.3
A. Goods and Services	3477.5	4008.6	−531.1
Goods	1499.1	2685.6	−1186.5
Transportation	300.3	533.9	−233.6
Travel	1279.6	227.2	1052.4
Other Services	398.5	561.9	−163.4
B. Income	165.8	498.3	−332.5
Compensation of employees	94.0	23.7	70.3
Investment Income	71.8	474.6	−402.8
C. Current Transfers	757.9	110.6	647.3
Official	53.5	7.7	45.8
Private	704.4	102.9	601.5
D. Capital Account	19.1	30.0	−10.9
Government capital transfers	4.1	0.0	4.1
Other sectors transfers	15.0	30.0	−15.0
E. Financial Account	1644.2	1415.8	228.4
Direct Investment	523.7	94.9	428.8
Other Investment	965.1	1299.1	−334.0
Reserves	155.4	21.8	133.6
F. Net errors & omissions	0.0	1.2	−1.2

Jamaica's simplified balance of payments account in millions of US$, 2004.

Source: Bank of Jamaica, Pamphlet No. 8: 'Balance of Payments made Simple' by Fedrica Jackson.

Some comments on Jamaica's balance of payments account

Current account

There is a large deficit in the trade in goods of US$1186.5 million. A large part of this deficit will be due to oil imports.

There is a large surplus in the trade in travel of US$1052.4 million. This surplus will be due to tourism.

However, there is an overall deficit in the balance of trade of US$531.1 million and an overall deficit in the current account of US$216.3 million.

Income

There is a deficit on income from investment. This means that the incomes that foreigners are receiving from their investments in Jamaica exceeds the incomes that Jamaicans are receiving from their investments abroad (by US$402.8 million).

Current transfers

There is a large surplus of US$601.5 million in private transfers. This is always a feature of Jamaica's balance of payments. Jamaicans living and working abroad are transferring large sums to Jamaica regularly.

Financial account

Direct investment shows a surplus of US $428.8 million. This shows strong inward investment in Jamaica. However, the income from this investment goes out of Jamaica on the current account and accounts for the deficit which we noted under the income section, e.g. the big hotel chains invest in Jamaica when they build the hotel complexes, but when the hotels are up and running the profits go out of Jamaica.

Surpluses and deficits

The balance of payments is made to balance. However, in practice, there will be surpluses and deficits in different parts of the account. A deficit or a surplus does not necessarily have to be settled. If there is a deficit to another country, there is a debt to that country and it is as if there is a borrowing of money. The deficit can be settled by a surplus in the following year. It can be settled by drawing on reserves. All countries hold reserves of foreign currencies and gold. Creditor countries will want to be paid in hard currency so reserves mean reserves of hard currencies. Countries are reluctant to use their reserves so they hope that credits will cover debits in the balance of payments.

However, if a deficit persists debts will mount and interest payments will become large or reserves will be used up. Other action must be taken.

A deficit in the current account of the balance of payments

There is a deficit in the trade balance because (a) $X < M$ or (b) $M > X$.

1 Foreigners are not buying enough of your goods and services to cover what your citizens are buying from foreigners.

2 Your citizens are buying more from foreigners than they are buying from you.

1 Reasons why your exports are not selling

- You cannot make foreigners buy your goods. Perhaps you are selling the wrong sort of goods. There may have been a change in taste away from the goods you sell or the quality is not good. Your prices may be too high.
- The anti-smoking campaign is gathering strength and tobacco-exporting countries are facing difficulties. It is easy to suggest 'diversifying' into another product, but it is often difficult to do. They are losing their traditional markets in the West. Therefore, they must look for new markets in the East. This seems to be a solution, but it may be only temporary.
- If your prices are too high, it may be because your costs are too high compared with your competitors. You must seek supply-side solutions in terms of better methods of production, perhaps substituting machines for labour.
- Your prices may be too high because your currency is overvalued. Foreigners

have to pay too much of their own currency for a unit of yours.
- Foreigners' incomes are too low and they cannot afford your goods.

2 Reasons why your citizens are importing too much

- Foreign goods are more attractive. They may be better made. For years, Japanese cars were being sold with radios, cassette recorders and air-conditioning as standard whereas they were optional extras on European cars. Japanese electrical goods, cameras and watches have been very attractive in foreign markets.
- Foreign prices are lower than domestic prices. This is the principal cause of the West's trade imbalance with China today. China's prices are low because the costs of production are low and labour costs are the main factor in this.
- Your currency is overvalued. One unit of your currency buys many units of the foreign currency. This makes imports appear cheap.
- Your incomes are too high and so your consumption expenditure is high. Some of this goes on imported goods, e.g. incomes are high in the United States and consumers import foreign goods. The US car industry has been in crisis because Americans are favouring foreign-made cars.

The results of persistent deficits

We have already seen that debts will build up and interest payments will become burdensome. Also, we have seen that reserves will be drained and no country wants this. On the other hand, there is a positive side to deficits. In the short term, living standards will rise as more goods and services from abroad are consumed, usually at lower prices which leaves more income for domestic goods as well.

Many countries have an unfavourable trade balance with China

Source: Stillpictures..

However, we must analyse the problem in more depth. More and more money being spent on imports reduces the money supply at home. This is deflationary and economic growth falls with loss of jobs and falling incomes. Balance of payments deficits, therefore, must not be allowed to be persistent deficits.

Solutions to persistent deficits

It seems to come down to prices in the end. In a previous chapter, we looked at protectionist measures like tariffs, quotas and exchange controls. These measures do reduce imports, but they involve interference with the workings of the free market and are usually rejected by economists. The International Monetary Fund's (IMF) economists are free marketeers and they reject tariffs and quotas, but may allow exchange controls. However, their preferred solution is **devaluation**.

> **Definition of a devaluation**
>
> A devaluation is the reduction in the value of a country's currency against all other currencies.

As seen earlier in the chapter, the IMF does not like competitive devaluations to gain trade advantages, but when a country calls in the IMF for help with balance of payments problems, it makes devaluation the key plank in the **Structural Adjustment Programme (SAP)**. Apart from devaluation, an SAP also includes removing protectionist measures, privatisation and liberalisation; in general, the efficiency of the free market.

Devaluation makes exports cheaper and imports dearer, so a country that devalues will export more and import less, and its balance of payments deficit will be removed. A devaluation really only works when the demand for exports and imports is price elastic.

Prime Minister Michael Manley signed a Loan Agreement with the IMF in 1977 which brought hardship to many Jamaicans.

Source: AP/EMPICS.

In 1977, Michael Manley, Prime Minister of Jamaica, was forced to sign a loan agreement with the IMF because of the debts that Jamaica had built up. The IMF's conditions for the loan included devaluation of the Jamaican $ against the US$. The SAP introduced was considered to have had a negative impact on the lives of the vast majority of Jamaicans. To go further: the SAP is blamed for all the economic and social problems that beset Jamaica since calling in the IMF! Jamaicans continued importing, but just had to pay far more for their imports. Jamaicans exported, but received far less for their exports, and so on …

The First President of Tanzania (then Tanganyika in 1961), Julius Nyerere maintained strongly that devaluation was just the wrong policy to be imposed when a country was in balance of payments difficulties. With devaluation after devaluation, foreigners would be paying next to nothing for Third World exports. He suggested exactly the opposite. Foreigners should pay more for Third World exports, not less. Revaluation of the currency would bring this about. However, the dilemma is that revaluation means higher prices and higher prices choke off demand. Foreign consumers would find other markets, e.g. there are many coffee exporting countries. Countries with **'chronic'** balance of payments problems have to call in the IMF and devaluation is one of the conditions of the package.

Examination questions

1 Distinguish clearly between a depreciation and a devaluation of a currency. *(10 marks)*

2 Compare and contrast a floating and a fixed exchange rate system. *(10 marks)*

3 Explain what is meant by the terms of trade. *(10 marks)*

4 a Why is a balance of payments deficit considered to be a problem? *(4 marks)*
   b Discuss the different policies which might be used to try and eliminate this deficit. *(6 marks)*

Part seven

Caribbean economies in a global environment

Caribbean economies at present

In this chapter you will be concentrating on Caribbean economies in the world today.

- You will be reminded of the common historical background of Caribbean economies
- Bearing in mind that no two economies are the same, you will be given some common characteristics and problems of Caribbean economies. These are sometimes interlinked, e.g. the reliance on tourism is both a characteristic and a problem
- You will then be introduced to 'trade blocs' and the theory behind them
- You will study CARICOM, looking at what the bloc involves and go on to consider a cost/benefit analysis of CARICOM and an appraisal of its performance

The characteristics of Caribbean economies

In a classification of economies of the world under such classes as Western industrialised countries, Middle Eastern oil producing countries, Pacific Rim countries, Third World countries etc., Caribbean countries are always given as a separate class because they do not belong to any other group. They are not South American, North American, Third World or any other classification. They are their own group.

Please note that Guyana is in South America but is classed as a Caribbean economy for historical reasons. Belize is in Central America but is classed as a Caribbean economy for the same reasons. The Bahamas are outside the Caribbean geographically but are increasingly linked to the Caribbean economically, as well as culturally and historically.

The classification of economies into groups is convenient, but it is dangerous because no two economies are the same. Obviously, within the Caribbean economies, we find one oil producer and exporter – Trinidad and Tobago. We find two rich in bauxite – Jamaica and Guyana. Belize exports timber. The Cayman Islands and the Bahamas have big offshore banking centres. Barbados has to a lesser degree, but tourism is more important there. Dominica still largely depends on agriculture. St Lucia has a diverse light manufacturing sector. St Vincent's agricultural sector is still dominated by bananas … and so on.

However, tourism is common to all Caribbean economies and more must be said about this later.

The historical background

A common link is that all Caribbean countries used to be colonies (some still are) of a European country. This historical link is reflected in the languages spoken: English in the ex-British colonies, French in the ex-French colonies, Spanish in the ex-Spanish colonies and Dutch in the ex-Dutch colonies. Denmark did have colonies, principally St Croix, St Thomas and St John in the Virgin Islands, but they are now the Virgin Islands of the United States and English is the official language.

In the 'old colonial system', the economies of the colonies were subservient to the mother countries, Spain, Britain, France and the Netherlands. They were plantation economies, chiefly of sugar and tobacco. They were also slave economies. The Caribbean colonies were part of the 'Triangle of Trade of the North Atlantic' – from Europe to West Africa with firearms and manufactured goods to pick up slaves. The Middle Passage was the voyage across the Atlantic to sell the slaves in the Caribbean. The third leg of the triangle was transporting the sugar, molasses, rum and tobacco back to the European mother countries.

The dependence of Caribbean economies on European mother countries has gone. Most Caribbean countries are independent countries. Their economies have changed and their trading patterns have changed as we saw in Chapter 16. Sugar and other tropical crops have survived, but their importance has declined fast and all economies have diversified since colonial times.

Present-day characteristics

(From now on we are going to concentrate on the English-speaking Caribbean and we shall not specify 'English-speaking' any further in the text, but take it for granted that those are the economies we are referring to.)

Human development

In the United Nations Development Programme's Report under the Human Development Index (HDI) (which ranks 177 countries of the world by an index based on (i) per capita GDP, (ii) life expectancy and (iii) education), five Caribbean countries rank in the high human development category which is an HDI of above 0.8. They are (in order of ranking): Barbados, St Kitts and Nevis, Bahamas, Trinidad and Tobago and Antigua and Barbuda.

The others all fall in the medium human development category which is an index of between 0.8 and 0.5. They are (in order of ranking): St Lucia, Jamaica, St Vincent and the Grenadines, Grenada, Dominica, Belize and Guyana.

Therefore, we could say that it is a characteristic of Caribbean economies to be in the medium human development category. More precisely, they lie between 0.888 (Barbados) and 0.719 (Guyana) in the HDI. We can also say that no Caribbean economy lies in the low human development category.

EXERCISE To what extent do you think the HDI is a useful method to compare countries?

Free market economies

In the Heritage Foundation's Index of Economic Freedom Rankings, which we examined in Chapter 7, we saw that Caribbean economies lie in the 'Mostly Free' category, the only exception being Guyana. We can thus say that it is a characteristic of Caribbean economies to be free market economies, Bahamas being the most free market economy and Guyana being the least (remember that all economies are 'mixed' economies!).

The size of GDP

By size of GDP, Caribbean economies are small. Out of 232 economies ranked in the world (in the CIA World Factbook), Trinidad and Tobago – 132nd ranking – is the largest in the Caribbean with its GDP at purchasing power parity US$11.5 billion and St Kitts and Nevis – 214th ranking – the smallest at US$340 million. Trinidad and Tobago by GDP is over 1,000 times smaller than the United States! Singapore's GDP is 11 times bigger than Jamaica's, but its population is only bigger by two thirds. (Jamaica, GDP US$11.3 billion, and Singapore, GDP US$131 billion)! Therefore we can characterise Caribbean economies as being small. Most fall in to the category of **microstates**.

> **Definition of a microstate**
> A microstate is a country with a population of under one million people.

Market size

Caribbean economies are characterised by a small market size. By this we mean the domestic market. The market can be measured by population size. This certainly shows how many consumers there are in the market. Their spending power is shown by per capita GDP. In the table below are selected economies by population and per capita GDP (the figures are approximate).

Table 21.1 Market size in the Caribbean

Country	Population	Per capita GDP (US$)
Antigua and Barbuda	69,000	11,000
Barbados	280,000	16,000
Belize	280,000	6,500
Guyana	765,000	3,800
Jamaica	2,700,000	4,100
St Kitts and Nevis	39,000	8,700
St Lucia	156,000	5,000
Trinidad and Tobago	1,270,000	10,500

Source: CIA World Factbook.

The size of markets is very small by population. Jamaica and Trinidad and Tobago are the only economies with over a million people. Most Caribbean economies are 250,000 or less, with some under 100,000.

The spending power varies but, apart from the top two, the spending power measured by per capita GDP is also low at under US$10,000 per capita. Some Caribbean economies have per capita GDPs at under US$5,000 or under US$14 per day. This does not give much spending power in the market.

Over-reliance on trade

Caribbean economies are characterised by their exports and imports forming a high percentage of GDP. Think of GDP as being the total value of goods and services produced in an economy in the year (the output method of calculating GDP). Think of imports being the goods and services consumed by the citizens in the economy, but produced abroad. Think of exports being the goods and services produced in the economy but not consumed by the citizens of that economy. There are not many goods and services left that are produced and consumed domestically in the economy when exports and imports form a high percentage of GDP.

Exports % of GDP, 2004	Imports % of GDP
Barbados 57% of GDP.	Jamaica 21% of GDP
Guyana 94% of GDP	Trinidad and Tobago 40% of GDP

In 2004, the value of Trinidad and Tobago's exports and imports combined was US$11.25 billion, while its GDP was US$11.5 billion!

You may think that this is not surprising as most economies in the Caribbean are island economies with limited resources. They have to import and, to pay for the imports, they have to export. This brings us to the next characteristic.

The crowded harbour of Jeremie, Haiti. Over-reliance on trade in Caribbean countries.

Source: Stillpictures.

Reliance on tourism

Barbados relies heavily on tourism, but to a lesser extent all Caribbean economies do, and if they do not at present, they are certainly trying to build up the tourist industry, e.g. Dominica. Trinidad and Tobago exports oil, but it also has a thriving tourist industry. Guyana is one economy in the Caribbean which does not list tourism in its top ten exports. There are comprehensive figures for 2002 from the World Travel and Tourism Council (WTTC) and the Caribbean Tourism Organisation (CTO).

Table 21.2 Reliance on tourism in Caribbean economies in 2002[a]			
Country	Tourism penetration ratio (Tourists/1,000)[b]	Revenue from tourism (US$ millions)[c]	Tourism % of GDP[d]
Antigua and Barbuda	No data	528	72
Bahamas	63	2,497	46
Barbados	56	1,032	37
Belize	16	194	23
Cayman Islands	152	468	31
Dominica	23	64	22
Grenada	25	99	23
Jamaica	14	2,025	27
St Kitts and Nevis	43	93	25
St Lucia	45	380	51
St Vincent and the Grenadines	No data	110	29
Trinidad and Tobago	No data	787	9

Notes:
(a) The year 2002 is the year after 9/11, and the terrorist attack on the United States. Therefore, all the figures are down by that factor. By 2004, the recovery of tourism was complete. For example, in 1999, the average contribution to GDP was 43% but in 2002, it was down to 33%.
(b) The tourism penetration ratio shows the number of tourists per 1,000 of the local population, but it does not tell of the interaction between tourists and the local population.
(c) Revenue from tourism is significant. In three economies it is over US$1 billion and in two economies it is over US$2 billion.
(d) With the exception of Trinidad and Tobago, the contribution of tourism to GDP is always over 20% and in two economies, Antigua and Barbuda and St Lucia, it is over 50%. Again, with the exception of Trinidad and Tobago, the contribution of tourism to GDP in Caribbean economies lies between 20% and 75%.

It is dangerous to generalise, but we can say that the smaller the economy, the bigger the contribution of tourism to GDP.

Tourism also provides between 20–60% of jobs in the Caribbean.

Think also that the tourist industry is growing and reliance on it will be growing too.

EXERCISE Find out as much as you can about tourism in your country. Do you think your country is over-dependent on tourism?

Lack of diversification

You may say that this contradicts the last point about the reliance on tourism. Caribbean economies have diversified from being plantation economies into tourist economies. This point needs consideration. With independence from the UK and with UK joining the European Union in 1973, Caribbean economies have tried to diversify, but have they succeeded?

EXERCISE To what extent would you describe your country's economy as diversified?

The economies of the Caribbean are still sugar producers, e.g. Barbados, Guyana, Jamaica and Trinidad and Tobago. The Eastern Caribbean islands still grow bananas. Bananas were still about 50% of Dominica's exports a few years ago as they were in Grenada, St Lucia (41% of exports) and St Vincent (39% of exports).

Caribbean economies have diversified into financial services, but it is chiefly manufacturing which has not been developed. Some Caribbean economies have diversified into light industries but they are not a significant part of GDP.

There is a case to be made for saying that Caribbean economies have diversified, but not enough.

EXERCISE To what extent would you say your country fulfills the characteristics of a Caribbean economy?

Economic problems associated with Caribbean economies

Many of the economic problems arise out of the characteristics of Caribbean economies listed above, but others are only partly related to these characteristics.

Small economies and small populations

There is something about a 'vicious circle' connected to this problem, i.e. the problem is aggravated by its own consequences. Small populations generate low demand; low demand is met by low supply and low output; low output generates low demand for labour; low demand for labour brings unemployment; low demand for labour brings low wages; low wages and unemployment brings low demand for goods and services … and so on.

Low domestic demand brings reliance on foreign demand; foreign demand is for exports; this is good except that it brings a reliance on exports and exports become a large percentage of GDP. Caribbean economies become reliant on foreign demand over which they have no control (it also brings vulnerability to trade shocks and this will be dealt with later).

Small markets, low levels of output and small GDPs cannot generate investment. Caribbean economies, especially the small ones, rely on overseas investment which can be withdrawn as easily as it is given. Inward investment (foreign direct investment

St Kitts enjoys relatively high levels of employment.

or FDI) is good for the infrastructure but some of the profits and interest go out in the current account of the balance of payments.

Endemic unemployment

Unemployment rates in Caribbean economies are high. ('Endemic' unemployment means that it is regularly found in the economy, or that it is built into the economic system.) St Kitts and Nevis is an exception in that unemployment is stated at 4.5%. However, throughout the rest of the Caribbean, unemployment rates are over 10%, ranging from 10% in Bahamas to 22% in St Vincent. The two biggest economies, Jamaica and Trinidad and Tobago, have unemployment rates of 16% and 14% respectively. The eastern Caribbean islands tend to have high rates of unemployment.

There are demand-side and supply-side reasons for unemployment. Demand for labour is derived demand, i.e. labour is demanded for the goods it produces. If there is a lack of demand for domestically produced goods, then there will be a lack of demand for labour. This brings us back to the point about small economies once again. Small populations with low incomes (as seen by per capita GDP) cannot generate the demand for jobs. There is endemic unemployment.

However, if the demand for imports is high (imports are a high percentage of GDP), demand is diverted from domestically produced goods to foreign goods. This diverts demand from domestic labour to foreign labour. Again, this suggests that unemployment is built into the economic system.

On the supply side, there are causes of high levels of unemployment in the Caribbean. The labour force is not equipped to do the jobs. The re-training of former manual workers is not available, or not effective enough, to meet the requirements of jobs available. There are high levels of literacy throughout the Caribbean, but there must be more **'techno-literacy'** to fit the requirements of the modern labour force. Consequently, the jobs are going abroad or high-tech jobs at home are going to foreigners.

As in the rest of the world, technological unemployment is being experienced in the Caribbean. Think of computerisation in the banking industry. Many jobs have been lost, or there could be many more jobs available in those economies that are expanding their financial services industries, if it had not been for the introduction of the new technology in offices.

Reliance on primary products

By 'primary products' we chiefly mean agricultural goods. Caribbean economies have diversified in modern times, but in many countries there is still a reliance on sugar, bananas, citrus and other fruits, coffee, cocoa, copra and spices for exports. The problem with relying on export revenue from primary products is that they are **income inelastic**, i.e. when world incomes rise, demand for primary products rises very little. Therefore, export revenue rises very little for Caribbean exporters of primary products when the world's incomes are rising. This can be shown very simply in a diagram.

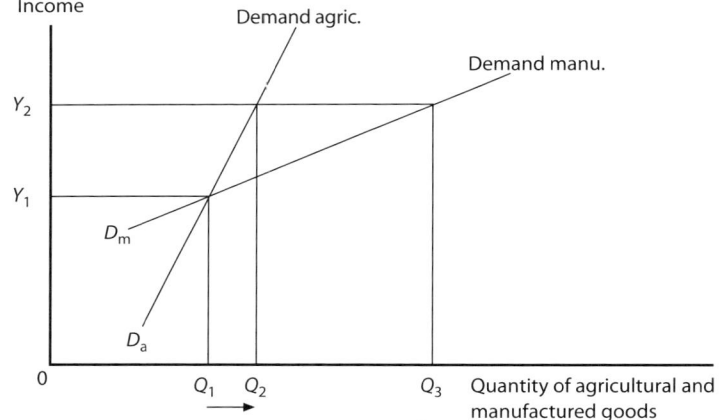

Fig. 21.1
Inelastic demand for agricultural goods

When world incomes rise from Y_1 to Y_2, demand for agricultural goods only increases from Q_1 to Q_2, whereas demand for manufactured goods increases from Q_1 to Q_3. This is because demand for agricultural goods is relatively income inelastic compared to the demand for manufactured goods.

'Brain drain'

Definition of the brain drain

The brain drain is the continuing loss of citizens of high intelligence and creativity through emigration.

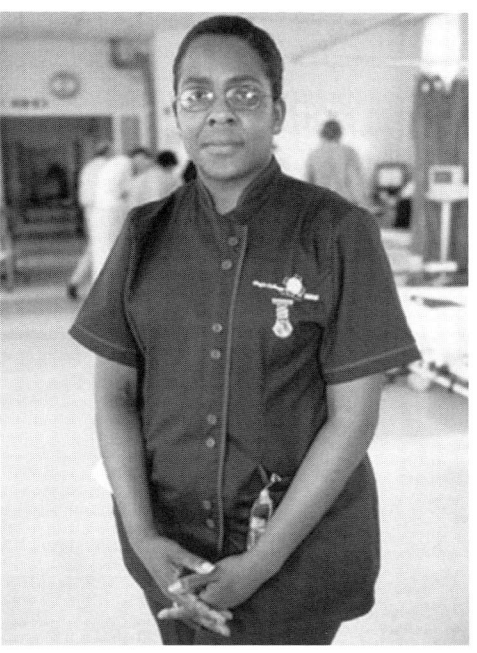

The 'brain drain' when qualified nurses seek jobs abroad.

The other side of the labour problem is that Caribbean citizens are being well educated to fill jobs, but these jobs are being taken abroad in Canada, the UK and the United States. Either there are not enough jobs available at home for their skills or that higher rates of pay overseas attract Caribbean labour. Caribbean economies, especially Jamaica, suffer from the 'brain drain'. It is a serious problem for Caribbean economies because (i) the investment that has been put into education does not benefit the Caribbean economy, but a foreign economy and (ii) Caribbean economies lose valuable labour resources and sectors of the economy suffer shortages of skilled labour.

The brain drain is particularly felt in the medical profession from nurses right up to surgeons.

The brain drain is mainly caused by wage differentials between western industrialised nations like Canada, the UK and the USA and Caribbean economies. A surgeon earns one-tenth in Jamaica of what he or she could earn in the above-mentioned countries and a nurse about one third.

There can be a system of 'bonding' which ties a recipient of state education to the domestic labour force for a number of years. However, the wage differential is sufficiently high to enable those going abroad to work to pay off their bond. On the other hand, bonding is not ethically desirable as it implies compulsion and force. You do not like to think that the nurse is working in the local medical service because she or he is forced to.

EXERCISE Do you know of people who have been part of the 'brain drain'? Where did they go? Try and find out, if you can, why they went.

External shocks

Caribbean economies which are so heavily reliant on trade are vulnerable to shocks which come from outside the economic system. It is best to give an example. In 1989, the Soviet Union, under the reforms of 'perestroika' (reconstruction) begun by General Secretary of the Communist Party Gorbachev, withdrew its support and subsidisation of the Cuban economy to the extent of US$4 to 6 billion a year. Between 1989 and 1993, Cuba went into deep recession from which it is only slowly recovering. This was a deep, sharp shock. Usually external shocks are not so brutal, but they are nevertheless severe.

The terrorist attack on the United States of 11 September 2001 made Americans stop flying, domestically and abroad. This seriously affected Caribbean economies as holidays were cancelled and bookings went down dramatically. Unlike Cuba's case, where Russian support was ended for good, recovery was quicker for Barbados, Jamaica and the other islands that had been hit hard, as Americans took to the air again and resumed their Caribbean holidays.

Caribbean economies are vulnerable to recessions in the economies of their trading partners. The last deep recession in the United Kingdom, from 1989 to 1993, affected tourism in the Caribbean. For over ten years now, the Caribbean economies have been spared the impact of recession abroad.

Reliance on tourism

Relying on a single source of revenue can be dangerous. There is an English saying: 'Do not put all your eggs in one basket.' What happens when you drop the basket? Caribbean economies derived 33% of their GDP from travel and tourism in 2002. Barbados and St Lucia are the Caribbean economies most reliant on tourism.

As pointed out before, in 1999 tourism contributed 43% of GDP. Just because of an external shock, Caribbean economies lost 10% of the contribution to GDP. This shows the vulnerability to the economy of relying on one source of revenue.

The **tourist multiplier** can be seen to be in operation. When tourist expenditure rises by $1,000,000, this creates incomes for Caribbean citizens. They will spend some of that $1,000,000 at home and that spending will create further incomes, and so on … The initial increase in expenditure by the tourists has created round after round of increased incomes and the GDP of the Caribbean economy increases by a multiplied amount, i.e. more than $1,000,000. If the GDP rises by $1,500,000, the tourist multiplier is 1.5:

$$\text{Tourist multiplier} = \frac{\text{Change in GPD}}{\text{Change in tourist expenditure}} \quad \text{(in symbols)} \quad \frac{\Delta Y}{\Delta J} = \frac{\$1,500,000}{\$1,000,000}$$

However, the tourist multiplier also works in reverse. If tourist expenditure falls, GDP will fall by a multiplied amount. This stresses the vulnerability of Caribbean economies to something over which they have no control.

The tourist multiplier is weaker than the investment multiplier because there are more leakages. We have seen that when a tourist stays in a hotel, some of that expenditure is leaked out of the Caribbean in profits. When a tourist drinks gin, some of that expenditure is leaked out of the Caribbean. Therefore, the tourist multiplier is weak, but it is still a multiplier.

20% to 60% of jobs in Caribbean economies depend on tourism. In 2004 travel and tourism created 2,416,500 jobs in Caribbean economies. If there is war, terrorism, recession or political change abroad, tourism can suffer and Caribbean economies will suffer. This time we are thinking of job losses and unemployment.

In 2006 there was a specific threat. The United States Homelands Department proposed the **Western Hemisphere Travel Initiative** in order to protect the borders of the United States. This is a consequence of 9/11. Under this initiative, US citizens without a passport (and many US citizens do not have a passport) can only visit US territories in the Caribbean if they are willing to pay about an extra US$400 for a family of four. Other Caribbean destinations could face economic loss because 51% of tourists come from the USA (up to 86% in the Bahamas).

The Western Hemisphere Travel Initiative brings out clearly how vulnerable the tourist industry is and how vulnerable Caribbean economies are when tourism is the mainstay of the economy.

A limited range of products

There is a limited range of products produced in Caribbean economies. There are agricultural products, such as sugar, bananas, coffee, citrus, cocoa, coconuts, copra, spices and corn, to name but a few. However, most economies produce these. When an economy has diversified into light industry, this usually means the production of soap, shoes, beverages, textiles, food processing and furniture. Jamaica has tried to diversify in agriculture, e.g. in horticulture and fish farming.

Diversification into light industry: a shoe factory in the Dominican Republic.
Source: Stillpictures.

When most economies are producing the same products there is little scope for integration. In Chapter 19, we saw the gains from trade to be had by specialisation and comparative advantage, but Caribbean economies seem unwilling to put these theories into practice and integrate their economies. The failure to integrate economies within the Caribbean is a problem.

Lack of competitiveness

This problem closely follows from the previous one about failure to integrate and enjoy the gains from specialisation. In major industries Caribbean economies do compete, as in tourism and financial services, and compete fiercely, but in other, smaller industries there is little competition. In competition, the strong prosper and the weak go under. There is an underlying feeling in Caribbean economies that each industry is a strategic industry and that each country must have an industry of its own. There is a strong element of history in this. Caribbean economies grew up with strong trade links to the outside world, but not strong trade links with each other so they all developed their own industries, some on a very small scale.

The rum industry can be used as an example. Each island, or almost each island, developed its own rum industry although it would have made economic sense for one island to specialise in rum and enjoy the economies of scale. However, the rum industries in each island developed without regard to economic theory and there was no competition.

Reliance on preferences

The Caribbean Community and Common Market, **CARICOM**, came into operation in August, 1973. It was the successor to the Caribbean Free Trade Association, **CARIFTA**, which linked the English-speaking countries of the Caribbean economically. Now CARICOM has 15 full members and five associate members (those that are not independent countries).

CARICOM is a trade bloc. It became the newest trade bloc in the world on 23 January, 2006. The purpose of forming a trade bloc is economic survival. CARICOM removes trade barriers between members, thus creating a free market, but places a common tariff against non-members, sometimes called 'third countries'. The trade bloc will be a protection against **globalisation** (see the next chapter) and competition from the rest of the world.

Within CARICOM, industries can grow and enjoy economies of scale protected from powerful competition from abroad by the tariffs. However, the preferential treatment enjoyed by members is a sure sign that Caribbean industries could not compete in the global market. The **World Trade Organisation (WTO)** wants the removal of preferential trading arrangements. The two preferential trading arrangements that are due to be removed from CARICOM members are those with the United Kingdom and the European Union. The preferential trading arrangements with the European Union were made under the Lome Convention. There are also preferential trading arrangements with the United States under the Caribbean Basin Initiative (CBI). The EU and the US will be under pressure from the WTO to end these preferences. These are the ones that Caribbean economies have relied on most. **Caricom Single Market and Economy (CMSE)** will become even more important for the survival of the Caribbean market.

The removal of preferences will certainly be a problem for Caribbean economies in the future. The theory is that with the protection that Caribbean countries have enjoyed, they will have grown strong enough to be able to survive without protection in the future (the 'infant industry argument'). This remains to be seen.

Trade blocs – CARICOM

The World Trade Organisation (WTO) is trying to free world trade from trade barriers, but increasingly countries are forming themselves into regional trade blocs as we can see in the map of the world below.

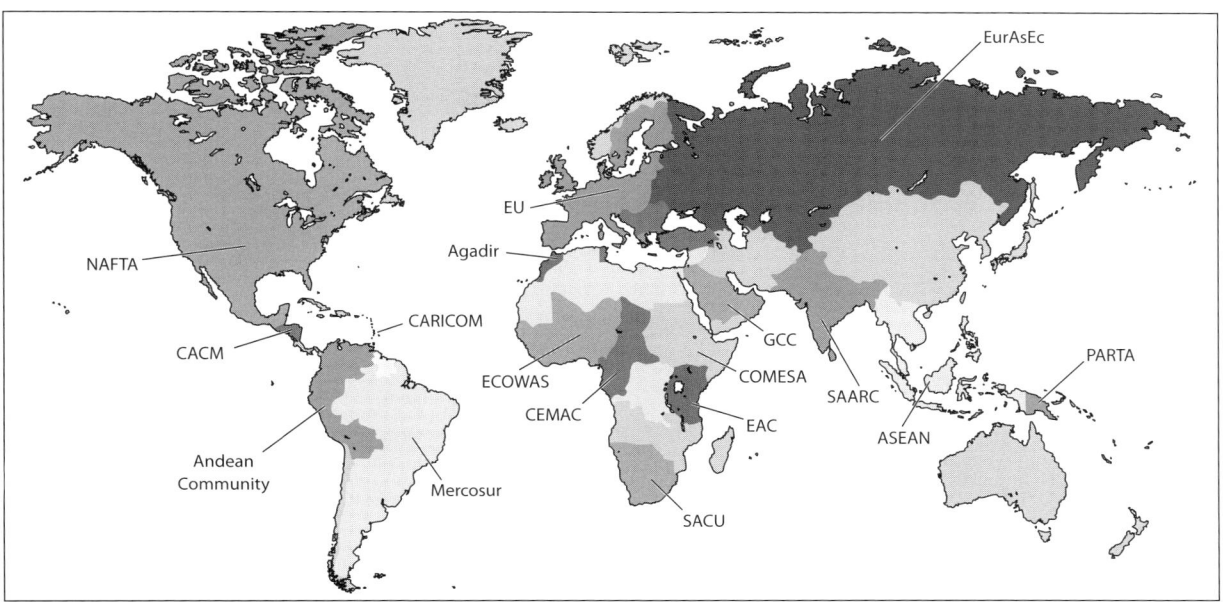

Map 21.2
Major trade blocs of the world

Definition of a trade bloc
A trade bloc is a large free trade area formed by a tariff and a trade agreement.

The four biggest trade blocs are:

- The European Union (EU).
- The North American Free Trade Area (NAFTA).
- The Association of South East Asian Nations (ASEAN).
- The Cairns Group (an informal group of agricultural exporters led by Australia and including many South American countries).

CARICOM is shown on the map in Fig. 21.2, but it is a relatively small trade bloc of approximately 14.5 million people. Its GDP is a little over US$64 billion.

Countries forming trade blocs aim to lower trade barriers between them and to stimulate regional trade with a view to encourage economic growth.

There are four types of trade blocs:

Free trade area

Members trade freely amongst themselves but each have their own trade barriers against countries outside of the free trade area. The North American Free Trade Area comprises Canada, Mexico and the United States and it used to be the largest Free Trade Area until the enlargement of the European Union (EU).

Customs union

Countries in customs unions surrender some of their control over trade policies. They have a Common External Tariff (CET) applied to all countries outside the union. The European Union is the largest and presents a common front in dealings with the World Trade Organisation.

Common market

In addition to being a Customs Union, there is the free movement of the factors of production, e.g. labour and capital. Mercosur is a common market of some South American countries.

Economic union

This is a common market that has gone further than trade in goods and services, common tariffs and the free movement of factors of production. There may be fixed exchange rates or even a single currency which implies a common monetary policy. There may be political integration with a common parliament and common policies, e.g. foreign policy and defence. The European Union is moving towards an economic union, but the consequent reduction in sovereignty (independence) is holding members back.

The economic theory behind trade blocs

A trade bloc brings **trade creation** and **trade diversion**. Trade creation is brought about because a trade bloc creates a bigger market than a single state can have. The enlarged market generates increased output. Countries will specialise, increase output and improve efficiency in production. Increased output brings economies of scale which should bring down prices in the trade bloc. Trade creation is always beneficial. However, would more trade be created if the world had no trade blocs?

Trade diversion is not always good. Production is diverted from countries outside the bloc to countries within the bloc. Those countries outside the bloc have a comparative advantage over those countries within the bloc.

Let us make up an example. Suppose St Kitts has a small textile industry making clothes for local consumption. This industry could not compete with world supply so membership of CARICOM would divert consumption from world supply to some CARICOM supplier – trade diversion. This is shown in the diagram below.

St Kitts and textiles

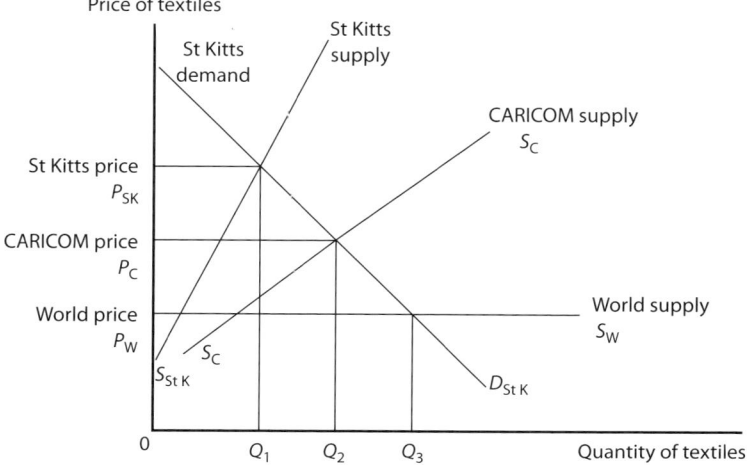

Fig. 21.3
The effect of trade diversion

World supply is sold at the world price, P_W. Before the trade bloc, citizens of St Kitts and Nevis could buy Q_3 of textiles at P_W, a big quantity at a low price. Local supply is inefficient and local suppliers can only supply Q_1 at price, P_{SK}. When St Kitts and Nevis join the trade bloc, CARICOM, trade is **diverted** from world suppliers outside the bloc to CARICOM suppliers. St Kitts and Nevis consumers now buy Q_2 textiles at price P_C. The trade bloc has caused a loss to St Kitts and Nevis consumers of $Q_3 - Q_2$ and a rise in price from P_W to P_C.

Is there any advantage? Yes, there is in that there has been a diversion of trade to a Caribbean supplier and Q_2 is a bigger quantity than Q_1 so the trade bloc supplier may be able to enjoy some economies of scale.

Trade creation is thus a benefit but trade diversion is a questionable benefit.

CARICOM: a cost–benefit analysis

> **Definition of cost–benefit analysis**
>
> Cost–benefit analysis is the weighing up of all of the costs and benefits, including the social costs and benefits, of a decision or project in order to be able to decide whether to proceed with it.

We shall deal with the benefits and costs of trade blocs in general and then apply them to CARICOM.

Benefits	Costs
Political	
a Bargaining power. As with trade unions, there is strength in unity. A customs union can enter into negotiations more effectively and will be more likely to make deals. b i) There is increased security in relations with fellow members. Conflict is unlikely. ii) There is increased security against non-members. c There can be regional agreement on domestic politics, e.g. democracy amongst member states can be reinforced under 'commitment mechanisms' (commitment to democracy in this case).	a Members have to sacrifice some measure of sovereignty when they allow the union to make security arrangements in a 'blanket fashion'. b When the union makes common cause on a political issue all members are unlikely to be in full agreement. The cost is a loss of voice by individual members.

Benefits	Costs
Economic	
a 'Scale and competition effects': removing trade barriers enlarges the market – (scale effect). Firms benefit from greater scale. They may be able to enjoy economies of scale. Removing trade barriers brings firms in member countries into closer competition. This will bring efficiency improvements (competition effect). Larger firms will attract investment in projects where size is important. Foreign Direct Investment (FDI) is of great benefit. b 'Trade and location effects': removing tariffs between members will switch demand towards supply from other members. Demand should switch to the members. Demand should switch to the lowest cost producer and aid efficiency. This is trade creation within the union. c Changes in location of production between members will occur determined by comparative advantage. There will be gains for members from comparative advantage. d Labour-intensive production will move to low-wage countries. The increased demand should pull up wages there. e Technology will be transferred between members.	a The costs are that greater scale and increased efficiency would probably have resulted from trade liberalisation with the world as the market (scale effect) and local firms facing competition from the rest of the world (competition effect). Members can no longer 'shop' in the world market. b Domestic production is lost when it cannot compete with the production of another member after tariffs have been removed between members. c Governments will lose tariff revenue. d If a member has comparative advantage because it had a head start in an industry or some natural advantage, income differentials between members could result.

CARICOM

From 1965 to 1972, there was the Caribbean Free Trade Association (CARIFTA) which was organised to continue the link between the English-speaking countries of the Caribbean after the break-up of the West Indies Federation in 1962. CARICOM was established by the Treaty of Chaguaramas. The first four members were Barbados, Guyana, Jamaica and Trinidad and Tobago. There are now fifteen full members and there are non English-speaking members, Haiti and Suriname. There are five associate members which are colonies or dependencies of the United Kingdom.

CARICOM is (i) a free trade area, (ii) a customs union and (iii) a common market, but whether it will go further into an economic union with a fixed exchange rate, or even a single currency with a common monetary policy, and further still into a political union with a common government, is doubtful. History is against it. Caribbean countries were colonies. Haiti fought bitterly against France for its independence. English-speaking countries won their independence from Britain. Having won independence after a long struggle, they are unlikely to surrender

CARICOM is the Caribbean trade bloc.

sovereignty to another body. There is a certain rivalry between Caribbean countries and it is a healthy rivalry (as in cricket).

In 2005, the leaders agreed to create the Caribbean Single Market and Economy (CSME). This is as far as integration has progressed. There is a CARICOM Secretariat, but that is a long way from a common government. The mission statement of the CARICOM Secretariat is: 'To provide dynamic leadership and service, in partnership with Community institutions and groups, toward the attainment of a viable, internationally competitive and sustainable Community, with improved quality of life for all.'

Barbados, Jamaica and Trinidad and Tobago are already signatories to CSME. It is hoped that ten of the remaining twelve members of CARICOM (not Bahamas and Haiti) will sign up to CSME.

There is also a sub-group among members of CARICOM, the Organisation of Eastern Caribbean States (OECS), which comprises seven full members and two associate members of CARICOM in the Eastern Caribbean. In some ways, this group is more closely integrated than CARICOM itself as there is a common central bank and a common currency.

One of the CARICOM institutions that students will be most familiar with is the **Caribbean Examinations Council (CXC)** which produces the syllabi and sets and marks the examinations that you all take.

Policy choices

There are four policy choices facing CARICOM.

1. With whom to make an agreement. Should CARICOM expand its membership? The debate is focused on the Dominican Republic. The Dominican Republic sought full membership in 2005, but its admission would be a big step for the other members to take as the Dominican Republic has a much larger economy and population than any existing member. The debate really hinges on whether to accept high income or low income partners (although Haiti has already been admitted). There has been a history of disagreement between CARICOM members and the Dominican Republic.

2. There is also the policy stance towards the outside world (outside the Caribbean). CARICOM has free trade agreements (FTAs) with a number of countries. There are already Preferential Agreements with Venezuela and Colombia and free trade agreements with Cuba, the Dominican Republic and Costa Rica.

   On the doorstep is the North American Free Trade Area (NAFTA), the second-largest trading bloc in the world. Surely CARICOM would benefit by some preferential trading agreements with NAFTA, more embracing than the present Caribbean Basin Initiative (CBI) with the United States?

   As ex-colonies, Caribbean countries have common ground with African and Pacific countries, and strong ethnic ties with African countries. The African, Caribbean and Pacific Group of countries is a very loose grouping which CARICOM may wish to strengthen.

3. The policy choice closest to the hearts of CARICOM members, however, concerns CARICOM itself. Do members want closer political and economic commitment to CARICOM? Do they want a single currency and a single monetary policy? Do they want common taxation? Do they want a CARICOM parliament, i.e. to put themselves under one government and surrender some degree of sovereignty?

4. CARICOM still has not decided on the range of activities which it should cover. It covers goods, services and factor mobility. Travel between member countries is already 'visa-free' and now the members are debating a CARICOM passport. In January 2005, Suriname launched the CARICOM passport. It was followed by St Vincent and the Grenadines in April and St Kitts and Nevis in October 2005. Probably all members will adopt the common passport when the stock of their existing passports runs out.

Future proposals that we have not already mentioned are for one airline and one stock exchange.

An appraisal of CARICOM

CARICOM has been in existence for 32 years and is growing larger in terms of the number of members, population and GDP. It is significant that no members have withdrawn from CARICOM in those 32 years. There are candidates for admission. In operation are a free trade area, a customs union and a single market, although not all members participate in this. There is visa-free travel within CARICOM and there will be a common passport.

There is a Heads of Government Conference where the heads of government from each member state meet and there are standing committees with responsibility for specific areas such as Health. We have seen that there is a Secretariat based in Georgetown, Guyana, to deal with day-to-day matters of CARICOM.

There are 14 CARICOM Institutions and these include the Caribbean Disaster Emergency Response Agency (CDERA), the Caribbean Meteorological Institute (CMI) and the Caribbean Environment Health Institute (CEHI). There are also four Associate Institutions including the Council for Trade and Economic Development (COTED), the Council for Foreign and Community Relations (COFCOR) and the Council for Human and Social Development (COHSOD).

The number of institutions is proof of positive action in CARICOM. In education we have only to think of CXC and the break with the examination boards of the United Kingdom. The syllabi are now geared to the interests and needs of Caribbean students. Another break with the United Kingdom was the setting up of the Caribbean Court of Justice. No longer are appeals heard in the House of Lords in the UK, but by the CCJ in the Caribbean.

The clearest way of appraising performance is to examine economic growth. For 40 years to 2002, economic growth in the Caribbean economies was 2.8%, which is a good average, but it should be higher for developing countries. The countries of the Eastern Caribbean tend to have the highest trend growth, up to 4.8% in St Vincent and the Grenadines. Haiti, Guyana and Jamaica have the lowest with only 1% in Haiti. However, Guyana is expected to grow at over 5% and Trinidad and Tobago by over 10% in the next few years.

The most successful sector in CARICOM economies has been the offshore financial sector. The Cayman Islands and Bahamas were always to the forefront in this market, but Barbados and Antigua and Barbuda are also doing well. There has been a small increase in light manufacturing, especially in clothing, where CARICOM members have a comparative advantage in high value-added goods such as made-to-measure clothing.

However, in trade overall, CARICOM has not been as successful as had been hoped in trade creation. 51% of Caribbean CARICOM exports go to NAFTA countries and the exports have fallen in percentage terms. It would be ideal if CARICOM could join NAFTA and enjoy parity with the existing NAFTA countries.

Tourism is the most dynamic export segment in CARICOM. This export market is highly competitive and Cuba and the Dominican Republic are CARICOM's biggest rivals. CARICOM countries are diversifying into eco-tourism (a strength of Cuba), sports, entertainment and health tourism.

However, overall Caricom has only gone part of the way towards achieving what it was set up for – trade creation and economic growth. CARICOM consists of many **microstates**: therefore the markets are too small for internal trade to be created. There is insufficient scale for more than one producer in each market, yet member countries continue to produce the same products. There is no chance of achieving the economies of scale unless members will sacrifice some domestic production. It must be said that CARICOM has not succeeded in promoting intra-regional trade as a trade bloc is supposed to do.

There has been some diversification, but not enough. There is still a concentration on a few products in a few markets.

Extra-regional trade for CARICOM is a result of preferential agreements which have secured markets in the past. However, the Lome Convention now embraces Spanish-speaking countries of the Caribbean which will bring unwanted competition to CARICOM members in trade with the European Union.

CARICOM is at a crossroads. The WTO is pushing for trade liberalisation and globalisation and preferential agreements will probably be ended. CARICOM can seek membership of bigger regional trade blocs. If not, the emerging regional trade blocs will be difficult to compete with. It will have to go further in its policies for trade creation. The economies of scale are not being reached under the present system of trade. Members will have to give up some sovereignty in their economic infrastructures. Perhaps they will have to accept monetary union and even a central policy-making institution.

Examination questions

1. **a** Explain how the Human Development Index is constructed. *(4 marks)*
   b How successful has it been as a means of comparing the quality of life in different countries? *(6 marks)*

2. **a** Outline the main characteristics of Caribbean economies. *(5 marks)*
   b Discuss the main problems facing Caribbean economies today. *(5 marks)*

3. Discuss, with the aid of examples, how external shocks can affect an economy. *(10 marks)*

4. Explain why economies should be as diversified as possible. *(10 marks)*

5. Explain what is meant by a multiplier. *(10 marks)*

6. Discuss the advantages and disadvantages of different forms of economic integration. *(10 marks)*

7. How successful do you think CARICOM has been as a regional economic unit? *(10 marks)*

Trade liberalisation, globalisation and their effects on Caribbean economies – E-commerce

In this chapter you will learn about the role and aims of the World Trade Organisation with regard to trade liberalisation and globalisation and the effects of trade liberalisation and globalisation on Caribbean economies. Finally, you will learn about E-commerce.

- You will learn how the World Trade Organisation developed historically from the Bretton Woods reorganisation of world trade after the Second World War through the General Agreement on Tariffs and Trade (GATT) to its present form
- You will see how the movement for trade liberalisation is supported by economic theory
- In contrast you will be given some arguments in favour of tariffs
- You will study the concept of 'globalisation'
- You will be shown how and why the WTO supports globalisation
- You will then be taken through the four main cases concerning the WTO and Caribbean economies: the Banana case, the Caribbean Basin Initiative case, the Sugar case and the tourism case
- The Structural Adjustment Programmes of the IMF are then explained
- You will study the effects of globalisation on Caribbean economies
- You will then consider the Caribbean Single market and Economy (CSME)
- Finally, there is a section on E-commerce

The World Trade Organisation

In July 1944, delegates from forty five countries met at Bretton Woods, New Hampshire, USA. The world had just passed through the Great Depression of the 1930s and the Second World War, which had started in 1939, was coming to an end. The delegates were determined to establish stability in the global economy so that trade could resume and flourish once the war was over. The two principal signatories to the Bretton Woods agreement were the UK and the USA, the victorious powers. John Maynard Keynes, the British Economist whom we have mentioned before, had much influence at the conference, but the USA, as the world's leading economy, was eager to take the dominant role in the post-war settlement. Out of Bretton Woods came a number of important initiatives.

Fixed exchange rates

The US dollar became the international currency. The dollar was fixed to gold at $35 per ounce of gold. All other currencies were fixed to the US$ so the dollar was known as the **'intervention currency'**. If all currencies were tied to the dollar, and the dollar was tied to gold, then the world was on a **'gold standard'**. This was intended to bring stability to the exchange rate market and encourage trade.

This latest gold standard lasted until 1973 when President Nixon devalued the dollar and floating exchange rates were introduced because the world had lost confidence in the stability of the dollar.

The International Monetary Fund

At Bretton Woods, the International Monetary Fund (IMF) was set up. Its aim was to **'facilitate the expansion and balanced growth of international trade'** and **'to contribute to the promotion and maintenance of high levels of employment and income'**.

The IMF was to oversee the fixed exchange rate system outlined above. In the Great Depression, countries had devalued their currencies in order to obtain an advantage over their rivals in trade, the so-called **'beggar-my-neighbour'** policies. Devaluation made exports cheaper so that the devaluing country sold more goods which led to increased production and lower unemployment which was so widespread in the 1930s. Instead competitive devaluations just caused chaos in foreign exchange markets and trade was discouraged.

> **Definition of a beggar-my-neighbour policy**
> A beggar-my-neighbour policy refers to profit making at the expense of others.

In the 1930s it was either making sure that domestic employment was maintained by not trading (importing) with your neighbours or using competitive devaluation to attract foreign demand so that domestic industries could maintain employment. In both ways it was a case of **'exporting your unemployment'**.

The IMF was to enable currencies to be exchanged easily for each other so as to encourage international trade.

Finally, the IMF was meant to lend money to countries in difficulties with balance of payments problems so that they would not have to forgo imports and make their domestic economies suffer. Keynes foresaw that some countries would be in surplus and others in deficit. He thought that the surpluses should be used to help those in deficit by importing their goods. However, the United States delegates were against this and they stopped the IMF being an automatic dispenser of loans. The system of **'special drawing rights'** (SDRs) was set up whereby those countries that put the most into the IMF could take the most out when in difficulties. The USA's SDR Quota is about US$27 billion. The number of votes a country has in IMF decisions is also determined by the quota. Therefore, the United States is in a position to dominate the IMF.

The IMF is able to impose its own conditions on countries taking a loan when in balance of payments difficulties. This has led to the **'Structural adjustment programmes' (SAPs)** that we saw in Chapter 20.

After Bretton Woods, countries were still allowed to keep tariffs and other trade barriers, but they were meant to be reduced to open up trade. We will see this under the **General Agreement on Tariffs and Trade (GATT)** a little later.

The World Bank (the International Bank for Reconstruction and Development)

The **World Bank** (its full name is the 'International Bank for Reconstruction and Development' was also set up at Bretton Woods. As its full name suggests, its aim was to help economies that had been devastated by war to recover. Specifically, it was to make loans for infrastructure projects like roads, dams, airports, power plants, but also for agricultural recovery and education. These loans would be at lower rates of interest than commercial banks would offer.

The infrastructure of European countries had been most hard hit, but European countries were helped directly by the United States with the **Marshall Plan**. Therefore, the International Bank for Reconstruction and Development began helping the newly independent countries in the 1960s. In the 1980s, these countries began finding difficulties with their loan repayments and the **Third World Debt Crisis** began. In fact, it was Mexico in 1982 that first defaulted on its debt repayments which was hard to believe as it was an oil exporter!

The General Agreement on Tariffs and Trade

GATT is the direct forerunner to the WTO. GATT was set up to reduce trade barriers chiefly by removing or lowering tariffs throughout the world. There were seven rounds of tariff reductions under GATT. The last round was the 'Uruguay Round' in 1986. The final meeting of delegates for this round, taking place in Marrakech, Morocco, in 1994, replaced GATT with the World Trade Organisation. GATT lacked

Headquarters of the World Bank in Washington.

Source: AP/EMPICS.

status whereas the WTO is an internationally recognised organisation. In 1994 it had 137 members and 30 'observers'. Today it has 150 members. This is approaching the same number of the United Nations. It is difficult to stay outside the WTO because of the dangers of being unrepresented. Whereas GATT only dealt with trade in goods, WTO includes the **'General Agreement on Trade in Services' (GATS)** which includes banking, investment, telecommunications, transport, health, education, the environment and many more fields. We shall return to the WTO later.

Trade liberalisation

Definition of trade liberalisation
Trade liberalisation is the movement towards removing barriers that restrict the import and export of goods and services between countries.

Trade liberalisation is the movement towards removing barriers that restrict the import and export of goods and services between countries. The barriers that are being referred to specifically are tariffs, quotas and exchange controls.

Intellectual property rights are patents, copyrights and trademarks which protect the products of creative works and inventions, such as fuel-efficient engines and song-writing.

Subsidies are also considered as an unwelcome interference with free trade as they lower prices and increase output which gives a competitive edge to exports. Here is a reminder of how a subsidy works.

A subsidy is paid by the government to local banana growers. The effect of the subsidy is to shift the supply curve outwards to the right by the vertical amount of the subsidy, AB.

The new supply curve cuts the foreign demand curve at a lower price, P_2, and an increased quantity, Q_2, giving the local growers a competitive edge (unfairly, according to free traders).

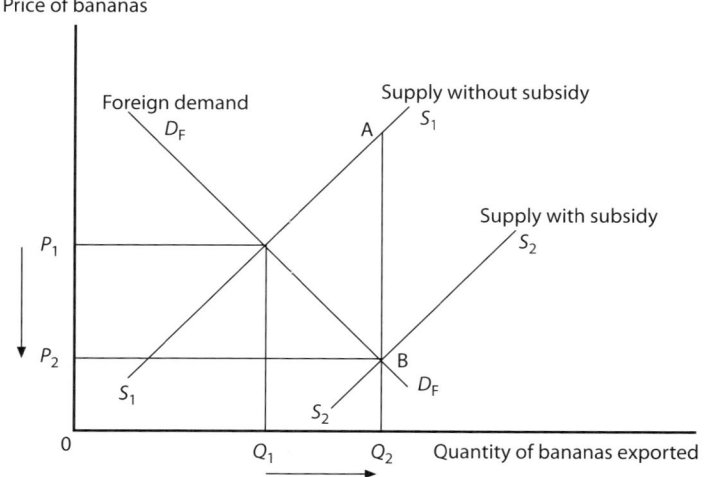

Fig. 22.1
The effect of a subsidy on exports

From the days of Adam Smith and David Ricardo, economists have stressed the virtues of free trade. Adam Smith first pointed out the gains from specialisation. If each worker specialised in what he or she was best at, output would increase. The worker becomes faster, more skilled at the job and invents better tools with which to perform the task. Unit costs go down and so goods become cheaper. The increased output is then traded and everyone gains in terms of more goods and services at lower prices.

On the other hand, if there is any interference with specialisation and free trade of surpluses, everyone loses.

David Ricardo brought us the theory of comparative advantage on a global scale. Each country should specialise in the production of a good in which it has a comparative advantage. As we saw in Chapter 16 on international trade, individual countries and the whole world gain from trade. Ricardo believed in free trade and proved it theoretically.

Suppose we have three imaginary Caribbean islands, Islands A, B and C. They all grow three crops; bananas, coffee and sugar. According to the Theory of Comparative Advantage, each island should specialise in growing what it has a comparative advantage in. World output would increase and each island would be better off with trade. Island A will specialise in bananas, Island B in coffee and Island C in sugar. By specialisation, the output of each crop will increase by so much that each island will have more than it had before and be able to trade the surplus to the other islands *and the rest of the world*.

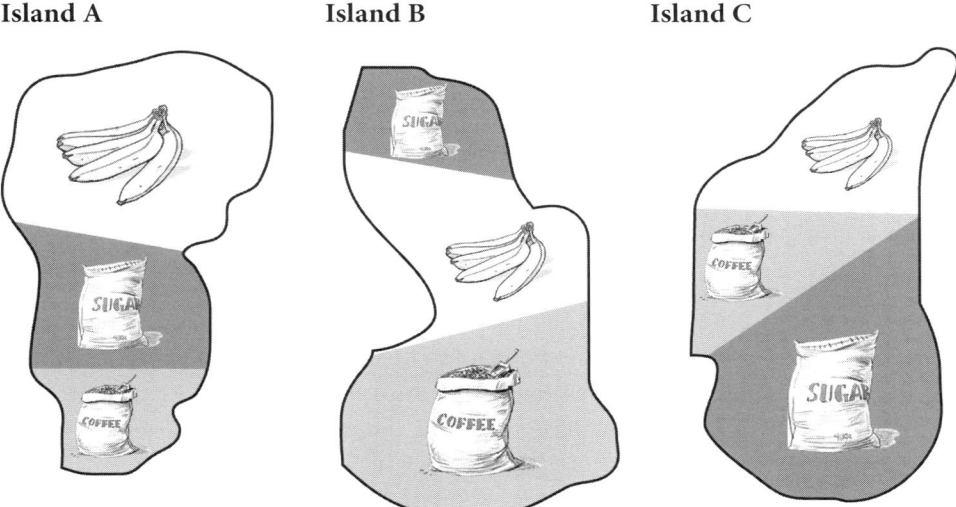

Fig. 22.2
Before specialisation

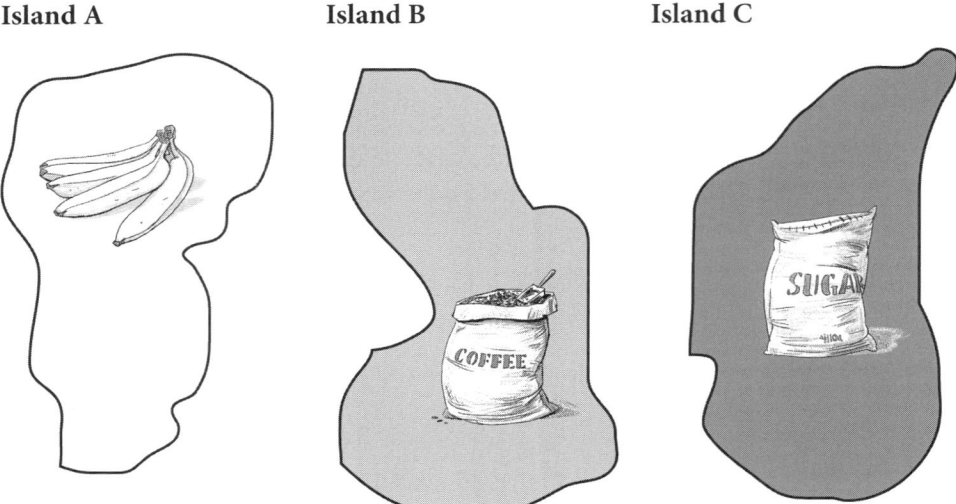

Fig. 22.3
After specialisation

If there is any interference with free trade, the world will not gain. For example, if Island A subsidised its production of sugar, it would destroy Island C's comparative advantage in sugar and the gains from trade would be taken away. Or, if Island B placed tariffs against Island A's bananas, Island A's comparative advantage would be destroyed and our mini world would be the loser again.

Liberalisation will allow comparative advantage to work and the world to gain from trade.

Arguments against comparative advantage and liberalisation

In the model above, the three islands are 'putting all their eggs in one basket'. If something goes wrong, then they are 'sunk'. Therefore, **'partial specialisation'** is practised by most countries. They specialise in what they are best at, but in the interests of self-sufficiency, they also produce other goods. For example, Island A will specialise in bananas, but will also produce some coffee and sugar in case something goes wrong with the banana market.

However, there is no point in holding on to an industry that is obsolete. This may be the case with the tobacco industry if the anti-smoking lobby persuades the world that smoking is harmful to health. It must be remembered that thousands of people earn their livelihood from the tobacco industry in a country, from the growers to the cigarette factory employees, and if the industry is written off suddenly because it has no future, those thousands will suffer a loss of livelihood. Therefore, the government must try to allow the industry to decline slowly, allowing time for tobacco-dependent workers to find alternative employment.

'Balanced trade' is the theory that explains why exclusive specialisation may give way to partial specialisation for reasons of self-sufficiency and security. Some economists suggest that a country should keep half its pre-liberalisation production of goods in which it does not have a comparative advantage for self-sufficiency and security reasons. The UK still maintains a beef industry even though it has no hope of competing with Argentina, Australia or Brazil.

There is also an argument for tariffs, in complete contradiction to liberalisation. Indian and Chinese textiles and clothing have advantages in production that the rest of the world cannot compete with. However, tariffs are in place in the United States and European countries against Far Eastern textile imports. Those who preach liberalisation would argue that these tariffs cause great welfare losses for Americans and Europeans because they cannot have huge quantities of textiles and clothing at low prices. However, the supporters of the tariffs argue that they must keep their own textile industries, and removal of tariffs would bring massive unemployment that the governments are not prepared to accept. Let us again go through the free trade versus tariff argument with the aid of a diagram.

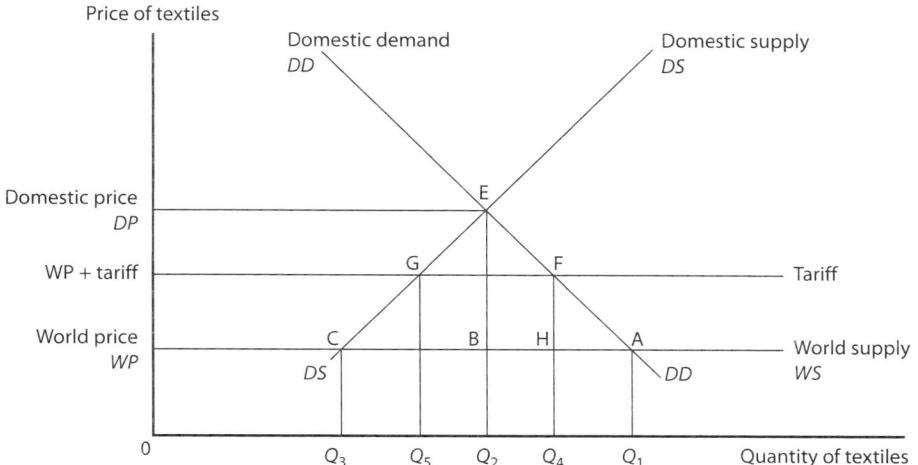

Fig. 22.4
For and against a tariff

Trade liberalisation

With free trade (before the tariff), the citizens of this country would be consuming quantity Q_1 of textiles at the world price, a very low price. They would enjoy a huge consumer surplus, measured by WP, DD, A (the triangle above WP to the left of the demand curve). A tariff would raise the price to WP + tariff and reduce the quantity to Q_2. A tariff would reduce consumer surplus by the area WP, WP + tariff, F, A, a considerable loss of consumer surplus. We can also talk about the **'welfare loss'** to society of this amount.

Domestic producers are inefficient in comparison with their foreign competitors. At WP, they can only produce Q_3. Free trade does not allow their inefficiency to be rewarded or increased. It holds their output on Q_3. The security argument is that if anything went wrong with the Far Eastern textile industry (it is hard to imagine what could go wrong, but perhaps there could be a break in diplomatic relations between the USA and China over Taiwan), the domestic industry could step into the breach and supply Q_2.

In favour of the tariff

The tariff brings revenue to the government. It is measured by the difference in price × the quantity sold: WP, WP + tariff, F, H. The only work that the government has to do for this revenue is in the collection of the tariff and the stopping of smuggling.

The consumers do lose $Q_1 - Q_4$ textile goods, but it can be argued that the loss is acceptable for the amount of jobs that are gained. The domestic textile industry is able to produce at quantity Q_5, an increase in domestic production of Q_3 to Q_5 which represents an increase in jobs in the domestic industry.

Trade liberalisation, therefore, does increase efficiency and the amount of world output. In theory, all countries will gain with trade liberalisation. They will gain products that they did not previously enjoy. They will enjoy more goods at lower prices. However, there are risks attached to liberalisation and **balanced trade** may be a better policy.

Economies of scale

Trade liberalisation will lead to increases in output as the volume of trade increases and increases in output will bring economic and social benefits in those countries where increased exports have resulted.

We need to remind ourselves about the benefits of large-scale production. The economic benefits are called **'economies of scale'**. When output increases, average costs decrease up to a point. This point can be at a very high level of output. It depends on the product. It is an argument in favour of mass production. In the manufacture of cars, the lowest-cost level of output is likely to be very high. Think of the large Japanese car plants. When the output is large enough, it can enjoy the economies of bulk buying, e.g. the steel, the technical economies, such as the introduction of robots, the managerial economies gained by bringing production units under central management and financial economies from large-scale investment. It is easily shown on a long run average total cost curve.

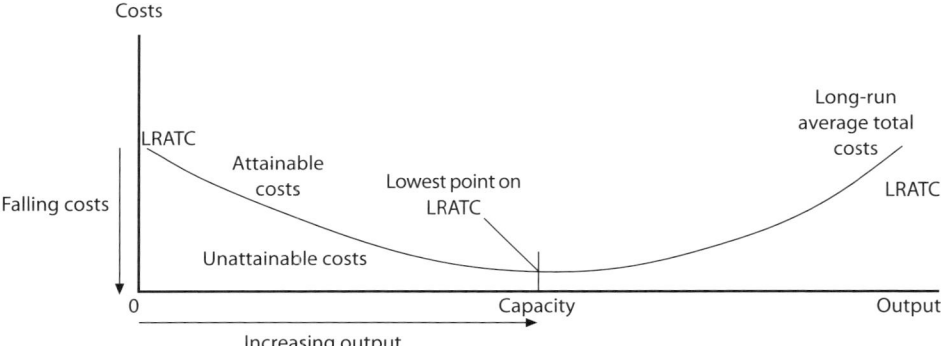

Fig. 22.5
The economies of scale

Definition of capacity

Capacity is the lowest point on the long-run average total cost curve.

LRATC is the long-run average total cost curve. Above this curve, costs are attainable but they could be lower (on the curve). Below the curve, costs are unattainable.

Costs fall up to a point, **capacity**, and then they rise. At capacity, the economies of scale have been reached.

Productive efficiency is: $\frac{\text{Total costs}}{\text{Output}}$ = Average costs at their lowest.

The social benefits of large-scale production are many. More jobs will be created (except where large-scale production has introduced labour-saving techniques). Lowest costs often means lowest prices. Large-scale production often attracts inward investment which helps the balance of payments and increases Gross Domestic Product which may translate into higher incomes.

Large-scale production is a spin off from trade liberalisation and globalisation as we shall see again in this chapter.

Outsourcing

In trade liberalisation, countries are free to produce wherever they wish. This is called 'outsourcing'.

> **Definition of outsourcing**
>
> Outsourcing is the obtaining of something from a supplier outside the business. It can also mean the contracting out of work or services with an external supplier.

Labour cannot move easily across borders. Labour in some parts of the world is low-wage labour. An economist would say that it makes good sense for a firm to produce where costs are lowest and sell where prices are highest. Therefore, firms may outsource to the Far East. For example, GAP and Nike, two huge US **multinational corporations**, outsource the manufacturing of their clothes and shoes to Indonesia where the workers are paid roughly a dollar a day.

> **Definition of a multinational corporation**
>
> A multinational corporation has its head office in one country and production and distribution units in other countries all over the world.

EXERCISE Try and find out which multinational companies are operating in your country.

There are skilled seamstresses in the United States but their wages are about 100 times higher than an Indonesian seamstress. Indonesia has a comparative advantage in the production of clothes and shoes and a free trader would argue for the gain from this comparative advantage. Employment is created in Indonesia where there would be unemployment. Everyone gains.

Do they? The US seamstress loses her job and perhaps has to work as a checkout girl in a supermarket. The skill is wasted. In fact, she may be a better seamstress than the woman in Indonesia, but the wage differential gives the work to the inferior worker so the job is not being done better.

Outsourcing is most common in computer programming where US and UK companies outsource to India. There may be better computer programmers in the

US and UK but the job is awarded by location, not skill. Free trade is not allocating according to skill. It would be better to have a free flow of labour between countries so that wage differentials would be eroded and production would be 'sourced' according to skill and efficiency.

Globalisation

> **Definition of globalisation**
>
> Globalisation is the extension of free trade throughout the world, increasing the opportunities for trade in goods, services, ideas and technology.

The opponents of globalisation might define it this way:

Globalisation is a deceitful term that hides the negative effects of profit-making multinational corporations, and the use of legal and financial means to get round local laws and standards in order to exploit the labour, goods and services of under-developed nations.

EXERCISE Do you think the advantages of globalisation outweigh the disadvantages? Consider how your country's culture is a product of globalisation.

The World Trade Organisation and globalisation

As the successor to GATT, the WTO is pledged to lower and remove barriers to trade throughout the world. It is committed to the extension of free trade throughout the world.

Like GATT, the WTO proceeds through successive rounds of talks through which trade barriers are further and further removed or reduced. One of the recent ones was the 'Doha Round' which focused on the enlargement of free markets for global corporations in agriculture. This gives the impression that the WTO is the driving force in globalisation, but this may not be the case.

There have been many trends since the Second World War in globalisation which have not been as a result of deliberate policy by any international body or national government. There has been an increase in trade and the movement of goods. We saw earlier in the book the movement of huge sums of money that has taken place since 1973 with the advent of 'petro-dollars' and electronic communication. People are moving about the world more freely and in greater numbers. Investment funds have also been crossing boundaries seeking the best returns. Technology has made huge leaps and spreads across boundaries very easily. Information is passed round the world, again electronically. There has been creeping globalisation for many years. More precisely, these trends can be divided into (1) economic, (2) cultural and (3) other trends.

Economic trends

a International trade has increased at a faster rate than the world economy has grown.

b Capital flows between countries have increased, especially foreign direct investment.

c Global financial institutions have been developed, not just the IMF and the World Bank, but many other development banks, e.g. the Caribbean Development Bank (CDB). This bank intends to be the leading development bank in the Caribbean, working towards social and economic development and the reduction of poverty in the region.

d The growth of multinational corporations in size and numbers and the outsourcing of production by these multinationals, often to developing countries.

e The growth of the WTO in membership, power and influence.

Cultural trends

a Westernisation is the trend for the English language to be studied and used by more and more countries. However, there are other aspects of Westernisation that have spread such as music and movies. Reggae has certainly made its contribution culturally.

b The growth of China is leading to **'Sinicisation'** ('Sinic' = 'Chinese'). Mandarin is the most widely spoken language in the world due to the sheer size of China's population over 1.3 billion), but increasingly it is being learnt in other countries.

c Travel and tourism is increasing yearly (9/11 was a temporary set-back) as Caribbean countries know well.

Food culture is one form of globalisation.

d Emigration (leaving a country) and immigration (entering a country) have increased. The one must balance with the other over the world as a whole but individually countries can either be net-emigration or net-immigration areas.

e Food culture: multinationals, e.g. McDonald's, Pizza Hut and Kentucky Fried Chicken have spread the consumption of fast food to over 80 countries. Jamaican meat patties have also spread to other countries. In the UK, a popular food is Chicken Tikka Masala, an Indian dish which originated in England 25 years ago and has been exported to India! This one dish embodies immigration, food culture and globalisation!

Other trends

a The development of telecommunications globally has been noted already, but the trend has been for rapid expansion. Communication satellites orbit the earth, mobile (cell) telephones are available even in the poorest countries*, and the Internet is a major source of information.

b E-commerce, the conducting of business through the Internet, is the fastest growing branch of retailing. We shall be dealing with this at the end of this chapter.

Sanctions

WTO has more power than GATT. If GATT wanted to impose sanctions on one of its members for not lowering tariffs as agreed, all members had to approve the sanctions. This is not the case with the WTO. It has a **Dispute Settlement Body (DSB)** that can apply tough trade sanctions when only one member has accused one other of breaking the global trade rules. 'Experts' hear the case in secret and if the DSB decides on sanctions, they are enforced unless *all* the other members protest. A unanimous protest is extremely unlikely. It is not surprising that some countries have not joined the WTO. However, staying outside has disadvantages.

The Banana case

Under the Lome Convention, the European Union had allowed preference to be given to bananas imported into Europe from the ex-European colonies of the Caribbean (and Africa and the Pacific, but it mainly concerned the Caribbean ex-colonies). Also, these bananas are grown more organically than the pesticide-intensive plantations of Dole and Chiquita, the two giant American banana companies. The European countries said that preference was a matter of internal national policy and not a matter for the WTO. The American banana companies argued that preference was unfair. The WTO supported the American companies, saying that 'the most favoured nation' clause in the WTO agreement demands that similar products from member countries must be treated equally. Caribbean countries like Dominica, Grenada, St Lucia and St Vincent and the Grenadines are threatened with a loss of market and the collapse of their main industry.

---

* In some Sub-Saharan African countries where the land lines are frequently breaking down, mobile phones have become the only means of telecommunication.

Nations use the DSB to pursue their own interests. In practice, the tendency has been for the most powerful nations to use the DSB to manoeuvre weak countries to the advantage of the strong and disadvantage of the weak.

National treatment clause

This clause in the WTO agreement lays down that a country may not discriminate against the products of another country for any reason at all, e.g. you cannot refuse to trade with a country on the grounds that its goods have been produced by child labour, or that labour is paid below a living wage (as in sweatshops in Indonesia perhaps). It is up to the importing country to prove these labour conditions exist and this is very difficult and unlikely to be accepted by the WTO which tends to take the side of the strong against the weak in the cause of globalisation. This is one reason for the huge demonstrations that sometimes accompany WTO meetings. Therefore, WTO meetings will be held more and more beyond the reach of demonstrators.

Multinational corporations

Perhaps the strongest force in globalisation are the multinational corporations. Even in 1997, the total sales of General Motors, at US$163 billion, exceeded the GDP of Thailand at $153 billion and Norway at $152 billion! The 1999 Human Development Report of the United Nations Development Programme showed that 50 of the largest economies in the world were not countries, but companies! Of course, such huge corporations have immense power. However, General Motors is engaged in the production and selling of motor vehicles and does not have the direct impact on globalisation that the oil companies like Exxon and Shell have or the clothing companies like Nike and GAP. A recent book, *The No-Nonsense Guide to Globalisation* by Wayne Ellwood, has called the impact of the multinationals a 'cultural and economic tsunami'!

Multinationals have achieved this impact because the movement of goods and investment has been freed in the move to trade liberalisation and globalisation under the direction of GATT and the WTO. The multinationals and the WTO work hand in hand. The multinationals want to be able to produce their goods where costs are lowest and sell them in any market in the world. The WTO supports this because it is free trade. The multinationals also want to be able to invest in whatever country they wish in order to set up a plant. It is hard for a member country of the WTO to resist because the multinationals would call in the **Dispute Settlement Body** and the multinationals would win the dispute.

We have said earlier that inward investment is a boost to the Balance of Payments and that the investment multiplier increases National Income by a multiplied amount, but sovereign countries should have the right to refuse a multinational entry into their economies. They may want to protect their own industries and help them to grow.

What seems to be more to the point is that the multinationals not only invest where and when they want but that they can withdraw their investments, or move them from one (developing) country to another suddenly. This can bring ruin to a struggling economy and cause thousands of job losses. The country's export earnings from the sale of the multinational's products are lost and it can do nothing about it.

The IMF supports the multinationals indirectly because, as part of any **structural adjustment programme (SAP),** debtor countries are forced to accept privatisation. In selling off government assets to the private sector, the door is opened to **foreign direct investment (FDI)** by multinationals. Once again we must consider the pros and cons of FDI.

Advantages of foreign direct investment (FDI)

FDI is inward investment and is a credit in the financial account of the balance of payments. It is an injection into the economy and raises the level of GDP by a multiplied amount. It may lead to the production of export goods which will improve the current account of the balance of payments.

Disadvantages of foreign direct investment

The profits from the investment often go out of the country to the owners of the multinationals and is thus a debit item in the current account of the balance of payments. Multinationals often employ expatriates in top and middle management positions or as experts. This (a) denies jobs to locals and (b) leads to remittances of salaries abroad. They may produce for the local market and cut out local suppliers.

The multinational may not be replacing imports and thus is not helping the Balance of Payments.

In Chapter 21 we said that, on balance, FDI was 'a good thing' for an economy. However, we can repeat that a sovereign country should have the right of refusal. There are other non-monetary considerations which we have not mentioned before. The total sales of many multinational corporations exceed the GDPs of even quite large countries. Imagine how far they exceed the GDPs of small developing countries. In such cases, the political power of the host country is overwhelmed by the power of the multinational. The host country may not be able to make the political decisions it wants to when they conflict with the interests of the multinational corporation.

It is likely that oil extraction will cause damage to the environment. No matter how much they protest to the contrary, oil companies cannot be environmentally friendly. Think of Shell and the extraction of oil in the Niger Delta. The local people protest the damage to the environment, but what would Nigeria do without the oil revenues?

In conclusion, the nature of Foreign Direct Investment from a multinational corporation is more important than its quantity to an individual country.

Effects of globalisation on Caribbean economies

Globalisation is here to stay. It is impossible to ignore globalisation and hope that it will go away. It is a fact of the world economic system and it presents both opportunities and threats to Caribbean economies. Globalisation can promote growth and help developing countries in their development. However, there are risks for developing countries, but the risks from denying globalisation and trying to stay outside the system are greater. Therefore, Caribbean economies must react to globalisation.

In 1994, Caribbean countries signed up to the WTO with reservations. While admitting that the WTO was a good idea, they said that they would have to be allowed to keep the special trade deals that allowed the smaller economies to survive. In the ten years that have followed the formation of the WTO, Caribbean countries have become less and less happy with globalisation as pursued by the WTO, especially with the Doha Round and the Hong Kong trade talks. It was called the 'development round' but the major world economies are forgetting about development issues. For example, the European Union is about to end the preferential agreements won in the Lome and Cotonou Agreements for African, Caribbean and Pacific states. These chiefly concern bananas and sugar, as we have seen before. However, compensation for ACP states for losing their markets is not being considered and they are not going to be given time to adjust to the loss of markets in Europe.

Caribbean representatives are arguing for 'social justice' by which they mean justice for ACP societies. They argue that if Caribbean needs are not met at Hong Kong, Caribbean countries will need aid packages similar to those given to African countries.

Let us take four issues in which Caribbean economies have not been well served by globalisation and the WTO. The first three of these arose in the second half of the 1990s and the repercussions are still significant today. The last one is a recent issue.

Chiquita bananas on sale in Ohio.

Source: AP/EMPICS.

The Banana case

This is by far the central issue posed by globalisation to the Caribbean, the Windward Islands in particular. In 1997, the US multinationals, Chiquita and Dole, began their (successful) attempt to have the European Union/African Caribbean Pacific (ACP) preferential banana agreements declared illegal by the WTO. The US government has backed Chiquita and Dole. In 1999, it placed strict tariffs against European goods entering the US in retaliation against the preferential agreements between the EU and the ACP over bananas. From January 2006, ACP and Latin American bananas will enter the EU under a single tariff. The productivity per acre in the Windward Islands is one quarter that of Central America. The plantations of Chiquita and Dole enjoy economies of scale and their labourers are paid very low wages.

Without preferential agreements, the Windward Islands cannot compete. They are turning their attention to the tourist market as are other Organisation of Eastern Caribbean States (OECS), but that market is very competitive.

The Caribbean Basin Initiative Case

In 1994, the North American Free Trade Area was formed to take effect in 1995. The United States, Canada and Mexico, under their NAFTA Agreement, ended at a stroke duty-free access their markets for Caribbean goods under the Caribbean Basin Initiative. Many Caribbean producers were hurt badly, but the Jamaican garment industry suffered most because its garments faced a 13% duty. It could not compete with Mexico and 9,000 jobs were lost in Jamaica. Also, foreign investors in the garment industry diverted their funds (FDI) from Jamaica to Mexico.

In 2005, the global system of garment quotas came to an end under the WTO agreement and China is likely to crush all competition in the future.

Caribbean countries tried three courses of action to overcome this blow to their economies from globalisation.

a They tried to enter NAFTA on the same terms as Canada and Mexico. The US Government denied **NAFTA Parity** to Caribbean countries.

b They tried to become members of NAFTA without any success. CARICOM decided that this would have no chance of success and abandoned the idea.

c Caribbean Basin economies, including Central American economies, formed themselves into a sort of pressure group called 'Smaller Economies for Free Trade Area of Americas' (FTAA). They urged NAFTA for special treatment for smaller economies. The small territories pleaded that they could not achieve the economies of scale and could not compete unless they could have free trade with NAFTA. The US government refused to recognise any definition of 'Smaller Economies'.

Britain's Prime Minister Tony Blair speaks with Arthur Owen, his counterpart from Barbados. Britain will press the EU to provide a fair deal for sugar-producing countries hit by drastic cuts in EU subsidies.

Source: AP/EMPICS.

The Sugar case

This is very similar to the Banana Case in that it involves a traditional agricultural export from the Caribbean, but this time the competition is from European beet sugar farmers. The CAP policy of the EU placed a very high tariff on imported sugar. Caribbean sugar does enter the European market but Caribbean producers do not receive European prices. The transition period for a further price cut on Caribbean sugar has been extended from two to four years, but by 2010 it will be very hard for Caribbean countries to export sugar to Europe at competitive prices.

Cruise liners threaten local services.

Source: AP/EMPICS.

The definition of 'tourism' case

This case is particularly taken up by Barbados, but it is a concern to all Caribbean tourist host countries and cruise ship venues. The WTO does not define cruise ships as tourism at present; it defines them as **'maritime transport services'**. Cruise ships are increasingly important to Caribbean economies, not only for the dues that cruise ships pay but also for the competition they pose for hotels, tours, attractions and entertainment. Cruise ships sell goods and services on board and the cruise lines direct their tourists to certain retail outlets on land. Caribbean economies want the WTO to bring tourism within external **services** trade negotiations.

On another issue related to tourism, Caribbean countries are pressing for a change. Caribbean countries have to import many items to support tourism, e.g. furniture and linen, pasta, wines and spirits, refrigerators, meats and fish. They also have to provide telecommunications, transport and insurance services of the highest quality. Caribbean economies want a reduction in tariffs on these imports.

If a Caribbean country wishes to reduce VAT on tourist goods, all Caribbean economies would have to do the same to stop one country having a competitive advantage. This would then come under the scrutiny of the WTO.

The Caribbean Single Market and Economy (CSME)

The global trend is for the world to become divided into more and more trade blocs. This seems to contradict globalisation when it is defined as 'the extension of free trade throughout the world' or 'a borderless world'. However, trade blocs are a response to globalisation and are a part of globalisation. CARICOM saw that a trade bloc was essential when its needs were apparently being overlooked by the WTO, the EU and the USA, as outlined in the cases of bananas, NAFTA membership, sugar and tourism. The ending of preferential trading arrangements with the UK and the EU was 'the straw that broke the camel's back'.

Therefore, coming into effect on 23 January, 2006, was the **CARICOM Single Market and Economy (CSME)**. It looks forward to full implementation in 2008. CSME goes beyond a free trade area in which there are no tariffs between members and a common tariff against third parties. It hopes to establish a Single Market and Economy which will have a common tax system and social services.*

After the experience of the past ten years of globalisation and disregard by the WTO, the CSME hopes to speak with a single, more powerful, voice in negotiations with the WTO and other blocs like NAFTA. At first, Barbados, Jamaica and Trinidad and Tobago agreed to CSME but the other members of CARICOM, with the exceptions of Bahamas and Haiti, will be members at the inauguration.

However, CSME as a trade bloc will still be small. Production and distribution units will still find it hard to achieve the economies of scale although costs should be lowered by larger scale operations. The markets will be small and have limited spending power.

Councils of the CSME

The three most important councils of the CSME are:

1 The Council for Trade and Economic Development (COTED) which deals with agriculture, trade, tourism and industry which are the key areas of economic growth, development and employment. The members of COTED are the CARICOM Ministers of these departments.

2 The Council for Human and Social Development (COHSOD) which embraces health, education and social services.

3 The Council of Finance and Planning (COFAP) which is made up of CARICOM Finance Ministers.

Therefore, the institutions are in place. There is the foundation for co-operation, but it remains to be seen whether the individual states will be prepared to lose a certain amount of sovereignty, e.g. in establishing a common tax system or common foreign policy.

---

* The Caribbean Court of Justice has already been set up. The following social services are expected. The free movement of goods, services, capital and people within the CSME. If there is to be free movement of people, there will be the transference of social security benefits. Any CARICOM-owned company will be able to operate in any CSME state. There will be a uniform system of public education. Uniform standards and quality in goods and services will be monitored and competition will be ensured amongst members.

Summary of the benefits to be gained from the CSME

1 A larger market; increased sales; scale economies; the attraction of foreign direct investment.

2 Trade creation; new trading partners.

3 Trade diversion according to comparative advantage.

4 Gains from trade by comparative advantage.

5 Free trade; no tariffs between members.

6 Tariff revenue from third parties.

7 Free movement of capital, goods, services and people.

8 Speaking with one voice; more influence on world stage; a common foreign policy.

Development strategies for Caribbean governments

a Membership of a larger trade bloc. This has failed in the past, but it may be worth taking up again. The CSME is still a small bloc. Regional trading blocs are much larger. Therefore, attachment to a larger bloc gives access to a larger market. Economies of scale would then follow whereas they are unlikely while still confined to the Caribbean market. Of course, NAFTA springs to mind. In the days of the Cold War with Cuba, the Caribbean was highly important for US security. Therefore, there was the Caribbean Basin Initiative. Perhaps security issues will arise again and closer alliance with Caribbean neighbours will be more important to the US. The political alliance may then be cemented by a trading agreement.

The South American Community of Nations (CSN) is a very large bloc of ten member states with a combined population of over 370 million.

A smaller regional bloc is the Central American Common Market (CACM).

At present, all the members of CARICOM (except Haiti and Suriname) and Anguilla, Bermuda, British Virgin Islands, Cayman Islands and Turks and Caicos Islands have preferential treatment from **CARIBCAN**, a Canadian Government programme which gives duty-free access to the Canadian market for all goods except textiles, footwear, leather goods, lubricating oils and methanol if they have proof that they are grown or manufactured in those Caribbean countries mentioned above. However, CARIBCAN is not a trade bloc, just a trade agreement.

There is something to be gained from attachment to one of these larger blocs.

b Stronger unification ties. The benefits of one voice in international forums have been noted. Even further unification could be pursued. Perhaps a common parliament for CSME following a common taxation (fiscal policy) and foreign policy. A Central Bank for CSME, and a single currency (monetary policy). One voice on tourism to end the internal competition which is hurting some Caribbean states is a strategy which comes to mind. A single airline for the CSME has been suggested.

c Diversification. As mentioned earlier, this is a strategy for which it is easier to say the word than implement the policy. However, diversification away from agriculture and into light industry is possible. The supply side strategy would be in education (already good), training, new technology and government assistance in start-up.

d Attracting foreign direct investment is a strategy already in operation in tourism. The limited size of the market in the CSME is a factor that works against FDI, but there are ways of attracting foreign investment such as a partnership with local governments and tax holidays whereby foreign companies would not pay taxes on their profits for the first two or three years.

E-commerce

E-commerce explained

Definition of E-Commerce
E-Commerce means electronic business.

The 'E' means 'electronically' via the Internet. Commerce is business in all its aspects: marketing, buying and selling, making payment, etc. There is B2B business which is 'business to business' and there is B2C business which is 'business to consumer'.

It is all done on the computer screen. The presentation, placement, display, stocking, selling and payment is automated through the screen.

Some people need to see, touch and feel goods before they buy and E-commerce is not for them; at least the touching and feeling are not possible.

An E-business creates a catalogue in which goods are displayed with descriptions and prices. However, there is not one page per good because that would necessitate thousands of pages. A database has been created with all the goods for sale. A template is presented on the screen which can be filled in and the product retrieved from the database when requested. This template will show a picture of the good, a description, its price and availability, the number of days between order and delivery and the method of delivery. Suppose a business is selling digital cameras which are always being improved; it deletes the old models from its database and adds the new models.

The consumer cannot turn pages on the screen! He or she is helped by a navigation system which is a set of links. The first link will be the product category, e.g. digital cameras. The next link will be the brand, and so on. Eventually, in under 10 seconds, the customer will have exactly the right product. This is called 'drilling down'.

Usually on the right hand side of the screen is a **'shopping basket'** or **'cart'** into which the customer places the good or goods if buying more than one item, e.g. 1) digital camera, 2) memory card and 3) camera case.

When the customer has finished shopping, he or she is invited to **'proceed to the checkout'**. The next screen will show the total order and the prices plus the delivery charge. (Note the language of the supermarket.)

Payment

Customers attracted to E-commerce, online shopping in particular, are often deterred by the method of payment. Payment has to be made by debit or credit card and the details have to be given of the type of card, the cardholder's name, account number, expiry date and so on. This information must not fall into the wrong hands. All payment methods involve a **secure socket layer (SSL)**. The information is encrypted or scrambled so that no one can access the information even if they somehow intercept it. The customer must have confidence in the payment system. If not, no business will be done.

'Receipts' are also given online when the order has been confirmed. Later, a delivery note will arrive with the goods, but no payment details are given on this note. However, before delivery, the customer is advised when the goods have been despatched.

The customer can usually 'track' the order by accessing his or her personal record.

E-commerce can be called **'armchair shopping'** and it is the fastest growing form of business because it is so convenient.

EXERCISE Visit Amazon.com (or any other Internet shopping site) and scroll through the screens to see how the system works. You do not have to buy anything!

The benefits of E-commerce

The world becomes one market. Goods can be bought in the US from anywhere in the world provided payment can be made. Debit cards and credit cards issued by companies like Visa and MasterCard will ensure this is possible.

Prices are competitive in E-commerce. In fact, they are usually much lower than on the High Street because the firm's overheads are much less. Delivery charges can be high, but usually the total price (price + delivery charge) is still below conventional retailing.

The range of products is far larger than can be found in a retail store. Anything from cars to flowers can be bought on line from the same website.

We have mentioned the convenience. E-commerce is conducted without leaving the house or place of work. There are no transport costs in getting to the market!

E-commerce is quick and time has an opportunity cost. The businessman using E-commerce can use the time saved making profit in some other activity.

E-commerce is safe and reliable. It has been up and running for years now and the systems have been perfected.

In general, E-commerce has expanded business and will go on expanding business. This will increase aggregate demand in the economy and raise the level of National Income, delivering all the benefits which flow from this.

The challenges of E-commerce

E-commerce tests the powers and capabilities of firms to enter a new world of business and to play their part in globalisation. This is a challenge. However, it is a challenge which must be met. If not, businesses will not compete in the global market.

To meet the challenge there will be a certain amount of investment required from a business. The new technology is obvious. However, there must also be training in the new expertise. There will be a change in the workforce. Apart from computer programmers, E-commerce operates through very specialised stock control, another field for expertise. There will be some laying off of workers in a business. Some workers will not have the skills to adapt.

In general, E-commerce saves on labour costs so there will be unemployment. The challenge to the economy as a whole is to absorb the redundant workers into other parts of the economy.

The banking system is challenged. It must be able to handle the payments required and some of them are across borders (E-commerce is global).

Like globalisation, E-commerce is here to stay and for an economy to be successful it will have to embrace E-commerce now or very soon in the future.

Examination questions

1. Explain what happened at Bretton Woods in 1944. *(10 marks)*

2. Discuss the role of the IMF and the World Bank. *(10 marks)*

3. Explain the difference between exclusive and partial specialisation. *(10 marks)*

4. **a** Define a multinational. *(3 marks)*
   b Discuss the advantages and disadvantages of a multinational. *(7 marks)*

5. **a** Explain the meaning of globalisation. *(3 marks)*
   b Discuss the advantages and disadvantages of globalisation. *(7 marks)*

6 Discuss the role of the World Trade Organisation in international trade. *(10 marks)*

7 Discuss why it might be useful to regard the Caribbean as a single market. *(10 marks)*

8 In a global economy, why are there regional trade blocs? *(10 marks)*

9 a Explain what is meant by e-commerce. *(3 marks)*
   b Why do you think this has been the fastest growing form of retailing in recent years? *(7 marks)*

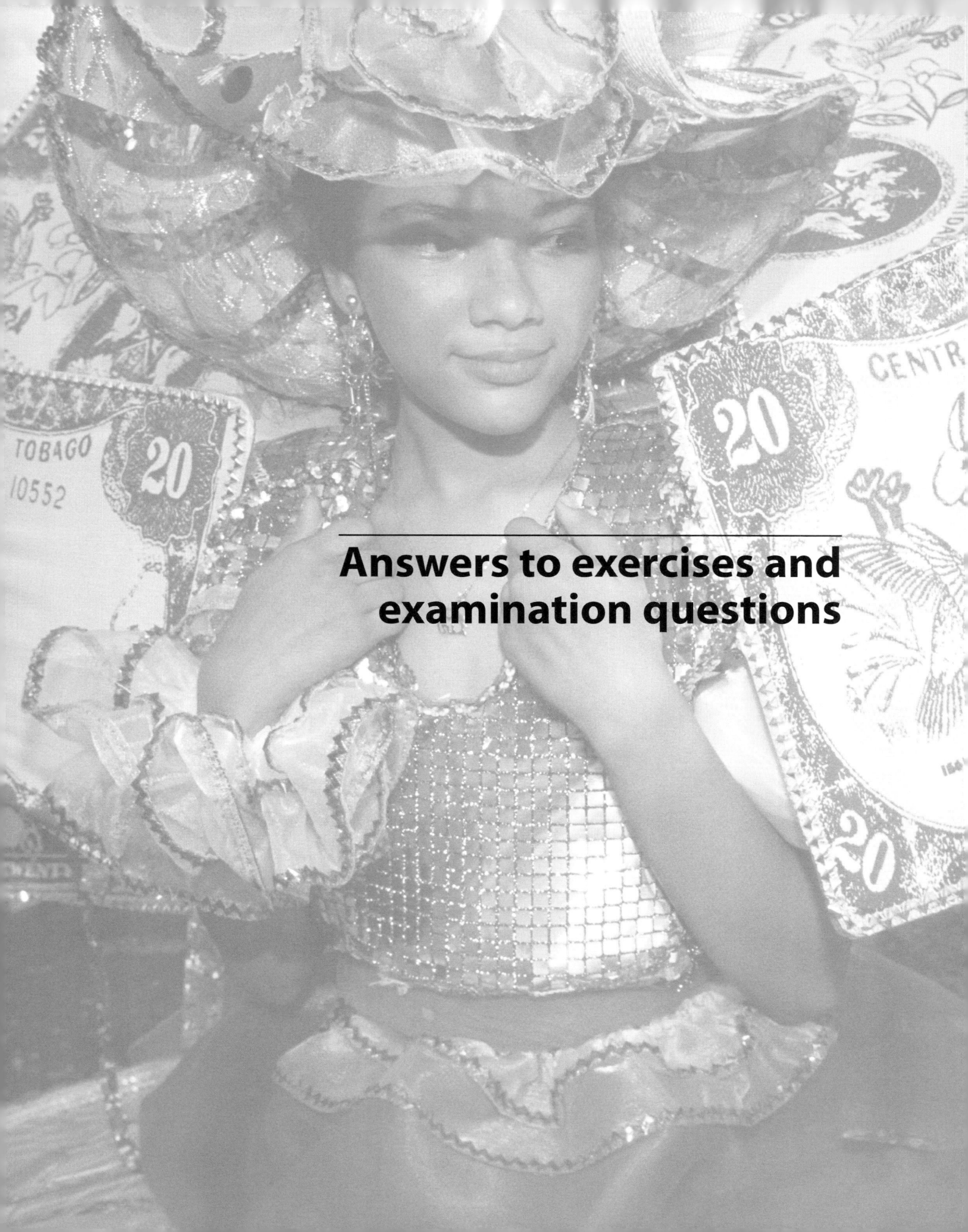
Answers to exercises and examination questions

Chapter 1

Exercises

Exercise: Consider why you, Bill Gates, the USA, Burkina Faso, Cuba and the Cayman Islands all face an economic problem.

Answer: Economics is essentially concerned with the problem of scarcity and the need to make choices. Resources are finite but our wants are infinite. All of the above will therefore need to make a choice between alternative uses of those scarce resources.

Exercise: Write down as many examples as you can of opportunity cost decisions you have taken in the last week or month, stating both what you chose and what you didn't choose.

Answer: Your decisions could include examples of money, i.e. what you spent your money on and what you didn't buy, and time, i.e. what you decided to do in a particular time period and what you decided not to do.

Exercise: Consider the likely advantages and disadvantages of private and state provision of education in a society.

Answer: Private education may be of a better quality with smaller class sizes but will involve payment of a fee; this will limit the number of people who will have access to it. State education will be available to everybody with the money for it raised from taxation but the class sizes may be much larger and it is possible that the quality of education may be lower.

Exercise: Look at the following five statements. For each one, say whether you think it is an example of a positive or a normative statement.

Answer: 1 – a positive statement
2 – a normative statement
3 – a normative statement
4 – a positive statement
5 – a normative statement

Exercise: Try and find out the private and public sector percentages in your country.

Answer: Answers to this exercise will vary from country to country. It might be useful to look at the figures for a number of countries in the West Indies and compare them.

Exercise: Try and find out some information about the Cuban revolution of 1959. From what you have discovered, do you think that the revolution has been successful in achieving what it set out to do?

Answer: The Communists under Fidel Castro took power in January 1959. The revolution has been successful in some respects, e.g. the quality of education and health care in Cuba is regarded as being of a relatively high standard. On the other hand, the issue of political rights and civil liberties is still a controversial one. Ultimately, you will have to make up your own mind on whether the advantages outweigh the disadvantages.

Exercise: What do you think are the advantages of universal secondary education for both the individual and the economy?

Answer: The individual will benefit by gaining a higher level of education; this will improve his or her knowledge and skills, enabling the person to obtain a better job with a higher wage or salary. The advantage for the economy is that productivity should increase leading to higher levels of Gross Domestic Product so that standards of living increase. Improvements in education are often seen as contributing to the shift of the production possibility curve to the right.

Examination questions

1 a You need to explain what is meant by a free market system in terms of its freedom from government intervention. Private enterprise will be crucial and resources will be allocated through the price system (the 'invisible hand' as Adam Smith called it).

A diagram would be useful to show how prices act as a signal in the market leading to the market being 'cleared'.

b You need to explain that despite the theoretical advantages of the free market economy, there are a number of disadvantages. For example, public goods might not be provided, and merit goods are likely to be under-consumed and demerit goods over-consumed. There are likely to be a number of externalities which require governments to intervene and there is also the problem of an unequal distribution of income and wealth in a free market which limits the extent of 'consumer sovereignty'.

2 a You need to explain what is meant by the concept of opportunity cost in terms of the next best alternative that is foregone. Resources are scarce and so decisions have to be made concerning their allocation; these decisions need to be seen in the context not only of what is decided but also of what is not chosen. It is important to stress that opportunity cost is concerned not just with any alternative that is foregone but with the next best alternative.

b There are a number of examples that could be given of opportunity cost in an economy. A common contrast is 'guns v butter', i.e. should limited resources be allocated to the production of armaments or food? Other examples might include whether to spend money on the construction of a new school or a new hospital, or whether to build a new housing development in an area of outstanding natural beauty.

3 This question covers similar ground to the previous one but focuses on one particular area of concern. It refers to the fact that protestors sometimes oppose the building of new motorways or airport runways. You need to explain how the concept of opportunity cost could be applied to such situations by discussing the money that would be involved in such projects and the alternative uses this money could be put to. You would also need to consider the land that would be required to build new motorways or airport runways and the alternative uses this land could be put to.

4 In the first part of the question, you would need to discuss the advantages of a free market. You could stress the fact that there is no need for government intervention and that all resources are allocated through the price mechanism; this acts as a signal in the economy which should be efficient and respond effectively to the decisions taken by consumers and producers. In the second part of the question, you would need to discuss the advantages of a planned economy. You could link the two parts by saying a little about the disadvantages of a free economy and why the planned economy aims to overcome these disadvantages, e.g. through the provision of public and merit goods so that everybody has access to such goods and services, irrespective of their income. The advantages of a five-year plan could also be discussed, stressing that a planned economy would try to allocate resources in the best interests of the people over a particular period of time.

5 You need to explain clearly the distinction between a normative statement, i.e. one based on an opinion or judgement, and a positive statement, i.e. one based on fact. There are many examples that could be included: normative statements often have 'ought' or 'should' in them indicating that they express an opinion or point of view.

Chapter 2

Exercises

Exercise: You have a certain amount of money to spend and this could be spent on a CD, a cinema ticket, a DVD or the entrance to a disco. Which would you choose? Consider the opportunity cost of your decision.

Answer: There is, of course, no right answer to this question. The decision of which one of the four alternatives to choose is entirely up to you. What is important is that you recognise that with a limited amount of money, you would not be able to obtain all four. Whichever one you choose, the opportunity cost is the next best alternative that you could have spent your money on.

Examination questions

1 You need to explain clearly what is meant by the four factors of production, i.e. land, labour, capital and enterprise. The question explicitly requires the use of examples so farming and fishing would be examples of land, labourers and teachers would be examples of labour, tools and machinery would be examples of capital (not to be confused with capital in the monetary sense) and two local examples of entrepreneurs would indicate enterprise.

2 You need to distinguish clearly between consumer and capital goods and, as in the previous question, give appropriate examples of each. A consumer good is one which is consumed directly, such as a television or a car, whereas a capital good is one which is used in the production process, such as a piece of equipment or a piece of machinery.

3 a In the first part of the question, you need to draw a production possibility curve and there are a number of examples of these in the book. In order to get full marks, the axes need to be clearly and correctly labelled.

   b In the second part of the question, you need to explain how it can be used to show the idea of a 'trade-off', i.e. a movement along the curve will represent an increase in the production of one thing, e.g. agricultural production, and a decrease in the production of something else, e.g. manufacturing production. The only way in which this 'trade-off' is avoided is if there is a movement from inside the curve to a position on the curve or if there is an outward shift of the curve.

4 In this question, you need to explain what is meant by economic efficiency in terms of its two elements, i.e. productive efficiency where production is at minimum average cost and allocative efficiency where price is equal to marginal cost. The question does not explicitly require a diagram but one could be included to aid the explanation.

5 You need to distinguish clearly between a movement along a production possibility curve, where there will be a 'trade-off' between the two types of production labelled on the horizontal and vertical axes, and a shift of the curve as a result of the increased quantity or quality of resources which will enable greater production of both. Again, a diagram is not explicitly asked for but examiners would expect one to help in the explanation.

Chapter 3

Exercises

Exercise: Can you think of any examples where you have been influenced by peer pressure?

Answer: This is a very personal question; some of you may be more easily influenced by peer pressure than others. Try and think of at least three examples.

Exercise: Consider whether your education is just a 'means to an end' or whether it has a value of its own. Which subjects do you think might be more useful in terms of the eventual earning power of individuals?

Answer: The answer will probably vary from one person to another. Some of you may simply see education as something that has to be 'got through' in order to gain the necessary qualifications to get a particular kind of job. Others may see education in a positive way, valuing it as something worthwhile in its own right. I suppose language, mathematics and science would be very important in terms of eventual earning power; I am biased but I would also put a case for Economics.

Exercise: Can you think of any other factors that could influence your decision to spend?

Answer: I suppose the most obvious one that is missing is the effect of advertising. The media exert a powerful influence on our behaviour. Another example might be seasonal or weather factors that could influence the demand for particular products at certain times of the year. You may well have thought of other examples.

Exercise: What is the opportunity cost of extracting bauxite from the land in Jamaica?

Answer: The opportunity cost is the next best alternative that is foregone as a result of the extraction of the bauxite. For example, this could be the delightful scenery that was ruined because of the mining operation.

Exercise: Research your own country and see if you can find any examples of environmental degradation and pollution.

Answer: The answer to this exercise will vary a great deal from one Caribbean country to another. It should be possible to find at least one example of environmental degradation and pollution in your own country.

Exercise: What is the opportunity cost for a Caribbean island of developing its tourist facilities?

Answer: Virtually every Caribbean country has been developing its tourist facilities. The opportunity cost needs to be seen in terms of the money, i.e. what else the money could have been spent on, such as schools or hospitals, or in terms of what else the land could have been used for, such as a public park. Certainly, many people would regard the building of large numbers of hotels as a possible 'eyesore'.

Exercise: Consider the potential advantages and disadvantages of trade unions. When you go out to work, do you think you would be keen to join one, assuming that there was a trade union in existence for you to join?

Answer: There are both potential advantages and disadvantages of trade unions. The advantages include the greater strength of workers because they are in a collective body and this should lead to better wages and salaries, better working conditions and improvements in other aspects of their working lives, such as improved pension provision. The disadvantages, however, could include the fact that their actions could lead to a strike which could be very disruptive; there is also the possibility that a firm cannot afford to pay the wages they are demanding, leading to its collapse. The decision as to whether you would choose to join one when you go out to work is, of course, a very personal one; you would need to weigh up the advantages and disadvantages of such an action before making a decision.

Exercise: Discuss whether a police force or a fire service should be run by the state or by private firms.

Answer: I think most people would feel that the police force ought to be run by the state; this would make it more likely that the police would act in the interests of everybody. There are, however, many examples of private security firms. The same argument would apply to the fire service; imagine if your property was on fire and you had fallen behind with your payments. It is generally felt that the financing of such services should come out of taxation.

Exercise: Consider the advantages and disadvantages of the state provision of education.

Answer: The main advantage of the state provision of education is that it should be available to everybody and so each person gets at least a minimum standard of education. The main disadvantage is that it is very expensive and so will constitute a significant proportion of a country's public expenditure budget.

Exercise: Compare and contrast the private and social benefits of a meningitis inoculation.

Answer: The private benefit on a meningitis inoculation is that it protects the individual from contracting the disease. This provides social benefit in that this individual will never be in a position to pass the disease on to others.

Exercise: The price of a cigarette is often about 80% tax. Do you think it right that governments tax such products so heavily?

Answer: Your answer is likely to be influenced by whether you are a smoker or not. If you are, you will probably argue that it isn't right. If you are not, you are more likely to stress the potentially harmful effects of smoking cigarettes and view them as good examples of a demerit good; in this case, you will probably agree with the high rates of taxation to try and reduce the consumption of them. The money raised through these taxes can then be spent in other areas of the economy.

Exercise: Do you think wages should be entirely determined by the free market forces of demand and supply without any government intervention?

Answer: The 'free market' approach would argue that the price of labour, just like any other price, should be determined by the interaction of the forces of demand and supply, i.e. a worker will get paid according to the value of his or her labour in that particular society. The alternative 'interventionist' approach would argue that this would leave many of the less skilled (or unskilled) or less educated (or uneducated) on extremely low wages; there is, therefore, a case for government intervention in the form of a minimum wage.

Examination questions

1 a   In the first part of the question, you need to distinguish clearly between the private and public sector of an economy, stressing that the main aim of firms in the former is profit maximisation whereas the main aim of the government in the public sector is to provide a service that is available to everybody, even if it makes a loss.

   b   In the second part of the question, you need to discuss the advantages and disadvantages of allocating resources through the public sector. The advantages are that all of the citizens should be able to benefit, even the poorer ones, and that the service will continue to operate, even if it makes a loss. The disadvantages are that resources in the public sector are not always allocated as efficiently as they are in the private sector and that a loss could have a damaging effect on a government's public finances.

2   You need to distinguish clearly between direct and indirect taxes, stressing that the former are taxes on income and the latter are taxes on expenditure. Examples of the former would include income tax, corporation tax and inheritance tax. Examples of the latter would include a sales tax, such as value added tax.

3 a   In the first part of the question, you need to give a clear definition of a trade union, such as that it is an organised body of workers who come together to create 'strength in numbers' to influence employers. This is usually achieved through collective bargaining but, if this fails, a union might resort to industrial action, such as a strike.

   b   In the second part of the question, you need to develop the explanation of why membership of a trade union might be beneficial. This could be in the form of increased pay, better working conditions, improved holiday entitlement and a satisfactory pension arrangement. Other examples of benefits could be given.

4   A public good is something which it would be almost impossible for a free market to provide. It would be difficult to charge a price because of the 'free rider' problem, i.e. of how to exclude those who haven't paid. Examples

would include defence and street lighting. A merit good is something which could be provided through a free market but it is likely that it would be under-consumed which would be disadvantageous to both individuals and the economy. Examples would include education and healthcare. A demerit good is something which is likely to be over-consumed in a free market, damaging the health of the people. Examples would include cigarettes and alcohol. These goods are taxed heavily to discourage consumption.

5 You need to compare and contrast the various influences on individuals in their spending decisions. There are a large number of such influences and these include income, price, the prices of substitute and complementary goods, occupation, lifestyle, social class, religion, geographical area, seasonal/weather factors and the media. You should note that the question explicitly requires you to compare and contrast these influences; a purely descriptive answer is, therefore, unlikely to gain more than half marks.

6 This question is concerned with the different influences on the behaviour of firms. These could include the search for profit, the need to maximise sales and therefore revenue, the need to gain greater market share, the recognition of building and maintaining customer loyalty, good relationships with the workforce and the creation of a positive image in the community.

Chapter 4

Exercises

Exercise: Consider the difference between 'production' and 'productivity'.

Answer: Production is the amount or quantity that has been made; productivity is the efficiency of how it has been made, usually expressed in output per worker over a given period of time.

Exercise: Consider the extent to which the green revolution has affected your country.

Answer: This will obviously vary from one Caribbean country to another. See if you can find some examples of how agricultural productivity has increased in certain areas.

Exercise: Place the following in the above categories of labour.

Answer: Surgeon
– professional, skilled, white collar.
Typist
– clerical, semi-skilled, white collar.
Builder
– manual, skilled, blue collar.
Cane cutter
– manual, skilled, blue collar.
School teacher
– professional, skilled, white collar.
Architect
– professional, skilled, white collar.
Farmer
– manual, skilled, blue collar.
Mechanic
– manual, skilled, blue collar.

It should be pointed out that for some of these, it is difficult to be precise, such as for the case of a farmer.

Exercise: To what extent do you think the brain drain has affected your country?

Answer: This will vary from one Caribbean country to another. See if you can find out information in particular areas of work, such as teachers, nurses or doctors.

Exercise: See if you can find some other examples of entrepreneurs. Explain what impact they have had in their particular industry.

Answer: The book gives a number of examples of entrepreneurs in the Caribbean. Try and find out the names of some others, especially in your own country, and investigate the impact and influence they have had.

Exercise: Choose three or four different occupations. Find out what average wages are in those occupations and draw a demand and supply diagram to explain them.

Answer: You should be able to find out some of the wages in different occupations in particular countries. You then need to draw some diagrams to show why the wages are at a particular level. For example, if an average wage is relatively high, it is likely to be a reflection of a high demand and a limited supply, such as in the case of doctors. If an average wage is relatively low, it is likely to be a reflection of a low demand and a large supply, such as in the case of labourers.

Examination questions

1 In this relatively straightforward question, you need to explain clearly what is meant by the four factors of production. You need to pay particular attention to the meaning of capital as a factor of production. Although the question does not specifically ask for examples of each factor, it would be a good idea to include them to show that you fully understand the differences between the four factors.

2 Whereas the first question was concerned with all four factors of production, this question focuses on just one of them. You need to describe clearly what the role of an entrepreneur is in terms of organising the other factors of production and, in doing so, how this involves an element of risk. Again, as in the previous question, the use of examples is advised.

3 You need to explain what is meant by a natural resource of a country and, on this occasion, the question does explicitly require you to use appropriate examples. The book refers to a number of these, such as bauxite.

4 This question is concerned with the combination of factors of production and specifically why that combination of resources might be changed. For example, a company might move away from a labour intensive type of production to a more capital intensive one, perhaps because labour has become relatively too expensive or scarce or because the price of capital equipment has become relatively cheaper.

5 A major factor influencing the choice of a particular job is the wage or salary but this question is concerned with the other possible factors which could influence this decision. These could include working conditions, the prospect of promotion, the distance to travel, the number of hours or the range of benefits available.

6 Some occupations are paid more than others and, in this question, you will need to discuss why this might be the case. A wage is really a price and, like any other price in a market, it is determined by the forces of demand and supply. A large demand and a limited supply will lead to high wages; a limited demand and a large supply will lead to low wages. Appropriate diagrams should be used to aid the discussion.

7 This question is concerned with different systems of production and, in particular, with the degree of labour or capital involved. If labour is significantly more important than capital, it will be regarded as labour intensive; if capital is significantly more important than labour, it will be regarded as capital intensive.

8 In this question, you will need to explain the rewards that are paid to the different factors of production, i.e. rent to land, wages and salaries to labour, interest to capital and profit to enterprise.

9 a In the first part of the question, you will need to explain what is meant by the specialisation of labour, i.e. where there is division of labour and how labour concentrates on particular aspects of the production process.

b In the second part of the question, you will need to explain how specialisation of labour can lead to greater productivity. You need to stress the advantages of the idea of splitting up the work and getting workers to concentrate on particular aspects rather than getting workers to do a little bit of everything. The outcome should be greater efficiency.

Chapter 5

Exercises

Exercise: Look in a newspaper and try and find examples of how the price of a particular model of a car changes over a number of years.

Answer: You should be able to find examples of particular cars that have fallen in value as they have got older, i.e. they have depreciated in value. Of course, you may also find examples of very special models of cars which have gone up in value, i.e. they have appreciated in value but these are the exception.

Exercise: Consider why some costs, such as electricity or telephone, have both fixed and variable elements.

Answer: It is not always easy to distinguish clearly between fixed and variable costs. For example, the cost of a telephone service will have a fixed element, which will need to be paid even if the telephone is never used, and a variable element, depending on how many calls are made and the time and distance of those calls.

Exercise: Try and think of some other examples which show the relationship between the average and the margin, such as the goals scored by a particular footballer.

Answer: All sports will provide opportunities; for example, the footballer who averages a goal every two games and then scores three in one game. Three is the marginal figure and it will pull up the average.

Exercise: Discuss whether the advantages of a large factory outweigh the disadvantages.

Answer: This will get you to think about the potential advantages of a large factory, which economists call economies of scale, and then to contrast these with the possible disadvantages if a factory gets too large, which are known as the diseconomies of scale. You may be able to find out information about particular large factories in your own country.

Examination questions

1. This question is concerned with the various economies of scale. You need to explain what the various economies are and it would be helpful if you gave examples of each one. It would also be a good idea to include a diagram to illustrate the concept.

2. In this question, you will need to distinguish clearly between a fixed cost, which doesn't vary with a change in output, such as interest payments on a loan, and a variable cost, which does vary with a change in output, such as the cost of raw materials or component parts. Again, a diagram would aid the distinction.

3. You will need to distinguish clearly between the economies and diseconomies of scale. You will stress the advantages of large factories but then contrast these with the possible disadvantages as a firm or factory becomes too large. Examples should be given of both and a diagram would be useful.

4. In this question, you will need to distinguish clearly between the average cost of production, i.e. the cost divided by the output, and the marginal cost, i.e. the cost of producing one more unit. Again, a diagram would be useful to aid the distinction.

5. The short-run is a period of time when it is not possible to change all of the factors of production and this is a major constraint on a firm. The long-run is a period of time when it is possible to change all of the factors of production and this gives a firm greater

freedom to take decisions. You need to point out that the short-term and long-term cannot be defined precisely in terms of particular periods of time as they will vary from one industry to another.

Chapter 6

Exercises

Exercise: Discuss why some goods, such as a bicycle, could be regarded as both a consumer good and a capital good.

Answer: If a bicycle is used by a person as a leisure activity, perhaps as a way of keeping fit, it would be regarded as a consumer good. However, if it is used as a means of delivering something to a customer, it would be regarded as a capital good.

Exercise: Can you think of any other examples of an inferior good?

Answer: The answer will vary from one economy to another. You need to think of something that would be bought by the less well-off and then be replaced by something better as they become more prosperous.

Exercise: Consider why governments provide merit goods.

Answer: A merit good is something which would be under-consumed in a free market if it was charged its real price, such as education and healthcare. Governments, therefore, provide such goods to encourage the consumption of something which has a particular merit and is therefore seen as worthwhile and important.

Examination questions

1   You need to distinguish clearly between a public good and a merit good. A public good is something which would be virtually impossible to charge a specific price for, such as a streetlight or a lighthouse. A merit good is something which could be provided in a market system but which is likely to be under-consumed, such as education or healthcare. Governments intervene in the market to provide such services, usually alongside the private provision of them.

2   You need to distinguish clearly between a consumer good, which is something that is bought by people for a particular use, such as a television, and a capital good, which is something that is used in the production of consumer goods, such as a particular piece of equipment. A capital good is not usually purchased for its own worth but for the output that it can help to produce.

3   You need to explain that a free good is something which is freely available and for which a price cannot be charged, such as air. There is enough air for everybody and if one person consumes the air, it doesn't deprive others of it.

4   You need to distinguish clearly between a normal good, the consumption of which goes up with a rise in income, and an inferior good, the consumption of which goes down with a rise in income. Most goods, such as cars, are normal goods; inferior goods are those goods which are relatively cheap, such as a bicycle, in contrast to a car. It should be pointed out that what is considered an inferior good will vary from one country to another.

5   You need to stress that a Giffen good is something the demand for which goes up when the price increases, such as the demand for potatoes during the Irish potato famine. A Veblen good also involves a rise in demand when there is a rise in price but whereas a Giffen good refers to very cheap goods, a Veblen good refers to relatively expensive goods and people demand more of them to 'show off'. This is known as conspicuous consumption.

6   You need to look at the two sides of the argument. Half of the marks will be allocated to a discussion of why education and

healthcare should be provided through the public sector, i.e. as examples of merit goods, they would be under-consumed in a free market and so governments need to provide at least a minimum provision (usually alongside private provision). The other half of the marks will be allocated to a discussion of why education and healthcare should be provided through the private sector, i.e. there is the possibility that this will lead to greater efficiency and a better quality of service.

Chapter 7

Exercises

Exercise: Which type of taxation system do you think is best? Explain your reasoning.

Answer: The answer will, of course, depend on one's own attitudes and opinions. The progressive system could be seen as being fairer as it takes a higher percentage of income from the better-off; it could, however, be criticised for the disincentive effect it could have on higher earners. The regressive system might be seen as fairer as it treats everybody equally by having a fixed rate; the problem, however, is that in terms of the percentage of income taken, it will hit the less well-off the hardest.

Exercise: See if you can find out how the percentage from each of the three sectors in your country has changed over the last hundred years.

Answer: The answer will vary from one country to another. As each country develops, the percentage of the primary and secondary sectors will decline and the percentage of the tertiary sector will increase but the actual outcome will vary a great deal depending on the extent of development in each country.

Exercise: The class is divided into three groups and each of these has to consider the advantages of one of the three types of economic system. Two or three people from each group then present their ideas to the rest of the class, leading on to a debate about the relative merits of each system.

Answer: It is, of course, impossible to predict the outcome, i.e. which one will be seen as the best of the three. The exercise will involve people presenting the arguments in what will, hopefully, be an interesting debate which will involve everybody in the class.

Examination questions

1 You need to discuss the three fundamental questions involved in the allocation of resources, i.e. what will be produced, how will it be produced and for whom will it be produced? It will help if you include examples to illustrate the importance of these three decisions in an economy.

2 You need to explain clearly what is meant by the circular flow of goods and services in an economy, i.e. the movement of goods and services, consumer expenditure, factors of production and factor incomes between firms and households in an economy. A diagram would aid the explanation.

3 In this question, you need to distinguish clearly between the three sectors of an economy, i.e. the primary, secondary and tertiary sectors. The question explicitly asks for examples and you should include a number of these for each of them. It would also be useful to indicate how the importance of the three sectors has changed over the years, making it clear that the precise proportion of each will vary greatly from one country to another.

4 In this question, you will need to explain clearly what is meant by command and free market economies and then go on to compare and contrast their relative advantages and disadvantages. It is not enough simply to describe the types of economy; you will need to compare them and then come to a reasoned judgement as to which you think is better and why.

5 This is an interesting question. You would need to discuss the free market first and consider its possible problems. In response to these problems, there is then a need for government intervention. For example, if a public good, such as defence, was not provided in a free market, it would become necessary for it to be provided by the government.

Chapter 8

Exercises

Exercise: Choose any one of these various markets and find out as much as possible about it. You can then give a presentation to the class.

Answer: It is entirely up to you as to which one you choose; select the one that you are most interested in.

Exercise: Choose another example, apart from CDs, such as DVDs or items of clothing. Do you think that the demand curve will be the same shape as for CDs?

Answer: The demand curve for the majority of goods tends to be the same as the one for CDs, i.e. it is downward sloping from left to right indicating that as the price falls, the level of demand is likely to rise. It would, however, be possible to think of some exceptions, such as very expensive items where the demand goes up as price rises.

Exercise: Explain why only the equilibrium price and quantity are possible in a free market.

Answer: In a free market, there is no government intervention and so prices are determined by the forces of demand and supply. Prices work as an 'invisible hand' giving out signals so that a market clearing price and quantity is established in what is called the equilibrium position.

Exercise: Try and think of some other examples of goods that are complements in joint demand.

There are many examples of these. You might have thought of CDs and CD players or DVDs and DVD players; if you have one, you need the other.

Exercise: If your income rose, how do you think that might affect your choice of products or services to buy?

Answer: Your demand for the vast majority of goods and services is likely to increase; these would be regarded as normal goods. However, there might be some goods or services that you demanded less as your income rose, such as cheaper kinds of food; these would be regarded as inferior goods.

Exercise: Can you think of another example of something that is in fashion at the moment, perhaps as the result of an advertising campaign?

Answer: You should probably be able to think of a range of different goods that have become popular as a result of an advertising campaign, such as MP3 players or digital cameras.

Exercise: Research the production of one particular product and see if you can find out what have been the main technological changes in this production.

Answer: You should be able to go on the Internet and select a particular product; there should be a lot of information relating to the technological developments in production.

Exercise: Do you think that it is right that a cartel, such as OPEC, can fix prices in this way?

Answer: I suppose the answer to this will depend on whether you live in an OPEC member country or not. If you do, you will probably defend the right of a cartel to fix prices to ensure that the country gets a good reward for a vital natural resource. In most other cases, you will argue that it isn't right and that prices of certain products, such as oil and petrol, are higher than they would otherwise be.

Examination questions

1. **a** You need to point out that a market in economics is anything that brings buyers and sellers together. It could be where these two come face to face, as in a traditional street market, but with technological developments today, it is not necessary for there to be such personal contact.

   b A goods or services market is where buyers and sellers of a good or service come together to reach an agreement. A factor market refers to the market for factors of production, i.e. land, labour, capital or enterprise. For example, the wage to be paid to a worker will be determined in the factor market.

2. You need to explain that a demand curve usually slopes downwards from left to right because people will usually only buy more of a good or service if the price falls; this is related to the concept of diminishing marginal utility. A supply curve, however, will slope in the opposite direction, upwards from left to right, as producers are only willing to supply more if the price rises.

3. You need to emphasise that a movement along a demand curve is when the price of that particular good or service changes but every other possible influence on demand remains constant. A shift of the demand curve is when these other influences on demand change, such as if there is a change in income or an advertising campaign. It would be useful to include a diagram to illustrate the difference.

4. Youneed to explain that a shift to the right of a supply curve means that more can be supplied at any given price. The factors that can cause this are those which increase the productivity, such as an improvement in technology. A diagram should be given to illustrate the shift of the supply curve to the right.

5. A quota is when there is a fixed limitation on something, such as a quota on the import of particular goods into a country. A subsidy is when money is given to support a firm, enabling it to cover its costs and possibly reduce prices, depending on the size of the subsidy.

6. A market system is where prices and output are determined by the interaction of the forces of demand and supply, establishing an equilibrium position without the need for government intervention. A diagram should be used to illustrate this position of equilibrium.

Chapter 9

Exercises

Exercise: Can you think of other examples of each of these five degrees of elasticity?

Answer: A box of matches could be regarded as an example of perfectly inelastic demand; an essential item of clothing, such as shoes, might be regarded as relatively inelastic; an item of clothing that is neither essential nor a luxury, such as a shirt, could be seen as an example of unitary elasticity; an expensive holiday tour could be seen as being relatively elastic; an agricultural product, such as apples, could be seen as being perfectly inelastic.

Exercise: Consider how a seller can use a knowledge of price elasticity of demand to his or her advantage.

Answer: If a seller knows that the demand for a good is relatively elastic, he or she will reduce the price to increase revenue; if a seller knows that the demand for a good is relatively inelastic, he or she will increase the price to increase revenue.

Exercise: Why might a good be regarded as an inferior good by one person and a normal good by another?

Answer: An inferior good is one for which the demand falls when a person's income rises. One person may become very rich so that he or she stops buying cheap food; in this case, the cheap food is an inferior good. Another person, however, may be very poor and so buys the cheap food; if his or her income rises a little, the person will still be relatively poor but will perhaps be able to buy more of the cheap food.

Exercise: Can you think of other examples of substitutes and complements?

Answer: You can probably think of many different examples of substitute goods, such as cassette players and CD players, and complementary goods, such as CDs and CD players.

Examination questions

1 a In the first part of the question, you need to explain clearly what is meant by the price elasticity of demand: i.e. the relationship between the proportionate change in the price of a good and the proportionate change in the demand for it. It is calculated by the percentage change in the quantity of a good demanded divided by the percentage change in the price of the good.

   b In the second part of the question, you need to compare and contrast the five degrees of price elasticity of demand: i.e. perfectly inelastic, inelastic, unitary elastic, elastic and perfectly elastic. You should include some examples to illustrate each of these and diagrams would help to distinguish between them.

2 In this question, you need to discuss the potential usefulness of price elasticity of demand to a business. If a business knows how demand is likely to change in response to a price change, it can take decisions about whether to raise or reduce price. If the demand is elastic, the price should be reduced in order to increase the revenue; if the demand is inelastic, the price should be raised to increase the revenue.

3 Income elasticity of demand shows the relationship between a proportionate change in income and a proportionate change in demand. It is measured by the percentage change in the quantity demanded and the percentage change in income. With most goods, demand goes up with an increase in income and these are called normal goods; with some goods, however, the demand goes down with an increase in income and these are called inferior goods. Cross elasticity of demand shows the relationship between a proportionate change in the quantity demanded of a good and the proportionate change in the price of another good. It is measured by the percentage change in the quantity demanded of a good divided by the percentage change in the price of another good. It is important to make clear whether the other good is a substitute or a complement.

4 The demand for soap is likely to be relatively inelastic, i.e. relatively low. The reason for this is that soap can be regarded as an essential good which is relatively cheap; the demand for it, therefore, is not likely to be affected very much by a change in price. The demand for a foreign holiday, however, is likely to be relatively elastic, i.e. relatively high. The reason for this is that foreign holidays can be regarded as a luxury good which is relatively expensive; the demand for it, therefore, is likely to be affected a great deal by a change in price.

Chapter 10

Exercises

Exercise: To what extent do you think that perfect competition is a theoretical idea without any real examples?

Answer: To some extent, you are likely to agree with this statement. Economists need to develop models of behaviour in different market structures and perfect competition is regarded as the opposite of monopoly. On the other hand, however, you could argue that some markets do get quite close to the model, such as a stock exchange.

Exercise: Consider the differences between normal and supernormal profits.

Answer: Normal profit can be regarded as that level of profit that is just enough to keep a firm in that particular line of business; supernormal profit can be regarded as the extra amount of profit that a firm can receive above normal profit.

Exercise: Discuss why monopolistic competition is closer to perfect competition than it is to monopoly.

Answer: Monopolistic competition consists of quite a large number of firms whereas a monopoly consists of just one firm. In monopolistic competition, only normal profits can be made in the long-run, as in perfect competition; in monopoly, supernormal profits can be made in the long-run. There are no barriers to entry in both monopolistic and perfect competition; in monopoly, there are very strong barriers to entry.

Exercise: Do you think it is right that many people on one air journey may have paid very different prices for their seats?

Answer: I suppose the answer depends on whether a person has paid a cheap rate or a more expensive price. The key point to stress is that the difference in price is not the result of a difference in costs.

Examination questions

1 **a** In the first part of the question, you need to explain the characteristics of perfect competition, such as that firms are price takers, goods are homogeneous and there are no barriers to entry meaning that only normal profits occur in the long-run. A diagram illustrating perfect competition would be useful.

   b In the second part of the question, you need to discuss whether perfect competition is purely a theoretical model which economists have devised or whether it has some basis in reality. Stock exchanges are sometimes said to be probably the best example.

2 You need to distinguish clearly between normal profits, which are those profits just enough to keep a firm in that particular line of business, and supernormal profits, which are those profits above normal profit. You should include diagrams to illustrate the two concepts.

3 You need to discuss the main features of monopolistic competition, such as that there are many firms in this market and that normal profits exist in the long-run because of the lack of barriers to entry, and monopoly, such as that there is just one seller and that supernormal profits exist in the long-run because of barriers to entry. Diagrams would help to make the differences between the two market structures clear.

4 In this question, you need to explain the conditions which are necessary for price discrimination to occur, such as that there must be monopoly power and the ability to separate markets according to their price elasticity of demand. It is also important that resale is not possible from one market to another.

5 **a** In the first part of the question, you need to explain clearly what is meant by an oligopolistic market structure in terms of it being characterised by a few firms in an industry and the existence of a high level of interdependence between firms. Firms tend to avoid competing on price and so there is a high level of price rigidity.

   b In the second part of the question, you need to explain what is meant by a kinked demand curve, stressing that this indicates the interdependence of firms with an elastic portion of the demand curve above the price and an inelastic portion below the price. This explains why price remains fairly rigid because the potential actions of other firms in the market need to be taken into account. It would be useful to include a diagram of the kinked demand curve.

6 This is an interesting question and requires you to compare and contrast the advantages and disadvantages of monopolies. It can certainly be argued that they are against the public interest in that they limit the degree of consumer choice and sovereignty and often charge prices that are higher than they might otherwise be. On the other hand, it could be argued that they do have some advantages; they tend to be large and so may benefit from economies of scale, leading to lower costs and, possibly, lower prices. You will need to consider both points of view and then come to a reasoned judgement.

Chapter 11

Exercises

Exercise: Consider the relative advantages and disadvantages of monopoly. Focus on one in your own country if there is a suitable example. On the whole, would you say monopolies are generally good or bad for an economy?

Answer: You need to consider the various advantages of monopoly, such as that it can benefit from economies of scale, and the various disadvantages, such as that it may produce a limited output at a higher price, and come to a judgement as to whether you think, on the whole, it is generally good or bad. It is probably an element of both but you need to consider whether the advantages outweigh the disadvantages or vice versa. It would be useful if you can refer to a particular monopoly in your own country.

Exercise: Look at some of the current advertising campaigns. Do you think that advertising is a good or bad feature of economies today?

Answer: You can choose which advertising campaigns you wish to research; you might like to select three or four. Advertising is a crucially important element of modern economies; you need to consider some of the main advantages and disadvantages of advertising campaigns and then come to a judgement as to whether, on the whole, it is a good or bad thing.

Exercise: Do you think that governments should ban smoking?

Answer: Cigarettes are an example of a demerit good and smoking clearly creates negative externalities. Your attitude to the question will probably depend on whether you smoke or not. If a government bans something, it may be difficult to enforce the ban. In most cases, governments place heavy taxes on the goods to try to discourage the level of consumption. You will need to make a decision as to whether a ban would be a good act to take or not for a government.

Exercise: Why is it sometimes quite difficult to be certain what is a public good in particular countries?

Answer: It is relatively easy to define a public good in terms of something that would be very difficult to provide through a market because of the difficulty of excluding 'free riders', i.e. those people who wouldn't pay. In reality, however, it is quite a difficult concept because what is provided by a government in one country might be provided through the market in another, such as fire or ambulance services.

Exercise: Find out how many people are unemployed in your country. Try and discover the reasons for the different types of unemployment there.

Answer: You should be able to find out how many people are unemployed in your country through published statistics or through the Internet. The more difficult part of the exercise is to discover the reasons for the different types of unemployment; you need to try and find out whether it is because of a decrease in the demand for particular products or resources, a technological development leading to a greater degree of capital intensive production or seasonal factors.

Exercise: Do you think that governments should intervene to try and reduce the inequality of income distribution in an economy?

Answer: This will depend, to some extent, on your own opinion. In a free market, it is very likely that there will be a great deal of inequality in the distribution of income. If you are a 'free marketeer' and generally opposed to government intervention in an economy, you will accept this as a natural outcome of a free market. However, if you are more inclined to favour different forms of government intervention, you will be more likely to believe that governments should intervene in an attempt to reduce the degree of inequality, such as through progressive taxation.

Examination questions

1. Allocative efficiency is where the price of a good or service is equal to the marginal cost of producing it, i.e. the value of it is the same for both consumers and producers. It would be useful to include a diagram to aid the explanation.

2. **a** In the first part of the question, you need to outline the main features of monopoly, such as that there is just one firm in the market which can make supernormal profits in the long run because of the existence of barriers to entry. A diagram to show monopoly would be useful.

   b In the second part of the question, you need to explain the advantages and disadvantages of monopoly. In terms of advantages, you could stress the potential to benefit from economies of scale, such as in terms of expenditure on research and development. In terms of disadvantages, you could consider the effect of monopoly on the output produced and the price charged, leading to inefficiency of production.

3. In this question, you need to distinguish clearly between positive externalities, which will benefit third parties, and negative externalities, which will make third parties worse off. You need to explain the concept of externalities and use examples to illustrate both positive and negative types.

4. You need to outline the main features of each of these three types of good. A public good would be very difficult to provide in a market because of the 'free rider' problem. A merit good could be provided in a market but it is likely that it would be under-consumed; governments therefore intervene to provide the service, usually in addition to a private sector. A demerit good is likely to be over-consumed in a market, such as tobacco or alcohol, and so governments intervene to discourage consumption, such as through a high rate of taxation.

5. There are many different types of unemployment that can occur in an economy and you need to distinguish clearly between them, such as frictional, structural, demand-deficient, cyclical, seasonal and technological. It would be useful to include some examples of each of these.

6. In this question, you need to distinguish clearly between absolute and relative poverty. Absolute poverty is when people cannot afford the basic necessities of life; relative poverty is when people are less well off than others in a particular society.

7. A business cycle is where levels of national income go up or down over a period of time. When an economy is doing well, it can lead to a boom when the cycle reaches a peak. When an economy is doing less well, it can lead to a slump when the cycle reaches a trough. This is why a general existence of unemployment is referred to as cyclical. It would be helpful to include a diagram of the business cycle.

8 Whereas question five was concerned with the various causes of unemployment, this question is concerned with the economic consequences of unemployment. Labour, like all factors of production, is an important resource and so any unemployment means that a resource is being wasted or under-utilised. The effect of this is that a country's GDP may be lower than it would otherwise be or, to put it another way, it is operating within its production possibility curve.

9 This question leads on logically from the previous one. If unemployment is seen as having bad economic consequences, it is only natural that governments will wish to create jobs, through fiscal and/or monetary measures. This should lead to an increase in GDP, economic growth and a movement to a position on a country's production possibility curve.

10 A 'multiplier effect' in an economy refers to the fact that expenditure by one of the elements that constitutes aggregate demand, such as government expenditure, can lead to an increase in income that is greater than the initial injection of money into the economy. One person's expenditure becomes another person's income and this process goes on and on throughout an economy. You need to explain how the multiplier can be calculated and a diagram would aid the explanation.

Chapter 12

Exercises

Exercise: Consider the various problems and disadvantages of barter. Imagine what would happen if all money disappeared and we were back to a situation of barter.

Answer: You need to make clear why barter was regarded as being very inconvenient. A major disadvantage was that it relied on what was called 'a double coincidence of wants', i.e. you had to find somebody who had something you wanted and who wanted to obtain something you had. Money is generally regarded as being much more convenient. Of course, in certain situations, barter can still exist, such as a means of exchange in prisons.

Exercise: Consider why inflation is considered to be such a bad situation for many people.

Answer: Inflation is a situation where the general level of prices is increasing over a period of time; it therefore means that a given sum of money will be worth less in terms of what it can buy. This will be especially bad for those people whose income does not rise as fast as the increase in prices.

Exercise: Draw a line across a page and call it the 'liquidity spectrum'. Make the left end the most liquid and the right end the least liquid. Place all of the items mentioned on the line, placing them in terms of their liquidity.

Answer: Cash is the most liquid asset and so this will be placed at the end on the left side. Money that is deposited for a long period of time, such as three or five years, will be much less liquid and so will be placed at the end on the right side.

Exercise: Find out the current rate of inflation in your country.

Answer: The rate of inflation is usually announced by the government or the central bank of a country. You should be able to find this rate, either in published sources or on the Internet. Inflation rates can vary a great deal between countries; prices have actually been falling in Japan in recent years whereas Argentina has had an inflation rate of over 1000 % p.a. The country with the highest rate of inflation today is probably Zimbabwe.

Examination questions

1 a In the first part of the question, you need to explain clearly what is meant by the term

barter, i.e. it is a means of directly exchanging one good or service for another without money acting as a means of exchange.

b In the second part of the question, you need to explain the main disadvantages of barter, such as the need for a 'double coincidence of wants' and the fact that it did not provide for portability or divisibility.

2 a In the first part of the question, you need to outline the main functions of money; these include money as a medium of exchange, a measure of value, a store of value and a standard of deferred payment.

b In the second part of the question, you need to explain the main characteristics of money; these include acceptability, divisibility, portability, durability and scarcity.

3 a In the first part of the question, you need to define inflation precisely in terms of a persistent tendency for the general level of prices in an economy to rise over a given period of time.

b In the second part of the question, you need to explain how the rate of inflation in an economy can be measured. You need to discuss the idea of a price index and how it is calculated. You need to explain the choice of a base year and the value of 100 given to this year. It will also be necessary to explain why various items in the basket of goods and services have different weights to reflect the proportion of income spent on them.

4 You need to explain that the nominal value of a given sum of money will be affected by inflation, i.e. the strength of its purchasing power will be reduced. The real value of a sum of money, however, takes into account the impact of inflation. For example, if your wage goes up by 5% but the prices in your country go up by 3%, you have had a real increase of 2%, i.e. the difference between 5% and 3%.

5 In this question, you need to explain the meaning of liquidity, i.e. the ease by which an asset can be turned into cash. Money is regarded as being the most liquid; deposit accounts that cannot be accessed for three or five years are regarded as relatively illiquid.

Chapter 13

Exercises

Exercise: Try and find out the names of the different financial intermediaries in your country.

Answer: You will need to research the financial system in your country and find out the names of the central bank, the commercial banks, the development banks, the stock exchange, the credit unions and the insurance companies.

Exercise: Consider the importance of the central bank in your country.

Answer: Central banks are extremely important in any economy, performing a range of crucial functions. You will need to find out as much as you can about the central bank in your country and then consider its importance. Most central banks have a website which should provide all the necessary information.

Exercise: Choose one or two firms that are listed on a stock exchange and follow the change in the price of the shares over a one or two week period.

Answer: This should be an interesting exercise. The price of shares can be very volatile and you need to think about why the price may go up or down.

Exercise: Try and find out something about a Development Project in your country. Where does the finance come from?

Answer: It should be possible to find out information about Development Projects in your country; there should be a website which contains relevant information, such as the sources of finance.

Exercise: Consider the conflict between liquidity and profitability for a bank.

Answer: A commercial bank needs, and is usually required, to keep a minimum of its assets in liquid form, i.e. money that can be given to customers. On the other hand, this will not make them a profit. This will come about by lending money and so there is always this clash between the need for liquidity and the search for profits.

Exercise: Why do you think Credit Unions are so popular in the Caribbean? Find out as much as you can about the ones which operate in your country.

Answer: The evidence shows that Credit Unions are very popular in Caribbean countries. You need to find out as much as you can about them and then explain the reasons for their popularity, especially the ones in your own country.

Examination questions

1 You need to distinguish clearly between maturity transformation and risk transformation. The first term refers to the fact that some customers will always be depositing money; this means that funds will be available to finance long-term loans. The second term refers to the ways in which financial intermediaries take the risk away from individuals.

2 In this question, you need to explain clearly the functions of a central bank, such as the issuing of notes and coins, acting as a bank to other banks as well as to the government, its role in relation to the exchange rate and its involvement in the implementation of monetary policy.

3 a In the first part of the question, you need to explain the meaning of a share, i.e. it is a part of the capital of a company.

   b In the second part of the question, you need to explain the functions of a stock exchange and then discuss its role in an economy. It is a way of buying and selling shares and this enables firms to raise finance; it thus plays a very important role in an economy.

4 Commercial banks need to take into account liquidity; i.e. they need to be able to meet the demand for money from customers, thus maintaining confidence in the financial system. They also need to take into account profitability so that it is possible to pay dividends to the shareholders. The problem is that to make the most profit, the assets need to be relatively illiquid.

5 a In the first part of the question, you need to explain what is meant by a credit union. You need to consider its functions and discuss why it can play an important role in the financial system.

   b In the second part of the question, you need to explain why they are so popular in Caribbean countries. You need to relate the general features of them to the particular circumstances of the Caribbean.

Chapter 14

Exercises

Exercise: Why do you think economists want to compare GDP figures over time and between countries?

Answer: Economists can make good use of GDP figures. They can be analysed in relation to one particular country over a period of time to see whether that country has had an increase in GDP and has, therefore, experienced economic growth. It is also useful to compare the figures at one point in time between countries to get an idea of standards of living, as long as the figures are adjusted to per capita or per head to take account of the population in different countries.

Exercise: Why do you think it is important to

take inflation into account when studying GDP figures?

Answer: The GDP of a country may have gone up by 5% in a year but if its inflation rate is 3%, it has really only gone up by 2% once the increase in prices has been taken into account. This adjustment to take inflation into account gives the 'real' figure.

Exercise: What do you think ought to be included in a definition of the "quality of life"?

Answer: This is an interesting question. The quality of life is a broader concept than the standard of living but not all economists agree on what should be included in it. Some of the factors that would be regarded as important are the teacher/pupil ratio, the doctor/patient ratio, the access to clean water or the level of literacy.

Examination questions

1. Gross National Product is the value of what has been produced within the geographical boundaries of a country by the nationals of that country and it takes into account the net property income from abroad. The National Income is the Net National Income at Factor Cost and takes into account the depreciation of capital assets.

2. In this question, you need to describe the three different methods of calculating Gross Domestic Product, i.e. the income, output and expenditure methods, and then explain the differences between them.

3. a In the first part of the question, you need to explain that real GDP is the figure that takes into account the rate of inflation.

   b In the second part of the question, you need to explain why it is important to use real GDP figures. If you did not, the figures might go up rapidly one year but this would not necessarily indicate a strong economy, simply that the prices were rising rapidly. For example, if GDP rose by 20% but the inflation rate was 25%, there would actually have been a fall in real terms of 5%.

4. a In the first part of the question, you need to explain what is meant by the Circular Flow of Income in an economy. You need to stress that it refers to the flow of income involving households, firms, the government and the effects of trade.

   b In the second part of the question, you need to compare and contrast the injections into the Circular Flow, such as investment, government expenditure and the money received from exports, and the leakages or withdrawals from it, such as savings, taxation and the money spent on imports.

5. In this question, you need to consider the limitations of the GDP figures in not always giving an indication of the standard of living of a country. For example, they do not include the figures from subsistence production, do-it-yourself or the hidden economy. On the other hand, they do include the figures from production which may not increase the standard of living, such as production of armaments or tobacco. They may also include the figures from factories which are responsible for polluting the environment.

6. The standard of living of a country has traditionally been defined by economists as the real GDP per capita. The quality of life, however, is a much wider term and takes into account both material and non-material elements, i.e. the qualitative as well as the quantitative dimension. The quality of life would include such things as the literacy rate, the health of the people and life expectancy.

Chapter 15

Exercises

Exercise: The principle of trying to balance revenue and expenditure is essentially the same for a government as it is for an individual. Draw up your own personal budget of income and expenditure over the period of a week or a month.

Answer: The purpose of this exercise is to get you thinking about the balance between income and expenditure. Governments are faced with the same sort of pressure as you and I; trying to keep a balance between the two. It will be interesting to see whether you still have some money left at the end of the period or whether you have over-spent.

Exercise: Do you agree with the principle of a progressive tax?

Answer: The answer to this question will largely depend on personal beliefs and opinions. If you think that governments ought to do something about the inequality of income, then your answer will probably be yes. If you don't like the idea of governments interfering in a free market, your answer will probably be no.

Exercise: What do you think the top rate of income tax should be in an economy?

Answer: It would be useful to find out what the top rate of income tax is in your country. In the UK, the top rate is 40% at the moment but in the past it has been as high as 83%.

Exercise: Explain why VAT is a regressive tax.

Answer: A sales tax will usually tax everybody at the same rate. In the UK at the moment, the rate is 17.5%. This may seem fair as everybody is taxed at the same rate. The problem, however, is that this will take a higher proportion of the income of a poor person than a rich person; that is why it is considered regressive.

Exercise: Do you think it is right that such a high proportion of the price of alcohol or cigarettes should be in the form of taxation?

Answer: This again may be a matter of opinion. Alcohol and tobacco are regarded as demerit goods and so taxation is used to make them much more expensive than they would otherwise be. The effect of this should be a reduction in consumption. Of course, it is difficult to know whether the percentage of tax should be 25% of the price, 50% of the price, 75% of the price or any other figure.

Exercise: Consider whether it is right to subsidise some types of production.

Answer: In a free market, there would be no government intervention and, therefore, no subsidies. Subsidies, however, can be justified if they help to keep down costs and, therefore, prices. This will mean that poorer people will be more able to buy these goods or services.

Exercise: Should we be worried about the size of a country's national debt?

Answer: I suppose the answer is: "it depends!" In one sense, it shouldn't be regarded as a problem as all governments need to borrow money for various reasons. On the other hand, it can be regarded as a problem because the size of the interest payments on the debt can be quite large and this will have an impact on a country's fiscal policy.

Examination questions

1 A direct tax is one that is imposed on income, such as income tax or corporation tax. An indirect tax is one that is imposed on expenditure, such as a sales tax.

2 A progressive tax, such as income tax, is one which takes a higher proportion of the income of the better-off. A regressive tax, such as a sales tax, is one which takes a higher proportion of the income of the less well-off. A proportional tax is one which takes the same proportion of the income of every person.

3 You will first need to draw a demand and supply diagram. Make sure that it is clearly drawn and correctly labelled. You then need to show the effect of the introduction of an indirect tax; this will be shown by the shift of the supply curve to the left, leading to an increase in price. You then need to show the effect of the introduction of a subsidy; this will

be shown by the shift of the supply curve to the right, leading to a reduction in price.

4 The aim of a budget should be to balance, i.e. where income equals expenditure. This, however, may not always happen. A government might wish to put more into an economy than it takes out; this will lead to a deficit budget. On the other hand, a government might want to put less into an economy than it takes out; this will lead to a surplus budget.

5 If a country borrows from a number of countries or from an international organisation, such as the World Bank, it is known as multilateral debt. If it borrows from just one country, it is known as bilateral debt.

Chapter 16

Exercises

Exercise: Find out the current rate of inflation in your country. Is the trend over the last few months upward or downwards?

Answer: You should be able to find out the current rate of inflation in your country from the Internet. You will need to look at the figures over a period of time and see whether the trend has been going up, going down or staying at about the same level.

Exercise: Try and think why falling prices might not be good for an economy.

Answer: Economists always stress that inflation is a problem but falling prices can also be considered a problem. For example, if prices are falling, firms will be discouraged from investing, especially if they think that prices will not cover costs. They may be forced to reduce costs and this could lead to an increase in unemployment.

Exercise: Try and find out what have been the main causes of inflation in your country.

Answer: This is a difficult question because it is not always easy to distinguish clearly between the different causes, such as demand-pull or cost-push. However, try and get some information from the Internet on your country's economy and see if you are able to see where the main pressures on prices have been coming from. For example, are the pressures mainly coming from within the country or is it largely a question of imported inflation?

Exercise: Think about who is likely to benefit from inflation and who is likely to be badly affected by it.

Answer: People whose income is rising more than the rate of inflation will have less cause to worry. Those whose income is rising less than the rate of inflation, or those on fixed incomes, will have more cause to worry.

Examination questions

1 **a** In the first part of the question, you need to explain what is meant by inflation, i.e. it is a situation where the general level of prices is persistently increasing over a period of time.

   b In the second part of the question, you need to compare and contrast the possible causes of inflation. You will need to look at demand-pull, cost-push, monetary factors and imported inflation.

2 In this question, you need to discuss both the beneficial and the unfavourable consequences of inflation. Firms may well benefit if prices have gone up by more than costs as this is likely to lead to greater profits. Those people on fixed incomes, however, such as pensioners, will be worse off because they won't be able to keep up with the rising prices, leading to a fall in their standard of living.

3 Inflation is a situation of rising prices over a period of time whereas deflation is a situation of falling prices over a period of time. You need to stress that both can have damaging effects on an economy, even though this will be for different reasons.

4 You need to explain clearly what is meant by the Quantity Theory of Money by discussing the Fisher Equation of MV=PT. You need to explain what each of these means and how they relate to each other. You then need to explain how this can be used to explain what the rate of inflation will be. This monetarist explanation of the cause of inflation has been a very influential theory.

Chapter 17

Exercises

Exercise: Do you think it is better for firms to operate in the private rather than the public sector?

Answer: Privatisation is generally regarded as a process that should lead to greater efficiency so that the consumer benefits. The problem, however, is that greater efficiency often means reducing costs and this could lead to some people losing their jobs, leading to an increase in unemployment. Public sector provision, on the other hand, is not under the same pressure to make a profit, meaning that there will perhaps be less unemployment.

Exercise: Can you think of any other examples of technological improvements that have increased output and productivity?

Answer: You should be able to think of a number of examples of technological improvements. For example, the greater use of computers in many different areas of production has lead to much greater levels of efficiency.

Examination questions

1 One of the most important macro-economic aims of government is to keep down the rate of inflation. For example, in the UK at the moment, the government aims to keep the rate no higher than 2%. The reason for this is that inflation has a number of negative consequences in an economy and you need to discuss these. For example, if the price of goods goes up too much, they may become uncompetitive in world markets and foreign demand will consequently fall.

2 The focus is often on reducing demand as a way of bringing down inflation. The focus of this question, however, is the supply side. You need to think of ways in which supply can be improved, leading to a greater degree of efficiency. For example, improved education and training would improve the quality of the workforce.

3 You need not only to describe monetary and fiscal policies as methods of controlling inflation but also to compare and contrast them, coming to a judgement as to which might be more appropriate in particular circumstances and why. Monetary policy will focus on the money supply and the rate of interest; fiscal policy will focus on the use of taxation to reduce spending power and on the decision of government to reduce its expenditure.

4 The marginal efficiency of investment is the return from each additional amount of money spent on investment. It is shown in a diagram as a downward sloping curve, i.e. as the rate of interest falls, the MEI is likely to encourage a greater level of investment.

5 The consumption function shows the link between a change in income and a change in consumption. It would be useful to include a diagram, showing the consumption function sloping upwards. The steepness of the curve will show the degree to which consumption will change as a result of a change in income.

Chapter 18

Exercises

Exercise: Find out the current rate of unemployment in your country. Is the trend over the past few months upward or downward?

Answer: You should be able to find the current rate of unemployment in your country on the Internet. Governments usually give details of such figures on its website. You need to look at the figures over a period of time and say whether the trend has been upward, downward or relatively constant.

Exercise: Consider some of the practical difficulties in measuring unemployment.

Answer: It is not always easy comparing unemployment figures from different countries because the way of measuring unemployment can vary a great deal from one country to another. For example, some countries only count those who are actively seeking work while others only count those who are signing on for benefits.

Exercise: Consider the various disadvantages of being unemployed.

Answer: I think that there are two ways of looking at this. Firstly, the disadvantages to the individual who may become bored and feel rejected; this situation could lead to criminal activity. Secondly, the disadvantages to the economy which is losing the output which that worker could have produced. The GDP of the country would therefore be lower than it would have otherwise have been.

Exercise: Find out if there is a minimum wage in your country and, if so, what it is.

Answer: Many of the countries in the world have a legally enforceable minimum wage. You will need to find out if your country has introduced this and, if it has, what the rate is at the moment.

Exercise: Find out information about another trade union in the Caribbean. When you go out to work, do you think you would be likely to join a trade union?

Answer: The book contains a lot of information about the OWTU but you need to find out information about another trade union in the Caribbean. Find out when it was set up, who it represents, how many members it has and how powerful it is. Whether you would join a trade union when you go out to work is, of course, a matter of personal choice. You might like to think of all the possible reasons why you would join a trade union and all the possible reasons why you wouldn't.

Examination questions

1 It is important that economists have figures on the number of people unemployed in particular countries but this question is concerned with the difficulties of accurately collecting this information. You need to consider some of these problems, such as the fact that people may have a job which they are not declaring and still trying to claim benefit. Also, there may be people who are unemployed who would like to have a job but who are not actively searching for one at a particular time.

2 There are many different possible causes of unemployment in an economy and you need to compare and contrast these, such as frictional, seasonal, casual, regional, technological and cyclical.

3 Some countries have introduced a minimum wage. The argument in favour of it is that in a free market, without any government intervention, some people may be paid a very low wage that it is virtually impossible to live on; there is, therefore, a need for the government to introduce legislation to provide for a basic minimum wage. On the other hand, those that believe in a free market argue that it represents unnecessary intervention by the government. Wages are determined by demand and supply and if a worker gets a low wage, this might encourage him or her to get a better education or new skills. A diagram would be useful to aid the discussion.

4 a In the first part of the question, you need to explain what is meant by a trade union, i.e. it is an organised group of workers who

come together to negotiate with the employers in an attempt to improve the pay, working conditions and various benefits of the employees.

b In the second part of the question, you need to discuss both the advantages and disadvantages of trade unions in an economy. The advantages include the fact that they may well contribute to better wages and working conditions and that this would be likely to lead to greater efficiency and productivity. The disadvantages are that the wages negotiated may be more than the firms can afford and possibly put some of them out of business; there is also the argument that trade union action can sometimes lead to strikes which are very disruptive in an economy.

5 You need to discuss the economic consequences of unemployment, stressing the waste of an important economic resource. The GDP of an economy will therefore be lower than it otherwise might have been. It may also lead to lower levels of spending in an area, leading to even greater unemployment. In countries which provide benefits to unemployed workers, it creates a huge burden on the state, especially if the revenue from taxation is lower because of the unemployment.

6 In this question, you need to describe the various functions of trade unions. The book includes those of the OWTU but you might be able to think of some others. You then need to say which one of the various functions you think is the most important and why. I suppose most people would say that the main function is to try and get as high a wage agreed as possible so as to give the workers the best possible standard of living. You, however, may think that another one of the functions is more important but you must say why you think so.

Chapter 19

Exercises

Exercise: Is the world population now too large?

Answer: The world population is now over six billion people. Whether this figure is too large or not is a matter of opinion. The problem, of course, is not the size of the population in itself but the relationship between it and the resources available in the world to feed this number of people.

Exercise: Think of as many goods and services as you can that are imported into your country.

Answer: This should be an interesting exercise. Every country in the world imports a great deal of goods and services; see if you can think of as many as possible in your own country.

Exercise: Do you think it is right that governments sometimes protect infant and declining industries?

Answer: The free market argument is that governments shouldn't intervene to protect any industry. It could be argued, however, that protectionism is necessary, at least for a certain period of time, to protect the 'sunrise' industries until they get themselves established and the 'sunset' industries so that workers can be retrained to work in other industries.

Exercise: If the Grenada Government subsidises its banana growers so that they can sell at low prices abroad, is this not 'dumping'? Argue the case for and against this subsidy.

Answer: A subsidy is an intervention in a free market by a government and so the main argument against it is that it is an interference; industries should be encouraged 'to stand on their own feet' and not be protected by governments. The main argument in favour of it is that the government in Grenada believes that the industry needs support, especially given the importance of the industry to the island's economy.

Examination questions

1. In this question, you need to distinguish clearly between an open and a closed economy. A closed economy is one which does not engage in any form of trade in goods or services with other countries; an open economy is the opposite, i.e. one which is fully engaged in the import and export of goods and services.

2. There is a range of different possible protectionist policies and you need to compare and contrast these. You are likely to include tariffs, quotas, exchange controls, subsidies and administration arrangements.

3. You need to explain clearly what is meant by the theory of comparative advantage in terms of international specialisation and the various factor endowments in different countries. The key part of the theory is that a country will have a comparative advantage over another country in the production of a good if it can produce that good at a lower opportunity cost. A table with the production of two goods would help to illustrate the theory.

4. The theory of comparative advantage would suggest that countries would operate on the principle of total specialisation. The reality, however, is that although this might be fine in theory, in practice many countries will be reluctant to give up entirely the production of certain goods. For example, they may feel that this would lead to a significant increase in unemployment.

5. You will need to explain the various gains from trade and these will include such things as greater choice for consumers, advantages to producers from economies of scale, greater efficiency and, therefore, greater world output and, consequently, an increase in standards of living.

6. Some countries decide to use protectionist policies to support particular industries. For example, these are likely to include infant or sunrise industries, declining or sunset industries and those key industries which might be regarded as being of crucial importance, perhaps for military or strategic reasons.

Chapter 20

Exercises

Exercise: Consider what happened to the Terms of Trade when oil prices quadrupled in 1973-74 from the point of view of (a) oil exporting and (b) oil importing countries.

Answer: The Terms of Trade shows the relationship between the index of export prices and the index of import prices. If oil prices quadrupled, this would be good for the oil exporting countries, making the Terms of Trade better, and bad for the oil importing countries, making the Terms of Trade worse.

Exercise: Calculate the Terms of Trade Index when the export price index is 103 and the import price index is 87.

Answer: To calculate the Terms of Trade, it is the Index of Export Prices divided by the Index of Import Prices. In this case, therefore, it is 103 divided by 87, multiplied by 100, which is 118.39.

Exercise: Consider the good and bad aspects of changes in the Terms of Trade for Caribbean countries.

Answer: If a Caribbean country's currency rose in value, this would lead to a fall in the price of imports and so the Terms of Trade would move in a favourable direction. If there is a fall in the price of agricultural exports, such as bananas or sugar, the Terms of Trade will move in an unfavourable direction.

Exercise: Find out the rate of exchange of your country's currency against the U.S. dollar.

Answer: This should be relatively easy to find out as exchange rates are usually put in the newspapers each day.

Exercise: If there was a target rate, what action would the Bank of Jamaica take if the Jamaican $ was falling in value?

Answer: If the rate was falling, the central bank would need to intervene by buying Jamaican dollars on the foreign exchange market; this increase in demand should reverse the fall in value and start bringing the value up.

Examination questions

1. These two terms can often be confused. A depreciation of a currency means that it has fallen in value as a result of developments in a free market, e.g. the demand for it has fallen. A devaluation of a currency operates in a fixed exchange rate system when a government decides to reduce the value of its currency on the foreign exchange market (the government will then need to intervene in the market to ensure that the value remains constant).

2. A floating exchange rate system is a free market one where the value of a currency is determined by the demand for and supply of the currency; if it goes up, it appreciates in value and if it goes down, it depreciates in value. A fixed exchange rate system is one where the value is determined not by free market forces in the foreign exchange market but by the government which decides what its value should be. If the rate is increased, it is a revaluation and if it is decreased, it is a devaluation.

3. You need to explain clearly what is meant by the Terms of Trade, i.e. it is the ratio of the export price index in relation to the import price index and it is calculated by dividing the former by the latter to give a figure above or below 100.

4. a In the first part of the question, you need to explain why a balance of payments deficit is regarded as a problem. You need to state that this means that the value of the imports is greater than the value of the exports or, to put it another way, the country is living beyond its means.

   b There are two ways to reduce or eliminate this deficit: encourage exports or discourage imports. Exports will be encouraged if production becomes more efficient, prices are kept down and the goods can compete in the international market on the basis of good quality and reasonable prices. Imports will be discouraged if the government tries to dampen down demand, such as by raising interest rates, or by imposing protectionist policies, either to raise the price of imports (through a tariff) or to restrict the quantity of them (through a quota).

Chapter 21

Exercises

Exercise: To what extent do you think the HDI is a useful method to compare countries?

Answer: In the past, the usual way to compare countries was to consider the real GDP per capita. The HDI (Human Development Index) is an improvement in that it takes into account a wider range of features. You need to be aware of what it does include (and, at the same time, what is excluded from it). Most economists would argue that, although not perfect, it is a useful method to compare countries.

Exercise: Find out as much as you can about tourism in your country. Do you think your country is over-dependent on tourism?

Answer: Tourism is a big industry in Caribbean countries and so you should be able to find out quite a lot about it. It will be a matter of personal judgement whether you think that your country is over-dependent on tourism but, in order to answer the question, you will need to find out just how important the tourism industry is in comparison to other industries in the country.

Exercise: To what extent would you describe your country's economy as diversified?

Answer: This really follows on from the previous exercise. You need to find out about the different industries that operate in your country and then come to a judgement as to how diversified it is. Are there dozens of different industries or are there just a few?

Exercise: To what extent would you say your country fulfils the characteristics of a Caribbean economy?

Answer: There are a number of common features in each of the Caribbean countries but, at the same time, each is in some way distinctive. You need to think about the typical characteristics of Caribbean countries and then form a judgement about the extent to which your country corresponds to these. Again, as with many of the questions, it will be, to some extent, a matter of opinion.

Exercise: Do you know of people who have been part of the "brain drain"? Where did they go? Try and find out if you can why they went.

Answer: How successful you are in answering this question will depend on whether you know of people who have left your country to work abroad. Hopefully, you will know of at least one person; if so, find out as much information as you can, such as why did they go, where did they go, whether they think it was a good decision and whether they would ever come back permanently.

Examination questions

1 a In the first part of the question, you need to explain how the Human Development Index is constructed. There are three elements to it and you need to describe clearly what these are.

  b In the second part of the question, you need to discuss how successful it has been as a means of comparing the quality of life in different countries. You can explain how it is an improvement on previous indicators, such as real GDP per capita, because it takes into account more features. However, you could consider other aspects of quality of life that are not included within it.

2 a In the first part of the question, you need to consider the main characteristics of Caribbean economies. Each one will be, in some way, different from others in the Caribbean but there are some broad similarities and you need to discuss these, such as the fact that all of them are relatively small in population.

  b In the second part of the question, you need to consider the main problems facing Caribbean economies today. Again, as in the first part, although each country may well have particular problems, all of the countries in the Caribbean will, to some extent, share certain problems, such as a high level of exports and imports, a reliance on tourism, a lack of diversification, low domestic demand and relatively high rates of unemployment.

3 In this question, you need to discuss how external shocks can affect an economy, such as any slump in world trade, which will affect demand for exports from the Caribbean, or any terrorist attacks, which will affect the demand for holidays abroad, such as in the Caribbean.

4 You need to explain why economies need to be as diversified as possible. For example, you could discuss the dangers of over-dependence on certain products; if the demand for that product falls, or the price of it falls, this could have a damaging effect on an economy. The more diversified an economy is, the lower the

risk involved compared to reliance on just one or two products.

5 In this question, you need to explain clearly what is meant by the multiplier. It is the degree to which a given injection into an economy will eventually lead to an increase in the national income. For example, if the Jamaican Government injects 100 million dollars into an economy and the national income increases by 200 million Jamaican dollars, the multiplier will be two.

6 You need to discuss the advantages and disadvantages of different forms of economic integration. You need to consider the different types of integration including a free trade area, a customs union, a common market and an economic union. It would be useful if you could give some examples of each of these. You then need to compare and contrast the advantages and disadvantages of each of these.

7 This question focuses on one particular example of integration, CARICOM, and you need to demonstrate a good knowledge and understanding of this trade bloc. You need to consider both its strengths and its weaknesses and then come to a judgement as to how successful you think it has been.

Chapter 22

Exercises

Exercise: Try and find out which multinational companies are operating in your country.

Answer: There is almost certainly going to be at least one multinational company operating in your country so you should not have too much trouble finding out about them.

Exercise: Do you think the advantages of globalisation outweigh the disadvantages? Consider how your country's culture is a product of globalisation.

Answer: Globalisation is a very controversial subject and people are divided as to whether it is good or bad. You need to compare and contrast all of the various advantages and disadvantages and come to a judgement as to the overall verdict. You then need to consider the most significant cultural features of your own country and see which ones have come in from outside.

Exercise: Visit Amazon.com (or any other Internet shopping site) and scroll through the screens to see how the system works. You do not have to buy anything!

Answer: E-commerce has been growing rapidly in recent years and you need to be aware of examples of how it operates.

Examination questions

1 Bretton Woods in 1944 was significant because the conference held there established fixed exchange rates, the International Monetary Fund, the system of Special Drawing Rights and the World Bank. You need to say something about each of these.

2 This question is concerned with two of the international bodies set up in 1944, the International Monetary Fund and the World Bank. You need to explain the functions and responsibilities of these and discuss their role over the last sixty years.

3 The theory of comparative advantage shows the importance of specialisation and so it would be expected that countries would totally specialise on what they are best at. The reality, however, is that countries often tend to have partial specialisation. You need to explain the differences between exclusive and partial specialisation and explain why the latter exists.

4 a In the first part of the question, you need to define clearly what is meant by a multinational, i.e. it is a firm which produces in more than one country. You need to stress that just because a firm may sell in many countries, this does not, by itself, make it a multinational.

   b In the second part of the question, you need to discuss the advantages and disadvantages of a multinational. There are a number of potential advantages, such as the fact that they can provide jobs, but there are also a number of disadvantages, such as the fact that the profits, after local tax has been deducted, return to the multinational's home country.

5 a In the first part of the question, you need to explain the meaning of globalisation. There are a number of different ways of defining it but it is essentially the extension of trade throughout the world so that national boundaries become less significant.

   b In the second part of the question, you need to discuss the advantages and disadvantages of globalisation. There is a lot to be said for it in terms of encouraging international trade and allowing countries to engage in the exporting and importing of a wide variety of goods and services. There are, however, a number of disadvantages, such as the fact that wherever you are in the world, you are likely to find many of the same multinational companies operating, possibly reflecting a degree of exploitation.

6 The World Trade Organisation is the successor to GATT (the General Agreement on Tariffs and Trade) and, in this question, you need to explain what it is and discuss its role in international trade. Its aim is to encourage free trade through a series of 'rounds' and you need to consider how successful these have been so far.

7 There are many different countries in the Caribbean and, although many of them share similar economic characteristics, they are all, to some extent, distinct. Many regional trade blocs have been established in the world and in this question, therefore, you need to consider the extent to which the Caribbean should be regarded as a single market.

8 In this question, you need to consider why regional trade blocs exist in the world despite the moves towards free trade. Many countries in particular areas of the world have formed close economic links with neighbouring countries and you need to discuss the reasons for this. You also need to point out that the degree of integration within these trade blocs can vary a great deal.

9 a In the first part of the question, you need to explain what is meant by E-commerce, i.e. the development of electronic business through the extensive use of computer technology.

   b This has been the fastest growing form of retailing in recent years and you need to consider the possible reasons for this. There are a number of possible advantages which you could mention, such as the convenience, the access to companies in different countries and the lower prices.

Index

absolute advantage 266, 267
absolute poverty 160
acceptability of money 170
accountants' profit 55
across the table bargaining 249
actuaries 189
adding value 39
advertising 136, 137
aggregate demand 161, 224–5
Aggregate Expenditure 199
aggregate supply 225–6
Agricultural Development Bank of Trinidad and Tobago 184
agriculture 82
allocative efficiency 19, 146–54
allocative inefficiency 147
Annual General Meeting AGM) 188, 191
Appraisal Report 185
appreciation 276, 277
arc elasticity 118
armchair shopping 329
Arthur, Owen 208
asset 186
Association of South East Asian Nations (ASEAN) 301
attainable costs 63
Automated Teller Machines (ATMs) 172
average costs 60, 62

backward sloping supply curve of labour 47
Bahamas, education in 92
balance of payments 207, 261, 279–82
 deficits of 260–1
 Jamaica 281–2
balance of trade 279
balanced trade 314–15, 316
balancing item 280
banana case 319–20, 324
Bank of Barbados 278
Bank of Jamaica 174, 182, 231, 276
Bank Rate 233
banking system 207
banknotes 171
Barbados Mutual Life Assurance 189
Barbados Securities Exchange 183
Barbados
 services in 74
 tourism 14
barrier to entry
 in monopoly 140–1
 in oligopoly 144–5
barter 94, 167
Base Rate 233
'basket' of shopping 174

Beacon Insurance Company 189
beggar-my-neighbour policies 310
bilateral trade 266
black market 97
bonding 297
boundary 16–17
brain drain 30, 44, 296–7
Branson, Richard 15
British Caribbean Insurance Company 189
broad money 173
broker 184
business cycle 93, 161–2

Cable and Wireless 148
Cairns Group 301
Canadian Development Bank 185
capacity 63, 316–17
capital 15, 16, 28, 29–30, 48–9, 184
 as resource 79
 return to 52–3
capital account 280
Capital Consumption 200, 205
capital good 16–17, 69
capitalist economy 7
Caribbean Basin Initiative (CBI) 300, 306, 324–5
Caribbean Community 259
Caribbean Community and Common Market (CARICOM) 259, 300–8, 324
 cost–benefit analysis 303–4
 policy choices 305–6
 appraisal 306–8
Caribbean Court of Justice 326
Caribbean Development Bank (CDB) 184, 185, 219, 319
Caribbean Disaster Emergency Response Agency (CDERA) 307
Caribbean economies
 characteristics 289
 diversification 294
 economic problems 294–300
 free market economies 29
 historical background 290
 market size 291–2
 over-reliance on trade 292–3
 present-day characteristics 290–4
 reliance on tourism 293
 size of GDP 291
 trade blocs 300–2, 302–3
Caribbean Environment Health Institute (CEHI) 307
Caribbean Examinations Council (CXC) 305
Caribbean Free Trade Association (CARIFTA) 259, 300, 304
Caribbean Freight Handlers 97

Caribbean Meterological Institute (CMI) 307
Caribbean Single Market and Economy (CSME) 259, 300, 305, 326–7, 327, 328
Caribbean Tourism Organisation (CTO) 293
Caribbean trade patterns 254–5
CARIBCAN 327
Caricom Single Market and Economy see Caribbean Single Market and Economy
cartel 104, 114–15, 141
Castro, Fidel 11
casual unemployment 245
catering 74
Cayman Islands
 economic problem of 3–4
 education 13, 75
 free market economy 20
 gap between rich and poor 158
 gas supply 10
 Hurricane Ivan 21, 201
 industrial relations 30–1, 32
 mixed economy 13
 public sector in 74
 taxation 34
 tourism 29
Cayman Islands Stock Exchange 183
Central American Common Market (CACM) 327
Central Bank of Barbados 173, 174, 277
Central Bank of Trinidad and Tobago 181, 232, 233, 276
central banks 35–6, 174, 178, 180–3, 232
ceteris paribus 24, 98, 109
cheques 172–3
China
 diplomatic relations with 259–60
 economic growth 201
choice 4–5
Choiseul Co-operative Credit Union 188
circular flow diagram 97, 98
circular flow of goods and services 81–2
circular flow of income 179–80
circular flow of the national income 205–7
classical unemployment 158
clearing banks 186
closed economies 253
coins 171
collective bargaining 31–2, 249
collectively consumed good 73
collusive oligopoly 143

command economy 4, 7, 11–12, 86–9
  advantages 87–9
  disadvantages 88–9
commercial banks 178, 186–7
commodity market 97
Common Agricultural Policy of the EU 156, 261
Common External Tariff (CET) 301
common market 302
communist economy 7
commuting to work 204
companies 191
Company/Corporation Income Tax (CIT) 212
comparative advantage 266, 268–70, 313
  arguments against 314
  theory of 265–70
competitiveness, lack of 299–300
complementary good 107–8
complements 107–8, 127, 128–9
Compton, Sir John 154
constant marginal rate of substitution 100
consumer durable good 69
consumer good 16, 69
Consumer Price Index (CPI) 174, 175, 198, 220, 272
consumer sovereignty 134
consumption 233–4
Consumption Expenditure 199
consumption function 235
contrived profits 263
co-operatives 188
corporate bonds 191
corporations 191
cost minimisation 27
cost of borrowing 232
cost of money 232
cost–benefit analysis 185, 303–4
cost–push inflation 225–6
costs of the factors of production 215
Cotonou Agreement 323
Council for Foreign and Community Relations (COFCOR) 307
Council for Human and Social Development (COHSOD) 307, 326
Council for Trade and Economic Development (COTED) 307, 326
Council of Finance and Planning (COFAP) 326
credit card company 172
credit cards 172
credit unions 178, 179, 187–8
creditors 169
cross elasticity of demand 126–7, 129
crowding out 218, 219

Cuba
  capital in 29–30
  command economy 11–12
  economic problem of 3–4
  economy 7
  gap between rich and poor 158–9
  industrial relations 30–1
  mixed economy 13
  nationalisation of tobacco industry 8
  private sector 74
  revolution (1959) 12
  services in 74, 92
  tourism 29
cultural trends 319–20
current account 279–80
current account of the balance of payments, deficit in 282–5
customs union 301
cyclical (demand-deficient) unemployment 155, 246

debentures 191
debit cards 172
debtors 169
declining industries, protection of 260
deficit financing 218, 219
deficits 279, 282, 283–5
deflation 220–1
degrees of elasticity 120
demand 98–101
  definition 98
  determinants of 106–10
demand and supply 256
demand curve 98, 99, 100
  effect of indirect tax on 215–16
  movements 114
  shifting 107–9
demand deficient unemployment 155, 246
demand–pull inflation 224–5
demand schedule 98, 99–100
demerit good 33, 73–4, 92–3, 151–2
denominations 170
deposit accounts 173, 187
depreciation 58, 200, 276, 277
derived demand, definition 50
determinants of supply 215
devaluation 275, 284
development banks 178, 184–6
differentiated product 136
diminishing marginal rate of substitution 99
diminishing returns: the law of diminishing returns 254
direct relationship between price and quantity 102

direct debits 187
direct tax 34, 211, 235–6
dirty floating 277
disamenities 204
discriminatory measures 260
diseconomies of scale 65
disequilibrium 206
disincentive
  definition 212
  of steep progressivity 212–13
Dispute Settlement Body (DSB) 319–20, 321
distribution of income 159
dividend 184
divisibility of money 170
division of labour and specialisation 44–6
Doha Round 318, 323
do-it-yourself (DIY) 203
dumping 261
durability of money 170

Eastern Caribbean Central Bank 35–6, 140, 180, 181, 190, 277
Eastern Caribbean Currency Authority 181
Eastern Caribbean Securities Exchange 183
EC Central Bank 36
e-commerce 319, 338–30
economic decision 4
economic development 201, 202
economic efficiency 18–19
economic freedom index 85–6
economic goods 68
economic growth 195, 201
economic problem 3, 15
economic recession 161–2
economic resources 15–16
economic systems 85–94
economic trends 319
economics, definition of 3
economically active part of the population 43, 44
economies of scale 63–5, 138–9, 179, 264, 316–17
economy 7
education 12, 13
  as intermediate 204
  level of 27
  productivity of labour force 44
  provision 33
education services 75
effective demand 98
elastic price elasticity of demand 120
elasticity, definition 116
emigration 319
employment 26, 260

energy as resource 5
enterprise 15, 16, 28, 49–50, 54–5
entrepreneurial ability 49
entrepreneurship 49
envelope curve 63
equilibrium 104, 206
equilibrium price 104–6
equilibrium quantity 105
equity 211
Ernst & Young 49
errors and omissions 280
European Monetary Union 278
European Union 158, 219, 261, 294, 300, 301, 302, 319–20, 323
excess demand 105
excess supply 105
exchange controls 264
exchange rate 258, 274–6
exchange rate systems 276–9
Exchequer 207
exclusive specialisation 266
expenditure-dampening 261
expenditure method 199, 207
exporting your unemployment 310
exports 255, 256
external benefits 150–1
external cost 151
external debt 219
external shocks 84, 297–8

factor cost 199
factor markets 97
factors of production 15–16, 40, 112–13
financial account 280
financial economies 65
financial instruments 189–91
financial intermediaries 177–9
firms, size of 138–9
First Citizens Bank (Trinidad and Tobago) 181, 187
fiscal policy 208–9, 211–19, 225, 235–9
Fisher equation 222–3
fishing 82, 94
fixed costs 57–8
fixed exchange rate 275, 277–8, 310
fixed factor 254
floating exchange rate 275, 276–7
Ford, Henry 45–6
Ford Motor Company 46
foreign direct investment (FDI) 295, 322–3
foreign exchange 265
foreign exchange market 97
foreign trade 207
free goods 68
free market economy 7, 9, 10, 86, 89–92
free riders 72
free trade 217, 259, 313–16
free trade area 301
Free Trade Area of Americas (FTAA) 324
freedom of entry 133
freely floating exchange rate 277
frictional unemployment 156–7, 244–5
Friedman, Milton 222
frontier 16–17

gap between rich and poor 158–9
Gates, Bill 3, 49, 142
General Agreement on Tariffs and Trade (GATT) 311–12, 318, 319
general consumption tax (GCT) 214
Giffen goods 71
globalisation 265, 300, 318–25
going rate 47
gold 169, 170
gold standard 310
Gonsalves, Dr Ralph 217
good
    definition 68
    types 68–72
    vs. services 67–8
government
    influence of 32–4
    in macroeconomy 35–6
government departments 36
government expenditure 199, 237
government securities 189
Green Revolution 20, 42, 43
Greenspan, Alan 272
Grenada
    Hurricane Ivan 21
    VAT 34
Gresham's Law 171
Gross Domestic Product (GDP) 74, 82, 83, 195, 196, 197–9, 200, 201, 236, 237, 291–2, 298
Gross Domestic Product (GDP) deflator 198
Gross National Product (GNP) 195, 199–200
Guardian Life of the Caribbean Limited 189

hard currencies 258
health service 67, 75
Heritage Foundation 85, 89, 93, 391
    Index of Freedom Rankings 291
hot money 279, 280
housing market 97
Human Development Index (HDI) 290

Hurricane Ivan 34, 201, 217
hyperinflation 229

immigration 319
imports 255, 256
imported inflation 226
improved technology 20
imputed rent 57
incidence of a tax 216
income, customer, changes in 109
income elasticity of demand 123–9
income inelasticity 296
income method 198–9, 206–7
index linking 228
Index of Economic Freedom Rankings (Heritage Foundation) 85, 93
indirect costs 58
indirect tax 34, 199, 211, 213–14, 236–7
individual demand 101
individual supply curve 103
individual supply of labour 46
industrial relations 30–2
    at national level 30–1
    within the firm 31–2
industries 83
inelastic price elasticity of demand 120
infant industries, protection of 259–60
inferior good 25, 69–71
inflation 168–70
    acceptable and unacceptable rates 221–2
    causes of 218, 222–6
    consequences 221, 227–9
    definition 175, 220
    measurement of 174–5
inflationary spiral 226
influences on individuals 24–7
    income 25, 26
    level of education 27
    occupation 26
    personal choice 24–5
    social pressures 25
influences on firms 27–32
information failure 149, 150
injections 205, 206
inputs 40, 57
institutional shareholders 189
insurance companies 178, 188–9
intellectual property 140, 312
Inter-American Development Bank, Bahamas 184
interdependence 144
interest 52
interest inelasticity 235

inter-generational theft 88, 218, 219
International Bank for
  Reconstruction and Development
  see World Bank
International Monetary Fund
  (IMF) 169, 264, 275, 284, 285,
  310–11, 319, 322
international trade
  factors that influence 256–61
  theory 265–70
international unemployment 158
intervention currency 310
inverse relationship 99
investment 27, 234–5
invisible balance of the current
  account 279
invisible hand 9, 80, 89
invisibles 279
inward investment 280
Irish Potato Famine 71
irrational demand curve 71
issue 190

Jamaica
  balance of payments account
    281–2
  as mixed economy 75
  bauxite in 28–9, 41, 42
  brain drain 44
  Budget 209–10
  economy 7
  education 13, 27
  health service in 75
  land 50
  minimum wage 34
  mixed economy 10
  National Poverty Eradication
    Programme 160
  private ownership 13
  railways 13
  services in 74
  Statistical Institute of Jamaica 174
  taxation 212, 214–15
  tourism in 74
Jamaica Railway Corporation 13
Jamaica Stock Exchange 183
Joint Stock Banks 186

Kaiser Aluminium 28
Keynes, John Maynard 224, 309
Keynesians 224
kinked demand curve 143–4

Laborie Co-operative Credit
  Union 188
labour 15, 16, 28, 30
  classification 43
  definition 43
  as resource 79
  return to 51–2
labour force 43
Laffer Curve 213
laissez-faire economy 7
land
  definition 40–1
  productivity 42
  as resource 15, 16, 28, 30, 79
  return to 50–1
  sustainable use 41
law of diminishing returns 254
law of large numbers 189
leakages 205–6
legal tender 168
leisure 203
liability 186
liberalisation 13
liquidity 53–6, 171
liquidity preference curve 54, 233
liquidity preference theory 53–4
loanable funds theory 53
local government bonds 191
Lome Agreement/Convention 300,
  319, 323
long run 62–3
  in perfect competition 135
long-run average total cost curve 63,
  316
Lorenz curve 159

macroeconomics 14
make the polluter pay policy 144
Malthus, Thomas 253
managed exchange rate 278–9
managed floating 277
Manley, Michael 284
margin 22
marginal cost 61, 62, 147–8
marginal cost pricing 148
marginal efficiency of
  investment 234
maritime transport services 325
market demand, definition 101
market demand curve 100
market failure 32
  failure under monopoly 148
  main consequences 154–62
  resources and 154–8
market forces 98
market price 106, 188
market supply curve 103
market supply of labour 46
markets 96–8
Marshall Plan 311
Marx, Karl 11, 155
maturity transformation 179, 183
menu costs 228, 229

mergers 141
merit goods 32–3, 73–4, 150
microeconomics 14
Microsoft 3, 49, 142
microstate 291, 307
Minimum Lending Rate 233
minimum wage 33–4, 247
ministries 36
mixed economy 7, 10, 12–14, 75, 86,
  92–4
Model T Ford 45, 46
Monetarists 224
monetary base 231
Monetary Economics 6
monetary GDP 198
monetary policy 223, 225, 230–3
  government and 35
  through interest rates 232–3
  see also fiscal policy
money 6, 167
  characteristics 170–1
  as dollar vote 9
  functions 168–9
money market 177
money substitutes 172–3, 178
Money Supply 173–4
monopolistic competition 135–9
monopoly 10, 139–43, 148
Most Favoured Nation (MFN)
  status 259
multilateral trade 266
multinational corporations 317,
  321–2
multiplier effect 161
municipal bonds 191
mutual organisations 188

narrow money 173
National Bank of Anguilla 187
national budget 207, 208–11
National Commerce Bank Group
  (Jamaica) 187
national debt 182, 189, 218
national income (NI) 195
national income accounting 195–207
nationalisation 13
natural monopoly 140
natural rate of unemployment 242
near money 171
negative externalities 151–2
net barter terms of trade
  (NBTT) 257, 271
Net National Income at Factor
  Cost 200
Net National Product 200
Net Property Income 199, 279–80
'next best' alternative forgone 5–6
Nixon, Gerald, visit to China 259–60

non-diminishing good 73
non-excludability 73
non-forgeability of money 171
non-rivalry 73
normal good 25, 69–70, 109
normal profit 135
Normal Trade Relations (NTR) 259
normative statements 8
North American Free Trade Area (NAFTA) 301, 306, 324–5
   NAFTA Parity 324
Nyere, Julius 284

oil 256, 323
   crisis (1973–4) 272, 280
Oilfields Workers' Trade Union of Trinidad and Tobago 31, 248–9
oligopoly 143–5
open economies 253
open market 96
open market operations (OMO) 231–2
operational balances 181
opportunity cost 52, 54, 55, 57
   production possibility curve and 17–18
Organisation of Eastern Caribbean States (OECS) 140, 324
Organisation of Petroleum Exporting Countries (OPEC) 104, 114–15, 143, 272
output method 197–8, 206
output per man hour 266
outputs 40, 57
outsourcing 317–18
overheads 58, 59, 64, 65
oversupply 146

par value 278
Pareto efficiency 18, 19, 91
parity 278
partial specialisation 266, 314
patent 140
Patterson, Prime Minister 10
peer pressure 25
pensions, index linked 228
per capita GDP 201–3, 204
perestroika 297
perfect competition 47–8, 105, 132–4
personal income tax (PIT) 212
persuasive advertising 149–50
petro-dollars 272, 280, 318
Ping Pong diplomacy 258
planned economy 7
Planning Institute of Jamaica 174
plant economies 64
plastic money 172
Plaza Agreement 275

pollution 204
population growth 42, 253
portability of money 170
positive externalities 150–1
positive statements 8
Post Office savings accounts 190
postage stamps 171
postal orders 171
poverty 160
poverty line 160
predatory dumping 261
predatory pricing 129
preferences, reliance on 300
premium 189
price 256, 257
price ceiling 33–4, 36
price discrimination 142–3
price elasticity of demand (PED) 116–20
   applications 121–3
   calculation from diagram 118–20
   calculation from schedule 117–18
   definition 116
   determinants 123
   inelasticity 216
price elasticity of supply 129–31
   calculation from diagram 130
   calculation from schedule 129–30
   definition 129
   determinants 130–1
price floor 33–4, 36
price mechanism 9–10, 89
price of good 107
price taker 133
primary products, reliance on 296
primary sector 82–3
private benefit 73
private goods 72–3
private sector services 74
privatisation 13, 239
producer, goals of 113
production possibility 14, 15–23
production possibility curve 16–17
   opportunity cost and 17–18
   point W 19–20
   shape 22
   shifting 20–2
Production Possibility Frontiers 155
production, definition 39
production-possibility frontier 269–70
productive efficiency 90
productivity, definition 39–40
productivity of labour 40
productivity of land 42
products, range of 299
profit 27, 39, 54–5, 134–5
profit maximisation 27–8, 39, 113

profit motive 39
progressive tax 80, 81, 211, 212
proportional tax 80, 81, 212, 214
protectionist measures 259–61
Provident Bank and Trust (Belize) 187
public benefit 73
public finance 195
public good 12, 32, 72–3, 152–3
   free rider problem 154
   non-excludability 153
   non-rivalry 154
public sector borrowing requirement (PSBR) 209, 218
public sector services 74
Purchasing Power Parity 196
pure profit 55

quality of life 201, 202, 203, 204
quantity theory of money 222–4
quota 104, 263

rate of interest, determination of 53–5
rates of inflation 220
Reagan, President 213
real GDP 198
real monetary values 227
real terms 168, 227
real value of money 169
real wage unemployment 158
redistribution of income 227
regional unemployment 246
regressive tax 80, 81, 212
regrettables 203–4
relative poverty 160
rent 39, 50, 57
Repo Rate 232–3
resource allocation 79
resources
   as influences on firms 28–9
   wastage of 154–8
restrictive trade practice 141
retail banks 187
revaluation 275–6
revenue maximisation 27, 28, 121
Ricardo, David 50, 266, 268, 313
risk premium 52
risk transformation 179
Royal Bank of Trinidad and Tobago 181
Royal St Lucia Police Co-operative Credit Union 188

sacrifice principle 34, 211
Samuelson, Paul 9
sanctions 319
saving 25

scarcity of money 171
search unemployment 157, 244–5
seasonal unemployment 157, 245
secondary sector 83
sectors of economy 82–4
secure socket layer (SSL) 329
security 189
self-employment 26
semi-fixed costs 59
semi-variable costs 59
service 84
   definition 68
   vs. goods 67–8
share 184, 191
short run 62–3, 135
   in perfect competition 135
short-run average total cost curve 63
sin taxes 215, 236
Sinicisation 319
Smith, Adam 9, 45, 313
snake in the tunnel 278
social cost 151
South American Community of Nations (CSN) 327
Soviet Union, former as command economy 12
special consumption tax (SCT) 214–15
special drawing rights (SDRs) 310
specialisation 265–6
spreading the risk 189
St Lucia Civil Service Co-operative Credit Union 188
St Lucia Teachers' Co-operative Credit Union 188
St Vincent, subsidies in 34, 35
standard of living 201
standing orders 187
state monopolies 141
state pension 198
stock 49
stock brokers 178, 183–4
Stock Exchange 97, 105, 178, 183–4, 191
Stock Market 134
straight-line supply curve 103
strategic industries 260
stretch 116
structural adjustment programme (SAP) 284, 311, 322
structural unemployment 155–6, 245–6
subsidies 34, 35, 217, 312
substitute good 108
substitutes 108–9, 127, 128–9
sugar case 325
sunrise industries 260
sunset industries 260
supernormal profit 138, 141
supply 102–3

definition 102
determinants of 111–14
supply curve 102
   effect of indirect tax on 215
   shifts in 111–13, 114
supply of labour 46–7
   to a firm 47–8
supply price 51
supply schedule 102–3
supply-side policies 230, 238–9
surplus 279, 282
sustainability 41

target exchange rate 277
tariff 260, 261–5
   advantages 315–16
   definition 261
taste, change in 110
taxation 34, 199, 207, 211–19
technical economies 64
technical efficiency 19
techno-literacy 296
technological unemployment 156, 246
technology 49, 113, 239
terms of trade 257, 271–4
tertiary sector 83–4
Thatcher, Margaret 213
Third World Debt Crisis 311
time as resource 4
time deposits 187
total costs 59–60
tourism 29, 74, 83, 84, 256, 298–9, 325
Tourism Product Development Company 74
tourist multiplier 298
trade blocs 300–2
trade creation 302–3
trade diversion 302
trade liberalisation 315–16
trade off 18
trade unions 30–1, 33, 52
   role of 248–9
   unemployment and 246–9
trade, gains from 264–5
traditional economy 94
transfer payments 198
transport 49, 74
transport infrastructure 12
Treasury 207
Treasury bills 190
Treasury bonds 190
Treasury notes 190
Trinidad and Tobago
   education in 75
   industrial relations 31
   minimum wage 34
   oil 41
   population growth rate 43

   services in 74
   trade pattern 2005 255–6
   transport in 74
Trinidad and Tobago Insurance Limited 189
Trinidad and Tobago Stock Exchange 183

umbrella curve 63
unattainable costs 63
underground market 97
undersupply 146, 151
unemployment 10, 94, 295–6
   causes 244–6
   definition 241
   disadvantages 243
   market failure and 154–8
   measurement of 241–3
   trade unions and 246–9
unemployment benefit 239
unitary elasticity 120
United Nations 197, 200, 201, 202
United Nations Development Programme (UNDP) 160, 290
United States of America (USA)
   economic problem 3
   roads 12
unrelated products 127
Uruguay Round 311
U-shaped curve 60, 61

value added 39
Value Added Tax (VAT) 34, 112, 214, 236
variable costs 27, 58–9
variable factor 254
Veblen goods 71–2
Virgin 15
visibles 279

wage 39, 51–2
weighting 174
weights 174
welfare loss 262, 315
welfare of society, decline in 162
Western Hemisphere Travel Initiative 299
whole supply curve 112, 113
Winkler, Anthony C. 40
win–win situation 265
World Bank (IBRD) 219, 311, 319
World Travel and Tourism Council (WTTC) 293
World Trade Organisation (WTO) 217, 261, 300, 301, 308, 309–12
   and globalisation 318–20
   national treatment clause 321